This book is an introduct   ...ic thought, mainly from
the twelfth to the fifteenth   .. emerges from the works of academic theologians and lawy   .u other sources, from Italian merchants' writings to vernacular poetry, parliamentary legislation, and manorial court rolls.

It raises a number of questions based on the Aristotelian idea of the mean, the balance and harmony underlying justice, as applied by medieval thinkers to the changing economy, and it attempts to relate theory to practice. How could private ownership of property be reconciled with God's gift of the earth to all in common? How could charity balance resources between rich and poor? What was money and how did it equalize the interests of buyer and seller? Did control of the standards of weights, measures, and coinage belong to the ruler or the people, or both? Could the 'balance of trade' be applied to the medieval economy? What were the just price and the just wage? How was a balance to be achieved between lender and borrower and how did the idea of usury change to reflect this? The answers emerge from a wide variety of ecclesiastical and secular sources.

DIANA WOOD is Senior Research Fellow in History, University of East Anglia, and Associate Tutor in Local History, Oxford University Department for Continuing Education. Her publications include *Clement VI: the Pontificate and Ideas of an Avignon Pope* (Cambridge, 1989).

Cambridge medieval textbooks

This is a series of specially commissioned textbooks for teachers and students, designed to complement the monograph series Cambridge Studies in Medieval Life and Thought by providing introductions to a range of topics in medieval history. This series combines both chronological and thematic approaches, and will deal with British and European topics. All volumes in the series will be published in hard covers and in paperback. For a list of titles in the series, see end of book.

MEDIEVAL ECONOMIC THOUGHT

DIANA WOOD

CAMBRIDGE UNIVERSITY PRESS

PUBLISHED BY THE PRESS SYNDICATE OF THE UNIVERSITY OF CAMBRIDGE
The Pitt Building, Trumpington Street, Cambridge, United Kingdom

CAMBRIDGE UNIVERSITY PRESS
The Edinburgh Building, Cambridge CB2 2RU, UK
40 West 20th Street, New York, NY 10011-4211, USA
477 Williamstown Road, Port Melbourne, VIC 3207, Australia
Ruiz de Alarcón 13, 28014 Madrid, Spain
Dock House, The Waterfront, Cape Town 8001, South Africa

http://www.cambridge.org

© Diana Wood, 2002

This book is in copyright. Subject to statutory exception
and to the provisions of relevant collective licensing agreements,
no reproduction of any part may take place without
the written permission of Cambridge University Press.

First published 2002

Printed in the United Kingdom at the University Press, Cambridge

Typeface Bembo 10/11.5 pt   *System* LATEX 2ε [TB]

A catalogue record for this book is available from the British Library

Library of Congress cataloguing in publication data
Wood, Diana, 1940–
Medieval economic thought / Diana Wood.
p. cm. – (Cambridge medieval textbooks)
Includes bibliographical references and index.
ISBN 0 521 45260 0 – ISBN 0 521 45893 5 (pbk.)
1. Economics – History – To 1800.   2. Aristotle – Contributions in
economics.   I. Title.   II. Series.
HB79 .W66 2002
330.15′12 – dc21   2002022274

ISBN 0 521 45260 0 hardback
ISBN 0 521 45893 5 paperback

In memory of Michael Wilks
and Roger Virgoe

CONTENTS

	Preface	page ix
	List of abbreviations	xi
	Introduction: problems, evidence, and background	1
1	Private property *versus* communal rights: the conflict of two laws	17
2	Wealth, beggary, and sufficiency	42
3	What is money?	69
4	Sovereign concerns: weights, measures, and coinage	89
5	The mercantile system	110
6	The just price and the just wage	132
7	The nature of usury: the usurer as winner	159
8	The theory of interest: the usurer as loser	181
	Conclusion	206
	Appendix Notes on the main writers and anonymous works mentioned in the text	210
	Glossary of terms	224
	Select bibliography	227
	Index	243

PREFACE

The subject of medieval economic thought is not in any sense a popular one – indeed, its mention is a positive conversation stopper. When I embarked upon it I had three basic assumptions. The first was that relatively little had been written about it. I could not have been more wrong. The bookshelves were already groaning, and the appearance of Odd Langholm's magisterial work, *Economics in the Medieval Schools*, in 1992 totally transformed the approach to the subject. The second assumption was that it would be possible to write about economic thought in isolation from economic practice. Those who were kind enough to read the first draft of my typescript soon pointed out this error. The result has been an attempt to integrate theory and practice, while desperately trying to keep the book to a manageable length. I am well aware that I have had to skate over many highly controversial areas of medieval economic history which deserve far deeper discussion than was possible here. The third assumption was that it should be feasible for someone like myself with no training in economics, but with experience in teaching medieval economic and social history (the two being inseparable) and the history of political ideas to write about medieval economic thought. I offer no judgement on this.

Anyone studying medieval economic history becomes aware of immense local variations. These exist not just in geographical, geological, or climatic terms, but also in what actually happened, in economic and social reactions, and in a mass of local custom and legislation. This makes generalization difficult and oversimplification an ever-present danger. The point has been underlined in a recent study by John Hatcher and Mark Bailey, *Modelling the Middle Ages: the History and Theory of England's Economic Development* (Oxford, 2001), which unfortunately appeared too late for me to take full account of it. The danger applies especially in a book of this type, where practical examples cited in support of theories are random ones. Above all, the problem of oversimplification occurs in the Glossary of Terms, but bearing this in mind, it still seemed worthwhile to include it.

I have amassed many debts of gratitude during the several years over which the writing of this book has been spread, and it is a pleasure to acknowledge them. My warmest thanks go to Anthony Tuck, who was kind enough to read two successive drafts and has been a constant source of wisdom, encouragement, and advice, and to Robert Swanson for his meticulous comments and constructive suggestions, made at a time when I know he was overburdened. My thanks are also due to Rosamond Faith and Diana Perry, who also have read complete drafts and have made many helpful suggestions and saved me from many errors. In this case it is no mere convention to say that the errors which remain are all my own work.

I should also like to express my gratitude to Charles Ormerod, for keeping my computer running at all times and for photographing the Wenhaston Doom. I am grateful, too, to the many friends, colleagues, and students, both at the University of East Anglia and amongst the local historians at the Oxford University Department for Continuing Education, whose interest has encouraged me so much. The two very different scholars to whose memory the book is dedicated, Michael Wilks and Roger Virgoe, have both contributed in ways they can never know.

I also thank Professor Odd Langholm for kind permission to quote copiously from his published work, especially from *Economics in the Medieval Schools*, and to the editor of *Studies in Church History* for permission to use material due to appear in volume 37. Acknowledgement must also be made to the University of East Anglia for generous study-leave in the early stages of writing. I am grateful for the helpfulness of the staff of the various libraries in which I have worked, especially those of the Bodleian, the Oxford History Faculty Library, the Oxford Department for Continuing Education, and Balliol College, Oxford. William Davies of the Cambridge University Press has always been known to authors for his patience, but this time he has excelled himself. Both apologies and thanks are due to him. I should also like to record my thanks to Sheila Kane for copyediting and to Meg Davies for compiling the index.

My final and deepest debt of gratitude is to someone who wishes to remain anonymous, but without whose conversation, generosity, and encouragement the book would not have been started, far less finished.

ABBREVIATIONS

CChr.SL	*Corpus Christianorum, series Latina* (Turnhout, 1953–)
EconHR	*Economic History Review* (London, 1927–)
EEH	A. E. Bland, P. A. Brown, and R. H. Tawney, eds., *English Economic History: Select Documents* (London, 1914)
EETS	Early English Text Society (London, 1864–)
EHD	*English Historical Documents* (London, 1953–)
EHR	*English Historical Review* (London, 1886–)
HPT	*History of Political Thought* (Exeter, 1980–)
JEH	*Journal of Ecclesiastical History* (Cambridge, 1950–)
Langholm, *Economics*	Odd Langholm, *Economics in the Medieval Schools: Wealth, Exchange, Value, Money and Usury according to the Paris Theological Tradition, 1200–1350* (Leiden, 1992)
LCL	Loeb Classical Library
MGH	*Monumenta Germaniae historica inde ad a. 500 usque ad a. 1500*, ed. G. H. Pertz et al. (Hanover, Berlin, 1826–)
Noonan, *Scholastic Analysis*	J. T. Noonan, *The Scholastic Analysis of Usury* (Cambridge, MA, 1957)
P & P	*Past and Present. A Journal of Scientific History* (London, 1952–)
PG	*Patrologia Graeca*, ed. J. P. Migne, 161 vols. (Paris 1857–66)

PL	*Patrologia Latina*, ed. J. P. Migne, 217+4 index vols. (Paris, 1841–61)
RS	*Rerum Britannicarum medii aevi scriptores*, 99 vols. (London, 1858–1911) = *Rolls Series*
SCH	*Studies in Church History* (London/Cambridge/Oxford/Woodbridge, 1964–)
Speculum	*Speculum: a Journal of Medieval Studies* (Cambridge, MA, 1925–)
TRHS	*Transactions of the Royal Historical Society* (London, 1871–)

References to columns in canon law citations are to Ae. Friedberg, *Corpus iuris canonici*, 2 vols. (Leipzig, 1879).

Spellings in quotations from the Middle English prose dialogue *Dives and Pauper* have been modernized.

INTRODUCTION: PROBLEMS, EVIDENCE, AND BACKGROUND

There was once a hungry ass who was standing between two heaps of hay. Each heap was equal in every respect. Because the ass could not decide between the two, he starved to death. This famous story, wrongly attributed to the fourteenth-century philosopher John Buridan, and known as 'Buridan's Ass',[1] was about the difficulty of making moral decisions, but it can also serve as a useful introduction to medieval economic thought.

The Franciscan John Buridan was a scholastic, a product of the University of Paris, primarily a philosopher and a commentator on the works of Aristotle, but also a mathematician and a theologian. During the medieval period most economic ideas were framed by such people. The medieval world was not one of econometrics and global markets, but one of 'theological economy'. Economics as a discrete discipline did not exist, so that, strictly speaking, 'Medieval Economic Thought' is a misnomer. All thought, whether political, philosophical, legal, scientific, or economic would have been regarded as an aspect of theology. This means that much economic thought has to be harvested from theological works, written by scholastics, many of whom were mendicant friars. Not surprisingly, medieval economic ideas are heavily imbued with questions of ethics and morality, with the motives rather than the mechanics of economic life. It was not until the early Renaissance period that people started to reflect on specifically economic topics.

---

[1] *The Oxford Dictionary of the Christian Church*, 3rd edn, ed. E. A. Livingstone (Oxford, 1997), p. 254.

Economics at its most basic was, and is, concerned with material matters. Economic thought is concerned with all aspects of material resources and goods and with the underlying ideas that regulate their acquisition, consumption, supply, and distribution. In the course of these processes economic relationships are formed, and these are regulated by the society in which they occur and reflect its morality. Scholastic thinkers considered the society in which they lived to be the Roman Church. The morality which governed economic and, indeed, all relations was therefore the morality of the Church, in theory a universal Christian society.

THE CHURCH, SOCIETY, AND ECONOMY

The Church dominated all aspects of medieval life. It controlled education, and therefore the shaping of attitudes. In formal terms this meant first the monasteries and cathedral schools, and later the universities. Less formally, education took place through pastoral instruction in pulpit and confessional. In towns and villages, fairs and markets, the Church controlled the whole rhythm of life. Time was measured by church bells, the calendar by the liturgical year, and leisure by holy days. But it had a more personal and direct hold over the economic life of Christians. The pope, as the head of the Christian body, claimed to be the universal judge of all mankind. This meant that everyone was subject to the law of the Church, canon law, and the jurisdiction of the ecclesiastical courts. The legal competence of the 'courts Christian' was enormous and included most economic matters. The Church claimed jurisdiction over all cases involving the clergy, even those in the most minor orders. It judged all matters which involved an oath, which meant matrimonial and probate matters, invariably concerned with property, and a whole host of other things, including commercial contracts. In England offences committed on Sundays or major feast or fast days might also be heard in the church courts, on the basis that the defendant should have been in church at the time. In 1488, for example, Thomas Samson of St Peter's in Thanet found himself before a Canterbury church court for looting a shipwreck, simply because he had chosen All Saints' Day on which to do it. Lucas Pancake of Otterden was accused of shaving his beard on a Sunday.[2] Quite apart from the church courts, a priest might be used as arbiter in a secular dispute,

[2] Brian L. Woodcock, *Medieval Ecclesiastical Courts in the Diocese of Canterbury* (Oxford, 1952), pp. 80–1. On the competence of the 'courts Christian' see R. N. Swanson, *Church and Society in Late Medieval England* (Oxford, 1993), pp. 166–82; James A. Brundage, *Medieval Canon Law* (London and New York, 1995), pp. 70–97. On the pope's legal competence see M. J. Wilks, *The Problem of Sovereignty in the Later Middle Ages* (Cambridge, 1963), pp. 313–14.

Introduction 3

perhaps in the market-place, as a 'good' man. Ultimately the Church had jurisdiction over all sin. Even if a particular crime did not come before it on earth, it still controlled the inner forum of conscience. And if it could not judge publicly in this world, it could and did judge in the next. Depictions of the Last Judgement, with St Michael weighing souls in the balance, as in a commercial transaction, featured prominently on Doom paintings above the chancel arch of medieval churches as a potent reminder.[3]

The aim of the Christian society was salvation – union with God in Heaven – but it still had to exist on earth and therefore to concern itself with material matters. The Church was the largest landowner in Europe, much of the land being concentrated in the hands of bishops and abbots. Such men had to be responsible for the running of often vast estates, to say nothing of the responsibility of the pope himself for papal territories. Monks would be involved in the affairs of town and market-place through their lordship of boroughs, and in the country the parish priest would participate in the local economy as he disposed of tithe, often paid in kind, or the produce of his glebe land.[4] Both monasteries and parishes had a special responsibility for the care of the poor and disadvantaged, and so for the distribution of charity.

The other-worldly aim of the Church meant that in theory at least the concerns of this world were secondary. Temporal ends and temporal affairs, the merely transient and mundane, always had to be subordinated to the higher, spiritual purpose of life. Because material matters were thought to be of so little account, the Church put a firm brake on economic development. It actively discouraged people from wanting to better themselves because to be socially ambitious, to want to be upwardly mobile, was a sin. 'Let every man abide in the same calling wherein he was called',[5] advised St Paul, and this was how it had to be. A professor at the 'new' university of Vienna, Henry of Hesse (or Langenstein, d. 1397), enlarged on this. The only justifications for working to earn more than mere sustenance were to perform pious works, to make reasonable provision for future emergencies, or to support offspring.

Whoever has enough for these things but still works incessantly to gain riches or a higher social status, or so that later he may live without working, or so that his sons may be rich and great – all such are driven by damnable avarice, physical pleasure and pride.[6]

[3] See, for example, Eamon Duffy, *The Stripping of the Altars: Traditional Religion in England, 1400–1580* (New Haven, CT and London, 1993), plates 120–2, for reproductions, and the cover to this volume.
[4] Swanson, *Church and Society*, ch. 5, pp. 191–251.   [5] I Cor. 7.20.
[6] Henry of Hesse, *De contractibus*, in John Gerson, *Opera omnia*, 4 vols. (Cologne, 1483–4), 4, cap. 12, fol. 191ra.

This was hardly the commercial or entrepreneurial attitude necessary for an economic take-off.

Society was rigid and hierarchical. It was divided into two 'orders', those of priesthood and laity, and in theory the priests dominated the laity. Within each 'order' people were strictly graded according to the function they performed – very much a case of one person, one job. The whole society formed one great 'chain of being', which mirrored the organization of the society of the blessed in Heaven. Earthly society was part of a divine plan. In more natural terms, Thomas Aquinas likened it to a bee-hive:

Some gather honey, some build their dwelling with wax, while the queens do none of these things: and it must needs be so likewise with man... for instance, that some cultivate the land, that some have charge of animals, that some build houses, and so forth. And since man's life demands not only goods of the body, but also, and still more, goods of the soul, it is necessary for some to be busy about spiritual things for the betterment of others: and such must needs be exempt from the care of temporal things. This division of divers duties among divers persons is made by divine providence, according as some are more inclined to one duty than to others.[7]

Spiritual betterment was encouraged; economic betterment was not. In practice, people did rise, despite the moral censure. To stop this, the Church condemned anything or anyone involved in money-making. Trade and merchants were especially frowned upon. But above all an attitude of 'zero tolerance' was applied to the taking of interest on loans. The Church considered that anything returned to a lender which exceeded the principal was usury, a damnable sin. Nauseating tales reminded sermon audiences of the terrible fate of unrepentant usurers after death. Yet the effect of the usury ban, if strictly applied, would have been to starve the developing mercantile world of the credit on which it was largely based.

Part of the aim of this study is to show how the attitudes of the scholastics to economic matters changed – how the economy was justified, how trade and merchants became respectable, and how the concept of legitimate interest on a loan became separated from the crime of usury. But all this could happen only when the nature of society changed, and when the control of the Church was weakened.

By the end of the fourteenth century a complex and fundamental change in the nature and purpose of society was well under way. Very gradually, from being united, unique, and universal, it was becoming transformed into a collection of independent territories, directed towards national interests by national sovereign rulers. Eternal salvation and divine precepts

---

[7] Thomas Aquinas, *Summa contra gentiles*, trans. The English Dominican Fathers, 4 vols. (London, 1924–9), 3, 2, bk. 3, ch. 134, p. 142.

were still of paramount concern to Christians, as a growing preoccupation with Purgatory shows, but in this new climate the natural, material ends of man's life also mattered. What was natural and human and secular became as important as what was divine. It is hard to overestimate the significance of the change, far less to pinpoint the causes, for to attempt this is to become caught in an intricate web of cause and effect. The problem is that the fundamental change encompassed many others within itself, changes in every aspect of life – not only political, but also intellectual and economic.

THE ECONOMIC CHANGES

From the late twelfth century the European economy underwent a spectacular transformation. Every sector of it grew apace – rural, urban, and mercantile. Exactly what triggered this is difficult to say. Many historians attribute it to an unprecedented rise in population.[8] An ever-increasing number of people led to pressure on land and resources, which in turn led to more intensive farming and to reclamation of waste and marginal lands for agricultural use. It also led to intensified production for the market, to the development of local markets, and to the growth of internal trade and industry. International trade, too, was stimulated, and fairs developed, first in Champagne, and then throughout Europe. New contacts with the East brought new trading routes, and new commodities reached Western markets. But the most significant demonstration of all this increased activity was the rise and development of the towns and of urban culture. The towns were centres not just of commercial activity, but also of royal and ecclesiastical administration, and of religious and intellectual developments. The mendicant friars especially were drawn to the towns and made them rather than the countryside their centres. It was in the towns that commercial practices such as deposit and exchange banking developed, and legal devices such as bills of exchange and different types of partnership contract became increasingly common. The people responsible were the mercantile elite. Merchants and traders were becoming literate, as business methods

---

[8] The debate centres largely on the views of R. Brenner and M. M. Postan. See R. Brenner, 'Agrarian class structure and economic development in pre-industrial Europe', *P & P*, 70 (1976), pp. 30–75; M. M. Postan and J. Hatcher, 'Population and class relations in feudal society', *P & P*, 78 (1978), pp. 24–37. For a convenient summary see S. H. Rigby, *English Society in the Later Middle Ages: Class, Status and Gender* (London, 1995), pp. 127–43. See also T. Aston and C. H. E. Philpin, eds., *The Brenner Debate: Agrarian Class Structure and Economic Developments in Pre-industrial Europe* (Cambridge, 1985); John Hatcher and Mark Bailey, *Modelling the Middle Ages: the History and Theory of England's Economic Development* (Oxford, 2001), pp. 66–120.

became more complicated, although it is not clear how far they were literate in Latin before the fourteenth century. The business communities of northern Italy and Flanders led the way.[9] It was to be the merchants, especially the Florentines in the fifteenth century, who would express somewhat different views from the traditional ecclesiastical ones. But the people who were mainly responsible for accommodating all this dangerous novelty within the Christian tradition were the friars. Although they were supposed to shun the world and all its concerns, especially money, they lived and breathed the commercial atmosphere of the towns and adapted it for their own ends. Their achievement was 'to bring into balance and to keep in balance their strict refusals to touch money or participate in legal proceedings with their exploitation of the techniques of selling, bargaining and persuading'. They 'negotiated the Gospel without using money, thus exercising commerce as truly Christian merchants'.[10]

THE EVIDENCE

The majority of the works drawn on in this book are from the late medieval period, that is, from the thirteenth to the fifteenth centuries, the period when the friars were active. But thought rarely evolves in isolation, and the work of medieval thinkers was heavily, and often deliberately, derivative: there was no concept of plagiarism in the Middle Ages. Recent work, especially that of Odd Langholm, has demonstrated this imitative trait. It has meant that the pride of place formerly given to the Dominican Thomas Aquinas, for example, or the Franciscan Bernardino of Siena has been undermined. An introductory section to Langholm's *magnum opus* is headed 'Not only Aquinas'; and it is now widely acknowledged that Bernardino borrowed heavily from the thirteenth-century Franciscan Peter Olivi (d. 1298).[11]

Equally important is the fact that the economic ideas of the scholastics, the academic writers of the medieval period, were often embedded in commentaries on either the Bible or the works of Aristotle, or in biblically based sermons, and they cannot be understood without some knowledge of these. Their works are stuffed with classical and biblical quotations. In any event, medieval writers loved to quote. They may not have acknowledged their immediate predecessors, but they were ostentatiously aware of the patristic pedigree of many of their ideas. As well as the Bible and

[9] Robert S. Lopez, *The Commercial Revolution of the Middle Ages, 950–1350* (Cambridge, 1976), esp. pp. 56–122.
[10] Barbara H. Rosenwein and Lester K. Little, 'Social meaning in the monastic and mendicant spiritualities', *P & P*, 63 (1974), pp. 4–32, at pp. 28, 32.
[11] Langholm, *Economics*, p. 11, and pp. 345–6, and n. 1 for the debt of later thinkers to Olivi.

Introduction

Aristotle, their works are full of citations from authors such as Augustine, Jerome, and Ambrose. In order to clarify the late medieval ideas it has often been necessary to examine their pre-medieval ancestry.

The Bible, 'the sovereign textbook of the schools',[12] was studied, glossed, and commented upon more than any other work in the medieval period. It was the revelation of God himself, and as such was the repository of all truth and wisdom. As a fourteenth-century commentator Nicholas of Lyre observed: 'Whatever is repugnant to Holy Scripture is false. So Holy Scripture is not only Wisdom itself; it is also the understanding of this Wisdom.'[13] This could be, and was, applied to economics. The morality contained in the Bible is the foundation of many of the arguments which follow. The friars who often feature as Aristotelian commentators were first and foremost theologians and biblical commentators. As theologians, their work also rested on the intellectual developments which characterized the so-called renaissance of learning which took place during the 'long' twelfth century.[14]

During this revival the processes of rational analysis and systematization were combined to create three fundamental works. One of these was the *Sentences* of Peter Lombard (d. 1160), which covered all the main considerations of Christian theology – the Trinity, the Creation and the Fall of Man, the Incarnation and Christian moral principles, and the Sacraments. In the *Sentences* Peter tried to harmonize conflicting opinions. The result, as a thirteenth-century critic observed sourly, was a work so weighty that 'it takes a horse to carry it'.[15] Despite this inconvenience, it was adopted as the main theological textbook in the schools.

The search for order was applied not just to theology, but also to law. The second basic work was the reclassification and rearrangement of the *Corpus iuris civilis*, the whole body of the Emperor Justinian's Roman law texts, by a Bolognese lawyer, Irnerius, in the early twelfth century. He also added his own interlinear comments, or glosses, to the texts – a practice

---

[12] The phrase is the title of ch. 3 of R. W. Southern, *Scholastic Humanism and the Unification of Europe*, vol. 1: *Foundations* (Oxford, 1997). This chapter, pp. 102–33, provides the best introduction to the Bible's significance in scholastic thought and the methods of interpretation applied to it. See also Beryl Smalley, *The Study of the Bible in the Middle Ages* (Oxford, 1983).

[13] Nicholas of Lyre, Prologue to *Postills on the Bible*, quoted by Southern, *Scholastic Humanism*, 1, p. 110.

[14] See the excellent introduction to the debates surrounding the 'long' twelfth century and its renaissance in R. N. Swanson, *The Twelfth-century Renaissance* (Manchester, 1999), pp. 1–11, esp. 4–5. On the early participants, c. 1060–1160, and the social and intellectual climate in which they worked see Southern, *Scholastic Humanism*, 1.

[15] 'Roger Bacon deplores the preference given at Paris to the *Sentences* over Holy Scripture' (c. 1267), in Helene Wieruszowski, ed., *The Medieval University* (Princeton, NJ, 1966), pp. 146–7.

emulated by a long line of both Roman and canon lawyers for the rest of the medieval period. The third great systematization was the *Decretum* of Gratian, or *The Concord of Discordant Canons* (1140) – the subtitle adequately conveys its scholastic method – which was a collection of canon law texts, including conciliar canons, papal decretals, patristic writings, and even excerpts from civil law.

Of these three, the *Sentences* was really a *summa* of theological knowledge, and the adoption of Peter Lombard's work gave rise both to commentaries on his work directly, and to a whole series of theological *summae*, of which the great *Summa theologiae* of Aquinas is the best-known example. Many of these theological treatises adopt a question and answer method. The question is first posed, then opinions against it and for it are rehearsed, followed by the author's discussion and opinion, and then the replies to the contrary arguments. Additional chapters might be added. Another academic genre was the *quodlibet*, which was a formal academic debate – as opposed to a university lecture – or, as its name implies 'whatever anyone liked'. Theological treatises of every sort are an important source for economic ideas.

The major part of Justinian's codification of the law, the *Corpus iuris civilis*, started in 527, is the *Digest* or *Pandects* (promulgated 533), which is a collection of extracts from the work of classical jurists, especially Ulpian and Paul. It covers fifty books. The *Codex* (534) is a collection largely based, as the name implies, on the *Theodosian Code*, though with some additions by Justinian, and the *Institutes* (533) is an adaptation of a basic textbook by an obscure second-century lawyer called Gaius. Added to these were the *Novella*, or new laws, which were enacted after the completion of the *Codex*.

The texts of the *Corpus* were glossed and commented on extensively. In the thirteenth century a mass of texts and explanatory scholarship was condensed into the *Great Gloss* of Accursius. If the *Sentences* came to overshadow the Bible in the theological schools, the same might be said about the *Great Gloss* and the *Corpus iuris civilis* in the legal schools. The second half of the thirteenth century and the fourteenth century saw the rise of a new group of legal commentators, the dialecticians, of whom Bartolus of Sassoferrato and his pupil Baldus were among the most celebrated.[16]

Roman law embraced both equity and natural law ideas about the equality of men, which explains its fundamental importance for economic ideas, quite apart from the specifically economic and commercial matters

---

[16] On Roman law see Peter G. Stein, 'Roman law' in David Miller *et al.*, eds., *The Blackwell Encyclopedia of Political Thought*, rev. edn (Oxford, 1990), pp. 446–50; Swanson, *Twelfth-century Renaissance*, pp. 68–73; Southern, *Scholastic Humanism*, 1, pp. 272–84; Barry Nicholas, *An Introduction to Roman Law* (Oxford, 1962), esp. pp. 38–45.

Introduction 9

it discussed. As a 'pagan' source, it was less restricted than the Christian writings, and yet it enshrined many of the same principles. Many of the lawyers of the dialectical school were doctors of both laws, civil and canon, and commented on both.

Gratian's *Decretum*, although it was a private compilation, gained wide acceptance as authoritative. To it was added a further collection in 1234 by Pope Gregory IX, known as the *Decretales*, the *Liber Sextus*, added by Boniface VIII in 1298, and the *Clementines*, by Clement V in 1317. Later, in 1500, John XXII's *Extravagantes* (literally those 'wandering outside' the main collections) were added and the *Extravagantes communes*. Together with the *Decretum*, they contained all the authoritative canons of general councils and the papal decretals, and became known as the *Corpus iuris canonici*. These collections too were extensively summarized and commented upon. Commentators became known as 'Decretists' and 'Decretalists'. In the thirteenth century the *Glossa ordinaria* of Johannes Teutonicus became the most influential work of systematization on the *Decretum*. The most celebrated commentators of the thirteenth century to feature here were Huguccio, Hostiensis, and Raymond of Peñafort, and of the fourteenth, Johannes Andreae.[17]

The remainder of the evidence for medieval economic thought is more varied. It consists, for example, of pastoralia – confessors' manuals, treatises on the Virtues and the Vices, and sermons. These are valuable especially for what they say on avarice, and its progeny usury, and on topics such as poverty, charity, and almsgiving. A particularly rich source in England is vernacular literature. The best example is *Dives and Pauper* – the Rich Man and the Poor Man – a prose treatise written probably by a Franciscan in the early fifteenth century, based on an exposition of the Ten Commandments.[18] Then, at the close of the period, there are secular sources, such as parliamentary statutes, private letters, and wills, as well as the treatises of Italian humanists and the business writings of merchants. Finally there are local legal records, such as manorial court rolls and village by-laws, which are interesting as reflections of customary law rather than Roman civil law.

---

[17] On canon law see Brundage, *Medieval Canon Law*; Swanson, *Twelfth-century Renaissance*, pp. 73–7; and on Gratian, Southern, *Scholastic Humanism*, 1, pp. 283–318; Anders Winroth, *The Making of Gratian's 'Decretum'* (Cambridge, 2000).

[18] H. G. Pfander, '*Dives and Pauper*', *The Library*, 14 (1933), pp. 299–312; H. G. Richardson, '*Dives and Pauper*', ibid., 15 (1934), pp. 31–7; Anne Hudson and H. L. Spencer, 'Old author, new work: the sermons of MS Longleat 4', *Medium Aevum*, 53 (1984), pp. 220–38; M. Teresa Tavormina, 'Mathematical conjectures in a Middle English prose treatise: perfect numbers in *Dives and Pauper*', *Traditio*, 49 (1994), pp. 271–86, discusses an unusual aspect of the treatise.

Most of the sources outlined above are not specifically economic ones. The economic thought they contain is almost incidental. It is only at the end of the period that we find treatises specifically written on economic topics, such as the *De Moneta* of the late fourteenth-century writer Nicholas Oresme, pupil of John Buridan, or the *Libelle of Englysh Polycy*, a strongly protectionist trade treatise written in the fifteenth century to ensure that England should retain mastery of the 'narrow seas' during the final stages of the Hundred Years War with France.

No discussion of the evidence for medieval economic thought can hope to be exhaustive: the subject is as all-embracing as the economy itself. The problem has been one of abundance rather than scarcity, and because of this, works by English authors have been used wherever possible. Sometimes economic ideas appear in unexpected places, such as the works of Chaucer or Langland, or in popular sermons. Although England was economically less advanced than areas such as Flanders and Italy, thought knows no geographical boundaries, and English thinkers made important contributions to economic thought. Part of the reason for this was the strong tradition of Aristotelian translation and commentary at Oxford. Many of the English writers who discussed economic subjects did so in the course of commenting on the works of Aristotle, and Aristotle was a predominating influence on both the method and content of medieval economic thought.

THE INFLUENCE OF ARISTOTLE

The story of Buridan's ass probably came from Aristotle, and John Buridan was an Aristotelian commentator. Most of Aristotle's works had been lost to the Western world throughout the early medieval period, yet, despite this, his influence was never entirely absent. It was transmitted partly through the few works which were translated, and partly through the ideas and vocabulary of thinkers such as Cicero and Boethius. As Cary Nederman has observed, 'the Middle Ages knew two Aristotles: one was present throughout medieval times, if only in dim awareness; the other was disseminated rapidly beginning in the twelfth century and forced medieval thinkers to re-evaluate their cherished orthodoxies'.[19] When the bulk of the philosopher's works became available it was to some extent the result of contact with the Greek world, which had been made and strengthened by historical events, in particular by the crusades. These started in 1096

[19] Cary J. Nederman, 'Bracton on kingship revisited', *HPT*, 5 (1984), pp. 61–77, at p. 76, reprinted in Nederman, *Medieval Aristotelianism and its Limits* (Aldershot, 1997), no. 13 (same pagination). The volume includes several essays on the early dissemination of Aristotelian ideas.

Introduction 11

and enabled scholars to travel in search of new knowledge. The way was opened to Syria, to Antioch, and to Byzantium. The conquest of Muslim Spain in the eleventh century was also very important. It revealed the store of Jewish and Arabic learning. Spain attracted numerous scholars and became one of the main centres for Aristotelian translation. Sicily, too, which was home to both Muslims and Christians, provided the West with great intellectual riches after its conquest by the Normans and its recognition as a kingdom by the papacy in the early twelfth century.

The two main works of Aristotle on economics and politics did not reach the West until the thirteenth century. The *Nicomachean Ethics* was translated by Robert Grosseteste, Bishop of Lincoln, and others, and completed *c.* 1247 (although parts of it may have been available earlier), while the *Politics* was not translated until 1260–4 (by William of Moerbeke).[20] The Aristotelian emphasis on the natural political abilities of man – on the powers of natural reason – were the complete antithesis of the papal system of ideas, which was based on divine law and priestly authority. Various attempts were made to prohibit the teaching of the pagan philosopher's works on natural philosophy at the University of Paris, the most important of which was by Gregory IX, *Parens scientiarum* of 1231. A week later the Pope charged the Dominican friars with the task of 'Christianizing' Aristotle, that is, of purging his work of all that was offensive to the faithful.[21] Although the original commission never reported to the papacy, its work was carried on by Albert the Great, William of Moerbeke, and, above all, by Aquinas. Hence the formation of the Thomist synthesis. Hence, too, the fact that Aquinas dealt with 'material' matters, as Aristotle had done, and therefore acquired his reputation as the most influential medieval economic thinker.

The bulk of Aristotle's works on logic, which became known as the 'new logic', reached the West in the twelfth century,[22] before the *Ethics* or the *Politics*. The result was the development of a new analytical and logical approach to the study of theology in the schools by question and

---

[20] On the translations see M. T. d'Alverny, 'Translations and translators', in R. L. Benson, G. Constable, and C. D. Lanham, eds., *Renaissance and Renewal in the Twelfth Century* (Toronto and London, 1991), pp. 421–62; B. G. Dod, 'Aristoteles latinus', in *The Cambridge History of Later Medieval Philosophy*, ed. N. Kretsmann, A. Kenny, and J. Pinborug (Cambridge, 1982), pp. 45–79. For a convenient summary see David Knowles, *The Evolution of Medieval Thought*, 2nd edn, ed. D. E. Luscombe and C. N. L. Brooke (London and New York, 1988), pp. 171–4.

[21] On the prohibitions and their effectiveness see ibid., pp. 205–8; Frederick van Steenberghen, *The Philosophical Movement of the Thirteenth Century* (Edinburgh and London, 1955), esp. ch. 6 on the condemnation of 1277, pp. 94–115.

[22] For minor exceptions see R. R. Bolgar, *The Classical Heritage and its Beneficiaries* (Cambridge, 1954), pp. 153–4.

answer – that is, dialectics. A theological doctrine would be subjected to reasoned analysis rather than accepted as a matter of faith. The whole process was summed up neatly by Peter Abelard in the famous statement that 'Through doubting we come to inquiry, and through inquiry we perceive the truth.'[23]

LOGIC AND MATHEMATICS

Logic was closely linked with mathematics, for mathematics is a strictly logical subject. Alexander Murray has observed of arithmetic that 'In numbers, it was what the art of dialectic was in the less pure realm of words.'[24] An Oxford scholar, Adelard of Bath (fl. 1116–62), after extensive travel in Syria, Southern Italy, and Spain, absorbing Greek and Arabic learning, combined the two. On the one hand, he applied dialectic to theology; on the other, he translated Greek and Arabic scientific works and wrote a treatise on the astrolabe. But the appearance of the 'arithmetical mentality' was by no means confined to scholastic circles. Many factors contributed to it, among them the growth in popularity of the abacus as a reckoning tool, from the tenth century, and the gradual replacement of difficult Roman numerals by the easier Arabic ones from the twelfth. There is no doubt, too, that the demands of trade and commerce and those of both royal and ecclesiastical administration played their part.[25] Here counting, measuring, and reckoning had become part of the fabric of daily life, and increasingly such calculations were being made in terms of money. At all levels of society, to a greater or lesser degree, the development of the monetized economy and the consciousness of numbers were inseparable. Counting, measuring, and reckoning in terms of money, the instrument that 'measured all things', will feature a lot in the following pages, as will the nature and properties of money itself.

MATHEMATICS AND THE MEAN

Medieval commentators often saw money as a middle term, a mean, through which equilibrium could be reached between the two parties to an economic transaction. The idea of the mean was basic to most

---

[23] See in general the classic work of Charles Homer Haskins, *The Renaissance of the Twelfth Century* (repr. Cleveland and New York, 1970), esp. pp. 341–67; Jean Leclercq, 'The renewal of theology' in Benson, Constable, and Lanham, eds., *Renaissance and Renewal*, pp. 68–87; Knowles, *Evolution of Medieval Thought*, pt. 2, pp. 65–136, Swanson, *Twelfth-century Renaissance*, pp. 115–41; Southern, *Scholastic Humanism*, 1.

[24] Alexander Murray, *Reason and Society in the Middle Ages* (Oxford, 1978), p. 206.

[25] Ibid., pp. 188–203.

economic thought and was associated with notions of balance, equilibrium, or moderation. Appropriately it had an economic origin, in Greece of the seventh century BC. To relieve a severe economic crisis the oracle of Delphi preached the virtue of moderation, nothing in excess, and warned of the need for everything to have a limit. This was to have a profound effect, not only on the Greeks, but on the whole tradition of Western thought, and in many different ways. It was taken up by the Pythagoreans in the fifth century, the followers of the Ionian philosopher Pythagoras (c. 550 BC) who had founded a school in southern Italy. They saw everything in mathematical terms, specifically in terms of number. For example, justice was seen as a square number, that is, a number made up of equal parts, each of which had the same value as the overall number of those parts. In politics, stability was preserved by maintaining the balance between different parts of the State, and not allowing any one to become too wealthy or powerful. But strict numerical equality was not the only approach to the mean: harmony and balance might also be achieved through proportion. Pythagoras based his ideas of musical harmony not on numerical equalities, but on strict proportion.[26] Harmony involves the fitting together of opposite notes to form the inclusive sound of a chord. Because a chord is a perfect blending of opposites it came to signify a natural limit – nothing in excess, not too much and not too little.[27] Significantly, in English polyphonic music from the fifteenth to the seventeenth century a middle part was known as the 'meane', because it maintained the balance between the outer parts, thus preserving the link with the mathematical concept. The Pythagoreans had also suggested an alternative type of justice based on reciprocity or requital, the receiving of something in proportion to what had been given. The suggestion that there was more than one type of mathematical mean was to have profound significance for both economic thought and natural philosophy.

Aristotle was influenced by Pythagorean ideas, though whether directly or indirectly is impossible to say. He wrote in the *Nichomachean Ethics* that 'Virtue ... is a state of character concerned with choice, lying in a mean' – in other words, the virtuous person applied moderation to his decisions. Pythagorean ideas also underlay his famous discussion in *Ethics* (v, 5) on justice in economic exchange. For him there were two types of justice. One was 'directive' or 'corrective', which implied a strict numerical equality between buyer and seller. This was the arithmetical equality faced by

---

[26] Willi Apel, *Harvard Dictionary of Music*, 2nd edn (London, 1970), p. 709, 'Pythagorean hammers'.
[27] On Pythagoras and the mean see Ernest Barker, *Greek Political Theory* (London, 1918, repr. in paperback, 1960), pp. 53–4, 56–7. On the 'meane' see Apel, *Harvard Dictionary*, pp. 512–13.

Buridan's ass. The other was distributive justice, which was proportional – in effect, rendering to each his due – and was arrived at by geometrical rather than arithmetical methods.[28]

THE PLAN OF THE BOOK

The following pages are largely about how ideas of the mean, of moderation and limit, of equality and balance, underlay medieval economic thought, and how they were developed, changed, and adapted to fit the shifting economic circumstances from the twelfth to the fifteenth centuries. The starting point is the problem of property and equality. How could private ownership and the inequalities that resulted be justified when God had given the earth and its resources to all in common? The first chapter explores both the origin and definitions of property, the basis of all economic relationships, and the various solutions which were put forward to the conflict between divine-natural law, which decreed common ownership, and human law, which sanctioned private possession. Were there any answers which appeared to harmonize the two positions?

Chapter 2 looks at shifting attitudes to wealth and poverty against the background of social and economic change and explores the possible foreshadowing of the idea of the work ethic. It also tries to show how the mean of economic sufficiency – not too much and not too little - was applied in different ways to the balancing of resources between rich and poor; how it governed the workings of earthly charity, enabling both the donor and the recipient to maintain their own mean of sufficiency; and how good works might be used to balance the sinner's account with God at the final reckoning.

Chapter 3 examines scholastic ideas on the nature and roles of money, in terms of both the individual and the State, and how they developed within the context of the commercial revolution. Two distinct roles, based on the *Ethics* and the *Politics* of Aristotle and commentaries on them, emerged. Money was, first, an artificial measure of value, authorized by the State, against which all things could be gauged, but which had no other use. In other words, money was a mean between things of differing value and quality. Secondly, since it was given physical reality by coinage made of precious metal, it came to be seen as a commodity with a value that could rise and fall like that of any other commodity.

Chapter 4 describes how political changes were reflected in the control of weights, measures, and coinage. This control was one of the sovereign

---

[28] See the penetrating discussion by Joel Kaye, *Economy and Nature in the Fourteenth Century: Money, Market Exchange, and the Emergence of Scientific Thought* (Cambridge, 1998), pp. 37–47.

rights of the monarch, but the late medieval period saw the development of representative institutions, such as parliaments and estates and councils. There were demands for counsel and consent at every level of society, from the College of Cardinals down to the village community. In England, through the development of constitutional monarchy, a mean was gradually established between the powers of the monarch and the representative assembly of Parliament. It was logical that sovereign rights which had been exercised by the king would in practice, if not in theory, also become subject to counsel and consent in Parliament or other representative assembly, and be implemented at the local level by manorial or borough officials.

Chapter 5 examines some of the economic ideas which emerged in conjunction with the development of the national sovereign states and the question of whether they anticipated the ideas of the Mercantilists of the seventeenth and eighteenth centuries. Attitudes to trade and merchants gradually changed from vilification to state protection. Underlying the change was the development of economic humanism, which promoted individual entrepreneurship as being for the common good, and economic nationalism, which promoted the economic good of the State. These demanded balance – the one internal, the other external. People needed to impose a limit on their economic behaviour. If they either took too much out of the economy by overindulgence and spending, or consumed too little by hoarding goods or money they disturbed its natural movement and upset its balance. Economic nationalism demanded that the trading relationship with other nations achieved some sort of balance between imports and exports. In order to avoid loss a country needed to balance imports and exports; in order to dominate, it needed to export more than it imported.

Chapter 6 is concerned with balance and equilibrium because it is about justice, the justice which governed prices and wages. The just price was supposed to be a mean between buyer and seller, in which the interests of both were included. The just wage struck a balance between the interests of the employer and the employee. But was an exact mathematical balance necessarily an economic advantage?

Chapter 7 is about the mortal sin of usury, that is, making a charge for lending money, in effect, making a charge for the use of the money as well as demanding the return of the amount lent. The focus will be on the role of the usurer as the one who gained at the expense of the borrower, and therefore upset the balance of justice.

The final chapter looks at the role of the usurer as loser, when the balance of justice swung the other way. Against this background, the theory of interest – that is, the avoidance of loss – developed. This allowed the lender to maintain the same economic position as he had enjoyed before he had made a loan. Eventually this was to lead to a narrowing in scope and a redefinition of what constituted usury. This would sanction the idea that labour, expense, and risk justified a borrower in paying a lender an amount which exceeded the principal of the loan. The aim was to achieve a mean between the usually rich lender and the destitute borrower.

The principle of the mean was applied in a number of different ways and at different levels. The story of Buridan's ass is about economic choice, but it also symbolized the deeper issue of moral choice. On one level the mean was applied to the individual. Living a righteous life involved the voluntary limitation of appetites and desires and the avoidance of extremes. The Christian had to live in the world and survive, but this involved a permanent balancing act between the often incompatible needs of body and soul – physical comfort in this world against eternal salvation in the next, material claims against spiritual ones. On another level it was applied to the distribution of resources, both between rich and poor and between areas of plenty and of scarcity. It balanced the relationship between seller and buyer, producer and consumer, employer and employee, and between lender and borrower. The result is that medieval economic ideas are concerned not merely with the market-place, with trade, and with industry, but also with less easily definable matters such as poverty and charity. At the heart of the economy is property – things – whether defined as lands, goods, money, or less tangible assets such as rights. Property in one sense or another is constantly being acquired, bought, sold, redistributed, given, lent, or borrowed. This is why we must begin with it.

I

PRIVATE PROPERTY *VERSUS* COMMUNAL RIGHTS: THE CONFLICT OF TWO LAWS

INTRODUCTION: DEFINITIONS AND PROBLEMS

'Since all things are common by God's law and by law of nature, how may any man be lord of anything more than another?'[1] mused Dives, the rich man, in the early fifteenth-century treatise *Dives and Pauper*. The question was not a new one, and this chapter will examine various answers which were suggested, either by groups or individuals, to the disagreement between divine-natural law and human law. By the law of God and nature all things were given to everyone in common; by human law things were owned individually and divided unequally. Was it possible to reconcile these two extreme positions – to find a mean between them? Some solutions to be examined here were purely theoretical; others, from late medieval England, were both theoretical and practical. Before investigating them, however, property, the origin and basis of all economic life and attitudes, needs to be defined.

Property can be seen as the means to sustain life and as something to be enjoyed and shared. It can also be seen as the object of human greed, and its possession as a title to riches and to power over others. Medieval thinkers considered that both property and the subjection of one person to another were the result of sin. In Paradise there was no private property, for everything was held in common, and the fruits of the earth were naturally shared. But after the Fall, when human nature became corrupted by sin, human institutions such as government and property became necessary. They were seen as a divinely ordained remedy for sin, which would help to order human life in its degraded state.

---

[1] *Dives and Pauper*, pt. 2, Commandment VII, v, p. 138, lines 1–3.

In Roman law property was 'things', and the law of 'things' featured prominently in Justinian's textbook, the *Institutes*, although the law students were left to work out for themselves just what 'things' were. In its simplest form, property was any 'thing', material or immaterial, that was owned or possessed and had some economic value. The most obvious and important thing was immovable: it was land, the chief source of wealth, and, in a primitive economy, the means of production. But 'things' also included the immovable buildings erected on that land, the movable animals which grazed on it, the crops which grew on it, and an infinite variety of movable chattels. These might be natural raw materials or manufactured goods. A 'thing' might even be intangible, such as the labour of one's own body. It might be a legal right, such as a right of way. It might involve rights over someone, a master's rights over a slave, a husband's rights over a wife, a manorial lord's over a serf or villein. The possession of property was therefore inseparable from both political and legal rights.

We shall explore the problem of the two laws, divine-natural law and human law, as applied to the question of property. Law is the expression of the society which fashions it. Medieval society was permeated at every level by the dichotomy between the secular and the spiritual – empire and papacy, kingship and priesthood, laity and clergy, all reflecting the division into body and soul of man himself. Translated into terms of law, the duality was that between the law of God and of nature, and human positive law, both written and customary. In a Christian society the laws of God and of nature tended to be identified, if only because God was the author of nature – hence divine-natural law. Yet they might be approached differently, the one through scriptural revelation, the other through natural human reason. Not surprisingly, this divine-natural law took precedence over all human law, and it was immutable. As Gratian, summing up earlier views in his *Decretum*, explained: 'Whatever is accepted as customary or committed to writing, if it is contrary to natural law is to be considered null and void.'[2] That at least seemed unequivocal, until it was applied to property. 'The law of nature differs from custom and statute', Gratian observed, 'for by the law of nature all things are common to all men . . . by the law of custom or statute, this belongs to me, that belongs to someone else'.[3] It was human law that created the problem. It was human law that had sanctioned the unequal possession described by Dives.

The issue attracted attention from the twelfth century. This is the century which has been credited with the 'discovery of the individual',

---

[2] Gratian, *Decretum Gratiani*, in Ae. Friedberg, ed., *Corpus iuris canonici*, 1 (Leipzig, 1879), D. 8, *ante* c. 2, col. 13.
[3] Ibid., D. 8, *ante* c. 1, col. 12.

when people developed a new sense of self-awareness and of their individual abilities and rights. The explanations range from the heightened spirituality of the age, the growing popularity of natural law ideas, and the intellectual developments of the twelfth-century Renaissance to the development of a European commercial economy.[4] The resulting consciousness of 'self' led to an awareness of individual rights, political, social, and legal, of which the growing importance of personal status, family descent, and possession, especially of land, were indicative. In economic and social terms the rise in population led to land hunger, a growing sense of acquisitiveness, and disputes about property – a situation exacerbated in England by the anarchy of Stephen's reign (1135–54). In the towns, propertied people, *nouveaux riches*, started to emerge in the shape of merchants, whose urban resources were their own. The fact that money was circulating in the market-place as a medium of exchange was an indication that the goods for which that money was exchanged were privately owned. In legal terms twelfth-century England saw the development of the common law of real property, which gradually transformed the relationship of lords and their tenants, giving the tenants something like private ownership of the lands they occupied. Later a dramatic fall in population, occasioned largely by the pestilence of 1348 and subsequent years, led to shortages of both tenants and labourers, giving the survivors unprecedented bargaining power and opportunities for both social and geographical mobility. Lords had to adopt a more flexible attitude to them. By the end of the period not only was land let on terms which amounted to private ownership, but it was also tenanted by a wider spectrum of people than previously. A growing sense of individual rights and possession provided a fertile background for the debate about conflicting legal ideas on property.

ST AUGUSTINE'S SOLUTION: GOD AS AUTHOR OF HUMAN LAW

In the early fifth century St Augustine had recognized the problem of the conflicting laws. Rights of possession were firmly grounded on human law, whereas divine law had decreed that 'the earth and the fullness thereof' were the Lord's. God had fashioned rich and poor out of the same dust,

---

[4] For a summary of views, see Antony Black, 'The individual and society', in *The Cambridge History of Medieval Political Thought*, ed. J. H. Burns (Cambridge, 1991), pp. 588–9. See also Colin Morris, *The Discovery of the Individual, 1050–1200* (London, 1972); Swanson, *Twelfth-century Renaissance*, pp. 141–50; Caroline Walker Bynum, 'Did the twelfth century discover the individual?', *JEH*, 31 (1980), pp. 1–17, repr. in expanded form in *Jesus as Mother: Studies in the Spirituality of the High Middle Ages* (Berkeley, Los Angeles, and London, 1982), pp. 82–109; Walter Ullmann, *The Individual and Society in the Middle Ages* (London, 1967), pt. 3, pp. 101–51.

and the same earth supported both.[5] In other words, divine law indicated equality and the sharing of the earth. Augustine contrasted the state of man's innocence with the state of fallen man. Human institutions, in particular the rule of kings and the subjection of slaves, had not existed in the state of innocence: sin was the cause of subjection. The first just men were shepherds of flocks rather than kings of men, 'so that in this way God might convey the message of what was required by the order of nature, and what was demanded by the deserts of sinners'.[6] God was the source of all power, and he granted rulership to men entirely at his pleasure: 'We must ascribe to the true God alone the power to grant kingdoms and empires. He ... grants earthly kingdoms both to the good and to the evil, in accordance with his pleasure.'[7] Despite earthly rulers, God's providence continued to rule humanity: 'It is beyond anything incredible that he should have willed the kingdoms of men, their dominations and their servitudes, to be outside the range of the laws of his providence.'[8] It was not difficult for Augustine and later medieval thinkers to justify the existence of earthly rulers by reference to divine law, even if they had not existed in the state of innocence. But property was another matter. Yet Augustine implied that God had sanctioned private property as well, at least indirectly, for human law was the law of emperors and kings, and it was through them that God had distributed things to the human race: 'By the law of kings are possessions possessed', he declared.[9] God instituted rulers, and rulers legitimated private property in a world which continued to be ruled by God's providence. But that did not make it either 'right' or 'wrong' in a moral sense. For Augustine, earthly institutions and possessions were merely useful to man on his pilgrimage through this life, and were to be used accordingly. They must not be valued, far less loved or desired, for their own sake. He spelt out carefully that there were two distinct types of possessions, temporal and eternal, of which the temporal were merely fleeting:

> The temporal ones are health, wealth, honour, friends, houses, sons, a wife, and the rest of the things of this life where we travel as pilgrims. Let us place ourselves in the stopping-places of this life as passing pilgrims, not as permanent possessors.[10]

The pilgrim who made use of earthly and temporal things did not allow himself to become obsessed by them or distracted from his journey

---

[5] Augustine, *In Ioannis Evangelium Tractatus*, 6, 25–6: *CChr. SL*, 36, p. 66, lines 18–20.
[6] Augustine, *City of God*, trans. H. Bettenson, ed. D. Knowles, *Augustine: City of God* (Harmondsworth, 1972), bk. 19, ch. 16, pp. 874–5.
[7] Ibid., bk. 5, ch. 21, p. 215.   [8] Ibid., bk. 5, ch. 11, p. 196.
[9] Ibid.: Gratian D. 8, c. 1.   [10] Augustine, *Sermo* 80.7, *PL*, 38, col. 497.

towards God. They had to support him, rather than add to his burdens.[11] Augustine's reasoning is clear, even if his view of family and friends as temporal possessions seems strange. He had gone some way to solving the problem of the two laws by making God, at least indirectly, the author of human law. What he had not done was to explain how God had come to contradict himself by authorizing two apparently conflicting laws.

TOWARDS A SOLUTION: CHANGING NATURAL LAW

One way to solve the conflict was to remove it altogether by altering, or at least adjusting, natural law to the changed circumstances of human life after the Fall. It could then be brought into line with human law. Given that natural law was really divine-natural law, the law of God, attempting to change it was a daunting prospect, and both canonists and scholastics were cautious. But natural law was a flexible concept, which could be understood on different levels, from basic animal instinct to the sophisticated rules which made up the law of nations, international law. It was once described as a wheelbarrow into which anything could be dumped and which could be wheeled in any direction. Medieval thought was tidier, but it did exploit the flexibility of natural law in trying to resolve its contradiction with human law.

The twelfth-century canonist Rufinus arrived at a clumsy three-fold definition of natural law. The first two categories were based on Scripture: commands which ordered the performance of good acts, and prohibitions, which forbade the performance of bad ones. The third, known as demonstrations, was vaguer and more general, and included advice like 'Let all goods be held in common.'[12] It was this third category which was to present the most potential for change. With the Fall, human understanding of natural law, that is, of good and evil, had become clouded, but it had been restored through the 'commands' and 'prohibitions' of the Bible, which laid down principles of right and wrong. But these needed to be 'adorned' or supplemented by custom. They needed to be applied in specific situations. This was especially true of the 'liberty of all men and the common possession of things, for now, by civil law, this is my slave, that is your field'.[13] As Rufinus explained, although these things might seem contrary to natural law, they were necessary to restrain people and to prevent crime. They were a way of disciplining fallen humanity into following the commands and prohibitions of natural law, and so were not contrary

---

[11] Augustine, *City of God*, bk. 19, ch. 17, p. 877.
[12] Rufinus, *Summa Decretorum*, ed. Heinrich Singer (Paderborn, 1902), pp. 4–7, trans. Ewart Lewis, *Medieval Political Ideas*, 1 (New York, 1974), p. 38.
[13] Ibid.

to it.[14] This more flexible approach, governed by altered circumstances, would be followed later.

Thinkers soon abandoned the awkward three-fold classification of natural law and drew simply on the implication that there could be a difference between its strict letter and its application. One of the first was Alexander of Hales (d. 1245), a Gloucestershire born Franciscan who had been Archdeacon of Coventry before moving to Paris. In the *Summa* attributed to him[15] he suggested that the application of natural law should be flexible, although this did nothing to change its content. Although doctors might think drinking wine was healthy, they would hardly give it to a sick man. Man's sinful nature after the Fall was, in effect, sick, and while natural law decreed community of property for his 'healthy', innocent state of nature, it allowed private property in his fallen and diseased state. The basic natural law principle had not changed, merely its application in a particular situation.[16]

Thomas Aquinas pushed this a little further. For him, all law, including natural law and human law, if it derived from 'right reason', was derived from the eternal law of God.[17] If something followed 'right reason' it meant that it was for the common good, and anything for the common good therefore agreed with natural law. Aquinas was cautious about changing natural law. The first principles were unalterable, but on some 'particular and rare occasions' the 'secondary precepts', the particular conclusions from these first principles, might vary.[18] So far he had not gone much beyond Alexander. But he did go on to admit that natural law could be changed (and Aquinas actually uses the Latin verb *mutare*, to change) in two ways, either by additions to it or subtractions from it.[19] 'The individual holding of possessions is not... contrary to the natural law; it is what rational beings conclude as an addition to the natural law', he declared.[20]

One of the most colourful expressions of natural law adapting to circumstances was provided by the English Lancastrian lawyer Sir John Fortescue (c. 1394–c. 1476):

It is the same sun which condenses liquid mud into brick and melts frozen into flowing water; and the wind which kindles the lighted torch into flame is no other than that which cools the hot barley-porridge; for in these cases the qualities of

[14] Ibid., p. 39.
[15] For a summary of arguments on its authenticity, and for literature, see Langholm, *Economics*, pp. 118–20.
[16] Alexander of Hales, *Summa theologica*, 4 vols. (Quaracchi, 1924–48), 4, pt. 2, inq. 2, q. 3, 246, p. 348. Cf. Langholm, *Economics*, p. 124.
[17] Thomas Aquinas, *Summa theologiae: Latin text and English translation*, 61 vols., ed. T. Gilby et al. (London, 1964–80), 1a2ae, 93, 3, vol. 28, p. 59.
[18] Ibid., 94, 5, p. 93.   [19] Ibid.   [20] Ibid., 2a2ae, 66, 2, vol. 38, p. 69.

the objects cause the mutations which the objects themselves undergo; but the efficient cause... is not changed. Even so the equity of natural justice which once assigned to innocent man the common ownership of all things is none other than that equity which now, because of his sin, takes away from man... the good of common ownership.[21]

Fortescue, like others before him, implied that the first principles of natural law do not change, any more than the sun or the wind, but its effect in changed circumstances does. In theory at least the contradiction between natural and human law seemed to have been solved.

PRIVATE RIGHTS AND THE COMMON GOOD

The common possession laid down by divine-natural law benefited everyone; private possession benefited only the few. Could common and private possession be harmonized? One way to do this was to show that private possession was really for the common good. This is what Aquinas and others attempted.

Aquinas combined patristic and Aristotelian ideas. In book 2 of the *Politics*, Aristotle had supported private property against the community of wives and property recommended by Plato in his *Republic*. 'When everyone has his own sphere of interest there will not be the same ground for quarrels', he advised, 'And the amount of interest will increase, because each man will feel he is applying himself to what is his own.'[22] In other words, life will be harmonious and efficient. Aquinas also reckoned that it would be more peaceful under a system of private property. Combining Aristotle with patristic ideas, he explained that in the state of innocence men's wills were such that they could use things in common without danger of conflict. But now 'when owners multiply there has to be a division of possessions, because possession in common is fraught with discord, as the Philosopher says'.[23] Individual possession was necessary for human life:

First because each person takes more trouble to care for something that is his sole responsibility than what is held in common or by man – for in such a case each individual shirks the work and leaves the responsibility to somebody else... Second, because human affairs are more efficiently organized if each person

---

[21] Sir John Fortescue, *De natura legis naturae*, trans. Lewis, *Medieval Political Ideas*, 1, p. 134. For discussion and further examples see Richard Schlatter, *Private Property: the History of an Idea* (London, 1951), ch. 3.
[22] Aristotle, *The Politics*, trans. E. Barker (Oxford, 1946), II, v, 5, 1263a, p. 49.
[23] Thomas Aquinas, *Summa theologiae*, Ia, 98, 1 ad 3, vol. 13, p. 153.

has his own responsibility to discharge; there would be chaos if everybody cared for everything. Third, because men live together in greater peace where everyone is content with his task.[24]

Hard work, efficiency, and peace – on this basis private possession could be reconciled with the common good and with natural law.

PROPERTY AS NATURAL TO MAN

The next solution was to turn the possession of private property into a positive natural right by showing that its acquisition was the result of man's own labour. This bypassed the problem of the conflicting laws because it suggested that divine-natural law had sanctioned private property even in the state of innocence, so that the problem did not arise.

In justifying individual ownership, Aquinas had linked property and labour – common possession would lead to skiving. John of Paris (d. 1306), supporter of Philip IV in his dispute with Boniface VIII, was more specific about the connection in his *On Royal and Papal Power*. He was writing in order to distinguish the different spheres of authority of lay rulers and priests. Unlike Augustinian thinkers, he did not see civil society and institutions as the penalty for sin imposed by God. On the contrary, secular society and government were natural.[25] They were instituted before the priesthood, but even before this, lay property had been established as something natural to man. It was the result of his own labour.

> lay property is not granted to the community as a whole...but is acquired by individual people through their own skill, labour and diligence, and individuals, as individuals, have right and power over it and valid lordship... Thus neither prince nor pope has lordship or administration of such properties.[26]

This is a very radical viewpoint, as Janet Coleman has demonstrated, especially considering that John was writing as early as 1302.[27] It is a prelude to later ideas on the dignity and value of human labour.[28] It also enshrines the idea of privately owned property, for there is no sense of a lord and tenant relationship: on the contrary, it is the individual who has 'right and power...and valid lordship'.

Fortescue, too, saw the origin of individual property rights in labour, and regarded it as in a sense natural, although he followed the tradition

---

[24] Ibid., 2a2ae, 66, 2, vol. 38, p. 67.
[25] John of Paris, *On Royal and Papal Power*, ed. and trans. J. A. Watt (Toronto, 1971), ch. 1, p. 79.
[26] Ibid., ch. 7, p. 103.
[27] Janet Coleman, 'Medieval discussions of property: *Ratio* and *Dominium* according to John of Paris and Marsilius of Padua', *HPT*, 4 (1983), pp. 209–28, esp. 216–19.
[28] See ch. 2, pp. 52–3 below.

that property originated after the Fall. Natural law decreed one thing for man in his state of innocence, community of property, and another, private property, for his fallen state. He did not, however, separate the secular from the spiritual. All private property came to man through his own labour, and seemed to be blessed by God. He quoted God's words to Adam (Genesis 3.39): 'In the sweat of thy countenance shalt thou eat thy bread':

in which words there was granted to man property in the things which he *by his own sweat* [my italics] could obtain... For since the bread which man would acquire in sweat would be his own, and since no one could eat bread without the sweat of his own countenance, every man who did not sweat was forbidden to eat the bread which another had acquired by his sweat... And thus the inheritable ownership of things first broke forth. For by the words *bread* our elders teach us, we are to understand not only what is eaten and drunk but everything by which man is sustained; and by the word *sweat*, all the industry of man.[29]

Both John of Paris and Fortescue anticipated John Locke's idea that man by joining the labour of his body to something made it his property. John of Paris, like Locke, saw the origins of property in the state of innocence and therefore as natural, whereas Fortescue placed it after the Fall but gave it divine sanction.

THE MONASTIC SOLUTION: IMITATING JERUSALEM

The justification of private property was a way of sanctioning a life that was less than perfect. Life for the perfect was another matter entirely: it meant total renunciation of property and living a communal life. The Augustinian Giles of Rome (d. 1316), opponent of John of Paris, recognized that 'things being as they were', it was to the advantage of a city for the citizens to delight in private possessions. Since men were far from perfect they were content to live such a life. Those who decided to live without worldly possessions chose to live not as men but above men, living a Heavenly life. Such people, being so much better than others were not part of the State.[30] Nevertheless, for those who would be perfect, imitation of the apparently communal life of the first Christians at Jerusalem seemed to be the answer, despite the fact that the interpretation of the relevant biblical texts is disputed: community of property may not actually have been the rule at Jerusalem.[31] Gratian preserved a text, dubiously ascribed

[29] Fortescue, *De natura legis naturae*, trans. Lewis, *Medieval Political Ideas*, p. 135.
[30] Giles of Rome, *De regimine principum* (Rome, 1556), bk. II, pt. iii, ch. 6, p. 114r–v; ibid., ch. 5, p. 213v. For discussion see Langholm, *Economics*, p. 384; Schlatter, *Property*, pp. 56–65.
[31] A. J. and R. W. Carlyle, *A History of Mediaeval Political Theory in the West*, 1, *The Second Century to the Ninth* (Edinburgh and London, 1930), pp. 99–100, 135.

to Clement I, which recommended communal living for all who wanted to serve God and to imitate the apostolic life. The use of everything in the world ought to be common to all men, 'Clement' recommended. It was only through sin that individual possession, and the resulting conflict, had arisen. 'Just as the air cannot be divided nor the splendour of the sun, so the things given to all men in common should not be divided', he advised.[32] Counsel of perfection indeed, and it was followed, with varying degrees of success, by the monastic orders based on the Rule of St Benedict. In his Rule the saint ordered: 'Let no one presume to give or receive anything without the abbot's leave, or to have anything as his own... for monks should not have even their bodies and wills at their own disposal'; and he followed this with a reference to the Jerusalem community.[33]

Until the twelfth century, monasticism was regarded, in the words of a chronicler, as 'the surest road to Heaven'.[34] Then it became rather less sure. It was becoming obvious that while monks individually might be poor, the same could not be said of their institutions. The monasteries, especially the Benedictine ones, were becoming large property-owning corporations. Monks were able to renounce private possession, but they could not and did not renounce corporate possession. The consequence of wealth, much of it landed, as Barbara Harvey has observed, was that 'Benedictines were able to live like the nobility or gentry and... were almost obliged to do so.'[35] At the end of the medieval period, in 1535, the net income of Westminster, the second richest house in England, was a cool £2,800 a year, 17 per cent higher than in 1400.[36]

Benedictines paid the price, almost literally, of being too popular and well endowed in an age of heightened spirituality. The new devotional atmosphere was partly a reaction against the manifest wealth of the institutional Church and the increasing administrative efficiency of the papacy. But it was also the product of the quickening of the economy, of thriving trade and industry, urbanization, developing commerce, and with it the rise of a new merchant elite, all of which seemed to question traditional religious values. The whole of society appeared to be changing, and at such a time of upheaval, in some cases suffering, some preferred to concentrate on the next world rather than this. These reactions against materialism were at first channelled into Benedictine monasticism, but soon found expression in attempts to recreate the apostolic life of poverty and evangelization of the primitive Church. It was demonstrated both in the foundation of

---

[32] Gratian, *Decretum*, C. 12, q. 1, c. 2.
[33] *The Rule of St Benedict*, trans. Justin McCann (London, 1976), ch. 33, p. 40.
[34] William of Malmesbury, *Deeds of the Kings of the English*, EHD, 2, no. 118, p. 694.
[35] Barbara Harvey, *Living and Dying in England 1100–1540: the Monastic Experience* (Oxford, 1995), p. 1.
[36] Barbara Harvey, *Westminster Abbey and its Estates in the Middle Ages* (Oxford, 1977), p. 63.

the new and stricter monastic orders of the twelfth century, but also in alternative radical groups, such as the Waldensians, or Poor Men of Lyons (an instructive name – sometimes the groups were referred to generically as the 'Poor of Christ'), the Cathars, and the Humiliati.[37] Perhaps the most radical of all were the later Taborites, the extremist Hussite sect in Bohemia in the early fifteenth century. At the fortress of Tabor they lived a strict communal life. Their 'Articles' claimed: 'nothing is mine and nothing thine, but all is common, so everything shall be common to all forever and no one shall have anything of his own; because whoever owns anything himself commits a mortal sin'.[38] Even by the thirteenth century, however, the mantle of the 'Poor of Christ' was being assumed by the new mendicant orders, especially the Franciscans. Originally individual laymen, rather than monks cushioned by a property-owning institution, they have been regarded as the true heirs of the heretical Humiliati.[39]

THE MENDICANT SOLUTION: TOTAL POVERTY

The mendicant solution was to renounce all property, both individually and corporately. Implementing this, however, was not without problems, because in order to survive everyone needs a modicum of 'things'.

St Francis, whose life more than any other came to epitomize absolute poverty, arose from precisely the new mercantile elite against which religious movements were reacting. He was the son of a wealthy cloth merchant of Assisi. Francis himself was an extremist, totally dedicated to imitating not so much the poverty of the Apostles, but what he saw as that of Christ himself. In the Rule of 1223 he ordered his followers to renounce all property: 'The friars are to appropriate nothing for themselves, neither a house, nor a place, nor anything else. As "strangers and pilgrims [1 Peter 2.11]" in this world, who serve God in poverty and humility, they should beg alms trustingly.'[40] Above all, the Franciscans were to shun money. Brothers who worked were not to seek reward in coins or any

---

[37] Brenda Bolton, *The Medieval Reformation* (London, 1983), pp. 21–6.
[38] Josef Maček, *The Hussite Movement in Bohemia* (London and Prague, 1965), p. 114. John Wyclif, on whose ideas those of John Hus and his followers were ultimately based, did put forward the idea of property held in common, but it was not one of his main convictions and was not widely adopted by his followers: Anne Hudson, *Lollards and Their Books* (London and Roncaverte, 1985), p. 126.
[39] Brenda Bolton, 'The poverty of the Humiliati', in D. Flood, ed., *Poverty in the Middle Ages*, Franziskanische Forschungen, 27 (Werl, Westfalia, 1975), pp. 52–9; M. D. Lambert, *Franciscan Poverty: the Doctrine of the Absolute Poverty of Christ and the Apostles in the Franciscan Order: 1210–1323* (London, 1961), pp. 40–1.
[40] Francis of Assisi, *Rule of 1223*, ch. 6, ed. Marion A. Habig, *St Francis of Assisi: Writings and Early Biographies: English Omnibus of the Sources for the Life of St Francis*, 3rd edn rev. (London, 1979), p. 61.

substitute for coins – '*pecuniam aut denarios*' is the expression used.[41] They were not so much as to touch money: 'If ever we find money somewhere, we should think no more of it than of the dust we trample under our feet.'[42] The saint wanted his friars to be completely divorced from the commercial world of his childhood. Material life would deprive them of the love of Christ and of eternity and would drag them down with it to Hell.[43]

Total poverty may have been all very well when Francis had a mere handful of followers, but it was totally impractical when numbers expanded, even during the lifetime of the saint, to create a world-wide missionary order. The situation was not helped by the fact that his views on poverty were ambiguous. Francis himself was neither a legist nor an organizer. When, in 1219, he sailed away to Damietta to join forces with the crusading army there (in his case the battle was spiritual rather than physical), he wisely left the direction of the Order in other hands – notably those of Ugolino, later Gregory IX, who became its Cardinal-Protector. While retaining a natural authority, Francis never resumed official control.

Even during the founder's lifetime a number of related problems had started to emerge. How could the Order survive as a world-wide preaching organization if it could 'own' nothing? Was it possible to separate the ownership – dominion – of something, from its use? What exactly was meant by renunciation? Did the friars renounce property both individually *and* corporately? Overriding these questions was that of the exact nature of the poverty of Christ and the Apostles. Had they really been absolutely poor, and, if so, did they renounce both 'use' and dominion, in the sense of ownership? A variety of acrobatic legal solutions was worked out by both the Order and the papacy during the century following 1223, the Second Rule of St Francis.

Almost certainly the Cardinal-Protector Ugolino influenced Francis in drawing up the Second Rule.[44] The Rule was of great significance as being the thin end of the wedge between ownership, or dominion, and use. It introduced an intermediary, a financial agent or 'spiritual friend', who would stand between the friars and the world in order to provide clothes for the brethren and necessities for the sick.[45] Ugolino's views may have been coloured by an earlier incident which had prompted him to

---

[41] Francis, *Rule of 1221*, ed. Habig, *St Francis*, ch. 8, p. 38: for discussion see Lambert, *Franciscan Poverty*, pp. 38–40; Janet Coleman, 'Property and poverty', in Burns, ed., *Cambridge History of Medieval Political Thought*, pp. 607–48, at pp. 631–3.
[42] Francis, *Rule of 1221*, ch. 8, p. 38.   [43] Ibid., ch. 22, pp. 47–8.
[44] Habig, *St Francis*, p. 55, n. 7 for evidence. For discussion see pp. 54–7 and Lambert, *Franciscan Poverty*, pp. 1–30.
[45] Francis, *Rule of 1223*, ch. 4, p. 60.

distinguish between 'dominion' and 'use'. Francis had been furious when a house at Bologna had been referred to as the 'house of the brethren' – so furious that he had evicted the friars, allowing them to return only when Ugolino claimed that the house was 'his', and that they 'used' it only with his permission.[46] As pope, Gregory continued to reduce the impracticalities of total poverty. The real compromise, or mean solution, came with Innocent IV's *Ordinem vestram* (1245), which vested ownership of Franciscan property in the papacy, but allowed the brothers to retain its use. Compromises rarely satisfy, and this one led to both internal conflict and external attack, especially at Paris, leading to further compromises. The minister general, Bonaventure, in his *Apologia pauperum* tried to synthesize opposing viewpoints. Poverty was reaffirmed in that friars renounced all dominion (lordship) over property, both individually and collectively, and its possession. On the other hand, they were allowed to retain a limited 'use' of it – what became known as simple use – enough to sustain their lives. This was similar to the idea that by divine law all men were equal and shared the earth. In his bull *Exiit qui seminat* (1279), Nicholas III, drawing on Bonaventure, also tried to achieve a mean. He maintained the fiction that the pope was the owner of Franciscan property, but he also declared that 'apostolic poverty' was in accordance with the example of the life of Christ. He was giving official sanction to the poverty doctrine and extending direct papal protection to its practitioners. At least this warded off external attack, but it did nothing to soothe internal discord. Indeed, so serious did this become that in 1322 Pope John XXII renounced papal ownership of Franciscan property, and the next year, in *Cum inter nonnullos*, declared it heresy to say that Christ and the Apostles had owned nothing. He also beatified the Dominican Thomas Aquinas, whose moderate views on poverty had influenced him.[47]

Ideas about poverty and dominion, possession and use, were to be taken up by Richard Fitzralph, Archbishop of Armagh (c. 1295–1360) in his *De pauperie salvatoris*, written against the mendicant orders, in which he opposed the poverty doctrine. In England, especially, debates about poverty and dominion widened to embrace all the clergy. John Wyclif's fundamental idea on the connection between dominion and the state of grace

[46] Lambert, *Franciscan Poverty*, pp. 45, 87.
[47] On all this see C. H. Lawrence, *The Friars: the Impact of the Early Mendicant Movement on Western Society* (London, 1994), pp. 43–64; Lambert, *Franciscan Poverty*, esp. pp. 68–102, 126–48, 208–46; John Moorman, *A History of the Franciscan Order from its Origins to the Year 1517* (Oxford, 1968), pp. 140–54, 307–19; David Flood, 'Franciscan poverty: a brief survey', Introduction to Gedeon Gál and David Flood, eds., *Nicolaus Minorita: Chronica. Documentation on Pope John XXII, Michael of Cesena and The Poverty of Christ, with Summaries in English* (St Bonaventure, New York, 1996), pp. 31–53. For Aquinas's attitude to poverty see ch. 2, pp. 45–6, 55 below.

formed the basis for his, and others', demands for clerical poverty and the disendowment of the Church.[48] The far-reaching consequences of an apparently simple idea – total renunciation of property – espoused by a few friars to resolve the dichotomy between communal and private possession could hardly have been foreseen.

THE STEWARDSHIP SOLUTION: THE POPE AS STEWARD

In arriving at the legal fiction of owning all Franciscan property the papacy was echoing another solution to the opposition of common and private rights: the earth, and its resources, was owned perpetually by God, and Christians were merely stewards of it on God's behalf. The origins of the idea lie in the Old Testament conception of economic activity.[49] The People of Israel administered the earth on behalf of the Lord. They belonged to him, and everything they had was his. 'The Lord God took the man and put him into the garden to dress it and care for it' (Genesis 2.15). God's plan was that man should be the agent of economic growth. Under God, man was given dominion over the earth and encouraged to increase: 'Be fruitful and multiply, and replenish the earth and subdue it' (Genesis 1.28). Man's dominion over the earth was similar to that of God over man.[50] With the Fall, however, nature as well as man was changed, becoming less productive and less attractive: 'Thorns also and thistles shall it [the earth] bring forth to thee; and thou shalt eat the herb of the field; In the sweat of thy face shalt thou eat bread...' (Genesis 3.18–19). Scarcity had entered the world, acting as a catalyst to economic development. Adam was sent from the Garden of Eden 'to till the ground' (Genesis 4.23), and he and his descendants became farmers and shepherds. The accursed Cain and his progeny, unable to till the earth, diversified their economic activity, building cities, becoming herdsmen and manufacturers. The New Testament concentrated more on the kingdom which is 'not of this world', but even here the idea of stewardship was perpetuated in the parable of the talents (Matthew 25.14–30).

God retained lordship of property, but for practical purposes Christians administered it, or had the use of it. It belonged to the whole Christian society, the Church. All Christians were baptized into the Church; they became united within the mystical body of Christ. They were, in terms of Roman law, part of a legal corporation. And one of the hallmarks of

[48] On this see pp. 32–3 below.
[49] For what follows see Barry Gordon, *Economic Analysis before Adam Smith: Hesiod to Lessius* (London, 1975), ch. 4, pp. 70–82.
[50] Ibid., p. 73.

a corporation was that it could own property. The Bolognese canonist Johannes Andreae (d. 1348), who was probably only the second married layman to be a professor of canon law, pronounced that Christ himself had *dominium* of the goods of the Church.[51] The Christian corporation, however, differed from other corporations because their *personae* were simply legal fictions, whereas to Christians, Christ was no fiction. But the practical effect was the same, because Christ was not present on earth in physical terms any more than a fictitious legal person was. He therefore had to be re-presented, given physical embodiment, by an earthly vicar, in this case the pope. This meant that for practical purposes the pope had dominion of the property of the Church on behalf of Christ. As a fourteenth-century thinker, William of Sarzano (fl. 1316–33), writing for John XXII observed:

Although the possession, right, and dominion of ecclesiastical possessions can belong to various people, either singly or living communally . . . as secondary administrators, primarily and principally, all possession, right, and dominion is seen to belong to the person of the supreme pontiff . . . he is seen to be the *dominus* and principal steward of all ecclesiastical property . . .[52]

Some thinkers, like John of Paris, ascribed dominion of church property to the pope, and of secular property to the lay ruler.[53] A more extreme version of the idea awarded ownership of all property, both ecclesiastical and lay, to the Church. Giles of Rome declared:

there may be no lordship with justice over temporal things or lay persons or anything else which is not under the Church and through the Church: for example, this man or that cannot with justice possess a farm or a vineyard or anything else which he has unless he holds it under the Church and through the Church.[54]

The theory which left all property in the hands of an abstract body, the Church, the mystical body of Christ, was the perfect answer to the opposition between natural-divine law and human law, because it deprived individual Christians of dominion. All property was 'held', rather than 'owned', by them on behalf of the whole Christian society. Once the embarrassing right of ultimate ownership had been shed, Christians could truly claim to be 'the poor of Christ'.

[51] Johannes Andreae, *Commentaria ad Decretales* (Venice, 1581), II, xii, 4, p. 67vb.
[52] William of Sarzano, *Tractatus de Summi Pontificis*, ed. R. del Ponte, *Studi medievali*, ser. 3, 12 (1971), ch. 7, pp. 1044–5.
[53] John of Paris, *On Royal and Papal Power*, ch. 7, p. 104.
[54] Giles of Rome, *De ecclesiastica potestate*, trans. R. W. Dyson (Woodbridge, and Dover, NH, 1986), pt. 2, ch. 7, 8, p. 68.

JOHN WYCLIF'S SOLUTION: THE KING AS STEWARD

John Wyclif had his own way of removing the tension between the two laws. Well aware as he was of the niceties of papal theory, he simply adapted it in favour of the national English monarchy, so that the king became the vicar of God on earth.[55] Like Augustine, he thought that private property and other human institutions were the result of the Fall of man, introduced as a remedy for sin, and that they were contrary to man's ideal nature.[56] Unlike Augustine, he considered that kings existed before priests. Property had developed with kingship and was therefore part of secular lordship, which meant priests had no right to it: Christ's condemnations of riches, coupled with the exemplary communal life of the early Christians [Acts 4] amply demonstrated that. Any property that priests, or indeed laymen, held was the result of a royal grant, and was held from the king, on condition that it would be used for the good of the realm, and on the understanding that the grant was revokable.[57]

The problem of revoking the grant to the priests was an urgent one in the late fourteenth century. England was at war with France, and clerical wealth was clearly not being used for the good of the realm. Wyclif castigated the greedy and avaricious clergy for preying on the wealth of England during the national emergency. They were the worms in the 'stomach' of the body politic, which would ruin its health.[58] If they would not voluntarily renounce their wealth, and return to their former state of apostolic poverty, then the king, as the vicar of God, would have to confiscate it for the common good.[59] Disendowment of the English Church was discussed at the Parliament of 1371, and reported on by Wyclif. A 'certain peer, more skilled than the others' had argued that 'when war breaks out we must take from the endowed clergy a portion of their temporal possessions, as property which belongs to us and the kingdom in common, and so wisely defend the country with property which exists among us in superfluity'.[60]

Wyclif's followers, known as the Lollards, had absorbed his idea that Christ had dominion over property and that priests had no right to temporal possessions beyond what was needed for subsistence. In 1395 a document known as the 'Twelve Conclusions', which purported to be written

---

[55] In general see Michael Wilks, 'Predestination, property, and power: Wyclif's theory of dominion and grace', in Anne Hudson, ed., *Wyclif: Political Ideas and Practice: Papers by Michael Wilks* (Oxford, 2000), pp. 16–32, at pp. 25–31; and '*Thesaurus ecclesiae*', pp. 147–77, in ibid.
[56] Wilks, '*Thesaurus ecclesiae*', p. 156, n. 33. [57] Wilks, 'Predestination', pp. 30–1.
[58] Wilks, '*Thesaurus ecclesiae*', p. 166, n. 77. [59] Ibid., p. 164.
[60] Herbert B. Workman, *John Wyclif: a Study of the English Medieval Church*, 2 vols. (Oxford, 1926, repr. Hamden, CT, 1966), I, pp. 210–11.

by them, was nailed to the doors of Westminster Hall and St Paul's. It began, 'We, poor men, treasurers of Christ and his apostles...'.[61] This direct challenge to the pope's claims to be Christ's treasurer was not lost on Boniface IX, who wrote to Richard II and his bishops demanding that they suppress 'the crafty and daring sect who call themselves the poor men of Christ's treasury and of his apostles'.[62] The Conclusions were followed, probably in 1410, by a comprehensive bill for the disendowment of the Church, and the reallocation of its resources to the laity, from the king down to the beggars.[63]

The theory of dominion used by ecclesiastical writers, whether in support of the papacy, like Giles of Rome, or the king, like Wyclif, was ultimately dependent upon the lordship of God. Pope or king administered God's property as stewards, and Christian subjects held property from the steward. Since no one had strictly 'private' rights to dominion over property, the conflict between divine-natural and human law simply did not arise.

A SECULAR SOLUTION

In practice, there was a period in England, before the twelfth century, when the tension between the two laws did not arise, because there was no private ownership. Land was said to be held 'of' or 'from' a superior lord under certain conditions. It was only during the twelfth century that this started to change, and in practice, if not in strict theory, something like private ownership emerged.

In late Anglo-Saxon England aristocrats – earls or thegns – held land from the king in return for certain services, especially military ones. Less powerful aristocrats and freeman could enter into any one of a variety of dependent relationships with a lord, or perhaps more than one lord, a feature which has been termed 'serial lordship'. The lord might offer protection, both legal and physical, and exercise judicial rights over his dependant. Where land was involved, which it was not always, it might be held of the lord in return for services or rent rendered in kind, in money, or in labour.[64] No one actually owned land outright. The Norman Conquest resulted in a radical redistribution of land to William's followers, who also occupied it conditionally and not in full ownership under a system known

---

[61] *EHD* 4, no. 502, p. 848.   [62] Workman, *John Wyclif*, 2, p. 400.
[63] Anne Hudson, *The Premature Reformation* (Oxford, 1988), pp. 114–16; 334–44, esp. 339–40; Margaret Aston, '"Caim's Castles": poverty, politics, and disendowment', in Aston, *Faith and Fire: Popular and Unpopular Religion 1350–1600* (London and Rio Grande, 1993), pp. 95–131, esp. pp. 111–13.
[64] Robin Fleming, *Kings and Lords in Conquest England* (Cambridge, 1991), pp. 126–7. For further description of lordship and land tenure on the eve of the Conquest, see Ann Williams, *The English and the Norman Conquest* (Woodbridge, 1995), pp. 73–6, 191–2.

as feudal tenure.[65] The main features of this were vassalage and the fief, and both seem to have emerged more clearly in England than in France, where royal control was less centralized. Vassalage was the relationship between a freeman, the vassal, and his lord, which was sealed by an oath of fidelity. The lord offered protection and maintenance, and often the grant of a unit of land known as a fief, in return for service, largely military. The king's immediate tenants, his tenants-in-chief, endowed their own followers with portions of that land on similar terms, and these in their turn might also grant it to lesser men, thus making the lordship chain very complicated. At the base of society peasants held parcels of land from the lord of the manor in return for payment in kind and for labour services performed on the lord's demesne land, his home farm. The manor was not only the lord's house or hall at the centre of the estate, but also the smallest economic and social unit in the landholding chain and a unit of lordly jurisdiction. The existence of the manor pre-dated the Conquest, but increasingly it became assimilated with the system of feudal tenure, the ideas and language of which came to be applied at manorial level.[66]

The main division of the peasant tenants of the manor was into those who were free and those who were servile, known as villeins. The villeins were dependent and of low status, but were not legally defined as unfree and of servile status until the late twelfth century. The villein came to be regarded as no more than his lord's chattel, tied to both lord and landholding, bound to perform labour services on the lord's demesne, owning nothing himself, and ultimately himself saleable, usually with the land he occupied. His only recourse to justice was to that of his lord's court.[67] The lord was sovereign over his villeins, and his authority was the direct result of his dominion over land.

It is less clear how sovereign he was over his free tenants. The free tenants held their land in return for fixed charges and minimal services. They owned their goods and their labour and they had freedom of movement. The lord would have his own seigneurial court, to which the tenants, both free and unfree, were answerable, but the extent to which the king could and did intervene to protect free tenants is a matter of controversy. It is

[65] See E. A. R. Brown, 'The tyranny of a construct: feudalism and historians of medieval Europe', *American Historical Review*, 79 (1974), pp. 1063–88; Susan Reynolds, *Fiefs and Vassals: the Medieval Evidence Reinterpreted* (Oxford, 1994). For reviews of Reynolds's book, summarizing some aspects of the controversy see Frederick L. Cheyette in *Speculum*, 71 (1996), pp. 998–1006; Paul R. Hyams, 'The end of feudalism?', *Journal of Interdisciplinary History*, 27 (1996–7), pp. 655–62.

[66] See Rosamond Faith, *The English Peasantry and the Growth of Lordship* (Leicester, 1997), pp. 220–3, 255, on this assimilation.

[67] Paul R. Hyams, *King, Lords, and Peasants in Medieval England: the Common Law of Villeinage in the Twelfth and Thirteenth Centuries* (Oxford, 1980), pp. 3–65.

an aspect of the wider disagreement surrounding the 'birth of the English Common Law', a fixed body of law administered by the king's courts. Did it evolve gradually, building on pre-Conquest precedent,[68] or was it the deliberate creation of Henry II, or even Henry III or Edward I?[69] Most historians now attribute its beginnings to the introduction of property measures by Henry II, in particular the writ of right and the assizes of *novel disseisin* and *mort d'ancestor*. The effect of these was to diminish seigneurial jurisdiction over free men by making royal justice available to them in property litigation. The treatise on the English common law known as Glanvill, attributed to Ranulf de Glanvill (d. 1190), Henry II's Chief Justice, stated that no action could be brought against a free tenant by his lord in connection with the tenement unless the lord had a writ from the king or his justices.[70] Whether Henry really intended to undermine lordly jurisdiction or simply to develop it by making it more formal and bureaucratic is open to question.[71]

Whatever the intention, the effects on the concept of private ownership were profound. Feudal tenure has been described as the 'antithesis of private ownership'.[72] A tenant could not sell his holding without the consent of his lord, he could not leave it by will, nor did his family have any legal right to succeed to it. All that he had was 'seisin', or possession. The lord had lordship, or dominion, but unless he was the king, he was himself a tenant. The advent of the common law gave free tenants access to the royal courts and enabled them to assert hereditary claims to land if these had not been honoured and to recover land of which they had been unjustly dispossessed. This loss of lordly authority, and at the end of the period the substitution of the cash nexus for the personal bond of mutual contract and loyalty between lord and man, led to a distancing in the relationship between them. The law came to recognize that the tenant who had the immediate possession and use of land had 'dominion

[68] See, for example, J. H. Baker, *An Introduction to English Legal History*, 3rd edn (London, 1990), pp. 10–16; Paul Brand, 'The origins of English land law: Milsom and after', in *The Making of the Common Law* (London, 1992), p. 219, criticizing the views of S. F. C. Milsom, *The Legal Framework of English Feudalism* (Cambridge, 1976).

[69] Brand, '*Multis vigiliis excogitam et inventam*': Henry II and the creation of the English Common Law', in *Common Law*, pp. 77–102.

[70] Glanvill, *The Treatise on the Laws and Customs of the Realm of England commonly called Glanvill*, ed. and trans. G. D. H. Hall, Oxford Medieval Texts (Oxford, 1993), XII, 2, p. 137.

[71] Reynolds, *Fiefs and Vassals*, p. 379, considers that the new writs encouraged the development of seigneurial courts, against Milsom, *Legal Framework*, p. 36, who considers that the erosion of seigneurial jurisdiction was a 'juristic accident'. Brand, 'The origins of English land law', pp. 214–19, thinks that Henry II deliberately tried to enhance his own prestige and authority against the barons. See also Coleman, 'Property and poverty', esp. pp. 615–16.

[72] Baker, *English Legal History*, p. 262.

of use', as opposed to the ultimate and often distant dominion of the lord. Such a situation reflected the division of *dominium* arrived at by the Roman jurists in the thirteenth century – *dominium directum*, the lord's ultimate legal ownership of the land, and *dominium utilis*, the dominion of use of the tenant, which involved the right to 'use, have, and enjoy'. The lord's dominion was in practice reduced to no more than an economic right to exact dues. The tenant had become virtually a private owner: land in effect became freehold, and therefore saleable, and could be willed to heirs.

The villeins' position changed too, though more slowly. In addition to the commutation of labour services for money payments, a peasant land-market developed from the thirteenth century, which enabled villeins to buy and sell with the licence of the manorial court.[73] The richer ones could start to consolidate their arable holdings. In Warwickshire, Dyer has found examples of post-Black Death enclosure, where villeins started to enclose land for their own exclusive use.[74] The economic changes and social mobility of the fourteenth and fifteenth centuries led to a change in the concept of villeinage. As former villein lands were often let to substantial free tenants, villeinage became a matter of birth and personal status rather than landholding. Manorial tenants were increasingly given protection by copyhold tenure, by which they were given a copy of the entry in the manorial court roll which recorded their admission to the tenement. They may not have had the full protection of the common law, but they were moving towards it.

The growth of what amounted to private ownership, starting in the reign of Henry II, meant that the 'secular solution' of feudal tenure no longer applied. The problem of reconciling what amounted to private possession with what was demanded by divine-natural law had returned. One answer, at least in England, lay in property taxation.

TAXATION

The development of private property and national taxation in England are closely linked, if only because taxation was levied on property, whether land, movables, or income. Both were indicative of the gradual transition from a society dominated by feudal tenure to a national sovereign state ruled by king and Parliament. As part of this transition, customary feudal dues were gradually replaced by national levies.

---

[73] For discussion on aspects of this see P. D. A. Harvey, ed., *The Peasant Land Market in Medieval England* (Oxford, 1984).
[74] Christopher Dyer, *Warwickshire Farming, c. 1349–1530: Preparations for Agricultural Revolution*, Dugdale Society Occasional Papers, 27 (Oxford, 1981), pp. 7, 25–7.

Private property versus communal rights

The theory of taxation emerged in England in association with the idea of the community of the realm and the way in which this was represented. A sovereign ruler was thought to be the physical embodiment, or representative, of an abstract legal body, in this case the community of the realm, and to be totally identified with its interests. Thus John of Salisbury wrote in the mid-twelfth century, 'The prince is... the minister of the public utility and the servant of equity, and in him the public *persona* is borne.'[75] The ruler is no longer his own man: he has to remember that 'he does not owe his life to himself but to others'.[76]

A distinction existed between the ordinary revenues of a ruler and the extraordinary ones, which in theory were raised only in an emergency. In an important passage Aquinas distinguished between these and laid the foundations for later ideas on national taxation.

> It sometimes happens... that princes do not have revenues sufficient for the custody of the land and for other duties... and in such a case it is just that the subjects render payments from which their common utility can be cared for. And thence it is that in some lands, *by ancient custom* the lords impose fixed taxes on their subjects... And the same reason seems to apply if some new situation arises in which it is *necessary to spend more for the common utility*... for instance, if enemies invade the land... For then, in addition to the accustomed exactions, the princes of the lands can licitly exact from their subjects some payments on behalf of the common utility [emphasis added].[77]

The raising of extraordinary revenue was justified in an emergency situation where customary payments were not sufficient. Aquinas was highlighting two fundamental issues which would be developed later. First there was the idea that the ruler existed for the 'common utility', the 'custody of the land'. As already seen, Aquinas thought that individual possession was sanctioned by divine-natural law,[78] and although he does not say that the ruler is bound to protect private property, this is the implication. The idea had originated in the Roman Empire. Cicero had seen the whole purpose and origin of cities and commonwealths as the safeguarding of private property. This is why Nature had drawn men together. The statesman therefore had to 'make it his first care that everyone shall have what belongs to him and that private citizens suffer no invasion of their property rights by act of state'.[79] In England the celebrated clause 39 of Magna Carta by which the king had to protect a freeman from

---

[75] John of Salisbury, *Policraticus*, ed. and trans. Cary J. Nederman (Cambridge, 1990), bk. 4, ch. 2, p. 31.
[76] Ibid., ch. 3, p. 33.
[77] Thomas Aquinas, *De regimine Judaeorum*, trans. Lewis, *Medieval Political Ideas*, 1, p. 111.
[78] See above, p. 22.
[79] Cicero, *De officiis*, bk. 2, ch. 21, trans. Walter Miller, *LCL*, 21, p. 249.

being unjustly 'arrested or imprisoned or *disseised*' was an indication that the kingdom, as represented by the king, existed to protect property.[80] One of the accusations against Richard II in 1399 was that he had frequently declared, in the presence of various lords, that 'the lives of each of his subjects, together with their lands, tenements, goods and chattels were his, and subject to his will, regardless of any forfeiture, which is entirely contrary to the laws and customs of the kingdom'.[81] In the fifteenth century, when Parliament had become part of the constitution, Fortescue described England (in contrast to France) as a 'political and royal lordship' – a *dominium regale et politicum*.[82] One of the fruits of this was that the English were not 'examined or impleaded in respect of their chattels or possessions... except according to the laws of that land...'.[83]

The second issue was that of necessity. Aquinas stated that in cases 'where it is necessary to spend more for the common utility' the ruler could exact additional payments for the common good. This is an application of his theory of 'casual jurisdiction' by which a sovereign in normal circumstances is subject to law, but in an emergency can appeal above it to a higher law. The Roman law idea that 'necessity knows no law', was incorporated into canon law in the ninth century, and was used by Aquinas in more than one context.[84] Necessity became fundamental in discussions on emergency taxation and became synonymous with the emergency of war.

Almost inseparable from necessity was consent. For Aquinas the raising of emergency taxes was an attribute of sovereignty and needed no consultation or consent from the taxpayers. In practice in late medieval England it worked differently. The traditional way for the king to raise extraordinary revenue was by imposing aids on his tenants-in-chief, such as scutage (literally shield-money, paid in lieu of military service), or the three aids for the knighting of his eldest son, the dowry of his daughter, or the ransoming of his person.[85] From the twelfth century on this was increasingly inappropriate: it did not yield enough, it did not involve the wider community, and, apart possibly from scutage, it catered for the personal circumstances of a monarch who, in John of Salisbury's terms, had become a public person. Taxation needed to be for the good of the

---

[80] Magna Carta, clause 39, *EHD*, 3, no. 20, p. 320.
[81] *The Record and Process*, in Chris Given-Wilson, ed., *Chronicles of the Revolution, 1397–1400: the Reign of Richard II* (Manchester, 1993), no. 17, p. 180, cl. 26.
[82] Sir John Fortescue, *On the Laws and Governance of England*, ed. and trans. Shelley Lockwood (Cambridge, 1997). See J. H. Burns, 'Fortescue and the political theory of *dominium*', *Historical Journal*, 28 (1985), pp. 777–97.
[83] John Fortescue, *In Praise of the Laws of England*, ch. 36, pp. 52–3, in *On the Laws and Governance of England*, pp. 3–80.
[84] See below ch. 2, p. 60.   [85] Cf. Magna Carta, cl. 12, 15, *EHD* 3, no. 20, pp. 318–19.

Private property versus communal rights

whole community and to be paid by all freemen. At the same time the idea developed that, in the words of the Roman law maxim, 'What touches all should be approved by all', in other words, that consent was necessary before what amounted to private rights were invaded.[86] Initially this was sought in the king's Great Council. The form of taxation which evolved was the lay subsidy. Historians disagree about whether it evolved from the feudal gracious aid or, as seems more likely, from Roman law principles such as necessity and consent. The first one was the thirteenth levied on all free men in 1209 by John, after the assent of his council and for the defence of the realm.[87] The ideas of necessity and consent took a long time to evolve and the process is difficult to pinpoint because the English king acted as both feudal lord and national ruler during the transitional period, and it is not always clear in which capacity he was acting. The theory was that the ruler, the embodiment of the realm, had a right to demand aid from his subjects in an emergency which threatened that realm – that is, in a case of necessity. As this touched the property rights of all freemen, the king had to seek consent. The consent given by a representative gathering was binding, even on those who disagreed or who had not been present. It was given not to the raising of the tax, but to the admission that a case of necessity justifying an emergency levy existed. Once this was established, consent to the levy could not be refused, although bargaining about the amount set against redress of grievances might take place. Consent had become a formality.[88] It is true that Henry III was refused aid by the barons in the twenty years after 1237 on several occasions, but it has been convincingly argued by G. L. Harriss that this did not change its nature. The barons' refusal was based on their conviction that the wars in Gascony, for which the aid was asked, did not constitute a national emergency which threatened the safety of the realm, but were 'feudal' conflicts undertaken on the King's personal initiative.[89] In France, the right of consultation had

[86] Gaines Post, '*Plena potestas* and consent in medieval assemblies: a study in Romano-canonical procedure and the rise of representation, 1150–1325', in Post, *Studies in Medieval Legal Thought* (Princeton, NJ, 1964), pp. 91–162, esp. 114–17; Post, 'A Romano-canonical maxim *Quod omnes tangit* in Bracton and in early parliaments', in *Studies*, pp. 163–238, esp. 231–8; G. L. Harriss, *King, Parliament, and Public Finance in Medieval England to 1369* (Oxford, 1975), esp. pp. 21–6.
[87] Harriss, *King, Parliament, and Public Finance*, pp. 16–21, takes issue with Sydney Knox Mitchell, *Taxation in Medieval England* (New Haven, CT, 1951); Mitchell, *Studies in Taxation under John and Henry III* (New Haven, CT, 1914), and M. V. Clarke, *Medieval Representation and Consent* (London, 1936).
[88] Harriss, *King, Parliament, and Public Finance*, pp. 21–4; Post, '*Plena potestas*', pp. 114–17. See also J. G. Edwards, 'The *plena potestas* of English parliamentary representatives', in *Historical Studies of the English Parliament*, ed. E. B. Fryde and Edward Miller (Cambridge, 1970), pp. 136–49.
[89] Harriss, *King, Parliament and Public Finance*, pp. 35–48.

also developed, but here it concentrated not so much on the existence of an emergency situation as on when it was deemed to have ended, when, according to the ancient maxim 'the cause had ceased'.[90]

During the period when the English Parliament was developing, the issue of consent became prominent. In the Confirmation of the Charters, to which Edward I had to agree in 1297, he promised not to levy extraordinary taxes 'except with the common assent of all the realm and for the common profit of the same realm, saving the ancient aids and prises due and accustomed'. In the 'De tallagio non concedendo', probably drawn up by the barons, the common assent was spelt out as that of 'archbishops, bishops and other prelates, earls, barons, knights, burgesses and other free men of our realm'.[91] It was not, however, until 1340, under pressure of the Anglo-French war that Edward III conceded formally to the representatives of the community of the realm that they should not

> from henceforth [be] charged nor grieved to make [any] Aid, or to sustain Charge, if it be not by the common assent of the Prelates, Earls, Barons, and other great Men, and Commons of our said Realm of England, and that in Parliament.[92]

Fortescue in the next century was able to boast:

> Nor can the king... impose tallages, subsidies, or any other burdens on his subjects... without the concession or assent of his whole realm, expressed in his parliament...[93]

By placing consent to taxation within the framework of his balanced 'political and royal' constitution of king and Parliament, he was providing an answer to the conflict of the two laws on property, for private property was taxed for the common good. He was looking backwards to Aristotle who had not only favoured a mean or mixed constitution, but had also considered that 'the better system is that under which property is privately owned but is put to common use'.[94] He was also, once again, anticipating the ideas of John Locke.[95]

---

[90] E. A. R. Brown, '*Cessante causa* and the taxes of the last Capetians. The political applications of a philosophical maxim', in Joseph R. Strayer and Donald E. Queller, eds., *Post Scripta: Essays on Medieval Law and the Emergence of the European State in Honor of Gaines Post, Studia Gratiana*, 15 (1972), pp. 565–87; Nederman, 'Aristotle as authority: alternative Aristotelian sources of late medieval political theory', in Nederman, *Medieval Aristotelianism*, no. 15, pp. 31–44, at pp. 33–5.
[91] *EHD*, 3, no. 74, p. 486, clause 6; no. 75, p. 486, clause 1.
[92] *Statutes of the Realm*, I, 14 Edward III (1340), c. 1, col. 290.
[93] Fortescue, *In Praise of the Laws of England*, ch. 36, p. 52.
[94] Aristotle, *Politics*, II, v, 8, 1263a, p. 50.
[95] John Locke, *The Second Treatise of Government*, in Peter Laslett, ed., *Two Treatises of Government* (repr. Cambridge, 1988), ch. 10, sect. 140, p. 362.

CONCLUSION

Like his predecessors, Locke was to observe that 'God had given the earth to man in common'[96] and to muse on the 'partage of things in an inequality of private possessions'.[97] Medieval writers explained the problem as one of two conflicting laws, divine-natural law and human law which decreed different things. The solutions were roughly threefold. Some centred on the laws, suggesting either that God himself had authorized human law, that natural law could change according to circumstances, or that private possession was for the common good and was therefore according to natural law. Some centred on renunciation – either of the law or of private property. John of Paris and Fortescue bypassed the legal conflict by suggesting that private property was the result of man's own labour rather than a legal grant. Others renounced the ownership or dominion of private property, either retaining a limited 'use' of it, or vesting dominion in God and then holding it in stewardship from him, often through the intermediary of pope or king as his earthly vicar. Finally there was the English 'mean' solution where property was held privately but was taxed by a constitutional monarch with the consent of his magnates for the common good. For Locke the problem of the unequal partage of things lay not in the inconsistency of the two laws, but in the 'tacit and voluntary consent' of mankind to the use of money, which, being imperishable, allowed unlimited accumulation of wealth.[98] But that must be the subject of a later chapter.

[96] Ibid., ch. 5, sect. 26, p. 286, sect. 34, p. 291. [97] Ibid., sect. 50, p. 302. [98] Ibid.

2

WEALTH, BEGGARY, AND SUFFICIENCY

INTRODUCTION: RECIPROCITY AND THE MEAN

'Wealth and beggary are two extremes. The mean is sufficiency', declared Jean de Meun in the thirteenth-century French epic poem *The Romance of the Rose*.[1] This mean dictated the balancing of resources between haves and have-nots as a matter of justice. It also controlled the workings of charity, as almsgiving became more discriminatory and individuals tried to maintain their own status and to ensure that those beneath them maintained theirs.

Almsgiving and works of mercy assumed a society of unequals, in which charitable acts might help to redress the balance or make life fairer, either by redistributing material resources or by alleviating suffering. But everything had its price, and charity was no exception. Pious benefactors expected something in return for their benevolence, usually in the form of prayers for their salvation. The mentality of gift exchange and barter was never far below the surface. Reciprocity was closely linked with charity; rich and poor were bound together in a relationship of mutual, if hostile, necessity. Pauper, in *Dives and Pauper*, delivered a sermon on the Augustinian theme of 'The rich man and the poor be two things well needful each to other. And the rich man hath more need of the poor man's help than the poor of the rich.'[2] Inequality and reciprocity were part of the divine plan. As an English preacher Ralph of Acton appreciated:

[1] Jean de Meun, *The Romance of the Rose*, in Guillaume de Lorris and Jean de Meun, *The Romance of the Rose*, trans. Frances Morgan (Oxford, 1994), p. 173.
[2] *Dives and Pauper*, pt. 1, Holy Poverty, A, vii, p. 63, lines 15–34.

When God could have made all men strong, wise, and rich, he was unwilling to do so. He wished instead that these men should be strong, those weak; these wise, those foolish; these rich and these poor. For if all were strong, wise and wealthy, one would not be in need of the other.[3]

The Dominican Giordano of Pisa, preaching in Florence in 1304, intimated that without the poor, the salvation of the rich was improbable: 'Why are the poor given their station in life? So that the rich might earn eternal life through them.'[4]

This symbiotic relationship was a constant late medieval feature, despite changing attitudes to wealth and beggary. We shall see how for some poverty was transformed from a blessing to an evil, and riches from an evil to a positive good. As a result, donors of charity became more discriminating during their lifetimes, but more generous in making post-mortem bequests. Beggars became generally vilified as idlers and scroungers, raising the question of whether the idea of work acquired a new dignity.

The background to shifting attitudes is complex. In physical terms, changing economic circumstances contributed. Demographic crisis led to labour shortages, which generated an intolerant attitude to those who would not work. Some peasants and artisans who survived epidemics and war enjoyed better living standards and the trappings of higher social status, stimulating their appetites for further gains. Lords and employers reacted against this by trying to maintain or reimpose economic and social control. Directly or indirectly this led to popular resentment and rebellion – the Jacquerie in France in 1358, the revolt of the Ciompi in Florence in 1378, itself the climax of a series of disturbances, the English Peasants' Revolt of 1381, and that of the cloth workers of the Low Countries in 1382.

The intellectual backcloth was even more complicated. It encompassed developments in theological and legal thought in the schools, the commercial mentality of the market-place, and the increasing preoccupation by lay people with their destiny and status both in this world and the next. Added to this was the ferment of ideas associated with early Renaissance humanism.

ATTITUDES TO POVERTY

One thing was unchanging: physical repugnance at the smell and sight of the poor. Seneca had long ago pointed out that the wise man 'will not avert

---

[3] G. R. Owst, *Literature and Pulpit in Medieval England*, 2nd edn (Oxford, 1961), p. 561.
[4] Daniel R. Lesnick, *Preaching in Medieval Florence: the Social World of Franciscan and Dominican Spirituality* (Athens and London, 1989), p. 126.

his countenance or his sympathy from any one because he has a withered leg, or is emaciated and in rags, and is old and leans upon a staff'.[5] Jacques de Vitry (c. 1165–1240) a celebrated preacher, ultimately a bishop and a cardinal, issued a stark warning about hospital patients: 'One must have the courage of a martyr to overcome one's repugnance at the unbearable filth and stench of the patients.'[6] False Seeming, a character in the *Romance of the Rose*, reacted understandably: 'When I see those poor creatures naked on their stinking dung-heaps, shivering with cold, crying and moaning with hunger, I do not get involved.'[7] By the late fifteenth century, when almsgiving was thought to contribute directly to the donor's salvation, a Sienese Dominican declared that the more repulsive the beggar, the greater the charity shown by the almsgiver.[8]

In the twelfth century, when evangelical poverty movements like the Poor Men of Lyons and the Humiliati flourished, preachers increasingly identified the poor with Christ. Alan of Lille, preaching in 1189, asked, 'Where does Christ live? Only among the paupers of Christ, of whom he said "Blessed are the poor in spirit."'[9] Peter of Poitiers (d.c. 1216), a canon of St Victor in Paris, likened those who relieved the poor of the body of Christ, meaning the universal Church, to Mary Magdalen when she anointed Christ's feet.[10] Peter of Blois, archdeacon of London, called the poor man the 'vicar of Christ',[11] a title coming to be reserved for the pope alone.

In the thirteenth century the friars' debate on apostolic poverty examined in chapter 1 and their attempts to practise it among the urban poor gave the subject an even higher profile. In many of their sermons, as in the Dives and Lazarus parable, the poor were equated with the virtuous and the rich with the evil. A Polish Dominican, Peregrine of Oppeln, compared society to the Red Sea, where the big fish, the rich and powerful, motivated by selfishness and rebellion implanted by the devil, devoured the little fish, the poor. The red of the sea symbolized the blood of

[5] Seneca, *De clementia*, trans. John W. Basmore, LCL, 214, II, vi, 3, p. 443.
[6] Jacques de Vitry, *Historia occidentalis*, quoted in Michel Mollat, *The Poor in the Middle Ages: an Essay in Social History*, trans. Arthur Goldhammer (New Haven and London, 1986), p. 102.
[7] Jean de Meun, *Romance of the Rose*, p. 173.
[8] Bernadette Paton, *Preaching Friars and the Civic Ethos: Siena, 1380–1480* (London, 1992), p. 203.
[9] Mollat, *The Poor*, p. 113.
[10] Jean Longère, 'Pauvreté et richesse chez quelques prédicateurs durant le second moitie du XIIe siècle', in M. Mollat, ed., *Etudes sur l'histoire de la pauvreté (moyen âge au XVIe siècle)*, 2 vols. (Paris, 1974), I, pp. 255–73, at pp. 260–1.
[11] Mollat, *The Poor*, p. 108.

the victims.[12] In early fourteenth-century England a Franciscan, Nicholas Bozon, imagined the Judgement Seat:

> The righteous poor will stand up against the cruel rich at the day of Judgement... the simple folk will be exalted for their good deeds, and the haughty abased for their pride. Then God will do as the mender of old clothes, who turns the lappet to the front, and what was uppermost downwards...[13]

The English Dominican John Bromyard quoted Aesop's fable of the town mouse and the country mouse. The country mouse preferred his rural poverty to the splendour and luxury of his wealthy cousin. He at least could enjoy his rustic fare, beans and water, without fear of detection or of 'instruments for capturing mice'. In any case, the rich had acquired most of their wealth by dubious means, 'with troubled conscience and danger to their souls'.[14] In early fourteenth-century Florence, another Dominican, Giordano of Pisa, also highlighted the dishonesty of the rich: 'today there can be wealth in only two ways: either you have it as a legacy from your father who took it from others and stole it by usury, or you have it by doing the same yourself'.[15]

Not everyone saw wealth and poverty in such stark terms. As early as the second century, Clement of Alexandria had adopted a more moderate approach. He regarded Christ's command to the rich young man to sell all he had and follow him as purely metaphorical. There was no real advantage in poverty. Indeed, it could be a distraction from the worship of God. It was far better to have enough wealth to support yourself and to help the needy.[16] Centuries later Jean de Meun also questioned the import of Christ's command:

> Know, too, that when God commands the good man to sell all he has and give it to the poor and follow him [Mark 10.21], he does not therefore want him to serve him in beggary... He means rather that he should work with his hands and follow him with good works.[17]

Jean's attitude was very much in the spirit of Aquinas, who took another text, Matthew 10.10, where Christ commanded his disciples to provide 'nor scrip for your journey, neither two coats, neither shoes...'. Christ had not intended total poverty, but simply not carrying anything which

---

[12] Ibid., p. 130. [13] Owst, *Literature and Pulpit*, p. 299.
[14] John Bromyard, *Summa praedicantium*, 2, ch. 8, 'ministratio', sect. 31, fols. 32v–33r.
[15] Lesnick, *Preaching in Medieval Florence*, p. 123.
[16] Clement of Alexandria, *Quis dives salvetur*, chs. 11–13; *PG*, 9, cols. 615, 618; Carlyle, *History of Medieval Political Theory*, 1, p. 133.
[17] Jean de Meun, *The Romance of the Rose*, p. 175.

might be a distraction from man's true aim.[18] Aquinas did not see poverty as an unmitigated blessing; for some it might prove to be an evil:

> In so far as it removes the anxiety that is occasioned by riches it is useful to some... but it is harmful to some, who being freed from this anxiety, betake themselves to worse occupations.... In so far as poverty removes the good resulting from riches, namely the assistance of others and one's own support, it is simply an evil.[19]

The cracks in the 'rich = bad, poor = good' equation had begun to appear. Jean de Meun was in no doubt that poverty caused sin:

> And poverty is worse than death, for she torments and gnaws at soul and body, not just for an hour but as long as they dwell together, and brings them not only to condemnation but also to larceny and perjury and many other difficulties...[20]

These cracks deepened during the fourteenth century, partly due to economic circumstances. It was all very well for canonists like Johannes Andreae to insist that poverty was no kind of evil,[21] but that was just how it came to be seen. The shortage of labour resulting from the famines early in the century and the Black Death of 1348 led to new opportunities for peasants, artisans, and craftsmen. They were in a position to bargain. They could move from one master to another, one estate to another, from country to town, or from town to town in search of better conditions. In France and in Aragon ordinances condemned the outrageous wages being demanded by labourers.[22] The English Ordinance and Statute of Labourers, of 1349 and 1351 respectively, tried to impose a wage freeze and to restrict geographical mobility. Even worse, status was becoming a question of money rather than birth or breeding. In England, even before the Black Death, the canonist John of Ayton had complained that money – what he called 'the rotating wheel of rich fortune' – made serfs and villeins the equals of nobles and freemen. Indeed, 'villeins and simple folk' were disdaining 'holy rusticity and agriculture' in order to glory in 'disputes and legal assizes'.[23] The sumptuary legislation, especially that of 1363, gave concrete expression to feelings of instability – the world was

---

[18] Langholm, *Economics*, p. 209.
[19] Aquinas, *Summa contra gentiles*, bk. 3, ch. 133, vol. 3, p. 140.
[20] Jean de Meun, *Romance of the Rose*, lines 8107–11, p. 125.
[21] Johannes Andreae, *Glossa ordinaria ad Sext.*, 1, 3, 11, *Corpus iuris canonici*, 3 (Lyons, 1624), col. 45.
[22] John Day, 'Crises and trends in the late Middle Ages', in Day, *The Medieval Market Economy* (Oxford, 1987), p. 191.
[23] John of Ayton, *Commentaria ad Constitutiones Othonis et Othoboni*, in Lyndwood, *Provinciale* (Oxford, 1679), *ad v.* 'baronum', p. 122a; *ad v.* 'justitiam favor expellit [sic]', p. 78b.

topsy-turvy, the lower orders were getting out of hand, and all-important social distinctions were becoming blurred. The legislation regulated the food and above all the dress appropriate to each order, so that someone's social status was instantly recognizable. It drew attention to the 'outrageous and excessive apparel of divers people against their estate and degree, to the great destruction and impoverishment of all the land'.[24] It divided the different orders not just according to office or occupation, but also according to income. How effective it was is debatable. The fact that it was repealed the following year because it put 'the poor Commons... in danger and *subjection* [my italics]' and they felt they had been 'greatly burdened', may indicate that it was actually enforced briefly.[25] Yet at the end of the century the chronicler Henry Knighton still lamented that 'the lesser people were so puffed up... in their dress and their belongings... that one might scarcely distinguish one from another... not a humble man from a great man, not a needy from a rich man, not a servant from his master, not a priest from another man'.[26] In Italy, the chronicler Matteo Villani decried the arrogance of the *popolo minuto*, both men and women, which led them to eat and to dress inappropriately and to refuse to work at their normal tasks.[27]

Fear of the upwardly mobile, later to be coupled with suspicion of vagrants returning from the French war, led to a hardening in attitude to beggary in England. At a time of acute labour shortage, it is hardly surprising that lords and employers found it hard to bear the sight of the able-bodied begging. The Ordinance of Labourers of 1349 forbade the giving of alms to able-bodied vagrants:

And since many sturdy beggars... are refusing to work, and are spending their time instead in idleness and depravity, and sometimes in robberies and other crimes; let no one presume, on pain of imprisonment, to give anything by way of charity of alms to those who are perfectly able to work, or to support them in their idleness, so that they will be forced to work for a living.[28]

The Commons' petition against vagrants to the Good Parliament of 1376 also linked poverty, idleness, and criminality. Those who refused to work went about 'commonly robbing poor people in simple villages, by two,

---

[24] *EHD*, 4, no. 681, p. 1153. For discussion see Frances Elizabeth Baldwin, *Sumptuary Legislation and Personal Regulation in England* (Baltimore, MD, 1926), pp. 45–55.
[25] Ibid., p. 55.
[26] Henry Knighton, *Knighton's Chronicle 1337–1396*, ed. and trans. G. T. Martin, Oxford Medieval Texts (Oxford, 1995), p. 509.
[27] Matteo Villani, *Cronaca*, ed. F. Gherardi Dragomanni, *Croniche Storiche*, 5 (Florence, 1846), bk. 1, ch. 4, p. 13.
[28] Statute of Labourers, trans. and ed. Rosemary Horrox, *The Black Death* (Manchester, 1994), p. 289.

three, or four together, so that their malice is very hard to bear'.[29] An act of 1388 foreshadowed later settlement legislation: 'Anyone who goes begging and yet is able to work shall be treated like those who leave the town without a letter [patent of identification].' In the fifteenth century dislike of vagrants increased. An example is provided by an almshouse established in Romford, Essex, about 1450, to care for the transient poor. In 1480 windows were broken and inhabitants assaulted by the local people, who considered that it encouraged the 'wrong sort of person' to come to Romford, and by 1500 it was disused.[30] By the late fifteenth century, penalties imposed on able-bodied vagrants ranged from whipping or loss of their ears for first and second offences, to hanging for the third.[31] The hatred of idle but sturdy paupers and attempts to make them work were to be basic themes of Tudor and later poor-relief legislation.[32]

The climate in France was much the same. As early as the thirteenth century, Jean de Meun considered that 'an able-bodied man, if he does not have the means to live, should seek his living through the labour of his own hands and body, no matter how religious or anxious to serve God he may be'. He pointed out that Justinian had forbidden any able-bodied man to beg: 'It would be better to cripple him or make a public example of him than to support him in such wickedness', he concluded.[33] He was echoing the canonist Johannes Teutonicus, who cited the Roman law text which warned that a man able to work who accepted public relief was to be treated like a criminal and condemned to slavery.[34] William Durant the Younger, Bishop of Mende (d. 1330), declared: 'It is more useful to take bread away from someone who is hungry... than to break it with him and thus let him go on indulging his injustice.'[35] The Knight in *Le Songe du Vergier*, written during the time of Charles V, observed that 'When one sees a man asking publicly for alms, one fears that he has come to such misery by his own guilt.'[36]

This condemnatory attitude rubbed off on the beggars *par excellence*, the mendicant friars. Durant attacked their begging because it was a burden on society, and because it led to dependence on the wealthy. Friars should 'provide for themselves by their own hands, as the apostles did in

---

[29] R. B. Dobson, ed., *The Peasants' Revolt of 1381* (London, 1970), no. 7, p. 74.
[30] Marjorie Keniston McIntosh, *Autonomy and Community: the Royal Manor of Havering, 1200–1500* (Cambridge, 1986), pp. 238–9.
[31] *EHD*, 4, no. 568, p. 1003. For later legislation see W. E. Tate, *The Parish Chest*, 3rd edn (Cambridge, 1969), p. 190.
[32] For a list and summary see Paul Slack, *The English Poor Law, 1531–1782* (Basingstoke and London, 1990), pp. 59–64.
[33] Jean de Meun, *Romance of the Rose*, p. 174.   [34] Tierney, *Medieval Poor Law*, p. 58.
[35] Constantin Fasolt, *Council and Hierarchy: the Political Thought of William Durant the Younger* (Cambridge, 1991), p. 233.
[36] Mollat, *The Poor*, p. 253.

order not to be a burden unto others'.[37] The Aristotelian commentator Nicholas Oresme also thought that the friars should be forced to work.[38] Amongst English writers, Richard Fitzralph, Archbishop of Armagh, and John Wyclif and his followers condemned the idleness of the voluntary poor and thought that they should be made to work.[39] The Italian humanist Poggio Bracciolini complained about the hypocrites and parasites begging round the market-place in Florence. Under colour of religion they sought their sustenance without labour or sweat, professing absolute poverty and contempt for worldly goods. They made vast profits and totally consumed the fortunes of the citizens.[40]

The late medieval Italian view of wealth and beggary was partly coloured by civic humanism, which was built on mercantile foundations.[41] In Italy it was humanism which ultimately desanctified poverty. In essence, humanism drew attention to all that was natural and human – to man's human abilities, aims, and needs, to his natural dignity, and to his happiness in this life. It was the exact opposite of the theological values which had prevailed in the writing of the scholastics. When humanism was linked to civic pride, the pursuit of individual wealth for the good of the commune became not merely acceptable, but the goal of the mercantile elite. Poverty was a violation of human dignity and happiness and was damaging to the State. Hans Baron long ago drew attention to such attitudes among fifteenth-century Italian humanists, who were themselves building on foundations laid by lawyers such as Bartolus and Baldus de Ubaldis.[42] Poggio Bracciolini's contemporary and compatriot Matteo Palmieri provided a comprehensive summary of humanist attitudes. He urged poor citizens to work for the good of the city, adding:

Those who are lazy and indolent in a way that does harm to the city, and who can offer no just reason for their condition, should either be forced to work or be expelled from the Commune. The city would thus rid itself of that harmful part of the poorest class.[43]

---

[37] Fastolt, *William Durant*, p. 233.   [38] Mollat, *The Poor*, p. 253.
[39] James Donne Dawson, 'Richard Fitzralph and the fourteenth-century poverty controversies', *JEH*, 34 (1983), p. 342; Maria A. Moisa, 'Fourteenth-century preachers' views of the poor: class or status group?', in *Culture, Ideology and Politics: Essays for Eric Hobsbawm*, ed. R. Samuel and G. Stedman Jones (London, 1982), p. 163; Aston, 'Caim's Castles', p. 119.
[40] Poggio Bracciolini, *Dialogus contra Avaritiam (de avaritia)*, ed. G. Germano and A. Nardi (Livorno, 1994), XII, 7, p. 77. For discussion of the *De avaritia*, see Christian Bec, *Les Marchands écrivains à Florence, 1375–1434* (Paris, 1967), pp. 379–81.
[41] Hans Baron, 'Franciscan poverty and civic wealth as factors in the rise of humanist thought', *Speculum*, 13 (1938), pp. 1–37.
[42] Ibid., p. 17.
[43] Matteo Palmieri, *Della vita civile*, quoted in John F. McGovern, 'The rise of new economic attitudes – economic humanism, economic nationalism – during the later

In the preaching of the period, and following canon law, the needy came to be divided into the deserving – those like the friars who were deliberately poor, and those who had fallen into poverty blamelessly – and the undeserving, vagrants, lepers, the unemployed, and beggars, who were considered idle and degenerate.[44] Poverty became a civic evil while wealth became a civic good.

ATTITUDES TO WEALTH

The Bible was hostile to the well-to-do, with its condemnations of covetousness, its warnings of the obstacles to their salvation – the camel and the eye of the needle – and its emphasis on the blessedness of the poor. The patristic attitude was less aggressive. Some writers conceded that riches were not necessarily a bar to salvation if they were used rightly, and if they were not allowed to dominate their possessor.[45] Ambrose suggested that although great sums of money might be a temptation to the wicked, they were also an incentive to virtue.[46] Augustine's attitude to riches was neutral. Like other earthly things, they were useful and to be used by man on his pilgrimage through life, but not to be desired for their own sake.[47] This attitude seems to have endured until the twelfth century. St Bernard, the great Cistercian leader, wrote of gold and silver in his *De consideratione* to Pope Eugenius III: 'In themselves, as regards man's spiritual welfare, they are neither good nor bad, yet the use of them is good, the abuse is bad; anxiety about them is worse; the greed of gain still more disgraceful.'[48]

The thirteenth century brought fresh thoughts about wealth. Part of the reason for this, as in the case of thinking about poverty, was the obvious fact of the commercial revolution and the rise of the monied mercantile elite. In the cities the friars were living in the thick of this and were forced to grapple with the problems posed by the *nouveaux riches*. In theoretical terms

---

middle ages and the Renaissance, A.D. 1200–1550', *Traditio*, 26 (1970), pp. 217–53, at p. 235.

[44] Paton, *Preaching Friars*, pp. 198–203; Brian Pullan, *Rich and Poor in Renaissance Venice: the Social Institutions of a Catholic State to 1620* (Oxford, 1971), pp. 63–83, esp. pp. 68, 78, 81. Leprosy was seen as a punishment for sin, especially for pride and sexual depravity: see Carole Rawcliffe, *Medicine and Society in Later Medieval England* (Stroud, 1995), pp. 14–17. On the canon law aspects see pp. 60–1 below.

[45] On this see J. A. McGuckin, 'The vine and the elm tree: the patristic interpretation of Jesus' teachings on wealth', in W. J. Sheils and Diana Wood, eds., *The Church and Wealth*, SCH, 24 (Oxford, 1987), pp. 1–14.

[46] Ambrose, *Expositio Evangelii secundum Lucam*, bk. 5, 69, PL, 14, col. 1654.

[47] See p. 20 above.

[48] Bernard, *De consideratione*, trans. George Lewis (Oxford, 1908), bk. 2, ch. 6, p. 47.

the growing accessibility of Aristotle's works helped to provide them with some of the answers. In his *Ethics* Aristotle had suggested that the pursuit of the good, or virtue, required a certain amount of external prosperity – in other words, a mean of sufficiency.[49]

This influenced thirteenth-century commentators such as Albert the Great and Aquinas and their followers. Albert pointed out that excessive wealth might be a hindrance to the good life, but then so might excessive poverty, because it disturbed the harmony and competence of 'necessary personal faculties'.[50] Aquinas, too, struck a balance: 'riches are good forasmuch as they serve the use of virtue; and if this measure be exceeded, so that they hinder the practice of virtue, they are no longer to be reckoned as a good but as an evil'.[51] Jean de Meun summarized bluntly: 'The soul can be just as thoroughly ruined by excessive poverty as by excessive wealth; both wound with equal severity.'[52] In the mid-fifteenth century, Reginald Pecock, Bishop of St Asaph and then Chichester, tipped the balance in favour of wealth: 'perauenture more perel schal befalle in ouer greet pouerte than in ouer grete ricchessis'.[53]

Wealth was no longer evil, but was it a barrier to salvation? On the contrary, in 1304, Giordano of Pisa seemed to think that riches led to Heaven.

> Of many saints we read that they were very rich. They climbed up on this tower, or this mountain, and they were nearer to God. The more they had ... the higher they were, and the nearer to Heaven, grateful to God for it, and thanking him for it and loving him the more for it.[54]

Statistical analysis has confirmed that the majority of medieval saints were indeed of noble or upper-class origin.[55] Pauper, despite his mendicancy, was still able to reassure Dives that 'Christ excluded not you rich men from Heaven',[56] and he proceeded to instruct him just how he might squeeze through the eye of the needle.[57] Relieved, Dives confided, 'I was afraid that God did not love rich men', which prompted Pauper to hold up Abraham, Isaac, and Jacob and 'many thousand more' as examples

---

[49] Aristotle, *Ethics*, I, viii, p. 17.   [50] Langholm, *Economics*, p. 175.
[51] Aquinas, *Summa contra Gentiles*, bk. 3, ch. 133, vol. 3, pt. 2, p. 140.
[52] Jean de Meun, *Romance of the Rose*, lines 1239–43, p. 173.
[53] Reginald Pecock, *Repressor of Over Much Blaming of the Clergy*, 2, pt. 3, ch. 5, p. 304.
[54] A. Fanfani, *Catholicism, Protestantism, and Capitalism* (London, 1935), p. 125.
[55] Murray, *Reason and Society*, pp. 317–41, Appendix 1, pp. 405–12; André Vauchez, *Sainthood in the Later Middle Ages*, trans. Jean Birrell (Cambridge, 1988), pp. 157, 173–84, esp. table 6, p. 184 and table 8, p. 186.
[56] *Dives and Pauper*, pt. 1, Holy Poverty, A, iii, p. 55, lines 43–4.
[57] The 'needle' was a narrow gate into the city of Jerusalem. Camels had to be unloaded before they could pass through it. Cf. ibid., p. 55, lines 38–41.

of those who had been 'wel rich', and who now enjoyed the bliss of Heaven.[58] Pecock agreed with this. 'It is not forbodun of God eny man to be riche', he pointed out. With the grace which God gives to the rich man he may enter the kingdom of Heaven 'though he abide stille riche, and though withoute such grace it is ouer hard to him being riche for to entre'.[59]

The most dramatic changes in attitude appeared in tandem with the new views on poverty associated with humanism, described above. The Florentine Leonardo Bruni provides a good example. In the Preface to his translation of the pseudo-Aristotelian *Economics* (*c.* 1420) he observed: 'As health is the goal of medicine, so riches are the goal of the household. For riches are useful both for ornamenting their owners as well as for helping nature in the struggle for virtue.'[60] Matteo Palmieri, too, thought that riches were instruments in the pursuit of virtue.[61] Poggio Bracciolini turned ecclesiastical values on their head by predicting that without avarice civilized life would be destroyed.[62] Many of the Italian civic funeral orations of the fifteenth century praised deceased humanists for acquiring wealth by diligence and hard work, for the brilliance of their lifestyle, and for their contributions to the life of the city through charity, patronage of the arts, and financing of magnificent buildings.[63]

Were changing attitudes to wealth and beggary accompanied by a new attitude to work? Can we speak of the beginnings of a 'work ethic' in the medieval period?[64] Its development during the Protestant Reformation, especially among the Calvinists, was postulated by Max Weber early in the twentieth century. He saw it as a prelude to capitalism. The hallmarks of the work ethic were diligence, thrift, and self-discipline. Labour acquired dignity and value for its own sake, while worldly pleasure and idleness became anathema. Riches were an indication that their possessor was in a state of grace.[65]

Traditionally labour, especially manual labour, was seen as degrading. Associations with classical slavery and with the curse laid upon Adam at the Fall were enduring. Late medieval condemnations of idleness, however,

[58] *Dives and Pauper*, pt. 1, Holy Poverty, A, iii, p. 57, lines 1–8.
[59] Pecock, *Repressor*, 1, pt. 3, ch. 4, p. 296.
[60] McGovern, 'Economic attitudes', p. 236. See also Baron, 'Franciscan poverty', pp. 21–2.
[61] Baron, 'Franciscan poverty', p. 23.
[62] Poggio Bracciolini, *De avaritia*, XII, 6, p. 77.
[63] Baron, 'Franciscan poverty', pp. 22–3.
[64] Birgit van den Hoven, *Work in Ancient and Medieval Thought* (Amsterdam, 1996) has concluded on the basis of thirteenth-century *ad status* sermons that there was little change in attitude to labour.
[65] Max Weber, *The Protestant Ethic and the Spirit of Capitalism* (London, 1930, repr. London, 1992).

helped to establish the idea of work as a duty rather than a curse. Richard Fitzralph in damning mendicant idleness quoted II Thessalonians 3.10: 'if any would not work, neither should he eat'.[66] This does not suggest, however, that labour was dignified. The Italian citizens gained their wealth through diligence and hard work, but it was the wealth that mattered, and the ostentatious lifestyle that accompanied it, rather than the work. Poggio Bracciolini questioned whether anyone would work unless there was both reward and use attached to it.[67] As late as the end of the fifteenth century Leon Battista Alberti wrote: 'As for physical labor, we could almost call any form of it servitude, for... to be subject to another's commands is nothing but slavery.'[68] There was not much change there. As for being in a state of grace, some of the so-called merchant princes obtained a reputation for virtue, and were buried with honour, but the charitable bequests and restitution of ill-gotten gains in their wills show that they were uncertain of their salvation.[69] A few seeds of the later work ethic did exist in the late medieval period, especially in the Italian city-states, such as the emphasis on hard work and diligence, the hatred of idleness, and the praise of wealth. But there was no sense of worldly asceticism or of the dignity of labour, nor, without the theological underpinnings of the Calvinist creed, could the merchant princes be sure that their wealth indicated their eternal salvation.

AVARICE AND CHARITY: JUSTICE AND MERCY

Poggio Bracciolini wrote in praise of avarice, but at the end of the fifteenth century Alberti's views were still similar to those of the scholastics. He warned of the dangers of enslaving the soul to riches. The only point of wealth was to avoid servitude, and while riches were not to be scorned, 'cupidity', by which he meant avarice, had to be controlled.[70] The attitude of the scholastics to wealth and avarice had underlined the need for control and moderation. Avarice was the vice of immoderation, of unbounded appetite. Bonaventure, for example, pointed out that possession of riches bred cupidity in the owner, 'for it is difficult to have them and not to love them'.[71] The ideal was to control the mind so much that the craving for wealth was overcome, 'for no one acquires a thing if he lacks an acquisitive mind'.[72] Aquinas, too, stressed the virtue of moderation. If someone made

[66] Moisa, 'Fourteenth-century preachers' views', p. 166.
[67] Poggio Bracciolini, *De avaritia*, XI, 1, p. 76. Cf. McGovern, 'Economic attitudes', p. 235.
[68] Leon Battista Alberti, *The Family*, trans. Guido A. Guarino (Lewisburg, 1971), p. 153.
[69] See ch. 7, pp. 168–9, below.   [70] Alberti, *The Family*, p. 153.
[71] Langholm, *Economics*, p. 155.   [72] Ibid.

wealth his end it meant that he had an unlimited desire for it, but this desire should be limited to whatever is needed to support life.[73]

Aquinas had been trying to reconcile two apparently conflicting biblical texts: Ecclesiasticus 10.15, which attributed the root of all evil to pride, and I Timothy 6.10, which blamed avarice. Historians have noted a growing emphasis placed on avarice in late medieval literature and preaching, although there is not enough evidence to support the idea that it displaced the premier position of pride.[74] Certainly it was vividly described by popular writers. Jean de Meun told how the avaricious man 'aspires to drink the whole of the Seine but will never be able to do it, because there will always be some left'.[75] This was echoed in the next century in a preaching manual, the *Fasciculus morum*: 'when it [avarice] has gained the whole earth, it wants the sea; and after that, it soon craves for what is in the air. And by rising thus it knows no limit.'[76] William Langland, in *Piers Plowman*, gave a more homely example: avarice was 'as kind as a dog in a kitchen'.[77]

The self-control which conquered avarice could be seen as an aspect of charity, its opposing virtue, and one which had both a theological and a practical connotation.[78] John of Ayton described it as threefold – 'of God, of one's neighbours, and of one's own body'. The charity of God consisted in loving him more than oneself and so being able to withstand temptation to sin. The charity of neighbours involved loving them as oneself, without the hope of gain or the promptings of consanguinity, simply due to 'the fellowship of nature'. Charity of one's own body meant subjecting it to the spirit. It was a beast of burden to which a bag, some chaff, and a whip had to be attached: the bag, symbolizing penitential and 'supportive' works (presumably almsgiving), the chaff, those things necessary to sustain life, and the whip, an instrument with which to castigate the body for overindulgence.[79] All three aspects of charity implied limitation and control.

---

[73] Thomas Aquinas, *Summa theologiae*, 1a2ae, 30, 4, vol. 19, pp. 135–7.

[74] Morton W. Bloomfield, *The Seven Deadly Sins: an Introduction to the History of a Religious Concept, with Special Reference to Medieval English Literature* (East Lansing, MI, 1952), pp. 87–95; 182–3; J. Huizinga, *The Waning of the Middle Ages* (1924, repr. Harmondsworth, 1965), pp. 25–7; Lester K. Little, 'Pride goes before avarice: social change and the vices in Latin Christendom', *American Historical Review*, 76 (1971), pp. 16–59.

[75] Jean de Meun, *The Romance of the Rose*, p. 78.

[76] *Fasciculus morum: a Fourteenth-century Preachers' Handbook*, ed. and trans. Siegfried Wenzel (University Park, PA, and London, 1989), IV, ii, p. 315.

[77] William Langland, *Piers Plowman*, B, passus v, lines 260–2.

[78] For a summary of views on charity see Miri Rubin, *Charity and Community in Medieval Cambridge* (Cambridge, 1987), ch. 3, pp. 54–98.

[79] John of Ayton, *Ad Const. Othoboni, ad. v.* 'charitatem', p. 97a.

The most tangible expression of charity was in performing the Seven Corporal Acts of Mercy – feeding the hungry, providing drink for the thirsty, visiting the sick, clothing the naked, visiting the prisoner, sheltering the homeless, and burying the dead. Most of these involved an element of almsgiving. Yet there was some doubt about whether almsgiving was really an act of mercy or of justice, in the sense of redistributing and balancing resources between rich and poor. The problem had been pinpointed by the *Sentences* of Peter Lombard. He had quoted two apparently conflicting texts of Augustine: 'Justice is in the relief of misery' and 'Almsgiving is a work of mercy.'[80] The qualities of mercy, or loving kindness, and justice were closely related. As Bonaventure pointed out, 'If one does not love one's neighbour, it is not easy to do him justice.'[81]

Justice when applied to wealth and property meant equity in distribution. The conviction that almsgiving was a matter of justice had complex origins. It drew on ideas we have already encountered. Firstly the Aristotelian notion that property should be private in ownership, but common in use, and secondly that Christians had merely a stewardship of it on behalf of the Almighty.[82] As so often, Pauper, in *Dives and Pauper*, provided a good summary:

All that the rich man has passing his honest living after the degree of his dispensation it is other mens and not his, and he shall give well hard reckoning thereof at the doom... For rich men and lords in this world be God's bailiffs and God's reeves to ordain [= provide] for the poor folk and for to sustain the poor folk.[83]

He echoed a long patristic and canon-law tradition by reiterating that 'our superfluities belong to the poor'. Aquinas had declared:

according to natural law goods that are held in superabundance by some people should be used for the maintenance of the poor. This is the principle enunciated by Ambrose... It is the bread of the poor which you are holding back; it is the clothes of the naked which you are hoarding; it is the relief and liberation of the wretched which you are thwarting by burying your money away.[84]

In the end it was simply a matter of justice: almsgiving was the just return to the owners of what belonged to them, and what belonged to them was the superfluities of the rich. The Fathers of the early Church had been clear about that. Augustine had pointed out that 'those who possess superfluities possess alien goods',[85] and Pope Gregory the Great emphasized that when

---

[80] Peter Lombard, *Sententiae in IV Libros Distinctae*, 4 vols. (Rome 1981), bk. 3, dist. 15, ch. 5, p. 330 and bk. 3, dist. 33, ch. 1, p. 188. Cf. Tierney, *Medieval Poor Law*, p. 35.
[81] Langholm, *Economics*, p. 155. [82] See ch. 1, pp. 30–3, above.
[83] *Dives and Pauper*, pt. 2, Commandment VII, iv, p. 137, lines 64–70.
[84] Thomas Aquinas, *Summa theologiae*, 2a2ae, 66, 7, vol. 38, p. 81.
[85] Augustine, *Enarratio in Psalmos*, 147, 12, CChr.SL, 40, p. 2148.

we give necessities to the poor we are merely returning what is theirs.[86] It was only a short step to accusing the ungenerous of theft, or at least of harbouring stolen goods. Basil warned those who did not make offerings to God, 'whereby the poor may be fed' out of honest earnings, that 'robbery will be alleged against you'.[87] Not surprisingly the discussion in *Dives and Pauper* occurred under the heading of the Seventh Commandment 'Thou shalt not steal.' Pauper had both logic and tradition on his side when he declared that 'Withholding of alms from the poor needy folk is theft in the sight of God, for the covetous rich withdraw from the poor folk what belongs to them and misappropriate the poor men's goods, with which they should be succoured.'[88] The rich were worse than thieves; they were murderers. Ambrose had stated bluntly that those who do not feed the starving kill them.[89] This was taken up by Pauper, who dealt with it under the Fifth Commandment: Thou shalt not kill. 'If any man or woman dies for lack of help, then all those who should have helped, or might have helped, or who knew of the person's plight, but who would not help are guilty of manslaughter.'[90]

The idea that almsgiving was a matter of justice and the lack of it the equivalent of robbery or murder was the cold face of charity.

What about mercy? Albert the Great pointed out that for each individual there was a certain material status which was 'necessary' to that individual. True, Christ had advised men to give alms from their 'necessary' goods, but this was not a command, for commands applied only to superfluities.[91] Aquinas developed this. 'This... is what is actually commanded: to give alms out of our superfluous wealth; and to give alms to those in extreme need. Outside... that almsgiving... is a matter of counsel.'[92] Mercy involved an element of choice, whereas justice entailed returning what rightly belonged to the poor, and invited the idea that they had legal rights.

THE RIGHTS OF THE POOR

What were the rights of the poor, and how effective were they? In theory the Church was responsible for their care. Alexander III's Third Lateran

---

[86] Gregory I, *Regula pastoralis*, 3, ch. 21, *PL*, 77, col. 87.
[87] Basil, 'On mercy and justice', *Ascetical Works*, trans. Sister M. Monica Wagner, The Fathers of the Church, 9 (Washington, DC, 1962), p. 508.
[88] *Dives and Pauper*, pt. 2, Commandment VII, iv, p. 136, lines 27–31.
[89] Gratian, *Decretum*, D.88, c. 21, col. 302.
[90] *Dives and Pauper*, pt. 2, Commandment V, vii, pp. 13–14, lines 1–5.
[91] Albert the Great, *Super IV Sententiarum, Opera omnia*, 29 (Paris, 1894), dist. 15, art. 16, p. 496: cf. Langholm, *Economics*, p. 175.
[92] Thomas Aquinas, *Summa theologiae*, 2a2ae, 32, 5, vol. 34, p. 255.

Council of 1179 ordered churches to provide for all in need, both in the material and the spiritual sense.[93] From the fourth century onward the poor had been provided for out of tithe, the tenth part of a Christian's income, received by the Church in kind or occasionally in money. On the Continent it was divided into four parts, for the bishop, the clergy, the upkeep of the Church, and the poor, but in England the bypassing of the bishop resulted in a tripartite division. The development of the parish system transferred both the reception of tithe and the responsibility for poor relief to the parish. In practice, by the end of the overcrowded thirteenth century, the poor were being neglected. Even early in the century the canonist Johannes Teutonicus observed that the traditional quartering had broken down: 'Nowadays the bishops take everything for themselves.'[94] There is indirect evidence of this on the Continent, where the parishioners themselves assumed much of the responsibility for poor relief by the establishment of 'poor tables' (a table by the church door from which charity was administered).[95] This was so in Germany, the Low Countries, and France. In Spain the method was by 'poor plates'. In England the breakdown of the system was evidenced by the Franciscan Archbishop of Canterbury, John Pecham, who wrote to the rector of two Kentish parishes in 1284 complaining of the neglect of the poor, who were 'defrauded of all material and spiritual care'. He ordered his own proctor to spend 100 shillings on poor relief in each parish.[96] There is some evidence that English parishioners too were taking the initiative in providing for the needy. In the churchyard of Powerstock, Dorset, is a thirteenth-century dole table, admittedly a rare survival.[97] The Exeter diocesan statutes of 1287 show that alms-boxes were being placed in churches by the laity rather than the clergy.[98] By the first half of the fourteenth century John Bromyard was accusing the clergy of abusing the system, observing that they divided the goods of Christ, the Church, and the poor as the wolf divides its prey. Whatever they did not consume themselves they hid in chests, caskets, and treasure-chambers, sometimes underground.[99] This may not have been quite true: Richard Caistor, vicar of St Stephen's, Norwich,

---

[93] Alexander III, Third Lateran Council, clause 18, ed. John Gilchrist, *The Church and Economic Activity in the Middle Ages* (London, 1969), p. 170.
[94] G. C. Coulton, *The Medieval Village* (Cambridge 1925, repr. New York, 1989), p. 299.
[95] Mollat, *The Poor*, pp. 139–42.
[96] *Registrum Epistolarum Fratris Johannis Pecham*, ed. C. T. Martin, RS, 77 (2) (1884), p. 715.
[97] Stephen Friar, *The Local History Companion* (Stroud, 2001), p. 120.
[98] Alan Harding, *England in the Thirteenth Century* (Cambridge, 1993), p. 91. On the breakdown of the system see Christopher Dyer, *Standards of Living in the Later Middle Ages* (Cambridge, 1989), pp. 247–8; J. R. H. Moorman, *Church Life in England in the Thirteenth Century* (Cambridge, 1945), pp. 138–9.
[99] John Bromyard, *Summa*, 2, ch. 6, 'ordo clericalis', sect. 15, fol. 139v.

who died in 1420, left his money to the poor because 'according to the canons, the goods of the church are the goods of the poor'.[100]

In the thirteenth and early fourteenth centuries there were many more mouths to feed and many more 'miserable persons', so it was little wonder that the system buckled. But there was another reason: the system of appropriation. Many English parishes had been given by lay lords to monasteries or cathedral chapters after the Norman Conquest, which shifted the responsibility for the parish poor to them. Distance and an uncertain outcome meant that a journey to cathedral or monastery in search of alms was often not worth making.[101] At the local level the vicars or curates appointed to do the pastoral work could often barely maintain themselves, let alone the poor. In 1391 a parliamentary statute tried to enforce the charitable duties of appropriators. Another one, in 1403, ordered bishops to ensure that in the case of new appropriations 'a convenient sum' should be provided for the poor from the income of the parish; not much was.[102]

The monastery provided an alternative source of poor relief to the parish, justifiably since the tithes of the parish might well have been appropriated to it. Ideally charity should have been given to all suppliants indiscriminately, and in the immediate post-Conquest period this seems to have happened. Historians have suggested that discrimination started to be applied to recipients of monastic charity in the later Middle Ages, due both to demographic factors and a hardening in the attitude to beggary. Barbara Harvey, however, has demonstrated that discrimination was applied to giving handouts from the regular income of Benedictine monasteries administered by the almoner from as early as the mid-twelfth century. This can be explained by the severe inflation of the late twelfth and early thirteenth centuries, which deprived the black monks of real income, the drop in their popularity rating in favour of the newer orders, which robbed them of wealthy recruits and benefactors, and the increase in the number of urban paupers. Charity became directed more towards the poor living in institutions than to the rootless 'naked poor', and economies were made, such as cutting the daily distribution of food at abbey gates down to two or three times a week. The Cistercians, less targeted by the poor than the Benedictines, due to their remote locations, were also selective. They tended to support the sort of people who might later become *conversi*, or lay brothers, for on them the running of their economy depended.[103] By the early fourteenth century, due to

---

[100] N. Tanner, *The Church in Late Medieval Norwich, 1370–1532* (Toronto, 1984), p. 232.
[101] Moorman, *Church Life,* p. 139, and in general, Colin Platt, *The Parish Churches of Medieval England* (London, 1981), pp. 72–8.
[102] Dyer, *Standards of Living,* p. 248.   [103] Harvey, *Living and Dying,* pp. 7–23.

both inflation and the famines of 1315–22, many monks were themselves in need of charity, facing near-starvation and reduced to living on black bread and pottage.[104]

To some extent, as Barbara Harvey has also shown, the poor were compensated by an increase in funds given or left to monasteries for requiem masses or post-mortem anniversary commemorations, at which vast sums were shared by all paupers who attended. Here the monks were bound to honour the wishes of the testators, who wanted prayers for their salvation in return for their post-mortem charity. It was only from the mid-fourteenth century, with the general hardening in lay attitudes to beggary, that the testators themselves started to be more discriminatory, and the monks occasionally diverted their bequests to other charitable purposes.[105]

Monastic and parish charity might be supplemented by the generosity of the great. The Avignon popes in the fourteenth century set an example by distributing lavishly to the poor of the city, especially through the *pignotte*, the papal almonry.[106]

There were many generous princes, among them Louis VII, Louis IX, and Philip Augustus of France, the Emperor Henry V, and Henry II and King John of England.[107] The nobility followed their example. In addition, there was institutional charity in the form of hospitals, almshouses, and colleges. Whereas from the eleventh to the thirteenth centuries these were founded largely by bishops and abbots, by the fourteenth and fifteenth centuries the laity, especially the nobility and townspeople, were often responsible.[108]

If the poor could not depend on parish or monastic charity, and they lived in the wrong catchment area for episcopal, royal, or noble charity, how could they enforce their 'rights' to the goods of the rich? Johannes Teutonicus stressing these 'rights' suggested that an act of public denunciation and excommunication could be performed by a pauper against a rich man.[109] It sounds like the right of *diffidatio*, or defiance, which a vassal had against his lord when the lord violated the terms of a feudal contract.

---

[104] Mavis Mate, 'Coping with inflation: a fourteenth-century example', *Journal of Medieval History*, 4 (1978), pp. 95–106; Ian Kershaw, 'The great famine and agrarian crisis in England, 1315–1322', *P & P*, 59 (1973), p. 11.

[105] Harvey, *Living and Dying*, pp. 22–33.

[106] G. Mollat, *The Popes at Avignon 1305–1378*, trans. J. Love (London, 1963), pp. 316–17.

[107] Mollat, *The Poor*, pp. 96–7. For John see A. L. Poole, *From Domesday Book to Magna Carta, 1087–1216*, 2nd edn (Oxford, 1955), p. 428; Gilchrist, *The Church and Economic Activity in the Middle Ages*, p. 79.

[108] Rubin, *Charity and Community*, p. 94; Rubin, 'Development and change in English hospitals, 1100–1500', in L. Granshaw and R. Porter, eds., *The Hospital in History* (London, 1990), pp. 51–4.

[109] Tierney, *Medieval Poor Law*, p. 38; text at n. 33, pp. 147–8.

Probably this was not a practical suggestion; but what was practical was for someone to take what he needed as a matter of right.

The biblical basis of this was spelt out by Pauper. In Matthew 12. 1–4, Christ had defended his disciples against the Pharisees when they had illegally plucked and eaten ears of corn one Sabbath. He had excused them 'for need of hunger and said that they were unguilty and innocent', quoting the precedent of David and his followers who had eaten holy loaves in the tabernacle, something forbidden to all but the priests [1 Samuel, 21, 1–6]. Pauper added 'For it is a general rule in the law that need hath no law',[110] which indeed it was. The Roman legal maxim that necessity knows no law is often associated with Aquinas, who famously allowed a man in 'urgent and blatant' necessity to take what he needed if there was no alternative: this would be neither theft nor robbery.[111] In fact, Aquinas was not the first to say this, for Johannes Teutonicus[112] had already done so.

DISCRIMINATION IN GIVING

Who was to determine what constituted need? Who could say whether a suppliant was deserving, and did it really matter? After all, one of the greatest doctors of the early Church, John Chrysostom, had warned that if we are 'meddlesome' and examine lives we shall never have mercy on anyone.[113] Surely charity should be given to all indiscriminately, as suggested by Matthew 5.42 and Luke 6.3, 'Give to every man that asketh of thee'?

Practical circumstances conspired against the advice of both the Gospels and Chrysostom, as many early writers appreciated. Augustine, possibly echoing the first-century work known as the *Didache* or *The Teaching of the Twelve Apostles*, advised 'Let your alms sweat greatly in your hand, until you find a just person to whom you may give them.'[114] In the twelfth century Gratian assembled conflicting patristic texts about discrimination, which, as Brian Tierney has shown, gave rise to a fascinating debate among

---

[110] *Dives and Pauper*, pt. 2, Commandment VII, vi, p. 141, lines 15–24.
[111] Thomas Aquinas, *Summa theologiae*, 2a2ae, 66, 7, vol. 38, p. 81.
[112] Tierney, *Medieval Poor Law*, p. 147, n. 30.
[113] John Chrysostom, 'Sermon on almsgiving', in *St John Chrysostom on Repentance and Almsgiving*, trans. Gus George Christo, The Fathers of the Church, 96, sermon 10, p. 149 (26).
[114] Augustine, *Enarratio in Psalmos*, 102, 12, *CChr.SL*, 39, p. 2345. Cf. *The Didache or The Teaching of the Twelve Apostles*, ed. and trans. James A. Kleist, Ancient Christian Writers, 6 (Westminster, MD, 1948), ch. 1, 6, p. 16. On the dubious origins of the expression, which seems to have been pseudo-biblical, see Brian Tierney, 'The Decretists and the "Deserving poor"', *Comparative Studies in Society and History*, 1 (1958–9), pp. 360–73, at p. 363, n.15.

later canonists, who heaped up even more texts.[115] Two main principles emerged. The first was that if resources were low, discrimination should be applied. This was to be done according to a 'ladder of perfection' originally drawn up by Ambrose – one's parents, children, and household members before strangers.[116] Amongst the 'strangers' faithful Christians, the old, the sick, and those who fell blamelessly from wealth to poverty (a group labelled from the thirteenth century as the 'shame-faced poor') were to be preferred.[117] There was later some doubt about whether family and friends should be helped before strangers. The second principle, that of the 'undeserving' poor, that is, the idle but able-bodied, took longer to emerge, though the distinction was drawn from the twelfth century onward. Again the basis was patristic. Augustine especially had warned against giving to members of shameful professions – gladiators, actors, prostitutes, and the like.[118] Elsewhere he had warned that bread should not be given to someone who had led an evil life before becoming poor 'so that being led astray he may rejoice in injustice'.[119]

The idea of ordered charity was accepted by Aquinas and later writers.[120] Both the Dominican and Franciscan preachers of late medieval Siena recommended discrimination in giving, on the basis both of the suppliant's physical and moral state.[121] In England, Pauper explained that Christian charity excluded no one – neither man nor woman, no estate, no degree, no sect, neither heathen nor Christian – when they were in need.[122] But he cautioned:

Nevertheless us must keep order in giving and take need to the cause and to the manner of need in them that we give alms to, for why some be poor by their will and some against their will. And they that are poor by their will, some are poor for the love of God and some for the love of the world. They that be poor for the love of God must be helped passing other, for their poverty is profitable, perfect, and virtuous.[123]

Pauper was quite blatant about looking after his own interests: the mendicants were top of his list. Yet he did not totally exclude the undeserving

---

[115] Tierney, 'The Decretists and the "Deserving Poor"', pp. 360–73; *Medieval Poor Law*, pp. 55–62.
[116] Tierney, *Medieval Poor Law*, pp. 57, 150, n. 34.
[117] Gratian, *Decretum*, D. 86, cc. 14, 16, 17, cols. 300–1. Cf. Tierney, *Medieval Poor Law*, pp. 56–7.
[118] Gratian, *Decretum*, D. 86, cc. 7–10.
[119] Ibid., C. 5, q. 5, c. 2 and C. 23, q. 4, c. 37. Cf. Tierney, *Medieval Poor Law*, p. 58.
[120] Aquinas, *Summa theologiae*, 2a2ae, 32, 9 ad 2, vol. 34, p. 269.
[121] Paton, *Preaching Friars*, pp. 199–203.
[122] *Dives and Pauper*, pt. 2, Commandment IX, xiii, p. 286, lines 46–9.
[123] Ibid., lines 50–6.

poor: those who were poor 'only by sin... as they that waste their goods in lechery and gluttony, in pride and pleading and in misuse at the dice, in riot and in vanity. Such poor folk be last in the order of alms deeds, but their need be the more.'[124] Here he was more charitable than either Augustine or Johannes Teutonicus, and followed Ambrose in not excluding anyone. As for the rest, he followed Ambrose's scale, and was especially concerned with those who slid blamelessly into poverty 'for commonly such be shamefaced to ask'.[125]

A suppliant's need and moral condition influenced decisions about whether or not to give. The social status of donor or recipient, and what was considered sufficient to maintain it influenced what was given. In the early thirteenth century Cardinal Robert of Courçon recommended that through almsgiving a man should deprive himself to the extent that he was reduced to subsistence level.[126] The influence of Aristotle, however, was to change such ideas. He devoted a lengthy chapter to the virtue of liberality, which he defined as 'the mean with regard to wealth'. This applied both 'to the giving and taking of wealth, and especially in respect of giving. Now by "wealth" we mean all the things whose value is measured by money.'[127] Observing the mean in dealing with material goods meant, in effect, maintaining the 'sufficiency' recommended by Jean de Meun: 'The mean is called sufficiency, and that is where abundant virtues lie.'[128] 'Sufficiency' meant having whatever was necessary to maintain one's station in life. Pauper pinpointed this for both rich and poor:

> If the poor man have meat, drink and clothes he hath all that him needeth to his status and to his person. He careth not but for himself or few more. But the rich man careth for his person, for his status, for his great men, for his worship, for his goods. He hath need of much gold and silver and much money, many vitals. He hath need of many men's help, of servants, labourers, men of craft, or men of law, of great lordship, without which he may not maintain his status nor his riches.[129]

But how did this relate to almsgiving? Aristotle had suggested that giving – liberality – should be according to means: 'The term "liberality" is used relatively to a man's substance; for liberality resides not in the multitude of the gifts but in the state of character of the giver, and this is relative to the giver's substance.'[130] Aquinas warned more specifically that 'no one should live unbecomingly, and hence it would not do for a man to so impoverish himself by almsgiving that he could no longer live in decency

---

[124] Ibid., xiv, p. 287, lines 4–8.   [125] Ibid., xvi, p. 292, line 25.
[126] See Langholm, *Economics*, pp. 41–3.   [127] Aristotle, *Ethics*, IV, i, p. 79.
[128] Jean de Meun, *Romance of the Rose*, ch. 6, p. 173, lines 11241–2.
[129] *Dives and Pauper*, pt. 1, Holy Poverty, A, iv, p. 58, lines 42–50.
[130] Aristotle, *Ethics*, IV, i, p. 81.

on the residue according to his position and business commitments'.[131] He was flatly contradicting Robert of Courçon. Jean de Meun advised that 'since you are neither rich nor mean nor miserly you should give nice, reasonable little gifts... so that you do not fall into poverty and suffer harm and loss'.[132] Moderation had to be applied from the point of view of both donor and recipient. Pauper looked at both sides. He discussed those who had given too much to others and in so doing had impoverished themselves. They fell under the heading of people who were voluntarily poor for the sake of the world rather than for God. 'And these days', he commented, 'many folk divest themselves of their own property and take it to their children to make them great in the world, and many folk take so much heed to other men's profit that they take no heed for themselves and so fall into poverty and need.' These rash people should be helped rather than the involuntary poor, though they should be helped principally by those who had profited from their generosity. Unlike Aquinas, he saw people who had endangered their status as worthy of pity rather than condemnation. But, of course, they should not be helped before those who were poor for the love of God![133] As a mendicant, Pauper was without social status, replying evasively 'God knows' when Dives tried to discover it.[134] Nevertheless, he instructed Dives that in giving alms to 'them that be poor for Christ's sake and to the poor preachers', he should give 'of the better things, and help them worshipfully as God's friends and his Disciples'. To other folk, however, 'which the world has forsaken, not they the world' it was enough just to give relief 'for it is sin to give dainties to such poor common beggars when it be not convenient [= fitting] to them', and he cited various legal texts in support.[135] His own lack of estate did not prevent him from trying to keep others in theirs.

CREDIT IN HEAVEN

The material relationship between the rich and the poor was a symbiotic one, but this was even more true of their spiritual roles. Almsgiving opened the gates of Heaven. As Pauper saw it, either 'you must be poor or beg Heaven of the poor if you will come in Heaven'.[136] The idea originated with the early Church Fathers. Augustine provided a good example in a

---

[131] Thomas Aquinas, *Summa theologiae*, 2a2ae, 32, 6, vol. 34, p. 257.
[132] Jean de Meun, *Romance of the Rose*, ch. 5, p. 126, lines 8163–5.
[133] *Dives and Pauper*, pt. 2, Commandment IX, xiii, p. 286, lines 56–65.
[134] Ibid., pt. 1, Holy Poverty, A, iii, p. 53, lines 23–5. Cf. Moisa, 'Fourteenth-century preachers' views', pp. 161–3.
[135] *Dives and Pauper*, pt. 2, Commandment IX, xvi, p. 293, lines 40–6.
[136] Ibid., pt. 1, Holy Poverty, A, iii, p. 54, lines 9–14.

passage quoted in the *Fasciculus morum*: 'Almsgiving is a holy work which increases present merits, forgives sins, prolongs life, separates us from the devil, joins us to God, and calls his angels to our help.'[137] Such sentiments were epitomized in a popular proverb, of which Miri Rubin has found instances from Ælfric in the tenth century through to the late medieval period: 'Water extinguishes the burning fire and alms extinguish sin.'[138]

In the pre-Reformation period, concerns about personal salvation were focused on the doctrine of Purgatory. This was the intermediate place or state between Heaven and Hell where souls destined for ultimate salvation were purified in purgatorial fire, and penances unfulfilled on earth were completed. Although not fully enunciated until the twelfth century and defined officially at the Second Council of Lyons (1274), its foundations were patristic.[139] In early eighth-century England Bede's report of Drycthelm's vision of the afterlife contained a description of Purgatory in all but name.[140] It also mentioned the offering of prayers, fasting, alms, and especially masses by the living, which helped to set souls free from it. The notion that time in Purgatory could be lessened posed difficulties because earthly time does not exist in the afterlife, but the only way the purifying process could be envisaged was within a temporal framework.

In the late medieval period lay people were intent on working out their own salvation, and especially lessening their time of purgation. Part of the reason was disillusionment with the official Church – with worldly popes and prelates, opulent monks and friars, illiterate or absentee parish priests. The belief that almsgiving could lead to Heaven was to have both practical and spiritual repercussions.

One result was the foundation of charitable institutions throughout Europe, such as hospitals, hospices, and almshouses. Another was the appearance of gilds and fraternities. Gilds were founded to regulate a particular trade or industry and to look after the material needs of their members. Invariably, however, they were also religious bodies, concerned at least to

---

[137] Augustine, quoted in *Fasciculus morum*, v, xxii, p. 529.
[138] Rubin, *Charity and Community*, p. 64, n. 62.
[139] J. le Goff, *The Birth of Purgatory* (London, 1984). On its importance in late medieval England see Duffy, *Stripping of the Altars*, pp. 338–76; C. Burgess, '"A fond thing vainly imagined": an essay on Purgatory and pious motive in late medieval England', in S. J. Wright, ed., *Parish, Church, and People: Local Studies in Lay Religion, 1350–1750* (London, 1988), pp. 56–84; Virginia Bainbridge, 'The medieval way of death', in Michael Wilks, ed., *Prophecy and Eschatology, SCH*, subsidia 10 (1994), pp. 183–4, and for further literature.
[140] Bede, *Ecclesiastical History of the English People*, ed. Bertram Colgrave and R. A. B. Myors, Oxford Medieval Texts (Oxford, 1969), v, 12, pp. 489–97. The point is discussed by Aron I. Gurevich, *Medieval Popular Culture: Problems of Belief and Perception*, trans. János M. Bak and Paul A. Hollingsworth (Cambridge, 1988), pp. 117–18. Cf. ibid., pp. 142–3 on the early origins of the idea.

ensure that dead members were given a decent burial and that prayers were offered for them. The fraternities were more overtly religious and concerned specifically with salvation. One of their most important functions was to organize the funerals of members and to intercede for their souls. As has been observed, charity gradually changed from being vertical – handed down by church or monastery – to being horizontal – provided by one's colleagues, friends, and neighbours.[141]

Alms deeds were not always performed in life, and an area of considerable growth was that of post-mortem charity – charitable bequests to the poor, to almshouses and hospitals, to the local church, and to a lesser extent to monasteries and friaries. Provision was frequently made in wills for doles of food, clothing, or money to be paid to the poor at funerals in return for their prayers – and that was the whole point. The bell-man's round of the parish after a death, invoking prayers for the deceased, was taken as an open invitation to the funeral. Even if doles were not specifically mentioned in the will, the practice of paying them was almost invariable except at the funerals of the paupers themselves.[142]

Did post-mortem gifts benefit their donors? St Basil was blunt: 'One does not trade after the market is closed; he is not crowned who does not enter the lists until after the combat ceases.'[143] Late medieval English literature is heavy with such moralizing. John of Ayton, for example, recommended that 'Alms should much more be offered to the living, for sins are redeemed by alms. Money is vile, but mercy is precious.'[144] Pauper explained that 'Much better is he that hath grace to help himself afore his death with his own goods, for one penny shall profit more afore his death than twenty pennies after his death, and more profiteth one candle afore a man than twenty behind him.'[145] He followed this with a grim little tale about a wise fool and a 'natural' fool, and how the wise one allowed the other to burn to death in a baker's oven by betraying his trust. The two fools were the dead and their false executors.[146]

Post-mortem alms were not necessarily worthless, but those given from ill-gotten gains, especially usury, were. This point was stressed in patristic writing and canon law, and emerged in later pastoral literature. The *Fasciculus*, for example, underlined the point that 'bodily alms must be given from one's own property that has been justly and legally acquired,

---

[141] A. H. Bredero, 'Le Moyen âge et le purgatoire', *Revue d'histoire écclesiastique*, 78 (1983), pp. 429–52.
[142] Duffy, *Stripping of the Altars*, pp. 359–62 at p. 359.
[143] Basil, Sermon on Matthew 19, ed. M. P. McGuire (Washington, DC, 1927), pp 34–5.
[144] John of Ayton, *ad Const. Othoboni*, p. 121, *ad v.* 'propitiabiliter'.
[145] *Dives and Pauper*, pt. 2, Commandment IX, x, pp. 277–8.
[146] Ibid., xi, pp. 278–9.

not from what has been taken illegally and dishonestly from others... by such means as theft, usury, extortion, prostitution, and the like'.[147] For Pauper something was 'mis-gotten' when both the giving and the taking of the thing was against God's law. Among ill-gotten gains he lists the proceeds of simony, 'thing gotten by lechery and by sinful japery [cheating] of jugglers, of minstrels, of witches and of such other', and of bribes taken by 'officers of kings, princes, lords and ladies, of bishops and prelates', a revealing political comment.[148]

An important aspect of almsgiving was its method. If alms were given in the wrong way they would do their donor no good. Augustine had warned that 'If you give with sorrow you lose both your bread and the merit of your action.'[149] But it was not only a question of giving with a bad grace. Thomas Brinton, Bishop of Rochester, complained about the disagreeable attitude of some rich people, who before giving the poor the modicum due to them would provoke and insult them so much that they would have been better off without the alms.[150] Alms had to be given with pious intention and 'with a cheerful countenance'. Charity in this case really meant bene-volence – literally good will.

The *Fasciculus* author emphasized that the real point of almsgiving was to please God, and that a worldly motive would destroy the merit of the action:

He who puts coins in a bag with holes in knows when he puts them in but does not know when he loses them, and yet he puts them in and loses them at one and the same moment. In the same way he who gives alms or does some good deed out of pride or for worldly praise knows well when he does this but does not notice when he loses it, for he does it and loses it at one and the same moment.[151]

The author was right: the reason for almsgiving was to please God. It might incidently alleviate the suffering of a fellow human being, but the real point was the purchase of paradise. A benefactor always expected some return for his benefaction. If the rich gave to the poor, in life or in death, they expected the poor to pray for them in return. That was what would enable them to enter Heaven. Beneficiaries were bidden to pray for their testators; gifts and legacies to churches, especially memorials, were usually inscribed with the donor's name, in the hope that parishioners would pray for them. Offerings at shrines were made to encourage the saint to

---

[147] *Fasciculus morum*, v, xxii, p. 529.
[148] *Dives and Pauper*, pt. 2, Commandment VII, xi, p. 156, line 22; p. 157, lines 35–40.
[149] Augustine, *Enarratio in Psalmos*, 42, 8, CChr.SL, 38, p. 481, lines 14–15.
[150] Thomas Brinton, Sermon 44, ed. Sister Mary Aquinas Devlin, vol. 1, p. 196.
[151] *Fasciculus morum*, v, xxv, p. 545.

intercede with God for the donor. Reciprocity and mutuality entered even into the devotional sphere, and prayer and intercession were the currency. The afterlife became subject to what Chiffoleau has termed the 'mathematics of the soul'.[152] People tried to reckon the time they would have to spend in Purgatory, and how to 'balance' their account with God. They counted up the number of intercessors, the number of masses to be offered for them, the number of poor beneficiaries, and so on. Everything was given, in effect, a numerical value. In the early fifteenth century the eccentric wife of Lynn, Margery Kempe, saw salvation in terms of credit in Heaven. Christ, the executor of her will, promised, 'Daughter, I shall be a true executor to you and fulfil all of your will, and because of your great charity that you have to comfort all your fellow Christians, you shall have double reward in Heaven.'[153] Hers was, as has been suggested, a 'very material mysticism'.[154] But perhaps the most mathematical example of charity as an investment came from a story in the *Fasciculus*. A pious rich man had given to the poor at the instigation of his bishop, who had promised him a hundredfold reward and given him a promissory note for his donation. On his death, his wife and family tried to redeem the donation. The bishop took them to the grave, where the dead man lay peacefully, clutching a gold-lettered deed in his hand, which declared:

Let all present and future know that for the money I gave to Bishop Odo to be distributed for the use of the poor I have received a hundredfold return before my death in this world, namely the full remission of my sins, and in the future, as he had promised, eternal life.[155]

CONCLUSION

Attitudes to wealth and poverty had changed a good deal. By the fifteenth century poverty was no longer seen as an ideal, and wealth was regarded as praiseworthy, and even as an aid to salvation. Attitudes to 'beggary' had become harder and more discriminatory, both in theory and practice, and idleness was widely condemned. This is not, however, to suggest that labour acquired any particular dignity or that there was any sense of a medieval 'work ethic'. Charity, from being a largely monastic and clerical responsibility, had become the preserve of the laity. What did not

---

[152] Chiffoleau, *La Comptabilité*, p. 306.
[153] *The Book of Margery Kempe*, trans. B. A. Wineatt (Harmondsworth, 1985), ch. 8, p. 55.
[154] Sarah Beckwith, 'A very material mysticism', in D. Aers, ed., *Medieval Literature* (Brighton, 1986), pp. 34–57.
[155] *Fasciculus morum*, v, 26, p. 555, lines 7–19.

change was the underlying principle of balance. It might be applied to the redistribution of economic resources, or to maintaining one's own 'sufficiency' or that of one's suppliants as a mean between wealth and beggary. It also applied to the afterlife where the return for a charitable investment was not hard cash, but the prayers of the poor and ultimately credit in Heaven. The poor may have lost their high profile on earth, but in return they had gained a far more sublime one as the security guards of Heaven.

3

WHAT IS MONEY?

INTRODUCTION

The mathematics of the soul and the tendency to view sacred things in terms of economic exchange were reflections of the progressive dominance of the market-place and its dynamics in late medieval society. At the heart of this was money. Money bought and maintained property of all types; it was increasingly coming to buy status; it was the stuff of charitable handouts to the destitute and disabled, and it might be the means through which paradise was purchased. These roles have already been discussed. Those remaining, to be discussed in future chapters, were more complex, such as its role as price or wage, as commodity or investment, or as loan or credit. The nature and properties of money – the question of what it was and was not – were basic to much of the discussion about these functions, especially on credit and loans, and therefore form the main subject of this chapter.

Money, however, meant different things to different people, and the scholastic view was not the only one. Some simply worshipped it as a god. John Bromyard was following a long and hostile tradition of 'venality satire',[1] when he described how

a certain man used to say that if he wished a god other than the God of Heaven, he would choose money . . . for just as the man who has God is said to have everything, so the man who has money can have everything; for all things on earth and in Hell and in the Heavens, and even redemption from sin are bought with money.[2]

---
[1] John A. Yunck, *The Lineage of Lady Meed: the Development of Medieval Venality Satire* (Notre Dame, 1963).
[2] John Bromyard, *Summa praedicantium*, 1, ch. 27, 'avaritia', sect. 4, fol. 79r.

The silver pennies of late medieval England, each marked with a cross, according to Bromyard, were thought to have powers comparable with the Cross of Christ:

> He who has a purse copiously marked with the silver cross and always knows how to impart its abundant blessing can enter any court, and safely go wherever he wishes... This cross conquers, it reigns, and it wipes away the guilt from everything.[3]

By Shakespeare's time the word cross had become slang for coin.[4]

Money also fitted into another tradition, the political idea of society as a body. Both John of Salisbury in the twelfth century and Christine de Pisan in the fourteenth revived a classical fable from Aesop and Livy in which the stomach was the treasury of the body. The limbs rebelled against the incessant demands of the belly by starving it of food, that is, money, with the result that the whole body died.[5] In the fifteenth century the humanist Poggio Bracciolini adopted a more direct approach. 'Money', he declared, 'is necessary as the nerves that sustain the whole *res publica*. When copious misers exist they are considered to be its basis and foundation.'[6] The connection between the economic prosperity of a state and its political power was a constant theme in late medieval Europe.[7]

The ideas of the scholastics, based substantially on Aristotle, merged at various points with political ideas, particularly on the role of the ruler in relation to money. For the scholastics, money had two distinct roles. It was, firstly, an artificial measure of value, authorized by the State, against which all things could be gauged, but which had no other use. Secondly, since it was given physical reality by coinage made of precious metal, it came to be seen as a commodity with a value that could rise and fall, like that of any other commodity. These two ideas were given practical expression in the two types of money prevalent in the Middle Ages, actual money in circulation, and 'ghost' money, or money of account. Since money was made of imperishable and precious metal, it could also be used as a store of value, which might allow individuals to accumulate large sums of it. The two concepts of money, as artificial and 'useless', on the one hand,

---

[3] Ibid., ch. 17,'crux', sect. 37, fol. 168r.
[4] *Henry IV*, pt. 2, Act I, scene 2, where Falstaff is said to be 'too impatient to bear crosses', meaning both to carry money and to suffer being thwarted.
[5] John of Salisbury, *Policraticus*, ed. and trans. Cary J. Nederman (Cambridge, 1990), bk. 5, ch. 2, p. 67; Christine de Pisan, *The Book of the Body Politic*, pt. 3, ch. 1, ed. and trans. Cary J. Nederman and Kate Langdon Forhan, *Medieval Political Theory – a Reader: the Quest for the Body Politic, 1100–1400* (London and New York, 1993), p. 232. For further examples see E. H. Kantorowicz, *The King's Two Bodies* (Princeton, NJ, 1957), p. 184, n. 288.
[6] Poggio Bracciolini, *De avaritia*, XIV, 4, p. 79.
[7] See the discussion on economic nationalism in chapter 5, pp. 117–18, 121–7 below.

and as a commodity with an inherent value, on the other, were to clash in the debates about usury to be examined in chapters 7 and 8. As so often, the problem lay in finding a mean between them.

THE TWO ROLES: ARISTOTLE AND THE ORIGINS OF MONEY

Underlying much of the theorizing about the origins and properties of money were the *Ethics* and the *Politics* of Aristotle, in which he laid the foundations for the two basic interpretations of money – as an artificial measure of the value of things and as something of intrinsic value. In these two works the philosopher was trying to do different things, and this can lead to confusion in the interpretation both of his ideas on money and those of his commentators. The commentators examined the works separately, in some cases because translations of the *Ethics* became available in the West before those of the *Politics*. The treatment of money in the *Ethics* occurs during an attempt to define justice according to the principle of the mean; the treatment in the *Politics* occurs in a discussion of the association of the household as a stage in the evolution of political society.

In the *Ethics* just action is defined as 'intermediate between acting unjustly and being unjustly treated; for the one is to have too much and the other to have too little. Justice is a kind of mean ... because it relates to an intermediate amount, while injustice relates to the extremes.'[8] Aristotle applied this mean to economic exchange. He tried to establish equality between the things exchanged. He recognized that exchange is the basis of economic relationships between people: 'neither would there have been association if there were not exchange, nor exchange if there were not equality'.[9] The motivation for exchange is demand, but the precondition of exchange at this stage is that each of the two parties has something different to offer. Two doctors could not exchange with each other, but a doctor and a farmer could. This is where the problem lies: the things offered by different types of people will be diverse and not necessarily of equal value. There has to be some way of equalizing them, of deciding, for example, how many shoes are worth a house or a given quantity of food. This need to equalize things led to the introduction of money, which is a measure against which each thing can be valued. But there is still a missing link, because how can various things be measured against something which is in itself artificial? The way in which they are valued must be according to the demand for them, and the value of this demand is then measured by money. 'All goods must therefore be measured by some one thing ... Now this unit is in truth demand, which holds all things

---

[8] Aristotle, *Ethics*, v, v, p. 121.   [9] Ibid., p. 120.

together . . . but money has become by convention a sort of representative of demand.'[10] As a measure of value, money is entirely artificial: 'Money (*nomisma*) . . . exists not by nature but by law (*nomos*) and it is in our power to change it and make it useless',[11] Aristotle explains. In passing, he notes the common etymology of the Greek words for currency and law, *nomisma* and *nomos*.

The discussion of exchange in the *Politics* appears in the context of the household. Aristotle is concerned with the natural stages through which political society evolves – through household and village to the *polis* or citystate. Although this is a natural process, for, after all, man is naturally a political animal, it is not completely so, for someone deliberately has to *construct* the association.[12] The *polis*, once constructed, can take a variety of forms, or constitutions, not all of them necessarily aimed at the highest good.

One of the difficulties in interpreting Aristotle's work is that 'nature' can be understood on more than one level. The natural may be something instinctive, and therefore morally neutral, such as the 'natural' association of man and woman and the growth of the family, or it may be something far more complex, such as the *polis*, aimed at the good life, at justice or righteousness, which will cater for both the higher and the lower or instinctive parts of human nature. The real transition in the evolution of the state comes at the village stage, which caters for something 'more than daily recurrent needs'. This is when exchange is introduced, for having moved outside the immediate household, man is no longer economically selfsufficient. At the barter stage – the exchange of one essential commodity for another – exchange is considered natural and morally neutral. From this exchange, however, developed what Aristotle called 'chresmatic', the art of acquisition, which he considered unnatural and morally reprehensible. It originated through trade – import and export. People started to import what they lacked, and to export what they had in surplus. But because commodities were not necessarily portable,

men therefore agreed for the purpose of their exchanges to give and receive some commodity which . . . possessed the advantage of being easily handled for the purpose of getting the necessities of life. Such commodities were iron, silver, and other similar metals.[13]

THE NATURE AND USE OF MONEY

The problem which Aristotle bequeathed to the medieval world was to define the nature, and with it the function, of money. Was it simply an

---

[10] Ibid., p. 119.   [11] Aristotle, *Ethics*, v, v, p. 119.
[12] *Politics*, I, ii, 15, 1253a, p. 7.   [13] Ibid., I, ix, 8, 1257a, p. 24.

What is money? 73

artificial measure of value, given its own validity by the State, or did it have some inherent value of its own, due to its composition of precious metal? Was it, in effect, a commodity in its own right? These two views have become known respectively as the 'sign' theory (or, because it was adopted by the scholastics, the 'feudal' theory) and the metallist theory.[14] Aristotle himself was aware of both these approaches. In the *Politics*, he specifically notes the existence of the two views. The first is that money is of intrinsic value, and that wealth and money are synonymous. In this sense it is known as currency: 'those who hold the view often assume that wealth is simply a fund of currency, on the ground that the art of acquisition (in the form of retail trade for profit) is concerned with currency'. According to the second view, money 'is a sham and entirely a convention', useless for the necessary purposes of life. After all, according to the fable, Midas had starved in the midst of all his gold.[15] As so often with Aristotle, he arrives at a mean between the two views, and seems to subscribe to both. Yes, money is a convention, but in the *Politics* he adds that men agreed 'to give and receive some *commodity* which itself belonged to the category of useful things... such commodities were iron, silver, and other similar metals'.[16] The coexistence of the two views has enabled Eli Monroe, on the one hand, to laud Aristotle as 'heading a long line of "sound money" advocates',[17] while Barry Gordon, on the other, writes of his 'strong non-metallist emphasis'.[18]

Of Aristotle's successors, the Roman jurist Paul agreed that money was simply a creation of the law, a mere token. For him, money, when authorized by the State, overcame the difficulties of barter by providing a uniform measure. It 'serves for commerce and conveyance, on account not so much *of its substance* [my italics] as of its quantity' – by 'quantity' he means the public price set on it.[19] This was the view of the majority of Aristotelian commentators. Thomas Aquinas, following Aristotle, contrasted natural wealth, which satisfied natural needs, such as food and shelter, with manmade wealth: 'Artificial wealth comprises the things which of themselves satisfy no natural need, for example, money, which is a human contrivance to serve as a means of exchange, as a sort of measure of the value of things for sale.'[20] 'A sort of measure of the value of things for sale'

---

[14] For discussion and historiography, see Langholm, *Economics*, pp. 191–3; Gordon, *Economic Analysis*, pp. 162–6.
[15] Aristotle, *Politics*, I, ix, 10–11, 1257b, pp. 24–5.
[16] Ibid., 8, 1257a, p. 24. For discussion on Aristotle's application of the mean to these views see Ernest Barker, *The Political Thought of Plato and Aristotle* (repr. New York, 1959), p. 39–81.
[17] Arthur Eli Monroe, *Monetary Theory before Adam Smith* (Cambridge, MA, 1923), p. 7.
[18] Gordon, *Economic Analysis*, p. 134.   [19] *Digest*, 18, 1, 1.
[20] Thomas Aquinas, *Summa theologiae*, 1a2ae, 2, 1, vol. 41, p. 33.

meant in effect that money was a standard, a medium of exchange. As a standard it was different from other things. It could not itself be bought and sold. All that it could do was to provide a middle term, a mean or medium, between things which could be bought and sold. As an anonymous commentator on Grosseteste wrote: 'Money constitutes in a manner a middle term (medium), for it is a measure of all things, and so of their superior and inferior value.'[21] Albert the Great put it more geometrically: 'Coinage makes things to be exchanged equal, just as a measure makes equal things being measured by addition and subtraction.'[22] The role of money was to keep the balance between the goods being exchanged.

Aquinas had written of two types of wealth, but there were also two types of measure, a natural and an artificial. Things were measured 'by need, according to nature, and by money, according to human convention'.[23] This point was to be taken up by later commentators. The German Augustinian Henry of Friemar (d. 1340), for example, affirmed that 'human need is the true and natural measure of value, while money is a measure instituted by law'.[24] His contemporary, the Carmelite Guido Terreni, a theologian and canonist, and later bishop of Mallorca and then Elne, said much the same, adding that need was the natural measure because it was not deliberately invented. Need measured the accidental value which things had 'in use for the supply of human need'.[25] The idea of the 'double measure', the natural and the manufactured, underlined further the artificial character of money. It suggested that human need could be measured in terms of money, and this idea was to be fundamental to the theory of the just price which we shall discuss in a later chapter.

Measuring human need meant measuring the usefulness of things. Money itself was useful, but only as a measure of other things. Aquinas spelt out that

All other things from themselves have some utility: not so, however, money. But it is the measure of utility of other things, as is clear according to the Philosopher in the *Ethics*... And therefore the use of money does not have the measure of its utility from this money itself, but from the things which are measured by money according to the different persons who exchange money for goods.[26]

[21] Odd Langholm, *Wealth and Money in the Aristotelian Tradition* (Oslo, 1983), p. 69.
[22] Albert the Great, *Ethicorum*, bk. 5, tract 2, ch. 10, sect. 36, in *Opera omnia*, 7 (Paris, 1891), p. 360.
[23] Langholm, *Economics*, p. 230. See also *Wealth and Money*, pp. 49–50, where he suggests that this may have come from an ancient Greek commentary on the *Ethics*, which was translated by Grosseteste.
[24] Langholm, *Economics*, p. 545, transcribed from MS Basle UB F.I.14.
[25] Ibid., p. 502.
[26] Aquinas, *In quatuor libros Sententiarum*, III, 37, i, 6: cited by Gordon, *Economic Analysis*, p. 159.

For him the proper use of money was as an instrument of exchange: 'The prime and proper use of money is its use and disbursement in the way of ordinary transactions.'[27] This was to have important implications for the doctrine of usury, the subject of chapters 7 and 8, for it was linked with the Roman law idea that money was a fungible. A fungible was something which was consumed in use, as food and drink would be, or as money would be sunk or alienated in exchange. A fungible would perform only one service for its owner, unlike, say, a garment or a house. Fungibles could be counted, weighed, or measured, and the units were totally interchangeable and indistinguishable, because one unit could perform the service as well as another. As such, if they were borrowed, the same number, weight, or amount had to be returned, but not the actual unit which had been borrowed, because this would have been consumed or alienated in use. If someone borrowed a loaf of bread from a neighbour, then a loaf of similar size and weight would be returned instead of the original. The implication was, of course, that money too should be returned to its lender in the exact amount borrowed. In the medieval period usury did not mean, as now, taking an exorbitant rate of interest on a loan; it meant the taking of *any* interest on a loan. The exact amount of money borrowed was to be returned without addition or subtraction. There was an added dimension to the usury argument: since fungibles were consumed in use, it was not possible to separate ownership from use. (This was the very problem encountered by the Franciscans in their quest for total poverty described earlier:[28] did they need to own something in order to consume it?) Aquinas's classic definition of usury in the *Summa theologiae* embraced all these points:

> there are some things the use of which consists in their being consumed in the way in which we consume wine by using it for drinking and consume corn by using it for eating. We should not, therefore, reckon the use of such things apart from the things themselves. For, instead, when we grant to someone the use by that very fact we grant also the thing, and for this reason to lend things of this kind is to transfer the ownership, so that somebody who wanted to sell wine and the use of wine separately would be selling the same thing twice over or be selling something non-existent. And this would obviously be to commit the sin of injustice. By the same token, however, somebody commits an injustice if he lends corn or wine and asks for a twofold recompense – not merely the restoration of some equivalent but also a charge for its use, which is what usury strictly is.[29]

---

[27] Aquinas, *Summa theologiae*, 2a2ae, 78, art. 1, vol. 38, p. 235.
[28] See above, ch. 1, pp. 28–9.
[29] Aquinas, *Summa theologiae*, 2a2ae, 78, art. 1, vol. 38, p. 249. For discussion see Langholm, *Economics*, pp. 241–3.

Pauper, in *Dives and Pauper*, summarized: 'Many things there be that must not be used without waste and destruction of the thing, as meat and drink and such other, and in such the use may not be departed from the thing.' If the seller of a fungible charged for its use, 'He selleth that thing twice, and selleth thing that nought is, for the use is full waste of the thing.' Playing, like Aquinas, on the etymology of usury, he observed, 'The usurer selleth together the thing that he lendeth and the *use* of the thing and therefore *us*ury cometh of selling of the *use*.'[30]

The 'sign' theory of money, the conviction that money was an artificial, non-saleable measure of value, of which the only 'use' was to be alienated in exchange, was the one largely favoured by the scholastics. It was to be some time before most theorists started to consider that the metal content of money gave it independent value, and that such value, and therefore purchasing power, might vary according to market conditions, as it would with any other commodity. If the value of money could change, then it followed that there would be profit in buying and selling it. Aristotle himself had posed a problem for his commentators in the *Ethics*, the work in which he principally advanced the view that money was a measure of value. He pointed out that 'the same thing happens to money itself as to goods – it is not always worth the same; yet it tends to be steadier'.[31] In commenting on this, Aquinas had to admit that the value of money might fluctuate:

Money, however, like other things is actually subject to change. One does not always get for it what he desires because it is not always equal, that is, it is not always of the same value. But money should be established in such a way that it is more stable in the same value than are other things.[32]

It is tempting to accuse Aquinas of inconsistency, for this recognition seems very similar to the metallist approach, where money appears to take on a life independent of its role as a fixed and invariable measure instituted by law. The explanation, however, may lie in the contemporary state of affairs in which two types of money coexisted – money of account, appropriately labelled 'ghost money', and actual money in circulation.

GHOST MONEY: A MEASURE OF VALUE

'Ghost money' is indeed an apt name for money of account, because throughout the Middle Ages most of it had no physical, tangible presence:

---

[30] *Dives and Pauper*, pt. 2, Commandment VII, xxiv, p. 197, lines 42–5, 47–8; p. 196, lines 38–40. Cf. Langholm, *Economics*, p. 241, quoting from Aquinas, *De malo*, 'Usury derives from use.'
[31] Aristotle, *Ethics*, V, v, p. 120.
[32] Aquinas, *In decem libros Ethicorum*, V, 9: cited by Gordon, *Economic Analysis*, p. 166.

it existed only in the mind and in writing. It was a measure of value used for accounting purposes, and the value of other commodities, including actual coinage, would be measured against this standard. The system of money of account most common in medieval Europe was that of pounds, shillings, and pence, which was based on multiples of twelve (the duodecimal system), as opposed to ten (the decimal system). It was introduced possibly as early as the seventh century, but given prominence by the financial reforms of the Emperor Charlemagne in the late eighth century. The pound (*libra*) was actually a Roman silver weight then in use, and the idea was that 240 silver pennies should be struck out of every pound of silver. But at the time the basic money of account was still the Roman *solidus* or shilling. In order to maintain continuity, Charlemagne had to include the shilling, and it was reckoned as 12 silver pennies. This meant that 20 shillings (= 240 pence) were equal to a pound. In England this system, in both ghost and real money, lasted until 1971. In France the system of *livres*, or pounds, divided into twenty *sols*, each made up of 12 *deniers*, or pennies, lasted until the Revolution. During the early medieval period the coin in circulation, the only one actually minted, was the silver penny, or *denier*, or *pfennig*.

The accounting problem which gave rise to 'ghost money' was the small denominational value of the penny. Keeping accounts all in pennies was an accountant's nightmare. It would clearly be easier to think, and account, in terms of £20 10s 6d than in terms of 4,926 pennies. The ghost penny continued to feature in accounts, but as the economy became increasingly monetized, and coins became worn, clipped, or debased, the weight of the actual penny in circulation rarely coincided with its ghost value of a 240th part of a pound of silver.[33]

In early medieval Europe the system of wergeld payments provide a good example of 'ghost money' as a measure of value. The barbarian law codes assigned a monetary value, a wergeld, to both people (and to the individual limbs of their bodies) and to their property in detailed lists of compensations due for bodily injury, theft, murder, manslaughter, and for various misdemeanours. Everything and everybody quite literally had a price. For example, from the earliest known Anglo-Saxon laws, the dooms of Aethelberht of Kent (602–3) we read that 'If anyone lies with a maiden belonging to the king, he is to pay 50 shillings compensation.'[34] But of course 50 shillings would not have been paid, not just because the

---

[33] See Carlo M. Cipolla, *Money, Prices, and Civilization in the Mediterranean World, Fifth to Seventeenth Century* (Princeton, NJ, 1956), pp. 38–42 and Harry A. Miskimin, 'Price movements and specie debasement in France, 1295–1395', in Miskimin, *Cash, Credit and Crisis in Europe, 1300–1600* (London, 1989), no. 1, p. 235.

[34] Laws of Aethelberht, *EHD*, 1, no. 29, p. 357.

economy was largely non-monetary at that stage, but because neither the shilling, nor even the penny, was then in circulation. It was simply a way of evaluating the crime. The laws of the Ripuarian Franks, which were recodified in the late eighth or early ninth century, evaluated crimes in golden solidi (pounds). But they also provided a list of goods of equivalent value. Thus a cow was payment for 3 solidi, a sword in a sheath for 7 solidi, and so on.[35] In tenth-century Spain a *solidus* was considered to be worth either a ewe or a measure of corn (a *modius*, that is, a peck).[36] Again, the money was simply a unit of account. Sometimes things would be done the other way round, and in records of payment a money equivalent for the goods would be given – a candlestick worth ten denarii, for example.[37] Occasionally massive accounting exercises would be carried out in ghost money. The Domesday survey of 1086, for example, was really a great valuation of lands and services, comparing the monetary value in the time of Edward the Confessor with the 1086 value. But many of the values were given in pounds and shillings, and neither was minted at that time: they were purely accounting terms.

REAL MONEY: A MEDIUM OF EXCHANGE

Until the middle of the tenth century relatively little coinage changed hands in daily life. There were several reasons for this – among them lack of bullion, lack of expertise in coining, the uneven distribution of the coins which were in circulation, and lack of demand through international trade. What coinage there was would almost certainly have become concentrated in the hands of the lords, who would have needed things which could not necessarily be supplied by the local economy. The majority of payments by their dependants, however, in return for the occupation of land, would have been rendered in labour services or in kind. The local peasant economy would have functioned on a mixture of self-sufficiency, barter, and occasional money payments. It seems that virtually any commodity was acceptable as money. For example, in Anglo-Saxon England, the laws of King Ine of Wessex (688–94) stated that

> The *ceorl* (free peasant) who has hired another's yoke [of oxen], if he has enough to pay for it entirely in fodder – let one see that he pays in full; if he has not, he is to pay half in other goods.[38]

---

[35] Spufford, *Money and its Uses*, p. 35, citing Wilhelm Jesse, *Quellenbuch zur Mainz- und Geldgeschichte des Mittelalters* (Halle, 1924, repr. 1968), doc. 16.
[36] Cipolla, *Money, Prices, and Civilization*, p. 5.
[37] Murray, *Reason and Society*, p. 31, n. 19.
[38] Laws of Ine, *EHD*, 1, no 32, p. 371. cl. 60.

Often amounts due would be stated in optional terms – either money or goods, but almost certainly payment would have been made in goods. For example, in the laws of Aethelberht of Kent is the order that 'If anyone kill a man, he is to pay with his own money and unblemished goods, whatever their kind.'[39]

The 'take-off' into a monetary economy started about the year 950, and reached a climax in the first half of the eleventh century. It was caused partly by the great commercial development of the Ottonian Empire, with which England was closely linked, and by an influx of silver from Eastern Islam, combined with the discovery in the 960s of veins of silver in Germany, especially near Goslar, in the Harz Mountains.[40] Mines were usually worked for about a century before becoming exhausted, and in time the Goslar mines were succeeded by those at Freiberg, at Freisach in the Austrian Alps, at Jihlava in Bohemia, and finally – the most productive of all – at Kutná Hora in Bohemia, discovered in 1298. In Southern Europe silver was mined at Montieri in Tuscany, and then at Iglesias in Sardinia. The 'long thirteenth century' (c. 1160–c. 1330) was characterized by a 'silver rush'.[41]

The obvious result was that the economy of Western Europe became more monetized, although without necessarily becoming fully monetary. Whether we attribute the 'commercial revolution' which took place between the twelfth and early fourteenth centuries to demographic, political, or monetary factors, it is undeniable that the supply of bullion, the mint outputs, and the amount of money in circulation increased. For England, Mayhew has estimated that the amount in circulation grew from about £250,000 at the beginning of the thirteenth century, to a peak of about £1,100,000 in the early fourteenth century, and that the pattern throughout Europe was similar.[42] The result was that a greater proportion of transactions was carried out in 'real' money than previously. On English manorial estates, for example, both labour services and rents in kind were increasingly commuted for money payments. By 1279 the number of rents paid in money had overtaken the number paid in produce or labour services. The number of fairs and markets, where money changed hands, increased dramatically, in itself an indication of burgeoning trade. The amount of hard cash raised from country areas through taxation reached unprecedented heights in the early fourteenth century. At the local level the drop in the value of the English silver penny made it suitable for use in small

---

[39] Laws of Aethelberht, *EHD*, I, no. 29, cl. 30, p. 358.
[40] Spufford, *Uses of Money*, pp. 74–105; Murray, *Reason and Society*, pp. 27–58.
[41] Spufford, *Uses of Money*, pp. 109–131.
[42] N. J. Mayhew, 'Money and prices in England from Henry II to Edward II', *Agricultural History Review*, 35 (1987), pp. 125–6.

transactions, so that it increasingly replaced barter. The demand at this level for small change led to the issue of smaller units of currency, such as halfpennies and farthings.[43]

The debate about the causes of economic change applies not just to the economic 'take-off', but equally to the so-called Great Depression of the fourteenth and fifteenth centuries.[44] The damaging economic effects of war, famine, and plague epidemics were exacerbated by shortages of bullion, especially silver – the 'Great Bullion Famine' of *c.* 1395 to *c.* 1415, and the even more severe shortage from *c.* 1440 to 1460.[45] The lack of coinage led to a reversion to mixed payments – that is, partly in kind and partly in real money – and in some cases to barter. Dyer has shown that in England, for example, many local transactions which would previously have taken place for cash in the local market were carried out by barter.[46] In some areas, especially in the north-east, rents were once again being paid in produce. But this was offset by continuing commutation of labour services for money payments and did not imply a 'general retreat from monetized relationships between landlord and tenants'.[47] Effects of the bullion shortage were not limited to the agrarian sector. Workers in the English cloth industry in the fifteenth century were being paid only partly in money and mainly in kind, as is shown by many local complaints and by-laws on the subject. An act of Edward IV of 1464 laid down that carders, spinners, weavers, and fullers were to be paid 'lawful money for all their lawful wages', but continuing complaints suggest that it was largely ignored.[48] The situation in the Florentine cloth industry was similar.[49] In fourteenth-century France, Guido Terreni remarked on the practice of semi-direct exchange, where, if the value of one commodity did not equal another, its value would merely be topped up by a money payment.[50]

Developments in the scholastic attitude to 'real' money came with the changing economic circumstances of the fourteenth century. At a time

---

[43] Richard H. Britnell, *The Commercialisation of English Society, 1000–1500*, 2nd edn (Manchester, 1996), pp. 102–13.
[44] Day, 'Crises and trends in the Late Middle Ages', in *Medieval Market Economy*, pp. 185–224, with extensive bibliography at pp. 219–24.
[45] John Day, 'The Great Bullion Famine of the fifteenth century' and 'The question of monetary contraction in late medieval Europe', in *Medieval Market Economy*, pp. 1–54, 55–71, respectively. For further discussion see chapter 4, below.
[46] C. Dyer, 'The consumer and the market in the later middle ages', *EconHR*, ser. 2., 42 (1989), pp. 305–27.
[47] Britnell, *Commercialisation of English Society*, pp. 183–4.
[48] *Statutes of the Realm*, 2 (London, 1816), p. 406a.
[49] Raymond de Roover, *San Bernardino of Siena and Sant' Antonino of Florence: the Two Great Economic Thinkers of the Middle Ages* (Boston, MA, 1967), p. 26.
[50] Langholm, *Economics*, pp. 503–4.

of financial chaos, particularly in France, where successive monarchs had resorted to debasement to compensate for the lack of bullion, the whole subject of the metal content of the coinage was highlighted. With the changing values of actual money in circulation they were forced to recognize that money was also a commodity, and that its metal content was part of its essential character. One of the first to remark on this was paradoxically not a Frenchman but the rather neglected German Henry of Friemar, who recommended that money should be 'of precious metal, like gold or silver, so that a price can be put on goods easily and promptly according to its value'.[51] Money thus had a value of its own. The Frenchman Nicholas Oresme recommended that money should be made 'of precious and rare material, such as gold ... if there is not enough gold, money is also made of silver'.[52] The whole of his *De moneta* is concerned with the 'price' of money, and the effects of debasement. John Buridan, supposed originator of the fable of the ass, and Oresme's teacher, was also a metallist:

> The value of money must be measured by human need, for although we do not need gold or silver for our necessities, still the rich need them for their luxurious purposes. And therefore we see that gold and silver in the mass are of the same value, or about the same, as in money.[53]

Money was no longer a mere creature of the law, but something which had its own value as a commodity, due to its intrinsic metal content. Emphasis on its physical content underlay some important discussions in the late medieval period – the idea that money could act as a store of value and thus lead to accumulation and the extraordinary debate about whether money, being made of metal, was infertile, or whether it could become fertile and increase itself in a loan. These are the problems to be examined here. It also led to discussion of the ethics of altering the value of the coinage through changing its metal content, and, linked with this, the problem of how to maintain supplies of bullion. These are the problems which will be examined in chapter 5.

A STORE OF VALUE

The translator of the *De moneta* remarked that Oresme took no account of credit, nor of bills of exchange.[54] This is because Oresme was not

---

[51] Ibid., p. 546. Langholm has drawn attention to this hitherto neglected economic thinker.
[52] Nicholas Oresme, *The 'De moneta' of Nicholas Oresme and English Mint Documents* (London and Edinburgh, 1956), ed. and trans. Charles Johnson, ch. 2, pp. 5–6.
[53] John Buridan, *Questiones in decem libros Ethicorum*, bk 5, q. 17: cited by Gordon, *Economic Analysis*, p. 192.
[54] Charles Johnson, Introduction to *De moneta*, p. xi.

concerned with money as capital. He considered that money was 'an instrument artificially invented for the easier exchange of natural riches',[55] and even 'a balancing instrument for the exchange of natural riches'.[56] This was a thoroughly Aristotelian view. In the *Ethics*, however, Aristotle had added a third function to money: not only was it a measure of value and a medium of exchange, but, being durable, it was also a store of value. Money was, 'as it were our surety'.[57] This being so, it might allow someone to anticipate a future exchange.

> And for the future exchange – that if we do not need a thing now we shall have it if ever we do need it – money is as it were our surety; it must be possible for us to get what we want by bringing the money.[58]

Money overcame the problem of exchange over time. It solved the problem highlighted by the jurist Paul, and later by others: 'The coincidence was not always readily found, that when you had what I wanted I had what you were willing to give.'[59]

The other aspect of money as a store of value was in terms of accumulation. This relates to Aristotle's discussion in the *Politics* about trade as an unnatural activity – chresmatic. The difference between retail trade and the natural form of acquisition practised in the household was that the wealth produced by trade was unlimited. This was the danger. 'Currency is the starting-point, as it is also the goal, of exchange',[60] he warned. He recognized that the function of the art of acquisition was 'to discover the sources from which a fund of money can be derived'.[61] The idea of a 'fund of money' coupled with unlimited acquisition formed the basis of the sin of avarice, condemned by medieval preachers. In the seventeenth century John Locke would build on Aristotle's ideas when he attributed the corruption of human nature to the introduction of money. Before its introduction 'a Man had a Right to all he could imploy his Labour upon', so that there was 'no reason of quarrelling about Title, nor any doubt about the largeness of Possession it gave'.[62] Afterwards men

> by a tacit and voluntary consent, found out a way how a man may fairly possess more land than he himself can use the product of, by receiving in exchange for the overplus, Gold and Silver, which may be hoarded up . . . these metals not spoiling or decaying in the hands of the possessor.[63]

---

[55] Nicholas Oresme, *De moneta*, ch. 1, p. 5.   [56] Ibid., ch. 6, p. 10.
[57] Aristotle, *Ethics*, v, v, p. 120.   [58] Ibid.
[59] Paul, *Digest*, 18. 1. 1; Gordon, *Economic Analysis*, p. 134.
[60] Aristotle, *Politics*, I, ix, 1257b, 13, p. 25; ibid., 12.   [61] Ibid., 1257b, 9, p. 24.
[62] John Locke, *Second Treatise of Government*, ch. 5, p. 302, par. 51.
[63] Ibid., p. 302, par. 50.

The idea of money as a store of value might easily have led thinkers to consider such matters as saving or capital accumulation. Yet the view of most was the same as Aristotle's: 'Wealth consists more in use than in possession',[64] so they were hardly concerned about permanent possession or accumulation. Giles of Rome, relying heavily on Aristotle, warned that the artificial riches of gold, silver, and coinage brought no happiness. They were not riches in themselves, but always had to be measured against natural riches; their value was the result of men's decisions; they satisfied neither spiritual nor bodily needs.[65] Henry of Hesse linked accumulation with aspirations to social climbing and condemned it as damnable avarice.[66] Many of the theologians who discussed the problem, however, preferred the biblical approach. Here they were faced with two quotations from the New Testament: the Lord's Prayer (Luke 11.3), which invited them to pray for their daily bread and no more, and Christ's injunction in the Sermon on the Mount to 'take no thought for the morrow'(Matthew 6.34). Admittedly their effect was lessened by the example of the thrifty ant in Proverbs 6.7–8, which 'having no guide, overseer, or ruler, provideth her meat in the summer, and gathereth her food in the harvest'. Aquinas synthesized the Old and New Testaments by suggesting that 'take no thought' implied taking no thought for the morrow beyond its immediate needs:

> The ant shows solicitude at the seasonable time...Duly looking to the future belongs to prudence, yet such forethought and concern would be inordinate were a person to make temporal things...his purpose in life, or were he to seek superfluities beyond the needs of his present life or to anticipate the fitting time for solicitude.[67]

Henry of Ghent (d. 1293), while pointing out that Christ enjoined men to pray for no more than their daily bread, was more sympathetic to the savings of the laity than the clergy: 'Anxiety about the future is less justifiable in ministers of the Church than in lay and less perfect people.'[68] Guido Terreni advised people to pray only for what was necessary for adequate living, but added comfortingly that Christ did not forbid the possession of necessities 'nor a reasonable preparation for the morrow and days to come'.[69] These attitudes were reflected in the teaching of Walter of Henley, almost certainly a layman, in about 1286, on English estate management:

---

[64] Langholm, *Wealth and Money*, p. 66. Cf. Aristotle, *On Rhetoric*, bk. 1, ch. 5, sect. 7, 1361a, p. 59.
[65] Giles of Rome, *De regimine principum*, bk. 1, pt. i, ch. 7, pp. 13v–14r.
[66] See Introduction, p. 3, above.
[67] Thomas Aquinas, *Summa theologiae*, 2a2ae, 55, 8 ad 1 and 2, vol. 38, p. 163.
[68] Langholm, *Economics*, p. 253.   [69] Ibid., p. 497.

If youe may youre landes amende, eyther by tillage (thrifte) or by stock of cattaile or by any other provision above the yearly extente putte (turne) that overpluis into money, for if corne fayle [or stock die] or fier doe happen or any other mischaunce then wille that be somwhat woorth to you which you have in coyne.[70]

For all their attempts to compromise, the scholastics adopted a negative attitude to accumulation, and there is very little sense of the building up of financial capital in their writings. This is hardly surprising. It was not part of their intention to encourage something which could divert men from the otherworldly end of life and concentrate their minds and hearts on something very much of this world. The change in attitude was to come later, within the humanist climate of fifteenth-century Italy, as part of the change in attitude to wealth.

THE STERILITY DOCTRINE

The nature of money as precious metal enabled it to be considered as a store of wealth. It was precisely this metal content which gave rise to the very important idea of the sterility of money which was to dominate discussion, and especially condemnation, of usury. For example, both Basil and Ambrose had observed that usury made gold breed gold.[71] There were also Roman law origins, for the *Digest* of Justinian stated that money had no natural fruit.[72] But above all the origins lay in the Latin translation of a passage from Aristotle's *Politics*. After discussing the 'natural' economic acquisition involved in managing the household Aristotle turned to retail trade. This he condemned, since money was both the starting point and the goal and because there was no limit to it. Its most extreme form was usury, because it made a profit from money itself, instead of from the process of exchange that it should have served:

Currency came into existence merely as a means of exchange; usury tries to make it increase [as though it were an end in itself]. This is the reason why usury is called by the word we commonly use [the word *tokos*, which in Greek also means 'breed' or 'offspring']; for as the offspring resembles its parent, so the interest bred by money is like the principal which breeds it ... Hence we can understand why, of all modes of acquisition, usury is the most unnatural.[73]

Later arguments about Aristotle's ideas turned on the Latin translation of two words. One of these was the word for retail trade, which the translator

[70] Walter of Henley, *Husbandry*, ed. Dorothea Oschinsky, *Walter of Henley and Other Treatises on Estate Management and Accounting* (Oxford, 1971), ch. 4, p. 309.
[71] Basil, *Homily on Luke*, in Gratian, *Decretum*, D. 47, c. 8, col. 171. Cf. Ambrose, *De Tobia admonitio*, 1, chs. 12–13, *PL*, 14, cols. 774–7.
[72] Paul, *Digest*, 7.5.2,5,6,7,10, cited in Noonan, *Scholastic Analysis of Usury*, p. 54.
[73] Aristotle, *Politics*, I, x, 4, 1258b, p. 29.

William of Moerbeke wrongly rendered as *campsoria*, or money-changing. Whereas Aristotle himself had condemned retail trade as a whole, most scholastics damned economic activities which involved money alone.[74] The other word was *tokos*, which had the double meaning of both offspring and usury, and it was this which gave rise to the biological metaphor of barren money.

It is difficult to assess how seriously the scholastics took the ridiculous image of artificial money reproducing itself, although many of them cited it. The German papal supporter Conrad of Megenberg, writing in the mid-fourteenth century, provided a typical expression of revulsion in biological terms:

> Those who practice usury do something detestable and against nature, for it is against nature for an artificial thing to multiply itself. This is proper to natural things, so that they join together and multiply according to species. A sheep brings forth a sheep; an ox begets an ox. But how can a saw generate a saw, or a house bring forth a house? If a craftsman with a hammer makes another hammer, it is not the work of the hammer but rather of the craftsman's skill.[75]

Yet many of the scholastics appreciated that the point Aristotle was trying to make was not that money could not increase, because it was all too clear that in practice it could and did. His point was that to make it do so was to abuse the purpose for which it was invented, that of facilitating exchange. Aquinas considered that when money increased by means of money it was a kind of birth. But this was unnatural, for according to its nature money should be obtained for natural objects and not for money.[76] The Franciscan Richard of Middleton (d. 1302), possibly an Englishman, declared that money was invented to be a medium, price, and measure in buying and selling, not to be bought and sold itself: this was an abuse of its purpose.[77]

The reproductive argument easily lent itself to ribaldry. In the nineteenth century Jeremy Bentham famously poked fun at Aristotle: 'that great philosopher... notwithstanding the uncommon pains he had bestowed on the subject of generation, had never been able to discover in any one piece of money, any organs for generating any other'.[78] Perhaps because it was ludicrous, the sterility argument came to be expressed in less physical ways. The thinker largely responsible for this, as Odd Langholm has shown, was a little-known fourteenth-century Augustinian Hermit,

---

[74] Noonan, *Scholastic Analysis of Usury*, p. 47; Langholm, *Aristotelian Analysis of Usury*, p. 57; *Economics*, p. 265.
[75] Conrad of Megenberg, *Yconomica*, 1, 4, ch. 18, p. 348.
[76] Langholm, *Economics*, p. 237.   [77] Ibid., p. 337.
[78] Jeremy Bentham, *Defence of Usury*, ed. W. Stark, *Jeremy Bentham's Economic Writings*, 1 (London, 1952), letter 10, p. 158.

Gerardo of Siena (d. c. 1336), although his ideas were to be taken over, with modifications, by the fourteenth-century canonist Johannes Andreae, whose name is more usually attached to them.

Gerardo discussed loans of all fungibles, not just money. The essence of his case is that usury is vicious and unnatural not for reproductive reasons, but 'because it makes a natural thing overprice its nature and an artificial thing overprice its art, which is most contrary to nature'.[79] All fungibles have an inherent value. This is determined and assigned either by God and nature, in the case of natural things, or by art, in the case of artificial things. It is tied to the weight or measure or number of the fungible. Provided the thing is not damaged or altered in any way that would change its weight, measure, or number, this value is fixed. Fungibles, however, also have another, artificial value, which is determined by the market forces of supply and demand, or by comparability with the value of other things for which they might be exchanged. But no matter what happens to the artificial market value, provided the fungible remains unaltered, its true, inherent value remains constant. This depends on the nature of the thing in terms of its weight, measure, quantity, or quality. It is quite separate from its market value. Ultimately a litre of wine will retain its natural value as such, and taste as good, regardless of the fluctuations in its market price. The same is true of artificial money. Ten pence, provided they are not clipped or debased in any way (although Gerardo does not actually discuss this possibility), will still be ten pence, because this is their value determined by art. By arguing in terms of the inherent and natural value of fungibles, as opposed to the market value, Gerardo was able to state the sterility argument without resorting to biological imagery. The conclusion, predictably, when applied to usury was that it was malicious and unnatural because it made natural things overprice their natural value, and artificial things, especially money, overprice the value assigned to them by art. Anything which had a fixed value, whether God-given or artificial, was incapable of increasing itself in a loan.

Gerardo's focusing on two values of money, an inherent and unchanging one, and an artificial, market value, which can vary according to market conditions, is a variation on the Aristotelian theme of the two types of money examined in this chapter. The notion that money is a 'sham and entirely a convention', authorized by the State, and useless for anything other than to be a measure of exchange developed in the medieval period into the 'ghost money' used for accounting. This was the value usually considered artificial, because it did not coincide with the actual currency in circulation. The other view, that money was something of intrinsic

[79] Langholm, *Economics*, p. 555.

value, because of its composition of precious metal, a commodity whose worth could fluctuate like any other, was more often thought of as the inherent and true value. What Gerardo appeared to have done was to reverse the true and the artificial, making the market, commodity value the artificial, and the fixed, ghostly value, the true and inherent one. It really boiled down to a question of terminology and who was valuing the money. The peasant purchaser in the market-place would have seen the commodity value as the true one, because of its purchasing power. But medieval accounts clerks would have been more likely to agree with Gerardo that the unvarying 'ghost' value was the true one.

CONCLUSION: THE PROPERTIES OF MONEY

The first function of money on which our discussion has focused was to act as an artificial measure of value authorized by the State – a function which was reflected in 'ghost money' or money of account. The second was to be a medium of exchange, having been invented to overcome the inconveniences of barter, such as the transport of goods over long distances and the lack of coincidence between the needs of potential sellers and buyers and the value of their goods. Thirdly, and more debatably, it could be an imperishable store of value, which would allow people to anticipate future purchases.

In order to fulfil these functions money had to have certain properties. It had, for example, to be marked with the stamp of the ruler, as a guarantee of its genuineness. It had to be available in small enough units, not only for portability, but because, in an age before milled edges, it was more difficult to 'clip' a small coin than a large one. Aristotle had suggested various properties – for example, that money had to be portable and composed of a precious metal. He explained that initially the value of metal used in exchange was determined by its size and weight, but 'finally a stamp was imposed on the metal, which, serving as a definite indication of the quantity, would save men the trouble of determining the value on each occasion'.[80] Aristotelian commentators gradually amassed a list of essential monetary properties. Henry of Friemar (d. 1340) produced a particularly comprehensive list:

The first is that it be of very small size, so that subtraction cannot be made from it without easy detection, which would not be the case if it were of large size and ample form. The second is that it be impressed with the stamp of some prince, for otherwise anybody might fabricate and falsify money, by which equality in exchange would be done away with. The third is that it be of due weight, for

---

[80] Aristotle, *Politics*, I, ix, 1257a, 8, p. 24.

otherwise a fixed price cannot be put on commodities by means of it. The fourth is that it endure long without corruption, for otherwise future demand cannot be provided for by means of it... The fifth is that it be of a precious material, like gold or silver, so that a price can be put on goods easily and promptly according to its value.[81]

This list provides a convenient summary of the nature and functions of money as a medium of exchange, as an equalizer in transactions, as a store of value, and as a commodity with a value of its own. It also highlights the role of the sovereign in issuing, authorizing, and controlling the coinage to be examined next. But perhaps the most enduring property of money, its roundness, had been appreciated by Augustine: 'What is so uncertain as something that rolls away? It is appropriate that money is round, because it never stays in one place.'[82]

[81] Langholm, *Economics*, p. 546, transcribed from MS Basel UB F. I. 14, fols. 135rb–va.
[82] Augustine, *Enarratio in Psalmos*, 83, 3, *CChr.SL,* 39, p. 1147.

4

SOVEREIGN CONCERNS: WEIGHTS, MEASURES, AND COINAGE

INTRODUCTION: THE CONNECTION

The connection between weights, measures, and coinage was a close one in the medieval period, for control of all of them was part of the exercise of sovereignty. As the Dominican Ptolemy of Lucca (d. *c.* 1328), pupil of Aquinas, appreciated:

> weights and measures... are as necessary as the coinage for preserving the government of any lordship, since they are used in the payment of tributes, since their use decreases quarrels and protects fidelity in purchases and sales, and, finally, since they, like coins, are instruments of human life and, even more than coinage, imitate natural action... it seems that weights and measures take their origin from nature more than coinage does, and therefore they are even more necessary in a republic or kingdom.[1]

Our aim is to pinpoint the origins of weights, measures, and coinage, before exploring the development of sovereign rights to control their standards.

Control of the standards enabled a ruler, or his deputy, to regulate the most vital aspects of people's existence. The standard controlled the boundaries of the all-important land on which they lived, and which provided sustenance for them and their dependants and a surplus for the market. Within the market the standard controlled the amount or size of essential commodities – food and drink, and the cloth which covered human nakedness. Weights and measures regulated exchange just as much

---

[1] Ptolemy of Lucca, *De regimine principum*, trans. James M. Blythe, *On the Government of Rulers: De Regimine Principum, Ptolemy of Lucca with portions attributed to Thomas Aquinas* (Philadelphia, PA, 1997), bk. 2, ch. 14, p. 136.

as money did. They were the other side of the price equation, price being value measured in terms of money – so much or so many for a given amount of coinage. If the value of that coinage were to change, or to be deliberately altered, the effect on local trade and on all money payments could cause untold hardship.

In the early medieval period the establishment of control of weights, measures, and coinage coincided with the establishment of sovereign powers over a people. The late medieval period witnessed the development of representative institutions and demands for counsel and consent at every level of society. If the sovereignty wielded over different states was less absolute than in the earlier period, it followed logically that the exercise of rights once exclusive to a sovereign ruler, the control of the standards, might in practice, if not in theory, also become subject to counsel and consent in Parliament or other representative assembly, and be implemented at the level of manorial or borough official. The debate about standards and sovereignty became particularly intense when it was applied to the ruler's right to manipulate the coinage.

ORIGINS OF 'THE STANDARD'

The idea of the 'measure' or standard in Greek thought was inseparable from the concept of the mean, or moderation, and also that of justice. This being so, the idea that the measure was something divine can be traced back at least to Plato. The measure, like justice itself, seemed for Plato to be 'a pattern laid up in the heavens'. The philosopher thought that everything existed on two levels – that of Reality and that of Actuality. On the upper level of Reality were universals, and these had a real existence. On the lower, earthly level of Actuality, were particulars, which were mere forms or shadows of the universals, and did not have a real existence. In terms of measure, or standard, it meant that things on the earthly level had to coincide as nearly as possible with the pattern on the universal level. The Sophist Protagoras had asserted that 'Man is the measure of all things', and this was the view that Plato aimed to counter. In the *Laws* he claimed, 'Now it is God who is, for you and me, of a truth the "measure of all things", much more truly than, as they say, "man".'[2] Plato, was, of course, advancing a philosophical concept here, but like all great works and ideas, it can be applied in different ways, and, indeed, can be applied to measure in a physical as well as an intellectual context. The things on Plato's level of actuality – what we should call the 'real world' – did indeed take their measure from universals, from standards which existed on the otherworldly level.

[2] Plato, *Laws*, bk. 4, 716, pp. 100–1.

Although the God envisaged by Plato was not the Christian Deity, the idea that God was, in effect, the standard of all things, reappeared in the Bible. It began with the Prophets. They assigned the creation of weights and measures to God, and therefore saw the whole system as good and just. Solomon wrote in Wisdom 11.21,'Thou hast ordered all things in measure and weight and number', and Isaiah 40, 12 asked: 'Who hath measured the waters in the hollow of his hand, and meted out heaven with the span, and comprehended the dust of the earth in a measure, and weighed the mountains in scales, and the hills in a balance?' The creation of the system was coterminous with the creation of the world. Because it was the work of the Almighty it was thought to be just. Solomon wrote that 'A just weight and balance are the Lord's; all the weights of the bag are his work' (Proverbs, 16.11). Justice implied judgement. In the Sermon on the Mount Christ warned, 'With what judgment ye judge, ye shall be judged: and with what measure ye mete, it shall be measured to you again' (Matthew 7.2).[3] The whole concept of weighing and measuring was thus fundamental to the Christian faith (as it was to Judaism and Islam), and was closely associated with the Day of Judgement and the salvation of the soul. On the Day of Judgement men's souls would be weighed in the balance. Countless medieval paintings, stained-glass windows, and church carvings showed the Archangel Michael with his scales weighing souls and assigning them to Heaven or Hell.

The idea that control over standards was divine was reflected in Athens, where the standard weights and measures were dedicated to the gods by being kept on the Acropolis. In Rome they were kept on the Capitoline Hill, in Jerusalem they were placed in the Temple, and in Constantinople, the Emperor Justinian had them kept in the Basilica of Hagia Sophia.[4] Legend had it that money, too, had originated on the Capitoline Hill in Rome, on the site of a temple built in honour of the goddess Juno Moneta (the Monitress) – hence the Latin word *moneta*, money.

Christian monarchs were considered to be God's representatives on earth, and of no monarch was this more true than the pope, the vicar of Christ on earth, who wielded a plenitude of jurisdictional power thought to encompass the whole world. In the early fourteenth century Giles of Rome linked papal sovereignty directly with divine power over weight and measure and number. He based his words on Augustine's twofold interpretation of the words of Solomon, 'You have ordered all things in measure and number and weight.'

---

[3] Cf. Mark 4.24; Luke 6.38.
[4] Witold Kula, *Measures and Men*, trans. R. Szreter (Princeton, NJ, 1986), pp. 14, 18, 81.

We can apply these words to the Church, that is, to the Supreme Pontiff; for we may say that the Supreme Pontiff orders the whole Church in number, weight, and measure in that he disposes all things within the Church in such a way that they have their own number, their own weight, and their own measure. Or, according to the other interpretation [of Augustine] he orders all things in number, weight and measure in that he alone, who is number without number, weight without limit and measure without measure (because his own power is without limit of number, weight and measure) disposes all things.[5]

The right of the sovereign to control the coinage – to issue it, to circulate it, and to decree its weight – if not divine, at least had biblical sanction. Roman law had decreed that the emperor controlled the coinage,[6] and this was recognized by Christ in his advice to 'Render to Caesar the things which are Caesar's' (Matthew 22.20–1).

In practice, during the early medieval period the standardization of weights and measures, the reform and standardization of the coinage, and the control of trade often coincided with the establishment of effective sovereign power. One of the best examples is Charles the Great, the Emperor Charlemagne. He tried to standardize weights and measures.[7] He also introduced far-reaching reforms of the coinage, and he controlled trade strictly, to the extent that he made a trade treaty with the powerful Anglo-Saxon King Offa of Mercia (d. 796), and later imposed the first trade embargo on England. The coincidence between sovereignty and control of the standards was especially well illustrated in early medieval England. Offa himself established a uniform coinage, the silver penny, weighing 24 grains (to coincide with Charlemagne's reforms) and simultaneously established the Anglo-Saxon standard weight, the silver pound. Twenty of Offa's pennies made an ounce, and twelve ounces amounted to a pound. This weight later became known as the tower pound.[8] Alfred the Great of Wessex (871–99) who defended the Anglo-Saxons against the Vikings, and was 'ruler of all England not subject to the Danes', kept a strict control over the coinage, and made astute use of the process of demonetization (calling in existing coins after declaring them worthless for purposes of exchange, and recoining them at a profit).[9] He also actively encouraged trade, especially in the south-west.[10] His grandson Athelstan (924–39), briefly the

---

[5] Giles of Rome, *De ecclesiastica potestate*, trans. R. W. Dyson (Woodbridge, 1986), pt. 3, ch. 12, p. 203.
[6] Monroe, *Monetary Theory before Adam Smith*, p. 33.   [7] Kula, *Measures and Men*, p. 114.
[8] Ronald Edward Zupko, *British Weights and Measures: a History from Antiquity to the Seventeenth Century* (Madison, WI, 1977), p. 11.
[9] Janet L. Nelson, 'Wealth and wisdom: the politics of Alfred the Great', *Kings and Kingship, Acta*, 11 (1984), pp. 39–43.
[10] J. R. Maddicott, 'Trade and industry and the wealth of King Alfred', *P & P*, 123 (1989), pp. 3–51.

first truly sovereign ruler of all the English, was also the first king to decree that 'there is to be one coinage over all the king's dominion'.[11] Edgar the Peaceable (959–75), in the year of his high-profile coronation ceremony at Bath, 973, undertook a major reform of the coinage, so significant that it has been compared with decimalization. After that the coinage was re-issued and the types changed every six years.[12] Edgar specifically linked the standards of coinage and measurement when he laid down that 'One coinage is to be current throughout all the king's dominions, and no man is to refuse it; and the system of measurement as is observed in Winchester.'[13] At the Norman Conquest, William took over the Winchester standards of weights and measures, decreeing that they should be uniform throughout the realm and stamped with his seal to authenticate them. They were then moved to London, where they were kept in Edward the Confessor's Crypt Chapel of Westminster Abbey to symbolize the continuity of sovereignty.[14]

VARYING METROLOGICAL STANDARDS

It was one thing to decree that 'standards' of weights and measures should be the same throughout the realm, but quite another to enforce them. Repeated legislation demonstrated this: for example, Richard I's famous Assize of Measures of 1197 laid down that 'weights and measures...great and small, shall be of the same amount in the whole realm, according to the diversity of wares'.[15] There were to be many later attempts to impose the standard, including Magna Carta of 1215.[16] One of the most graphic was the Carta Mercatoria of 1303. Edward I ordered

> that in each market-town, and fair of our...realm and elsewhere within our power our weight be set in a fixed place, and before weighing the scales shall in the presence of buyer and seller be seen to be empty and the arms shall be level, and then the weigher shall weigh level, and when he has brought the balance level, forthwith move his hands away so that it remain level; and that throughout our realm and power there be one weight and one measure, and these shall be marked with the mark of our standard.[17]

The most obvious standard mark was the hall-mark applied to silver ware. In 1300 a statute of Edward I ordered that no silver ware was to leave the

---

[11] *EHD*, 1, no. 35, p. 384, cl. 14.
[12] R. M. Dolley and D. M. Metcalf, 'The reform of the coinage under Eadgar, a turning-point in the monetary policy of the English state', in R. H. M. Dolley, ed., *Anglo-Saxon Coins* (London, 1961), pp. 136–68, esp. p. 136.
[13] *EHD*, 1, no. 41, p. 397, clauses 8–8.1. [14] Zupko, *British Weights and Measures*, p. 15.
[15] *EEH*, section 6, no. 1, p. 154.
[16] Magna Carta, *EHD*, 3, no. 20, p. 320, cl. 35. For later examples see E. Lipson, *The Economic History of England*. 1. *The Middle Ages* (London, 1947), p. 299, n. 3.
[17] *EHD*, 3, no. 91, p. 516.

maker before it had been assayed by the wardens of the London goldsmiths' gild (the bulk of whose work was actually in silver) and marked with the leopard's head as proof of its quality. Other towns were to observe the London rules. In March 1327 the goldsmiths were granted a royal charter by Edward III recognizing them as the Goldsmiths' Company of London. It reinforced the statute and laid down that 'one or two men from every city or town shall come to London on behalf of their craft to fetch their certain touch of gold and silver, also the punch with the leopard's head with which to mark their work'.[18]

The goldsmiths' standards were easier to control than some others due to their tight organization. In other occupations enforcement was complicated because local standards, which had originated haphazardly, coexisted with the national ones. To begin with, measures developed anthropomorphically – people literally measured things by their own limbs – a foot, for example, a hand (still the measurement for horses today), or an ell (an elbow), or a pace, or even a hair's breadth. The unit of measurement used by the Germanic tribes, including the Angles and Saxons, was the foot, which was the length of twelve thumbs, or of thirty-six barley-corns laid end to end.[19] In some areas things had not progressed much by the thirteenth century, when the tenants of one of Glastonbury's manors owed the abbey kitchen thirty salmon a year, which had to be 'as thick at the tail as a man's wrist'.[20] A reeve on another Glastonbury manor claimed as his fee 'a stall full of [or a truss of?] hay as high as to a man's loins'.[21] Weights might become linked to occupation. Goods might be measured by the handful, the cartload, the wagonload, or as much as could be carried in a particular vessel.[22] The extent (survey) of a manor of Great Horwood (Bucks) of 1320 allowed a tenant 'one bunch of grass as much as he is able to lift with his handfork'.[23] Another tenant, William,

> at noon ... shall come to the lord's manse for his food at the lord's expense, husband and wife with his whole family bringing napkin, cup and dishes and they shall carry away all the scraps in their napkins and a cup full of beer.[24]

Handfuls, forkfuls, napkinfuls, were not the most precise of weights. Even the weight of money, the grain, had a haphazard agricultural origin. A thirteenth-century ordinance laid down that 'the English penny called

---

[18] T. F. Reddaway, *The Early History of the Goldsmiths' Company, 1327–1509* (London, 1975), pp. xxv–xxvi, 1–3, 222–4 (for text of charter).
[19] Zupko, *British Weights and Measures*, p. 10.   [20] Coulton, *Medieval Village*, p. 47.
[21] Ibid., p. 46.   [22] Kula, *Measures and Men*, pp. 4–5.
[23] *[Great Horwood] Extent of the Manor of the Lord Prior of Longville Gyfford*, ed. Warren O. Ault, *Open Field Farming in Medieval England* (London, 1972), no. 204, p. 169.
[24] Ibid., p. 170. For further examples see Coulton, *Medieval Village*, pp. 45–7.

the "sterling", round and without clipping, shall weigh 32 grains of wheat [that grew] in the middle of the ear'.[25] Land measurements too were vague but they were very important in an agrarian society, where the amount of land worked by a family could dictate starvation or survival. The English hide, the yardland, and the oxgang were all amounts of arable land that were supposed to support a family, and presumably would vary with the quality of the land, to say nothing of the size of the family. The number of acres (itself an imprecise measure) constituting a yardland or virgate could also vary. On the estates of Worcester Priory in 1240 estate surveyors were ordered to ask the revealing question 'How many acres make a yardland in various places?' when they conducted manorial surveys.[26] Equally variable were distances. Distances might be measured in terms of a stone's throw, a bowshot, the carrying distance of the voice, or walking distance from sunrise to sunset.[27] According to *The Laws and Customs of England*, a treatise attributed to the jurist Henry of Bracton, markets were to be sited so that anyone from the local area could walk comfortably to the market, transact his business, and walk back in daylight, a round trip of about 20 miles.[28] Measurements became especially contentious when they were applied to boundaries, for with boundaries were associated not merely possession, but also judicial rights. The medieval boundary between Huntingdonshire and Cambridgeshire apparently ran through the meres 'as far as a man might reach with his barge-pole to the shore'.[29]

Such customary weights and measures proved tenacious.[30] In 1340 Edward III's Parliament found it necessary to repeat that 'from henceforth one measure and one weight shall be throughout the realm of England'.[31] About ten years later the King had to admit defeat and to recognize that the force of local custom could not in practice be overridden. He decreed that 'all the measures . . . shall be according to the King's standard . . . saving the rents and farms of the lords, which shall be measured by such Measures as they were wont in Times past'.[32] It is one thing to legislate about measurement, but quite another to change the way people left to themselves will measure. There are many nowadays who, despite metrication, still think in terms of pints and gallons, rather than litres, yards and miles, rather than metres and kilometres, and many who still cook according to pounds

---

[25] *EHD*, 3, no. 218, p. 856.
[26] R. H. Hilton, *A Medieval Society: the West Midlands at the End of the Thirteenth Century* (London, 1966), pp. 114–15.
[27] Kula, *Measures and Men*, p. 5.   [28] Henry of Bracton, *De legibus*, 3, p. 198.
[29] Coulton, *Medieval Village*, p. 48.
[30] For some observations on this point see Kula, *Measures and Men*, ch. 15.
[31] Lipson, *Economic History*, p. 299, and n. 3 for other statutes.
[32] *Statutes of the Realm*, 1 (London, 1810), 25 Edward III (1351–2), p. 3216, c. 10.

and ounces, or who would like to 'shed a few pounds' of their own body weight.

Even where official standards were recognized, they were difficult to impose. Although they were the standards of the sovereign, in practice, copies of them would be kept in the castle, the manor, the abbey, the town hall, or the market-place. And they were merely copies – more or less accurate according to the skill of the local craftsmen who fashioned them. Since they were made of natural materials, such as wood or brass, they were liable to shrink or expand with changing weather conditions, and were subject to wear and tear.[33]

POLICING THE STANDARDS

The theoretical power of the monarch over weights and measures was absolute, and to demonstrate this the standards were stamped with his official stamp. Imposing these standards at local level was a different matter. Richard I recognized this in his Assize of Measures in 1197, which made certain people in each city and borough responsible for enforcing and authenticating the standards. Enforcement was difficult. In rural areas such responsibilities were an essential part of lordship. Usually they would be granted by the king with the land and handed on in subsequent grants. At local level such control could cause considerable resentment, for it could be seen by the lower orders as yet one more instrument of oligarchic or seigneurial oppression.[34] The appearance of the lord's surveyor with his measuring rod was an occasion of fear and apprehension. Not only did he use the lord's measure, which might be smaller than the customary measure, but his visit might mean that a peasant had tilled over a neighbour's boundary, or, far worse, it might be the prelude to the enclosure of the land and eviction of the tenant.[35] On some manors the scales were a manorial monopoly, and the peasant would have to pay to use them. In the towns, too, during the fairs, tradesmen might be forced to use the municipal scales, or to rent them, for which they would be charged.[36] In the Carta Mercatoria Edward I was forced to recognize this state of affairs. He decreed 'that each man may have scales of a quarter and less', but was forced to add, 'where that is not against the lord of the place or a liberty granted by us or our ancestors, or against the hitherto-observed custom of towns or fairs'.[37] In practice, it nearly always would have been.

Complications could arise in both country and town where lordship was divided. It could happen that in one village different measures might be

[33] Zupko, *British Weights and Measures*, pp. 30–1.
[34] Le Goff, *Medieval Civilization*, p. 303.   [35] Kula, *Measures and Men*, p. 14.
[36] Ibid., p. 21.   [37] *EHD*, 3, no. 91, p. 516.

used for the payment of tithe, purchases in the market, and the payment of manorial dues.[38] Until the early eighteenth century Winchester had both a local bushel and a larger College bushel. When rents were paid in corn and subsequently commuted for money payment the larger College bushel was used.[39] In a society of interlocking jurisdictions this would have seemed perfectly natural.

Often the demarcation line between urban and rural jurisdiction was unclear, especially where a borough had been carved out of a manor by its lord. The problem of policing standards in towns, as centres of trade, was both harder and more necessary. Policing involved three elements, inspection, verification, and enforcement, which included judgement and punishment. In 1266 Henry III tried to divide these functions between commissioners, who inspected and verified, and juries, who enforced and punished. When this cumbersome system failed, commissioners were authorized to inspect, verify, and enforce, but their greed and dishonesty, combined with hostility from local market officials, meant this scheme also faltered. By the end of the period metrological duties were granted to a variety of people – ecclesiastical and royal dignitaries, heads of religious houses, manorial lords, legal officials, such as justices, sheriffs, and coroners, and even to the chancellors of the universities of Oxford and Cambridge (1327 and 1378 respectively).[40]

The term 'assize' has more than one meaning. It could mean a legal regulation of weight, measure, quantity, quality, and price of articles, or it could be a session where weights and measures of things were examined, later known as an assay. Our concern here is with the first of these. In some assizes weights and measures were inseparably linked to price. The assize of bread, for example, fixed the price and weight of bread according to a sliding scale based on the current price of wheat. The assize of ale worked in the same way, determining the price of a gallon of ale according to the price of grain. The assizes, of course, had to be decided locally, because of local variations in price, and they also had to be enforced locally and constantly revised. For example, at Southampton the assizes were ordered once a month or at least four times a year to 'be well kept in all points according to the price of corn'.[41] Local legislation was supplemented by central, also linking price and weight. Thus Henry III's Assize of Bread and Ale (1266) fixed the price of ale, and decreed the weight of a farthing (a quarter of a penny) loaf of bread.[42] Sometimes, if market conditions

---

[38] Kula, *Measures and Men*, p. 19.
[39] William Beveridge, *Prices and Wages in England from the Twelfth to the Nineteenth Century*, I (London, 1939), p. 15.
[40] Ibid., pp. 35–59.   [41] Lipson, *Economic History*, p. 294.
[42] Ibid.; see also Zupko, *British Weights and Measures*, pp. 19–20.

changed, perhaps in the aftermath of a bad harvest, it was easier to reduce the weight of a standard loaf of bread than it was to increase the price. For one thing, people were used to paying a farthing for a loaf. For another, since the farthing was the smallest unit of coinage in circulation, the only way to have increased the price of a loaf would have been to double it to a halfpenny, which would have been unjust. Reducing the size of the loaf was both more subtle and more acceptable.[43]

The assizes, especially that of ale, were more honoured in the breach than the observance. In Norwich, for example, most wives brewed ale and sold it to their neighbours above the statutory price. Amercements for this offence were one of the most lucrative sources of income for the city officials, who expected, even hoped, that the assize would be broken. The fines seem to have been regarded as 'a sort of excise licence'.[44]

OFFENCES AGAINST WEIGHTS AND MEASURES

More serious were offences involving deliberate falsification of weights and measures. The records are heavy with examples. But these were far from new, for both the Old and the New Testaments had warned against them. Falsification of weight or measure was a crime against the justice of God, as the laws of Leviticus made clear (19.35–6). A passage in Deuteronomy (25.13–15) hinted at the death penalty for an offence which was to be common in medieval England:

> Thou shalt not have in thy bag divers weights, a great and a small. Thou shalt not have in thine house divers measures, a great and a small. But thou shalt have a perfect and just weight, a perfect and just measure shalt thou have: that thy days may be lengthened in the land which the Lord thy God giveth thee.

In the Sermon on the Mount Christ warned, 'With what judgment ye judge, ye shall be judged: and with what measure ye mete, it shall be measured to you again' (Matthew 7.2).[45]

John Bromyard testified to the manipulation of weights in late medieval England – how the fraudulent weighed down the balance 'to press it down without good and true weight'; how they would 'mingle bad and extraneous matter with the stuff that is to be weighed in sly fashion, like those who mix sand with wool, or wet the wool to make it weigh heavier',[46] and more in the same vein. In London in 1487 a baker's servant inserted a piece of iron, weighing about 6s 8d into a loaf to make it weigh more 'in deceit of the people'.[47] The records are full of such examples.

---

[43] See Kula, *Measures and Men*, p. 102.   [44] Coulton, *Medieval Village*, p. 61.
[45] Cf. Mark 4.24; Luke 6.38.   [46] Owst, *Literature and Pulpit*, p. 354.
[47] Riley, *Memorials of London*, p. 498.

Measurements could be manipulated too, especially in the cloth industry. In the poem *Piers Plowman*, 'Avarice' became a draper. He learnt how to stretch the selvedges ('drawe the lyser along') to make the cloth look longer. He also mastered the craft of piercing the richest cloth, the 'rays', with a packing-needle, plaiting them together, and then putting them in a press until 10 or 12 yards were drawn out to 13.[48] Much the same was happening in contemporary Florence.[49]

Sometimes the actual measure or the balance would be faked. A favourite trick was to keep two measures, ostensibly of the same capacity, as had been hinted at in Deuteronomy. The greater would be used when someone was buying and the smaller when selling. Bromyard disclosed that when friends lent out measures they would always ask whether they were to be used for buying or selling.[50] A treatise of about 1440 on how to hold a manorial court ordered inquiries to be made 'if there be any among you who use double measures, a greater to buy with and a smaller to sell with, or use false balances, weights, yards, ells'.[51] Walter of Henley advised, 'If you bee to selle (by weight) bee well advised for theare is muche fraude to suche as cannot espie it.'[52] Sometimes false weights or balances were used to weigh coinage. Avarice's wife, who at one stage in a colourful career was a cloth weaver, used a false weight to weigh out the pounds with which she paid her spinsters. Avarice himself admitted that it weighed a quarter of a pound more than on his own *auncel*, a type of balance in itself sufficiently suspect to be condemned by two statutes of Edward III.[53]

Even the aristocrats of the market, the gold and silversmiths, were guilty. The charter of 1327 censored goldsmiths for keeping their shops in 'dark lanes and obscure streets' in London, and for buying suspect articles of gold and silver, which they then melted down, turned into plate, and sold to passing merchants for export.[54]

Crime was not confined to lay people. About the year 1335, Salomon de Ripple, a monk of St Augustine's Canterbury, and the abbot's deputy for the receipt of tenths and fifteenths for the diocese, devised a balance which he called a 'pennypise'. At the time the coinage in circulation was of light weight, but Salomon managed to get hold of a pound's worth of old, heavy pennies, against which he weighed what was received in the

---

[48] William Langland, *Piers Plowman*, B, passus v, lines 209–14, pp. 146–8.
[49] De Roover, *San Bernardino*, p. 13.
[50] John Bromyard, *Summa praedicantium*, 2, ch. vi, 'mercatio', sect 8, fols. 20v–21r.
[51] *EHD*, 4, no. 355, p. 551.   [52] Walter of Henley, *Husbandry*, ch. 23, p. 341.
[53] William Langland, *Piers Plowman*, B, passus v, lines 215–18, p. 148. For condemnation see *Statutes of the Realm*, 1, 25 Edward III (1351–2), c. 9, p. 321b. In general, see Zupko, *British Weights and Measures*, pp. 23, 25.
[54] Reddaway, *Goldsmiths' Company*, p. 223.

lighter coinage. People found that they were having to pay anything from 3s 4d to 5s extra. The unsuspecting abbot was fined £80 for his deputy's offence, and made to repay all that had been unjustly exacted.[55]

SOVEREIGNTY LIMITED: CONTROL OF THE COINAGE

Control of the coinage was a royal prerogative. In the mid-thirteenth century Gerald of Abbeville (d. 1272), chancellor of the University of Paris and opponent of Aquinas, stated the royal position succinctly: 'To strike money and to protect it are the prerogatives of the king.'[56] It was far more important than control of weights and measures and differed from them. There could never be any question of tolerating local variations in the weight or fineness of the coinage. There was therefore no question of devolving enforcement of standards to local level. As the control of metrological standards became decentralized, control of the coinage became more centralized. Accordingly, the complaint about Brother Salomon was laid directly before the King's council, rather than the Archbishop's court, and the King himself ordered an inquiry.[57] Offences against standards of the coinage, such as clipping or counterfeiting, were habitually dealt with in the king's court rather than at borough level. The penalties were unremitting. Edward I's Statute of Westminster I (1275) made counterfeiting money a major offence, comparable with forging the king's seal and 'treason touching the king himself'.[58] Edward III's Statute of Treasons of 1352 was to reiterate this.[59] In November 1278 there was a mass arrest of Jews and goldsmiths, including some officials of the royal mint. Of those found guilty of coin-clipping, many were hanged, drawn, and quartered, including a Christian moneyer and an assayer, while the rest were severely fined. In general, Christians were treated more leniently than Jews.[60]

The minting of money was also gradually centralized. In late Anglo-Saxon England most boroughs had possessed a mint. By the reign of Henry III, twenty-one are known to have existed, but this total was reduced to a dozen by Edward I's reign. By the fourteenth century, London and Canterbury had become predominant, with other mints being brought

---

[55] Rogers Ruding, *Annals of the Coinage of Great Britain and its Dependencies*, 3rd edn, 1 (London, 1840), p. 211.
[56] Gerald of Abbeville, *Quodlibet*, VII, 4: transcribed and translated in Langholm, *Economics*, p. 279.
[57] Ibid., pp. 149–52.
[58] Statute of Westminster I (3 Edw. I), cl. 15: *EHD*, 3, no. 47, p. 401.
[59] *EHD*, 4, no. 214, p. 403.
[60] Mavis Mate, 'Monetary policies in England, 1272–1307', *British Numismatic Journal*, 41 (1972), pp. 34–79, at pp. 38–9.

into service only occasionally during recoinages.[61] The reduced supply of bullion during the reign of Edward III led to the closure of Canterbury and the transfer of its staff to London, thus achieving complete centralization. The Calais mint, established in 1363 in connection with the wool staple there, enjoyed two brief periods of activity up to about 1440. Rather than being in competition with London, Mayhew has suggested that it was 'an outlying branch of the London establishment'.[62] Both King and Parliament regarded the coinage and its standards as something of the utmost importance.

Why was this? The overriding reason was that the state of the coinage affected every order of society and all sectors of the economy. The state of the coinage and the quantity of it in circulation profoundly influenced prices of essential goods in the market-place. It could lead to inflation, on the one hand, or deflation, on the other. As historians now realize, it was just as likely to cause economic change as factors such as supply and demand, based on rising or falling population numbers, warfare, or climatic change.[63] It was also closely tied to international economic relations, especially to the balance of trade.

An issue much discussed by scholastic thinkers in connection with sovereignty was that of currency manipulation – alteration of the value of the coinage. This could be achieved in two ways. The first, and potentially more damaging way was by adulterating the content of the coinage. Coins were bi-metallic, composed of both precious and base metal, and

---

[61] N. J. Mayhew, 'From regional to central minting, 1158–1464', in C. E. Challis, ed., *A New History of the Royal Mint* (Cambridge, 1992), pp. 83–6; 143–7.

[62] Ibid., p. 152.

[63] See, for example, Michael Prestwich, 'Currency and the economy of early fourteenth-century England', in N. J. Mayhew, ed., *Edwardian Monetary Affairs*, British Archaeological Report, 36 (Oxford, 1977), pp. 45–58; Mavis Mate, 'The role of gold coinage in the English economy, 1338–1400', *British Numismatic Chronicle*, ser. 7, 18 (1978), pp. 126–41; Mate, 'High prices in early fourteenth-century England', *EconHR*, ser. 2, 28 (1975), pp. 1–16; N. J. Mayhew, 'Numismatic evidence and falling prices in the fourteenth century', *EconHR*, ser. 2, 27 (1974), pp. 1–15; Mayhew, 'Money and prices in England from Henry II to Edward III', *Agricultural History Review*, 35 (1987), pp. 121–32; Harry A. Miskimin, 'Monetary movements and market structure - forces for contraction in fourteenth- and fifteenth-century England', reprinted in Miskimin, *Cash, Credit and Crisis in Europe, 1300–1600* (London, 1989), no. 7; John Day, 'Late medieval price movements and the "crisis of feudalism"', and 'The Fisher equation and medieval monetary history', reprinted in Day, *Medieval Market Economy*, pp. 90–107, 108–15, respectively; John H. Munro, 'Bullionism and the bill of exchange in England, 1272–1663: a study in monetary management and popular prejudice', in University of California, Los Angeles, Centre for Medieval and Renaissance Studies, *The Dawn of Modern Banking* (New Haven, CT and London, 1979), esp. pp. 176–8; W. C. Robinson, 'Money, population and economic change in late medieval Europe', *EconHR*, ser. 2, 12 (1959), pp. 63–76.

a ruler could change the ratio of one to the other. The second way of changing the value was by reducing the weight of the coins while retaining their face value. Such alterations were possible only in a system where the coinage had intrinsic value.

Frequently the motive was profit. As the French writer Nicholas Oresme explained:

> I am of the opinion that the main and final cause why the prince pretends to the power of altering the coinage is the profit or gain he can get from it; it would otherwise be vain to make so many and so great changes.[64]

The profit was known as seignorage. People would bring in their old coinage to the mint (and if it had been demonetized there was little practical alternative, since it would be worthless in exchange). They would receive in exchange new coinage, which did not coincide with the intrinsic value of the coinage they had surrendered. Seignorage was, in effect, an underhand form of taxation. The French monarchy, with its frequent debasements, made a great deal out of it, often as an alternative to war taxation. Philip IV, the Fair, apparently derived over half of his total income from it in 1298–99; Philip VI Valois (1328–50), during the Hundred Years War with England, derived nearly 70 per cent of his in 1349, and his son John the Good (1350–64) emulated him.[65]

Most thinkers condemned a practice so manifestly dishonest, because of the harm it inflicted on the people. Indeed, in that respect it was little different from dishonestly altering a pair of scales. Ptolemy of Lucca recalled an old saying that 'Money is from *monere* (to warn), because it warns against fraud.' While endorsing the right of the sovereign to issue and authorize money, he advised the greatest caution:

> Any prince or king ought to be moderate in altering or diminishing the weight or metal, because this results in harm to the people, since it is a measure of things, and therefore to alter money or coin amounts to the same thing as altering a pair of scales or any kind of weight.[66]

William Durant the Younger also made the connection between altering the standards of the coinage and of weights and measures, and condemned rulers who

> debilitate the coinage and defraud the commonwealth of legitimate weights and measures. By so doing they cause and encourage a universal rise in prices and similar kinds of fraud, endangering their souls and the souls of others. This is

---

[64] Nicholas Oresme, *De moneta*, ch. 25, p. 24.
[65] H. A. Miskimin, *Money, Prices, and Foreign Exchange in Fourteenth-century France* (New Haven, CT, 1963), pp. 42–3; Spufford, *Money and its Use*, pp. 301–5; Munro, *Wool, Cloth, and Gold*, p. 22.
[66] Langholm, *Economics*, p. 457.

why there exist unequal weights, coins that are not worth their value, all sorts of sophisticated and fraudulent practices... and why all subjects, the great, the middling, and the small, are being plundered.[67]

An English official of the royal Mint, Richard Leicester, in 1381–82, reiterated the harm to the people: 'And to change the money in any manner seems to me universal damage to the lords, commons and all the realm.'[68] Nicholas Oresme in his *De moneta* warned that the alteration of the coinage for profit was a crime against both God and the People, against both divine and natural law. Such alterations amounted to fraud. The prince's stamp on a coin was supposed to denote the purity of the material and its proportions, and to change these was to falsify the coinage.[69] While debasement lasted, 'money rents, yearly pensions, rates of hire, cesses [taxes] and the like, cannot be well and justly taxed or valued... Neither can money safely be lent or credit given.'[70] The only people who would profit would be the unjust and the undeserving, namely, the money-changers, bankers, bullion dealers, and the like.[71]

The effects of alterations of the coinage on the economy could indeed cause great hardship. The most obvious effect of debasement or devaluation would be an inflationary rise in prices, which would hit everyone in society, especially the poor. Equally, those on fixed incomes, such as landlords, would suffer because the amount of money they would be receiving in the new coinage would no longer correspond to the amount originally set. Those not on fixed incomes, such as merchants, were likely to favour debasement. A return to strong currency meant that all those people holding debased currency would suffer, since a reduced value would be put on it to encourage circulation of the new money. The probable result, again hitting the poorest in society, would be deflation and falling prices. But taxes and dues would not necessarily adjust, so those who had to render a fixed amount would be hard hit. As early as the twelfth century, the Paris theologian Peter the Chanter (d. 1197) had condemned the king who meddled with the value of new money by doubling its value as immoral. This would in effect double the amount the peasants owed in census debts. As Peter observed, the king might just as well double the feudal services of his vassals.[72] This was illustrated later, in 1306, when

---

[67] Constantin Fasolt, *Council and Hierarchy: the Political Thought of William Durant the Younger* (Cambridge, 1991), pp. 230–1.
[68] 'Opinions of Officers of the Mint on the State of English Money', 1381–2, *EEH*, section 7, no. 9, p. 221.
[69] Oresme, *De moneta*, ch. 13, pp. 21–2.   [70] Ibid., ch. 20, p. 33.
[71] Ibid., ch. 21, p. 34.
[72] J. W. Baldwin, *The Medieval Theories of the Just Price: Romanists, Canonists and Theologians in the Twelfth and Thirteenth Centuries*, Transactions of the American Philosophical Society, n.s. 49, pt. 4 (Philadelphia, 1959), Appendix A, p. 80.

Philip the Fair restored good money after a debasement. The result was rent riots in Paris, with people refusing to pay their rent in the new money, because it contained three times as much silver as the old.[73]

Some thinkers, appreciating the hardship which was caused by debasement, saw the ruler who resorted to it as a tyrant, in the Aristotelian sense that he was acting in his own selfish interests rather than those of his people. The Dominican theologian and canonist Peter de la Palu (d. 1342), for example, considered that a ruler who debased the coinage was no king, but a tyrant: 'If the king alters money for his own utility and to the detriment of his subjects, he is a tyrant rather than a king.' He did, however, allow that the king could alter the coinage if the needs of his kingdom dictated it, and if other ways of raising money would be more harmful to his subjects, in other words if he was not motivated solely by his own interests.[74] In his commentary on the *Ethics*, the contemporary French Carmelite Guido Terreni (d. 1342) emphasized that money was instituted by the prince and the community together for the common good. After all, Aristotle had said in both the *Ethics* and the *Politics* that money existed by convention and that it was in the power of the *community* to change its value or render it useless.[75] If the prince altered the value by himself, against the interests of the community, then he was a tyrant:

since it is to the good of the community that commodities should be equalized better, therefore it can be altered by the will of the prince and the community as long as it yields to the common good, for if this were to be done against the common good and for the good of the prince and so as to harm the citizens, it would be unjust and such a prince would be a tyrant.[76]

Oresme too was to take up the theme of tyranny, stating graphically: 'The amount of the prince's profit is necessarily that of the community's loss. But whatever loss the prince inflicts on the community is injustice and the act of a tyrant and not of a king, as Aristotle says.'[77] Ultimately, he warned, this would lead to the destruction of the kingdom. It would result in the transformation of the whole realm from a kingdom to a tyranny, and 'a dominion which is turned from a kingdom to a tyranny is bound to have a speedy end'.[78]

Oresme's views on sovereignty and debasement are of particular interest because the *De moneta* was very much a 'tract for the times'. He composed

---

[73] R. Cazelles, 'Quelques reflections à propos des mutations de la monnaie royale française (1295–1360)', *Le Moyen âge*, 72 (1966), p. 258.
[74] Langholm, *Economics*, p. 490. For Aristotle's definition of a tyrant see *Politics*, v, x, 9, 1311a, p. 236.
[75] Aristotle, *Ethics*, v, v, p. 120. *Politics*, I, ix, 11, 1257b, p. 25.
[76] Langholm, *Economics*, pp. 504–5. [77] Oresme, *De moneta*, ch. 15, p. 24.
[78] Ibid., ch. 26, p. 47; ch. 25, p. 46.

the shorter French version probably in 1355, when successive debasements of the currency had virtually crippled the French landowners. Between 1355 and 1358 there was growing opposition to the policies of John II from a group of nobles who demanded an end to debasement and a strong monetary policy. The capture by the English of John II at the Battle of Poitiers (1356) and the subsequent demand for a huge ransom made matters worse. Oresme's treatise was originally written for the opposition party, but by the time he wrote the longer Latin version, the 'opposition' had come to power as advisers of the new king, Charles V, Oresme himself among them. He was ultimately rewarded for his services to the government with the bishopric of Lisieux.[79] Meanwhile he had become one of Charles V's chaplains, and for him had undertaken translations into French of both Aristotle's *Ethics* and *Politics*, works which profoundly influenced the King's economic and political ideas.

Oresme was to address the question of whether money was owned by the ruler or the community, and on the basis of communal ownership to attack the right of the sovereign to debase the currency without consent. The question of whether the ruler or the community 'owned' the money in circulation was inseparable from the wider discussion on whether the ruler was absolute or was limited by the community. If the community owned and controlled money, then the implication was that the community was sovereign rather than the prince. This, in its turn, was linked with issues of representation and of 'counsel and consent'. Was a community more truly represented by one person, be he pope, emperor, or king, or by an assembly such as a general council, electoral college, or parliamentary assembly? If the wider body, rather than the monarch, was the true representative of the community, then that is where sovereignty lay.

The medieval and the modern ideas of representation are different. In the twelfth century John of Salisbury had provided a good example of the medieval version in his *Policraticus*. He used the metaphor of the State as a human body, an abstract corporate entity into which all were united. The person who re-presented, that is gave flesh and blood to, this body was the ruler, whom John described as a 'public man, the man of the State', who belonged entirely to his subjects. When he came to discuss the ownership of money John adopted the same approach:

while it is expedient for the king to be extremely wealthy, still he must count his wealth as the people's. He does not, therefore, truly own that which he possesses in the name of someone else, nor are the goods of the fisc, which are conceded to be public, his own private property. Nor is this a surprise, since he is not his own person but that of his subjects.[80]

---

[79] Spufford, *Money and its Use*, pp. 300–1.
[80] John of Salisbury, *Policraticus*, bk. 4, ch 5, p. 40.

Oresme's approach differed from this because in his discussion of the community's ownership of money, he seemed to anticipate the modern concept of representation, where individuals themselves are represented, rather than the abstract, corporate entity of the community. At first he wrote of the ruler as the 'public person' in much the same way as John of Salisbury:

> Money is essentially established and devised for the good of the community. And since the prince is the most public person and of the highest authority, it follows that he should make the money for the community and stamp it with a suitable design.[81]

In his insistence that the ruler was the most public person (*personam publicam*) and of the greatest authority (*maioris auctoritatis*), he appeared to be using the medieval idea of representation. When he examines the ownership of money the issue becomes less clear. Here he seems to advocate individual ownership of money on the basis of the labour and goods which each person has given for it:

> Although it is the duty of the prince to put his stamp on the money for the common good, he is not the lord or owner of the money current in his principality. For money is a balancing instrument for the exchange of natural wealth ... It is therefore the property of those who possess such wealth. For if a man gives bread or bodily labour in exchange for money, the money he receives is as much his as the bread or bodily labour of which he (unless he were a slave) was free to dispose.[82]

Oresme concluded by applying a mean: 'Thus money belongs to the community *and* to individuals (*communitatis et singularium personarum*).'[83] Unfortunately he did not enlarge on these provocative statements.

Oresme was in no doubt that the sovereign prerogative of controlling the coinage belonged to the community, whether corporately or individually. He suggested that by debasing 'its' money, the community could raise funds to deal with emergencies such as war or the ransom of the prince:

> On the basis that the community owns the money in circulation, the community can alter it at will. It can therefore alter it after any fashion, make what gain it will from it and treat it as its own, especially if it needs a large sum of money for war or for the ransom of its prince from captivity or some accident of the kind.[84]

Traditionally, as we saw in chapter 1, it was the prerogative of the ruler to raise money in cases of necessity without having to resort to the consent of his magnates.[85] According to Oresme, it was for the community to decide what constituted an emergency and to act accordingly.[86] If the ruler was

---

[81] Oresme, *De moneta*, ch. 5, p. 10.   [82] Ibid., ch. 6, p. 10.
[83] Ibid., p. 11.   [84] Ibid., ch. 22, p. 35.
[85] See chapter 1, pp. 37–8 above.   [86] Oresme, *De moneta*, ch. 24, p. 39.

unable to assemble the community to consult it, he was not allowed the prerogative of acting on his own initiative: 'the prince cannot make these changes or receive profit in this way either by the regular common law or by privilege, gift, grant, bargain or any other authority or means whatever, nor can it be his right in virtue of his lordship or otherwise'. He added, somewhat defensively, that this was no infringement of his royal majesty, as flatterers, intriguers, and traitors to the commonwealth alleged,[87] but it is difficult to see how the removal of the use of the royal prerogative in cases of necessity could be anything less than this. Oresme was not an original economic thinker, for Odd Langholm has demonstrated that both his ideas and those of his teacher, John Buridan, are derivative, in many cases from earlier, unpublished Aristotelian commentaries.[88] His political ideas, however, have some distinctly modern elements, and in his thought about monetary matters, politics and economics are inseparable.

DEBASEMENT IN FRANCE AND ENGLAND

The constitutional situation in France and England differed, although in both countries the connection between the economy and the constitution was close. In late medieval France the concept of an institution claiming to be the representative of the whole country was less developed than in England. Much of the country was in the hands of great feudal rulers, so that, in effect, sovereignty was decentralized. In England, as we have already shown, the centralization of royal justice had led to the weakening of the jurisdictional powers of lords at the local level,[89] but they were compensated by gaining a share in the authority of the ruler at national level through their role in the developing institution of Parliament. In each country the constitutional situation was reflected in the policies adopted on coinage.

The French clergy seem to have taken on board the idea that money belonged to the community. Starting in 1303–4 they tried to persuade the King to seek the consent of bishops and magnates to alterations in the coinage. In the 1320s and 1330s Philip VI Valois went through the motions of consultation, but the opening of the Hundred Years War soon showed how little store he set by it, as the large seignorage profits indicated.[90] Then, early in 1347, at a critical stage in the war, Philip VI issued an ordinance declaring that the making, the provision, and the total control of money pertained solely to 'us and our royal majesty ... as it pleases us, and as it seems good to us for the good and profit of us, of our kingdom,

---

[87] Ibid., ch. 14, p. 41.
[88] See Langholm, *Wealth and Money*, which is largely devoted to this.
[89] See ch. 1, pp. 35–6 above. [90] Spufford, *Money and its Uses*, pp. 304–5.

and of our subjects, and the exercise of our right'.[91] There was no question of consultation. One way of demonstrating control was to make the royal money dominant throughout the land, which meant suppressing the feudal coinages. In 1226 Louis VII declared that his own money was to be current over the whole of France, whereas feudal money was restricted to its place of origin. Louis IX, St Louis, confirmed this in 1262, and forbade any baron who did not enjoy coinage rights to use any but the King's money. In 1319 the Crown started to buy some of the feudal coinages.[92] By the mid-fourteenth century the process was complete.[93]

By the late fourteenth and fifteenth centuries, however, rulers had started to take notice of Oresme. Charles V, his patron, did eventually return to 'sound money'. In Flanders Duke Philip the Bold and Duke John the Fearless of Burgundy, apparently both influenced by Oresme's doctrine of sound money, refused to debase or devalue the silver coinage, until forced to do so.[94] This was despite a severe bullion shortage, for which debasement was usually considered a remedy.

In England, unlike France, the principle that the community 'owned' the money in circulation, and that the approval of Parliament was necessary for any alterations to it was more firmly established than in France. Parliament strictly curtailed the king's sovereign rights over the coinage, which ensured that alterations when made were not for the king's profit, but because they were necessary to counteract the shortage of bullion. It was a condition of the Ordinances of 1311 imposed by the barons that Edward II should make alterations to the coinage only 'by the common counsel of his baronage and that in Parliament', because 'every time a change...is made...the whole people suffers greatly in many ways'.[95] Only once in the late medieval period did the king debase the coinage, in the sense of adulterating it. This was from 1335 to 1344, when shortage of bullion led Edward III to reduce the fineness of farthings and halfpennies, coins which would have been restricted to domestic use and would not have damaged the reputation of English money abroad. Parliament made him restore the fineness of the coins in 1344, and the experiment was not repeated, despite its success in attracting bullion to the Mint. Subsequent alterations were by weight alone. The four reductions in weight between 1344 and June 1351 provoked such a furore that in the Statute of Purveyors

---

[91] Cazelles, 'Quelques reflections', p. 96.
[92] Miskimin, 'Price movements and specie debasements', pp. 250–1 summarizes the various measures.
[93] Miskimin, *Money, Prices, and Foreign Exchange*, pp. 47–52.
[94] Spufford, *Money and its Uses*, p. 311; John Day, 'The Great Bullion Famine', in *Medieval Market Economy*, pp. 14, 16.
[95] *EHD*, 3, no. 100, p. 536, cl. 30.

of January 1352 the King was compelled by Parliament to promise to restore the coinage to its 'ancient state', and never to alter its weight or fineness again. The standard established in 1351 lasted for more than half a century. The reductions in weight by Henry IV in 1411–12 and Edward IV in 1464 were both made with the consent of Parliament.[96] As Munro says, 'No other West European nation even approached such conservatism in its mint policies.'[97] The sound English currency was to lead to other problems, connected with shortage of bullion, as will be seen in chapter 5. Nevertheless, the 'royal and political dominion', the 'mean' constitution of the sovereignty of the king in Parliament, enabled the English people to avoid some of the monetary hardships suffered by their French counterparts.

CONCLUSION

This chapter has explored the divine origins attributed to weights and measures and coinage, and the confused origins of weights and measures in practice. Control over their standards emerged as a sovereign attribute and developed in tandem with the establishment of political authority. With the subsequent weakening of the powers of the monarch, and the corresponding growth of representative institutions, control of the standards became subject to consultation and consent, especially by the English Parliament. Just how closely the different standards were still thought to be related, however, was demonstrated in the opinion of one of the Officers of the Mint, a goldsmith, in 1381 on a problem for which an obvious remedy would have been debasement. Instead of acknowledging and rejecting this, as the other officials had done, he recommended 'that there be one weight and one measure throughout the realm and that no subtle weight be suffered'.[98] A simple return to a universal standard was all that he thought was needed.

[96] Mayhew, 'From regional to central minting', pp. 144–8.
[97] Munro, 'Bullionism and the bill of exchange', pp. 190–1, quotation at p. 191.
[98] 'Opinions of Officers of the Mint', p. 222.

5

THE MERCANTILE SYSTEM

The sovereign rights to control the standards of weights, measures, and coinage discussed in chapter 4 had traditionally been royal prerogatives. They had emerged at a time when the European economy was still predominantly rural, the idea of the nation-state, if it existed at all, was in its infancy, and notions such as representation of the community and constitutional monarchy had not appeared. All this was to change, and discussion about trade, merchants, and a set of ideas attached to the 'mercantile system' fitted firmly into the new climate of the commercial revolution, the development of national sovereign rights, and demands for participation and consent.

The term 'the mercantile system' was first used in England by Adam Smith in *The Wealth of Nations* (1776) to describe what he termed the 'system of commerce' as opposed to that of agriculture. This is the broad subject of this chapter, and although it is treated by scholastics, many of the ideas are found in secular sources, such as parliamentary legislation, merchants' manuals, and vernacular literature. 'The mercantile system' gradually became synonymous with a set of economic ideas enunciated in the seventeenth century in both France and England and later known as mercantilism. Its founding father was Thomas Mun (1571–1641), a director of the East India Company. Mercantilism is a blanket term and as such has given rise to exasperated controversy. This has increased because there was no definitive work about it, merely writings on particular aspects, and these contain diverse views. Nevertheless, Adam Smith gave a certain coherence to it by attacking some of its fundamental tenets.

It would be a dangerous anachronism to suggest that fully-fledged mercantilism existed in the medieval period, hence the choice of 'the mercantile system' as the chapter title. Nevertheless, certain ideas current by the end of the period did foreshadow it, and these are the ideas on which we shall focus. The basis of the mercantile system was the desire to develop the power and wealth of a nation. The resources of the world were thought to be constant, and through trade they were transferred from one nation to another. One nation's gain was another nation's loss, so that the aim of each one was to maintain a balance in favour of itself. Some of the means to this were protection of the home industry, the granting of monopolies to traders, wage restraints, the restriction of exports of raw materials, coupled with an emphasis on exporting finished products, and the control of the sea.[1] Another aspect of the mercantile system was bullionism. Adam Smith castigated the Mercantilists for confusing wealth with money, so that the accumulation of bullion and specie (coinage) became all-important. This was inseparable from trade, because trade between nations controlled the flow of bullion in and out of a country, especially if it did not mine its own precious metals. In theory, if imports balanced exports, no money needed to change hands. If more goods were imported than exported, then either bullion or specie had to be exported to make up the deficit. If the situation were reversed then bullion flowed in to pay for exports. Rulers tried to oversee all these matters in the interests of the common good, to ensure that there was a favourable balance of trade with other countries, and to take whatever measures were necessary to maintain the supply of bullion to the mints. But before any of these policies could be developed, let alone implemented, the traditional scholastic hostility to trade and merchants needed to be overcome, and the merchant valued for his contribution to the wealth of the nation. The changing attitudes to trade and merchants need to be examined before ideas about the balance of internal and external trade, and late medieval views on bullionism and its connection with that balance.

TRADE AND MERCHANTS: CONDEMNATION

The store of ideas on trade and merchants inherited from classical and biblical sources was a mixed, if not contradictory, one. Aristotle regarded retail trade which involved the making of a profit as unnatural, in contrast to barter. He therefore banned merchants from his ideal State.[2] Plato, while disapproving of retail trade, grudgingly allowed foreign merchants a role in his city-state, because they contributed to 'the even and proportionate

---

[1] Jacob Viner, 'Mercantilist thought', in Jacob Viner, *Essays on the Intellectual History of Economics*, ed. Douglas A. Irwin (Princeton, NJ, 1991), pp. 263–75; Thomas A. Horne, 'Mercantilism', *The Blackwell Encyclopaedia of Political Thought* (Oxford, 1991), pp. 335–6.
[2] Aristotle, *Politics*, VII, ix, 3, 1328b, p. 301.

diffusion' of commodities.³ A contemporary even suggested giving free seats at festivals to merchants and ship-owners as a mark of respect, in the hope that more trade would be attracted to Athens, thus generating customs revenue.⁴

Medieval writers seemed to delight in hostile precedents such as Aristotle. When it came to the Bible, they again looked for condemnatory texts. They cited such texts as Ecclesiasticus 26.29, 'A merchant shall hardly keep himself from doing wrong', or 27.2, 'As a nail sticketh fast between the joinings of the stones; so doth sin stick close between buying and selling.' In terms of the Gospels, they were more likely to dwell on Christ's expulsion of the buyers and sellers from the Temple (Matthew 21.12–13) than on the Parable of the Talents.

The early medieval view duplicated Ecclesiasticus: sin always wedged itself between buying and selling, and merchants were invariable sinners. Gratian heaped many of the condemnatory texts into the sections on usury and penance in the *Decretum*. Among them was a famous warning to penitents from Pope Leo the Great (440–61) to avoid the dangerous business of trade because it was virtually impossible to avoid sin when buying and selling.⁵ Although Gratian was responsible for most of the *Decretum*, about 160 texts, known as *palea* (a pun on the name of the canonist apparently responsible for them), were added later in the twelfth century. Among them were three about merchants.⁶ One of them was from the late Roman philosopher and statesman Cassiodorus (*c.* 490–585). He described merchants as 'abominations', who barely considering the justice of God were 'polluted with immoderate striving for money', and who 'burdened their wares more with lies than with prices'.⁷ Another text, the *palea Eiciens*, was from a commentary on Matthew 21 – the expulsion from the Temple. This was falsely attributed to John Chrysostom (and referred to as Pseudo-Chrysostom), although it was probably by a heretical writer of the fifth or sixth century. Christ's action in driving out the buyers and sellers showed that it was seldom if ever possible for a merchant to please God. No Christian should be a merchant, lies and cheating being mandatory in buying and selling. But not all buyers and sellers were merchants: some were craftsmen who skilfully transformed raw material which they bought into finished wares and then sold for profit. They were exonerated. Only those who sold things unaltered for profit were really merchants, the ones

---

[3] Plato, *Laws*, xi, 918, pp. 311, 314.   [4] Gordon, *Economic Analysis*, p. 17.
[5] Gratian, *Decretum*, D. 5, c. 2, col. 1240.
[6] For full discussion of these see John W. Baldwin, 'The medieval merchant before the bar of canon law', *Papers of the Michigan Academy of Science, Arts, and Letters*, 44 (1959), pp. 287–99, on which I depend for what follows.
[7] Gratian, *Decretum*, D. 88, c. 13, col. 310.

who had been thrown out, signifying that they should be thrown out of the Church.[8] The most damaging extract was one from Augustine's commentary on an alternative version of Psalm 71.15–16: 'My mouth shall show forth thy righteousness and thy salvation all the day. Because I know nothing of business [rather than the alternative, "the numbers thereof"] I will go in the strength of the Lord God.' The implication was that those who *did* know something about business would not 'go in the strength of the Lord God'. Augustine took this to mean that Christians should not be involved in trade.[9]

The canonists examined the morality of merchants who bought cheap and sold dear. Gratian condemned the practice as 'shameful gain' (*turpe lucrum*).[10] This seems to have become an accepted definition of commerce – buying cheap and selling dear. Twelfth-century Decretists such as Rufinus and Huguccio worried about whether such action could ever be morally justified. Like the Pseudo-Chrysostom, Rufinus allowed craftsmen who fashioned something out of the raw materials they had bought to charge for their skill and labour, to recoup their expenses, and even to make a profit in the process. He also allowed someone to buy cheap and sell dear if circumstances forced him to, particularly if he had not originally bought with the intention of reselling. But deliberately buying cheap to sell dear was shameful if it involved neither labour nor costs, but relied on watching the market in order to buy up supplies in times of plenty to profit by reselling them in times of dearth. On the other hand, labour or heavy expenditure could transform such a sale into an honourable one.[11] Huguccio was more concerned with the merchant's intention, which had to be a right one. If greed was paramount, then selling dear was immoral, but if the intention was merely to provide for himself and his dependants, then the merchant's activity was justified.[12]

The impression, at least from late medieval England, was that in practice many merchants were guilty of shameful gain. Given the nature of commerce, merchants were more prone to avarice than other people, and the opportunities for transgressing the rules of justice, that is, upsetting the balance of interests between seller and buyer, were legion. Bishop Brinton of Rochester provided a summary of mercantile misdemeanours:

these days, false merchants infringe the rules of justice. In the whole craft such dishonesty is used in measurement, in loans, in weights, in the balance [or in

---

[8] Ibid., c. 9, cols. 308–9. For discussion of this passage see Langholm, *Economics*, pp. 102–3.
[9] Gratian, *Decretum*, D. 88, c. 12, cols. 309–10. For discussion see Langholm, *Economics*, pp. 128–9.
[10] Gratian, *Decretum*, C. 14, q. 4, c. 9, col. 737.
[11] Baldwin, 'The medieval merchant', pp. 294–5. [12] Ibid., pp. 295–7.

coinage – *stateris*], in deceitful mixtures and false oaths, that anyone, no matter who, will try to deceive his neighbour, whom he should rather serve in mutual charity.[13]

Not for nothing have the Middle Ages been termed 'a paradise for tricksters and the great age of fraud'.[14] In England the rolls of Parliament, the records of local courts, chronicles, poems, plays, sermons, confessors' manuals, and indeed literature of every type provide a positive litany of mercantile fraud and chicanery – of the nails lodged between the stones of buying and selling. Not that the problem was limited to England, as the catalogue of crimes recorded by the German Augustinian Henry of Friemar in the fourteenth century and Saint Bernardino of Siena and Saint Antoninus of Florence in the fifteenth make clear.[15] Especially fraudulent were the wool and cloth merchants, and the victuallers – the brewers, bakers, and above all the butchers. Legislative attempts to curb such vice in England had started in the tenth century, when Athelstan ordered that all commercial transactions were to take place within a town and before witnesses,[16] and efforts were to continue throughout the medieval period.

Predictably the worst offences, or at least those which feature most in the records, were those against weights and measures described in chapter 4. Yet appearances could be deceptive too. Richard I dealt with what was later called 'false shewing':

It is forbidden to all merchants throughout the whole of the realm that any merchant set in front of his shop red or black cloths or shields [blinds?] or any other thing, whereby the buyers' eyes are often deceived in the choice of good cloth.[17]

The winding and wrapping of wool also lent itself to chicanery. An act of Edward IV of 1463 complained of how

daily great deceipt is done in the winding, wrapping and making of fleeces of wool within this realm, by the owners of the same wool, by putting into the fleeces locks of wool and pieces of much worse wool than the fleece is, and also putting in the same fleeces, tar, stones, sand, grass, or dirt, to the great damage of the buyer...[18]

Turning to the victuallers, John Bromyard complained of butchers who painted the eyes of rotten sheep carcasses with blood to make them look

---

[13] Thomas Brinton, sermon 48, 1, p. 215. Cf. Owst, *Literature and Pulpit*, p. 353, whose punctuation I have preferred.
[14] Le Goff, *Medieval Civilization*, p. 304.
[15] Langholm, *Economics*, p. 542 (Henry of Friemar); Antoninus of Florence, *Summa moralis*, pt. 3, tit. 8, ch. 4: cited by Bede Jarrett, *Social Theories*, p. 159; Iris Origo, *The World of San Bernardino* (New York, 1962), pp. 80–1.
[16] II Athelstan, 924–39, clauses 12, 13.1, *EHD*, 1, no.35, p. 384.
[17] *EEH*, section 6, no. 1, p. 155.   [18] *EHD*, 4, no. 602, p. 1041.

fresh.[19] A similar crime was highlighted in 1475 when the gild of cooks in London petitioned that 'no one of the craft shall bake, roast, or boil flesh or fish two times to sell, under penalty [for thereby putrifying flesh might be passed off as fresh]'.[20] The French preacher Jacques de Vitry would have been at home in London. He related a tale of a butcher's customer who opened negotiations for a reduction in price with the reminder that he had been buying that butcher's meat for seven years. 'Seven years of eating my meat, and you are still alive!' exclaimed the butcher in surprise.[21] Bakers, too, had their own brands of chicanery. They might bake loaves with 'bad dough within and good dough without', as a certain Alan de Lyndeseye did in London in 1316.[22] The same year two bakers were pilloried for baking bread of 'false, putrid and rotten materials through which persons who bought such bread were deceived and might be killed'.[23] Sometimes the punishment really fitted the crime, as when a seller of unsound wine in London was made to drink a measure of it before the rest was poured over his head.[24] Finally there were livestock traders, especially horse-dealers, who resembled shady secondhand car dealers in hiding the faults of the animal, or selling 'a crokyd hors for a clene'.[25]

Given such indictments, could a merchant or tradesman be saved? Did Heaven have a trademen's entrance? From the twelfth century on, canonists and theologians laboured to justify the activities of the merchant, even to hold out the hope of Heaven to him, and to make trade appear 'respectable'. Scholastic theologians began to allow that merchants might be saved, especially if their intentions were right.

CHANGING ATTITUDES: THE TRADESMAN'S ENTRANCE TO HEAVEN

Augustine had laid the foundations for change by allowing a merchant to speak for himself. He justified his occupation because he carried goods over long distances, which entitled him to earn his living, for was not the labourer 'worthy of his hire'? The apparently mandatory lying and perjury of merchants was nothing to do with commerce as such, but was the fault of the individual: 'If I am evil, it was not trade that made me so,

---

[19] John Bromyard, *Summa praedicantium*, 2, ch. 7, 'ornatus', art. 4, fol. 160a.
[20] *EHD*, 4, no. 646d, p. 1102.
[21] Quoted by Baldwin, *Peter the Chanter*, 1, p. 265.
[22] *EEH*, section 6, no. 3, p. 157.   [23] Riley, *Memorials of London*, p. 121.
[24] *EHD*, 4, no. 616, p. 1059.
[25] John Bromyard, *Summa praedicantium*, 2, ch. 6, 'mercatio', arts 11–12, p. 21r. For other examples see Owst, *Literature and Pulpit*, pp. 25, 35.

but my own iniquity', the merchant admitted.[26] Another merchant who spoke for himself was imagined by the tenth-century abbot of Eynsham in Oxfordshire, Ælfric. In a few sentences of his *Colloquy*, Ælfric touched on many of the points which were to exercise later thinkers:

Master What do you say merchant?
Merchant I say that I am useful both to king and ealdormen, and to the wealthy and to all people.
Master And how?
Merchant I board my ship with my cargo and sail to lands overseas, and sell my goods, and buy precious things which aren't produced in this country. And in great danger on the sea I bring them back to you here: and sometimes I suffer shipwreck with the loss of all my goods, scarcely escaping alive.

...

Master Do you want to sell your goods here for just what you paid for them there?
Merchant I don't want to. What would my labour benefit me then? I want to sell dearer here than I buy there so that I gain some profit, with which I may feed myself and my wife and my sons.[27]

Several important ideas emerge – risk and labour as titles to profit, justification of buying cheap to sell dear on the basis of a right intention, and the usefulness of the merchant to the realm.

The gradual transformation of attitudes is illustrated by papal views. In the year 1078 a council at Rome had condemned merchants by stating that it was impossible for either merchants or soldiers to pursue their trades without sinning, and denied them the hope of eternal salvation unless they could find other work.[28] Yet in 1199 Pope Innocent III canonized the merchant Homobonus of Cremona within two years of his death.[29]

Two of the most interesting theological justifications of mercantile activity were written by Englishmen – Thomas, rector of Chobham, in Surrey, later subdean of Salisbury, and Alexander of Hales. Both touch on issues raised by Ælfric. In his great *Summa* for confessors, completed about 1216, Thomas allowed laymen to buy things cheap and sell them dear without alteration or improvement, because they were redistributing goods from areas of plenty to those of scarcity. Like the canonists, he allowed merchants to recover their original outlay, and to charge for labour, transport,

---

[26] Gratian, *Decretum*, D. 88, c. 9, cols. 308–9: Augustine, *Enarratio in Psalmos*, 70, 17, *CChr.SL*, 39, p. 955, lines 53–4.
[27] Ælfric, *Colloquy*, ed. Michael Swanton, *Anglo-Saxon Prose*, pp. 111–12.
[28] Gordon, *Economic Analysis*, p. 171.
[29] On him see Diana M. Webb, 'A saint and his money: perceptions of urban wealth in the lives of Italian saints', in Sheils and Wood, eds., *The Church and Wealth*, SCH, 24 (1987), pp. 61–73.

and expenses.[30] Alexander of Hales, too, found that much commerce was morally justifiable, especially if the intention of the merchant was a moral one. His most significant contribution was to allow a merchant to profit from the risk involved in storage rather than, like Ælfric, transport. The importance of this, as Langholm has pointed out, is that it deliberately introduced the element of time into the argument.[31]

Aquinas's views, too, were reminiscent of Ælfric's. He stressed the right intention of the merchant, labour as an entitlement to profit, and the usefulness of the merchant to the State:

> And this is the way in which commerce can become justifiable. This is exemplified by the man who uses moderate business profits to provide for his household, or to help the poor; or in order to ensure that the country does not run short of essential supplies, and who makes a profit as it were to compensate for his work and not for its own sake.[32]

The idea that merchants should contribute to the common good was one that was to become very influential, especially in the early Renaissance period, when the merchant's position was to become respected, and even honoured.

THE EXALTATION OF THE MERCHANT

Underlying the shift in attitude to merchants was both economic nationalism and economic humanism, the one advocating the wealth of the State, starting with that of the ruler, the other the wealth of the individual.[33] As early as the twelfth century Richard fitz Nigel (d. 1198), Henry II's treasurer and Bishop of London, linked strong government with sound economic foundations. Kings, he recommended,

> should be served for the preservation ... of the worldly wealth which pertains to them by virtue of their office. . . . Moreover the abundance of resources, or the lack of them exalts or humbles the power of princes. For those who are lacking in them become a prey to their enemies, whilst those who are well supplied with them despoil their foes.[34]

A century later Giles of Rome switched the emphasis to the people. People needed to live in society, because no one was economically self-sufficient.

---

[30] Thomas of Chobham, *Summa confessorum*, art. 6, d. 4, q. 10, pp. 301–2. For discussion see Langholm, *Economics*, pp. 54–5.
[31] Langholm, *Economics*, pp. 130–1.
[32] Thomas Aquinas, *Summa theologiae*, 2a2ae, 77, 4, vol. 38, p. 229.
[33] McGovern, 'The rise of new economic attitudes', pp. 217–53.
[34] Richard fitz Nigel, *Dialogue of the Exchequer*, EHD, I, no. 70, p. 491.

They needed one another to make good their economic deficiencies, not just of corn, but of all food.[35] The only way they could get what they needed was to exchange the things they had in abundance for those which they did not have. For this, buying, selling, exchange, and contract were necessary, and the State existed to make these easier.[36] Material goods were instrumental in the pursuit of the end for which political life was instituted. Kings and princes therefore had to rule their kingdoms so that their subjects should be rich in material goods, to the extent that they are able to live well.[37] Ptolemy of Lucca recognized that 'A king...needs artificial riches, such as gold, silver, other metals, and the coins minted from them, to defend his government.'[38] In fifteenth-century England John Fortescue provided a particularly good example of economic nationalism. He devoted a chapter of *The Governance of England* to 'The Harm that cometh of a King's Poverty', concluding: 'But we most hold it to be undoubted, that there may no realm prosper, nor be worshipful, under a poor king.'[39] He hoped that 'we should first have unity and peace within our land, riches and prosperity, and be *the mightiest and most wealthy realm of the world*' (my italics).[40]

The exaltation of the merchant developed in parallel with this economic nationalism. In the fourteenth century the Italian civilian Bartolus, a friend of Dante and Petrarch, and his pupil Baldus, praised trade and commerce as the foundations of political power, and also encouraged the development of a large and prosperous merchant class in the cities.[41] The two things had become linked. On such foundations the Italian humanists built. To take a random example, Coluccio Salutati, the Florentine chancellor, writing in 1381, regarded merchants as vital to the life of man: 'This type of man is necessary to the progress of human society: we cannot live without him.'[42] One of the high points of economic humanism was undoubtedly Poggio Bracciolini's dialogue on avarice.[43] Without the cupidity which motivated economic life, all liberality would cease, 'all the magnificence of cities would be removed, all culture and ornament would be destroyed, no temples would be built, no colonnades, no palaces, all arts would cease, and then confusion of our lives and of the republic would follow'.[44] It sounds like the description Hobbes gave of the state of nature in his *Leviathan*.

[35] Giles of Rome, *De regimine principum*, bk. II, pt. 1, ch. 1.
[36] Ibid., bk. III, pt. ii, ch. 32, p. 320v.   [37] Ibid., ch. 8, p. 279r.
[38] Ptolemy of Lucca, *De regimine principum*, bk. 2, ch. 7, p. 117.
[39] Fortescue, *Governance of England*, ch. 5, pp. 92–3.
[40] Ibid., Appendix B (alternative version of ch. 16), p. 138.
[41] Baron, 'Franciscan poverty', pp. 17–18.   [42] Ibid., p. 226, n. 42.
[43] Bec, *Les Marchands écrivains*, p. 380.
[44] Poggio Bracciolini, *De avaritio*, XII, 6, p. 77. Cf. McGovern, 'Economic attitudes', p. 235.

A genre which especially enshrined the 'virtues' of the merchant and advocated economic nationalism was the manual of commercial practice.[45] In 1458 the Ragusan merchant Benedetto Cotrugli, operating from Naples, wrote a handbook *On Commerce and the Perfect Merchant*. 'The advancement, the comfort, the health of republics to a large extent proceed from merchants', he declared,[46] and wrote of the 'dignity and office of merchants'[47] – the sort of language more usually used to describe priests and kings. In terms of creditworthiness at least the merchant was rated above kings and princes – a revealing sidelight on contemporary politics:

> It is generally said that today [good] faith abides with merchants and men-at-arms... Neither kings nor princes nor any [other] rank of men enjoy as much reputation or credit as a good merchant... And whereas a simple and plain receipt of a merchant is valid even without witnesses, the rulers and any other people are not believed without an instrument and strong cautions.[48]

Merchants keep the best company. At home the merchant 'associates with an honourable family in continuous and virtuous activity', while outside it he associates with 'artisans, gentlemen, lords, princes, and prelates of every rank' and is frequently visited by great scholars.[49] And there can be no doubt about the usefulness of trade to the city:

> Through trade... sterile countries are provided with food and supplies and also enjoy many strange things which are imported from places where other commodities are lacking... [merchants] enable the poor to live; through their initiative in tax farming they promote the activity of administrators; through their exports and imports of merchandise they cause the customs and excises of the lords and republics to expand, and consequently they enlarge the public and common treasury.[50]

In Italy at least the merchant had become vital for the smooth functioning of the republic.

In contrast to the earlier view of the Pseudo-Chrysostom, it was no longer impossible for a merchant to please God. Some of them certainly tried hard. As early as 1253 an Italian firm opened its accounts with the words: 'In the name of God and of profit',[51] not appearing to see any contradiction. At the end of the century an anonymous Genoese notary advised: 'Make your weighing so accurate that you may not be

---

[45] For discussion see ibid., pp. 246–7.
[46] Robert S. Lopez and Irving W. Raymond, *Medieval Trade in the Mediterranean World: Illustrative Documents* (New York and London, 1955), no. 200, p. 416.
[47] Ibid., pp. 416–18. [48] Ibid., p. 418.
[49] Ibid., pp. 417–18. [50] Ibid., pp. 416–17.
[51] Raymond de Roover, 'The scholastic attitude toward trade and entrepreneurship', in *Business, Banking, and Economic Thought*, ed. Julius Kirschner (Chicago, IL, and London, 1974), pp. 336–45, at p. 345.

caught in error, remembering the scales in which you are going to be weighed.'[52] Until its failure in the mid-fourteenth century the books of the Bardi Company contained charitable accounts opened in the name of 'the Lord God'.[53] Perhaps as a result of such practices the Florentine Dominican Remigio de'Girolami (c. 1319) was certain that merchants could be saved.[54]

French views were similar. Christine de Pisan in the fifteenth century described merchants

> who give a tenth of their goods to the poor and who found many chapels, places of prayer, and hospitals for the poor. And so there are those of such goodness that if God pleases, they truly deserve merit in heaven and goodness and honour in the world.[55]

In fourteenth-century England, Brinton placed merchants firmly within the mystical body of society. 'Merchants and faithful mechanics' are the left hand, and 'citizens and burgesses, more or less in the middle, are its heart'.[56] The value of the merchant to the State seems to be taken for granted, but it is spelt out in the epitaph for Mayor Richard Whittington 'the sonne of marchaundye':

> That loodes sterre and chefe chosen floure.
> Whate hathe by hym oure England of honoure,
> And whate profite hathe bene of his richess,
> ...
> That penne and papere may not me suffice
> Him to describe, so high he was of prise.[57]

Fortescue regarded the numbers and wealth of merchants as attributable not to 'fortune', as the Italian humanists might have done, but to God himself:

> Yet the estate of merchants, of whom some are richer than all the justices of the realm, exceed the justices in number by thousands. This cannot be ascribed to fortune which is nothing, but, I think, is to be attributed only to the divine benediction. For the Lord says, in the words of the prophet, that 'the generation of the righteous shall be blessed'. (Ps.112.2).[58]

In England, as numerous East Anglian and Cotswold 'wool' churches, chantry chapels, stained-glass windows, elaborate tombs, and other benefactions testify, the righteous merchants themselves did not think that they were beyond salvation.

---

[52] Lopez and Raymond, *Medieval Trade*, no. 207, p. 425.
[53] Ibid., no. 202, p. 419, n. 12.   [54] Langholm, *Economics*, p. 462.
[55] Christine de Pisan, *Book of the Body Politic*, pp. 242–3.
[56] Thomas Brinton, Sermon 28, 1, p. 111. Cf. Owst, *Literature and Pulpit*, p. 554.
[57] *The Libelle of Englyshe Polycye*, ed. George Warner (Oxford, 1926), p. 25.
[58] John Fortescue, *In Praise of the Laws of England*, ch. 51, p. 75.

THE 'CIRCULAR FLOW OF WEALTH'

Successful economic nationalism demanded a healthy internal economy. Lois Roney has suggested that the controversial fourteenth-century poem *Wynnere and Wastoure*, probably written between 1352 and 1370, contains an early version of the 'circular flow' theory. According to this, the economy is seen as an organic whole, and all economic transactions are interrelated.[59] Ideally the different movements or flows should be in a state of equilibrium, so that the same money will go on circulating. This is really no more than a sophisticated way of looking at the Aristotelian theory of exchange. To take the Aristotelian examples of the farmer and the doctor, the farmer will pay for the services of the doctor, and with the money the doctor receives he will buy the produce of the farmer. A balanced economic relationship therefore exists between them. Applied to the national economy, there is a single store of resources, and money needs to be kept moving in a constant and balanced series of transactions for the health of the whole. The poem is largely a spirited debate between two household knights of the King, probably Edward III. Debate is a peaceful alternative to the armed conflict for which they had been poised. In general, Winner devotes his time to 'getting' rather than 'spending', while Waster does the opposite. On one level the poem describes individual economic behaviour. Winner manages his estates punctiliously and hoards his resources and capital. Waster, describing him, invokes the image of the miser who tosses and turns at night, sleepless with worry about his goods. He describes how Winner (who sounds like a merchant) has 'werpede [stored] thy wyde howses full of wolle sakkes, The bemys benden at the rofe, siche bakone there hynges, Stuffed are sterlynges [pounds] vndere stelen bowndes.'[60] Winner's self-confessed motto was, 'Aye when i gadir my gudes, than glades myn hert.'[61] Waster, by contrast, neglects his estates, which have fallen into ruin, fails to maintain his station in life, and spends his time in pleasure and debauchery. He underlines the futility of stockpiling goods and money. What is the point of hoarding them when 'Some rote, some ruste, some ratouns [rats] fede'?[62] Anyway, most of Winner's fortune will vanish after his death as his son and executors sue one another, or it falls into the hands of the friars 'to paint their pillars or plaster their walls' (so much for apostolic poverty!).[63]

The lifestyles described are individual ones, yet the arguments are all set within the framework of the national economy of England and the effects which the economic behaviour of the protagonists will produce. The two

[59] Lois Roney, 'Winner and Waster's "Wyse Wordes": teaching economics and nationalism in fourteenth-century England', *Speculum*, 69 (1994), pp. 1070–100, for what follows. *Wynnere and Wastoure*, ed. Stephanie Trigg, EETS, 297 (1990).
[60] Ibid., p. 9, lines 250–2. [61] Ibid., p. 9, line 227.
[62] Ibid., p. 9, lines 252–4. [63] Ibid., p. 11, lines 300–4.

are interdependent, for what Winner acquires, Waster consumes.[64] This interdependence and the need for equilibrium is neatly epitomized by the line 'Who so wele [wealth] schal wyn, a wastoure moste he fynde',[65] and by the King's observation to Waster that the more he wastes his wealth, the better Winner likes it.[66] Both consider their own economic philosophy to be patriotic and the other's to be damaging to the national economy. They represent extremes, on whom a mean needs to be imposed. They halt the circular flow of wealth by removing from the common economic stock without replacing – Winner by hoarding and Waster by non-productive spending. Both of these seem to have been particular problems in the mid-fourteenth century after military successes against France led to a deluge of booty into England. As Miskimin observes: 'There are only two possible responses to a sudden augmentation of assets – hoarding or spending.'[67] Waster's spending for consumption and display was representative of the spending of the aristocracy as a whole. Paradoxically, some of the display expenditure actually amounted to hoarding. The sumptuary legislation of 1363 and later was designed not only to ensure that people behaved and dressed in a manner appropriate to their social position, but also to ensure that supplies of precious metal were not locked up in costly dress and personal ornament at a time of bullion shortage. Luxury spending could also affect the balance of trade adversely, because most luxuries were imported. Hence the later comments in the *Libelle of Englyshe Polycye* about the great galleys of Venice and Florence, which

> Be wel ladene with thynges of complacence,
> All spicerye and other grocers ware,
> Wyth swete wynes, all manner of chaffare [merchandise],
> Apes and japes [buffooneries] and marmusettes [monkeys] taylede,
> Nifles [nicknacks], trifles that littel have availed.

In return for this frivolous merchandise the Italians exported England's 'best chaffare', the staple commodities of cloth, wool, and tin, and drained the country of gold.[68]

Winner's conduct was the alternative response to the 'sudden augmentation of assets', that is, hoarding. Again this may have been a comment on the contemporary economic situation. Munro has suggested that hoarding was a result of debasement of the coinage, and Edward III, as we saw in chapter 4, was forced to debase in the period to 1351.[69] Munro's suggestion

---

[64] Ibid., p. 9, lines 230–2. [65] Ibid., p. 13, line 390. [66] Ibid., p. 16, line 495.
[67] Miskimin, 'Monetary movements and market structure', in *Cash, Credit and Crisis*, no. 7, p. 486.
[68] *Libelle*, ed. Warner, p. 18, lines 345–9; p. 20, lines 374–6; p. 21, lines 396–8.
[69] Munro, *Wool, Cloth, and Gold*, p. 17.

is supported by the fact that the largest number of English coin hoards to be discovered all relate to the reign of Edward III.[70] Winner's 'sterlynges' stuffed 'vndere stelen bowndes' were a genuine economic problem.

'MERCANTILISM' AND THE BALANCE OF TRADE

By the late fourteenth century the conviction that trade was linked with national sovereignty was firmly in place. The conflicts which proliferated in late medieval Europe – between, for example, Bohemia and Poland, or different Italian city-states, or, perhaps above all, England and France in the Hundred Years War – were all wars about national sovereign status. Here trade could be a useful diplomatic weapon. The most obvious example is the manipulation of the English wool trade by Edward III in the early stages of the war with France. By dint of cutting off vital supplies of raw wool to the Flemish cloth industry and then masterminding an export scheme by a group of monopolists at the strategic moment, he hoped both to compel the deprived Flemings to ally with him and to raise vast sums for his war effort. As it happened, the scheme was a disaster.[71]

Sovereignty was not just a land issue, control of the sea was equally important. The anonymous author of the *Libelle of Englyshe Polycye* tried to formulate a national economic policy which would enable England both to strengthen its trading position and to triumph over its enemies.

> The trewe process of Englyshe polycye
> . . .
> Is thys, as who seith, south, north, est and west
> Cheryshe merchandyse, kepe thamryalte [naval supremacy]
> That we be maysteres of the narowe see.[72]

By 'the narrow sea', the author meant the Straits between Dover and Calais. In the 1380s Chaucer's merchant had also been concerned about trade protection:

> He wolde the see were kept for any thynge
> Bitwixe Middelburgh and Orewelle [Suffolk].[73]

---

[70] Ibid., p. 17, n. 19, citing J. D. A. Thompson, *Inventory of British Coin Hoards, 600–1500* (Oxford, 1956), p. xxvi and *passim*.
[71] E. B. Fryde, 'Edward III's wool monopoly of 1337', *History*, 37 (1952), repr. in Fryde, *Studies in Medieval Trade and Finance* (London, 1983), pp. 133–49.
[72] *Libelle*, p. 1.
[73] Geoffrey Chaucer, General Prologue to the *Canterbury Tales*, ed. Larry D. Benson, *The Riverside Chaucer*, 3rd edn (Oxford, 1988), p. 27, lines 276–7. Middelburgh was a port on the island of Walcheren on the Dutch coast, almost opposite Orwell. The wool staple was there from 1384 to 1388: T. H. Lloyd, *The English Wool Trade in the Middle Ages* (Cambridge, 1977), pp. 230–1.

His reasons were similar, since at the time (1384–8) the wool staple was at Middleburgh, and Orwell was the wool port for Ipswich. In the 1430s, when the *Libelle* was written, English commerce, especially the export of raw wool and cloth, was badly threatened due to the hostility of Philip the Good of Burgundy at a critical stage of the Hundred Years War. The wool staple was at Calais, and Dover was one of the ports from where wool was shipped. By commanding the Straits of Dover England would be able to control the commerce between Italy, Spain, and Brittany to the south, and Flanders, the Netherlands, and the Hanseatic towns to the north.[74]

A conviction underlying mercantilism was that the world contained a fixed amount of resources, which had to be 'balanced' in favour of the writer's homeland. One method was through protection. Edward III had damaged the export of English raw wool through embargoes, but he protected the production and export of English cloth, which relied on the raw material of English wool. Not only were minimal export dues imposed, but subjects were bidden to wear English cloth, and Flemish cloth weavers were invited to live in England and to share their expertise with their hosts.[75] A Yorkist partisan writing in the next century was equally concerned about balance. The export of raw wool to foreign competitors in the cloth industry meant that foreigners would have no need to buy English cloth:

> The second grievance is because wool and woolfells have course and passage out of the realm, wherefore all strangers take but little reward to buy our English cloth, but make it themselves. The remedy is this; let it be ordained that no wool or fell passes out of the country on pain of forfeiture of the goods, and the person to make fine with the king ...[76]

In 1463 several acts were passed to regulate the export of essential wool, to control the use of ships for import and export, to prohibit the import of corn when prices were low at home, and to forbid the import of a variety of wares, ranging from cloth and silk to playing-cards and tennis balls, because the English 'artificers cannot live by their mysteries and occupations, but divers of them ... are at this day unoccupied, and live miserably in great want, poverty, and need'.[77] At about the same time Fortescue recommended as a subject for discussion by the King's Council 'How the prices of merchandise grown in this land may be sustained and increased, and the prices of merchandise brought in to this land abated.'[78] The granting of monopolies, control of the sea, protection of the home

---

[74] G. A. Holmes, 'The *Libel of English Policy*', EHR, 76 (1961), pp. 193–216.
[75] A. R. Bridbury, *Medieval English Clothmaking: an Economic Survey* (London, 1982), pp. 101–4, has questioned protection policies, and therefore cost, as the major factor in the success of the English trade.
[76] *EHD*, 4, no. 600, p. 1039.   [77] Ibid., no. 602, pp. 1040–2.
[78] John Fortescue, *Governance of England*, ch. 15, p. 116.

industry, embargoes on exports, especially of raw materials, were all grist to the mill of the later mercantilists as they advised on how to swing the trade balance in favour of their national economy. Equally important to them was bullionism, the building up and conserving of supplies of precious metals to supply the mint.

BULLIONISM

In England the connection between balance of trade and bullionism was especially close, because in an area where there was no substantial mining of precious metals the only way they could enter the country was in payment for goods exported. If the balance of trade was favourable, then this is what happened. If it was unfavourable, then bullion would flow out to pay for goods imported. Thomas Mun provided a pithy summary: 'The ordinary means to increase our wealth and treasure is by *Forraign Trade*, wherein wee must ever observe this rule: to sell more to strangers yearly than wee consume of theirs in value.'[79]

There is controversy about how far such ideas were current in late medieval England. In the late fourteenth and early fifteenth centuries there was an acute shortage of silver throughout Europe, caused in part by an unfavourable balance of trade with the Levant, known as the 'Great Bullion Famine'.[80] In 1381–2, at the beginning of the crisis, the opinions of the officers of the Mint were canvassed on the 'right feeble' state of English money, and the lack of bullion. They were reinforced by the grim warning that unless something was done, 'where you think to have 5s. you will not have 4s.'. Richard Leicester's complaint was that 'the land spends too much in merchandise, as in grocery, mercery and peltry, or wines, red, white and sweet, and also in exchanges made to the Court of Rome in divers ways'. In practice, by the 1380s less money was being exported to the papal curia than at the beginning of the century. Between 1303 and 1311 the Pope had managed to extract some £40,000.[81] Leicester's remedy was that 'each merchant bringing merchandise into England take out of the commodities of the land as much as his merchandise aforesaid shall amount to; and that none carry gold or silver beyond the sea'. The result would be that 'the money that is in England will remain, and *great quantity of money and bullion will come from the parts beyond the sea*' (emphasis added).[82] Leicester's colleague Richard Aylesbury maintained that:

---

[79] Thomas Mun, *England's Treasure by Forraign Trade or The Ballance of our Forraign Trade is the Rule of our Treasure* (London, 1664), in J. R. M. McCulloch, ed., *Early English Tracts on Commerce* (Cambridge, 1970), pp. 115–209, ch. 2, p. 125.
[80] Day, 'The Great Bullion Famine', in Day, *Medieval Market Economy*, pp. 1–54.
[81] T. H. Lloyd, 'Overseas trade and the English money supply in the fourteenth century', in Mayhew, ed., *Edwardian Monetary Affairs*, pp. 96–124, at pp. 102, 105, 117.
[82] 'Opinions of Officers of the Mint', pp. 220–1.

if the merchandise which goes out of England be well and rightly governed, the money that is in England will remain and *great plenty of money will come from beyond the sea*, that is to say, let not more strange merchandise come within the realm than to the value of the denizen merchandise which passes out of the realm.[83]

The point at issue is how far these opinions foreshadowed ideas of the balance of trade as enunciated by Mun and others. Max Beer took William Cunningham to task in 1938 for calling Richard Aylesbury a mercantilist and making him into an international celebrity. Cunningham had confused two types of balance – in effect, the arithmetical balance of commutative justice and the proportional balance of distributive justice. The first type aimed at equality, the second at inequality, so that the 'balance' was in favour of one of the trading nations, and this was the type advocated by the mercantilists. Aylesbury appeared to be advocating an equal rather than a favourable balance.[84] In fact, both Leicester and Aylesbury appear to have confused the two. The idea that exports should balance imports certainly implies equality, but both officers are concerned with retaining bullion and attracting great quantities of money from overseas, which does not necessarily imply equality. Mathematically equal exchange seems to lead to a favourable balance of money and bullion. In practical terms there are some imponderables, such as differing prices in the trading nations and the currency exchange rates. In theoretical terms the fourteenth century was the time when notions of equality were changing, as exact, arithmetical justice gradually gave way to a justice based on geometrical, proportional equality.[85] It may be that in this transitional period the officers were not clear themselves about what was meant by balance or equality.

In the following century the author of the *Libelle of Englyshe Polycye* attacked the Italians for being economic parasites:

> Also they bere the golde out of thys londe
> And souke the thryfte [prosperity] awey oute of oure
>   honde;
> As the waffore [wasp] soukethe honye fro the bee,
> So mynúceth [diminishes] oure commodite.[86]

He did not discuss the balance of trade as such, but he was convinced that the whole well-being of England depended on the fostering of commerce:

---

[83] Ibid., p. 222.
[84] Max Beer, *Early British Economics from the Thirteenth to the Middle of the Eighteenth Century* (London, 1938), pp. 76–9, criticizing William Cunningham, *Growth of English Industry, Early and Middle Ages* (London, 1922), pp. 395–6. Lipson, *Economic History*, I, p. 532, n. 6 endorses Cunningham.
[85] See above, Introduction, pp. 13–14 and below, chapter 6, pp. 149–50. This is based on the work of Kaye, *Economy and Nature in the Fourteenth Century*.
[86] *Libelle*, p. 21.

> For yef marchaundes were cherisshede to here spede,
> We were not lykelye to fayle in ony nede.[87]

Similar sentiments appeared in another fifteenth-century work, *On England's Commercial Policy*. This listed three things as essential for 'sustenance' – meat, drink, and cloth, and indicated that England's surplus of cloth meant that 'we might rule and govern all Christian kings'.[88] It is true that none of these works describes a balance of trade in favour of England as Mun later expressed it, but the foundations had been laid.

Another later idea which seems to have been illustrated in practice in the medieval period was that of Gresham's law, named, probably erroneously, after Dr Thomas Gresham (1519–79), a financial adviser to Elizabeth I. His idea was that where two coinages circulate whose face values are different from their bullion content, the cheaper coin will drive out the dearer one: 'bad money drives out good'.[89] The better money will either be extracted from circulation and melted down or taken abroad, where it will command a higher price: 'men try to take their money to the places where they believe it to be worth most'. As Edward III complained in 1351, 'because our gold and silver coins are so much stronger and lower priced than coins of other kingdoms, merchants have been taking our said coins to foreign mints for their own gain, so that little coin remains in our kingdom'.[90] At a time when economies were fuelled by currencies of intrinsic value, debasement was often linked with the question of bullionism. Oresme observed, again anticipating Gresham:

alterations and debasements diminish the amount of gold and silver in the realm, since these metals, despite any embargo, are carried abroad, where they command a higher value. For men try to take their money to the places where they believe it to be worth most. And this reduces the material for money in the realm.[91]

The operation of Gresham's law, or a variation of it, is especially well illustrated in late medieval England. The relatively sound state of the English currency compared with those of other European states brought its own problems, those of clipping and counterfeiting, which led to the deterioration of the coinage. Edward I took draconian measures against

---

[87] Ibid., p. 25, lines 483–4.
[88] Anon, 'On England's Commercial Policy', *Political Poems and Songs*, RS, 14, 2 (1861), p. 283.
[89] A. E. Feavearyear, *The Pound Sterling: a History of English Money*, 2nd edn rev. E. Victor Morgan (Oxford, 1963), pp. 78–9; H. A. Miskimin, 'The enforcement of Gresham's law', in *Cash, Credit, and Crisis*, no. 9, pp. 147–61. In general see Raymond de Roover, *Gresham on Foreign Exchange* (Cambridge, MA, and London, 1949).
[90] T. Rymer, *Foedera*, 3, pt. 1 (1740, reprinted Farnborough, 1967), ann. 1351, p. 67a. 223–4.
[91] Nicholas Oresme, *De moneta*, ch. 20, p. 32.

coin-clippers in 1278, but it by no means eradicated them. Over a century later, in Langland's *Piers Plowman*, Avarice confessed to having learnt from Jews and Lombards how to weigh coins, clip the heaviest, and then lend them out 'for loue of the crosse', a nice *double entendre*, referring also to the cross on the back of the penny.[92] During the reign of Edward I the activities of Jews, private individuals, and corrupt mint officials in clipping coins, cutting them illegally to make halfpennies and farthings, and making defective new money all contributed to the poor state of the currency at a time of severe bullion shortage. Prices rose while confidence plummeted. The recoinage of 1279–81 was so successful in restoring stability, however, that it created another problem. Gresham's law operated again: 'men try to take their money to the places where they believe it to be worth most'. Initially merchants started to take English money abroad, rather than buying English goods with it. This enabled the princes of Europe, especially those of the Low Countries, to manufacture counterfeit English coins, known as crockards and pollards, of inferior weight and fineness for use in the wool trade. These soon found their way to England in large quantities, which served to encourage the export of genuine coins even more. Edward refused to debase the coinage, but instead ordered a recoinage of the counterfeit money, in the process of which he demonetized it, making 2 pollards worth 1 sterling. Although this restored the standard of the coinage, it caused considerable hardship to those who held pollards, because it halved the value of their money. Then, by the Statute of Stepney of May 1299, he forbade anyone to import crockards and pollards 'on pain of forfeiture of life and goods and whatever else he can forfeit', prohibited the export of English silver coin and plate, set up tables at Dover and other ports for changing money for travellers' necessary expenses, and appointed wardens in all ports to police the system.[93] By the end of Edward's reign the stability of the coinage had been restored, but the problem of foreign counterfeits was to recur in the 1340s, at a time of acute shortage of silver, with forgeries known as lusshebournes, and in the 1400s with the galley halfpence.

If Gresham's law operated where two silver coinages were in circulation, it also applied where both gold and silver were current. The principle again was that cheaper money, in this case silver, forced out the more intrinsically expensive gold. Gold was likely to flow away from regions where it was undervalued in terms of silver to where it was worth more,

[92] William Langland, *Piers Plowman*, B, passus v, lines 242–4, p. 150.
[93] This paragraph is based on Mate, 'Monetary policies in England', pp. 34–79. For the Statute see *EHD*, 4, no. 82, p. 494. On crockards and pollards see N. J. Mayhew and D. R. Walker, 'Crockards and pollards: imitation and the problem of fineness in a silver coinage', Mayhew, ed., *Edwardian Monetary Affairs*, pp. 125–46.

while silver would flow the other way. In the seventh century, there was a world redistribution of gold and silver, based on their relative prices. Gold moved from Europe, and silver flowed in – which was why the silver penny became current and the reforms of monarchs like Charlemagne and Offa were based on it. The gold moved towards Byzantium and the Islamic world, so that Byzantium lost its silver and acquired gold, which commanded a high price there. The Islamic Empire, where the gold–silver ratio was in between that of Europe and Byzantium, at least initially, kept a mathematical mean and maintained a bi-metallic currency in the eighth and ninth centuries.[94] Soon, however, the 'silver famine' became general throughout the Muslim world.

Silver returned to the East from Europe during the twelfth century, enabling it to revert to using silver as its main coinage. But of course this had the effect of disturbing the balance, and was ultimately to lead to a reverse movement: gold came West. During the thirteenth century, at about the same time that silver became predominant in the East, Europe started to introduce a bi-metallic currency. Ultimately this was to lead to the minting and circulation of gold coins throughout Europe, to what has been called the 'victory of gold', and to a corresponding shortage of silver. The turning-point occurred in 1252, when Florence issued a gold florin and Genoa a new genovivo.[95] This was followed in 1284 by the Venetian ducat. The gold came largely from West Africa, but early in the fourteenth century a rich new source in the kingdom of Hungary, at Kremnica in Slovakia, started to be mined, which encouraged the gradual spread of gold to the rest of Europe.[96]

Supply of gold bullion was not the only factor: there was also the question of demand. It was impractical to make large payments at home, and even more so abroad, in the small unit of the silver penny. In England, as in France, some gold coinage had been known during the thirteenth century. In both countries, however, there was a feeling that gold coinage was not 'real' money, and its use was limited to hoarding and to royal and noble almsgiving at shrines like that of St Thomas at Canterbury.[97] As late as 1307 the papal tax collectors had to transport £4,000 in silver from England as far as Paris before it could be exchanged for gold florins.[98] The

---

[94] Andrew Watson, 'Back to gold – and silver', *EconHR*, ser. 2, 20 (1967), pp. 1–34, at p. 5.
[95] Ibid.
[96] Spufford, *Money and its Use*, pp. 267–8. The standard account of mining is J. U. Nef, 'Mining and metallurgy in medieval civilisation' in *The Cambridge Economic History of Europe*, 2 (Cambridge, 1952): see esp. pp. 433–58.
[97] Spufford, *Money and its Use*, pp. 183–4.
[98] Ibid., p. 277; W. E. Lunt, *Papal Revenues in the Middle Ages*, 2 vols. (New York, 1934), 2, nos. 356–63, pp. 236–9, no. 378, pp. 257–9.

reason for English tardiness may have been that the commercial revolution occurred later in England than it did in Italy and the Low Countries. The export of raw wool also meant that England's trade balance with Europe was favourable in the thirteenth century, and there was therefore little need to export large amounts of bullion.[99]

In the early fourteenth century the price of gold in England in relation to silver was higher than on the Continent, and this was where the problem lay. The price encouraged Italian merchants and bankers, such as the Bardi and Peruzzi, to import gold into England, taking out silver in exchange. This led to a shortage of English currency, particularly silver, and the Florentine florin started to circulate. In 1331, in order to protect silver, Edward III insisted that gold coins should not be accepted as payment in England, and he set up exchange tables at the ports for French royals and Florentine florins to prevent any more entering the country.[100] The situation changed dramatically, however, when he was forced to borrow vast sums, largely from the Italians, to purchase continental allies at the outbreak of the Hundred Years War. Much of the money was conveyed in gold direct from the Bardi and Peruzzi in Florence to Valenciennes.[101] This situation emphasized the need for a gold coinage. Philip VI had already started to mint gold écus, in 1337, to buy potential allies. Edward III experimented first with a gold 'leopard' coin early in 1344, which failed, partly due to the reluctance of the English to accept it, but it was quickly followed by the gold noble. The profits of both the war and the wool trade, remitted to England in gold, ensured sufficient supplies for vast numbers of nobles to be struck until the 1360s. By the mid-fourteenth century gold coinage had triumphed over silver, both in England and throughout Europe.[102]

Gold in Europe, and especially in England, was overvalued in terms of silver, which meant that it was likely to flow in, while the copious silver for which it was exchanged, flowed out. Despite efforts to keep them out, there is evidence of large numbers of florins in England in the 1330s, and that they were being hoarded and used as security and to pay off debts.[103] The idea that 'all that is rare is expensive' did not apply, for in England

[99] Carlo M. Cipolla, 'Currency depreciation in medieval Europe', *EconHR*, ser. 2, 15 (1963), pp. 413–21, at p. 419.
[100] Mate, 'The role of gold coinage', p. 127.
[101] Spufford, *Money and its Use*, pp. 277–8. Prestwich, 'Currency and the economy', in Mayhew, ed., *Edwardian Monetary Affairs*, pp. 46–7 points out that money which would normally have come to England, such as customs revenue and wool profits, was being diverted to finance the war effort in the Low Countries.
[102] Spufford, *Money and its Use*, pp. 183–6, 267–82; Watson, 'Back to gold – and silver', pp. 1–7; Mate, 'The role of gold coinage', pp. 126–41, esp. 127–32.
[103] Mate, 'The role of gold coinage', p. 128; Prestwich, 'Currency and the economy', p. 48.

in the late 1330s silver was paradoxically both cheap in terms of gold and scarce. The 'Song against the King's Taxes' of 1339 recommended that Edward III should melt down his plate and coin it, so that he could stop using wooden tallies. He could then eat off wood and pay with silver, rather than vice versa.[104] In March 1340 Parliament ordered merchants to supply the mint with 2 marks in silver plate for every sack of wool they exported, a policy repeated in various forms on ten subsequent occasions up to 1470.[105] The European silver shortage started in the thirteenth century, and the first English 'bullionist' legislation forbidding the export of silver occurred in 1278. By 1344, the year the gold noble was issued, no gold in plate or bullion might be exported, and from 1364 all export of gold and silver without royal licence was banned.[106]

It seems that the English King and Parliament were capable of understanding the importance of building up supplies of bullion and specie. They could also appreciate the principle that cheap, or even bad, money drives out the good and more expensive. Perhaps Gresham's law should be renamed as the law of the Plantagenets.

CONCLUSION

The commercial climate of the late medieval period led to a transformation in views on trade and merchants. The merchant's role became pivotal in the economic nationalism that fuelled international politics and warfare. In the course of this, many of the principles which would later characterize 'the mercantile system', such as bullionism and the balance of trade, were expressed and implemented by legislation and action. There was also an awareness of the likely effects of debasement and of clipping and counterfeiting the coinage on the balance of trade and the economic health of the nation. The fact that some of these ideas, which foreshadowed those of the seventeenth and eighteenth centuries, found expression at this period is an indication that economic practice tends to anticipate economic theory.

---

[104] *Anglo-Norman Political Songs*, ed. Isabel S. T. Aspin, *Anglo-Norman Texts*, 11 (Oxford, 1953), p. 111.
[105] Munro, 'Bullionism and the bill of exchange', pp. 192–3.
[106] Ibid., p. 192, and see Appendix B for a list of export prohibitions.

6

THE JUST PRICE AND THE JUST WAGE

INTRODUCTION

Prices and wages were closely connected and often discussed together in the medieval period. According to a thirteenth-century Roman lawyer, 'A price is given according to the estimate of a thing, but a wage according to the estimate of the *use* of a thing.'[1] In estimating a wage, the 'thing' being used was labour: a wage was the price for the use of someone's labour. Yet often the labour of a craftsman or merchant was one of the factors taken into account when a price was fixed, so that, too, was to some extent a 'wage'. In scholastic literature prices tended to overshadow wages because scholastics were not usually wage-earners. Lawyers, however, were equally concerned with both, if only because they involved the legal concept of justice.

Justice became attached to prices and wages because both were the result of a balance, supposedly a fair one, achieved between two parties, seller and buyer or employer and employee. As Aquinas appreciated:

a reward is something repaid to someone in return for work, as a sort of price paid for it. Thus just as the payment of the just price for goods received from someone is an act of justice, so too the payment of a reward for work is an act of justice.[2]

Scholastics and lawyers built on different foundations – the former on divine law and on Aristotle's *Nicomachean Ethics* (v, v); the latter on certain

---

[1] Rolandino Passageri, *Summa totius artis notariae* (Venice, 1546), fol. 117v: quoted by Steven A. Epstein, 'The theory and practice of the just wage', *Journal of Medieval History*, 17 (1991), p. 59.
[2] Thomas Aquinas, *Summa theologiae*, 1a2ae, 114, 1, vol. 30, p. 203.

texts of Roman law. This often led them to differing conclusions. We shall explore these differing solutions, as well as those of various types of official – government, urban, market, or gild – to justice in the establishment and implementation of just wages and prices. It will be structured according to three methods of arriving at a figure for the price of goods or services: the first was to accept the current market price, later known as the 'natural price'; the second was for it to be fixed by a public authority; the third was for it to be freely negotiated. This method covered salaries as well as wages, and the social status of the individuals might well be a factor. These three were separate models, but it was quite likely that they would overlap, so that when the official or 'legal' price was fixed, reference would be made to the 'natural' one; when parties were haggling, they might well use either the 'legal' or the 'natural' price as a bench mark. Each of the three could be upset in different ways by fraud or deceit, especially by 'monopoly'. Whether all, or any, of these methods resulted in a 'just' price or wage, however, depended upon such questions as what was meant by terms such as justice and equality, and whether they were absolute or relative. Much of the foundation for such speculations lay in the Aristotelian tradition, which must be examined first.

JUSTICE AND THE ARISTOTELIAN TRADITION

In his *Nicomachean Ethics* (v, v) Aristotle set up a model of justice in exchange which is fundamental to the idea of the just price. He did not discuss the just wage as such, because the society in which he lived was based largely on slavery, but his model generated ideas amongst later commentators which were applicable to both subjects. Aristotle's real concern was to apply justice to exchange. In its widest sense he saw justice as a state of mind which disposed someone to act rightly. It was righteousness itself, and as such it was the epitome of all virtue. 'Justice . . . is not a part of virtue, but virtue entire.'[3] For him virtue consisted in a mean. The just or virtuous person was one who avoided all extremes, and whose disposition led him to apply the mean, or moderation, to his behaviour. Justice in the sense of righteousness was a universal quality. When he discussed justice in exchange, however, his concern was with 'particular' rather than universal justice – justice as applied to relationships between people. This was divided into two types. The first was distributive justice, which allotted things to people in proportion to either their status or their contribution to the community (and, of course, the two were often linked). It could be applied especially to the relationship between the individual and the

[3] Aristotle, *Ethics*, v, ii, p. 109.

State. In effect, whoever put in most should be able to take out most. This type of justice was arrived at by the application of a geometrical mean. This meant that it operated on the basis of proportion rather than of strict numerical equality, and therefore allowed some latitude. The other type of justice, corrective, or rectificatory, was based on the arithmetical mean, which entailed strict equality, like the heaps of hay facing Buridan's ass. Here status and proportion were not factors. Corrective justice sought to establish an equal relationship between two individuals, and was therefore the foundation of contracts of exchange, of buying and selling, of lending, borrowing, and hiring. Distributive, proportional, justice came to regulate public relationships, and was the foundation of public law, whereas corrective justice, which 'corrected' inequalities between people on a 'one to one' basis, regulated private matters.

Within this context Aristotle tried to describe the workings of justice – of equality – in exchange. It was a vitally important subject, because exchange was what cemented society together: 'for neither would there have been association if there were not exchange, nor exchange if there were not equality, nor equality if there were not commensurability'.[4] He set up different pairs of potential exchangers, a builder and a shoemaker, a farmer and a shoemaker, and a carpenter and a builder, who were attempting to trade their unequal products with each other – food for shoes, beds for a house, and so on. The problem was to show how these disparate things could be measured against one another – how they could become 'commensurate'. The way this was done was through an intermediate, money, which, as he asserted, 'measures all things, and therefore the excess and the defect – how many shoes are equal to a house or to a given amount of food'.[5] Of course, as Aristotle admitted, it was impossible that 'things differing so much should become commensurate, but with reference to *demand* they may become so sufficiently'.[6] What was being measured by money was human need. But while need was the predominant factor, the philosopher did not omit the 'wage' element, because he recognized that inherent in the price or value of the goods being exchanged was the 'labour' of the craftsmen involved: 'The builder, then, must get from the shoemaker the latter's work, and must himself give him in return his own.'[7]

Two historians of economic thought, Odd Langholm and Joel Kaye, have focused attention on *Ethics* (v, v). Langholm considers it important 'because it caused a cost and a demand interpretation of value to rub repeatedly against one another in the Aristotelian commentary tradition' (something to be discussed later).[8] Joel Kaye has concentrated on the fact

---

[4] Ibid., v, v, p. 120.   [5] Ibid., p. 119.   [6] Ibid., pp. 120–1.
[7] Ibid., p. 118.   [8] Langholm, *Economics*, p. 412.

that the equality achieved between Aristotle's disparate pairs of exchangers was geometrical, proportional equality, rather than strict arithmetical equality. From the late thirteenth century the concept of equality found in the works of the scholastics gradually changed from the arithmetical to the geometrical. Proportional equality was something which prevailed in the market-place, and it was the actual dynamics of the market which, consciously or unconsciously, influenced the ideas of the scholastics on the just price.[9]

The current market price

Raymond de Roover long ago argued that far from being an ivory-towered scholastic concept, the just price was 'simply the current market price'.[10] While there is no doubt of the existence of the 'current market price', and that it was recognized as such, by scholastics, by lawyers, and by officials whose duty it was to enforce it, it is less clear whether it was actually 'just'. Moreover, discussions on the current market price were set within the context of a localized market, without any attempt to place it within the national economy. The influence of local supply and demand, and of the labour and expenses of the seller were discussed, but not issues of the wider economy, such as the level or state of the coinage in circulation, which, as we have seen, could also affect prices.[11]

The legal origins of the idea of the current market price went back a long way. A celebrated Roman law text in the *Digest* affirmed that the value of a thing was the price for which it could be sold, in other words, the current market price.[12] Canon law supplied *Placuit*, originally a capitulary of Carloman of the Franks of 884. The clergy were to order their parishioners not to charge strangers more for things than the price charged in the local market, otherwise the travellers could refer the matter to the priest, who was then to set the price 'with humanity'.[13] These were current prices, but not necessarily just. Nevertheless, the Englishman Alexander of Hales, commenting on *Placuit*, connected justice with the normal price of things. In listing the conditions under which trade was licit, he suggested that it should be conducted 'by a just estimation of the thing, and by commerce, according to the way it is commonly sold in that city or place where trade occurs'.[14] Albert the Great declared that

---

[9] Kaye, *Economy and Nature*.
[10] Raymond de Roover, 'The concept of the just price: theory and economic policy', *Journal of Economic History*, 18 (1958), pp. 418–38.
[11] See ch. 5, pp. 101–4 and 101, n. 63, above.
[12] *Digest*, 36, 1, 1, 16.   [13] *Decretales*, 3, 17, 1, col. 518.
[14] Alexander of Hales, *Summa theologica*, 4 vols. (Quaracchi, 1924–48), 4, pt. 2, bk. 3, tract 2, sect. 2, q. 11, tit. 3, 490, p. 723b.

the just price was what goods were worth according to the estimation of the market at the time of the sale.[15] Aquinas was more cautious. He told a story (borrowed from Cicero) of a wheat seller approaching a city during a famine. The seller knew that others were following him and that when they arrived the increased supply of wheat would drive the price down. Should the seller admit this, or should he simply sell his wheat at the current market price, the price which he 'finds'? Aquinas reluctantly allowed him to sell, but added that 'a disclosure or a reduction in price would spell more abounding virtue, yet is not required in strict justice'.[16] 'Strict justice' seemed to involve accepting the market price, even if justice in this case had parted company from virtue.

The word 'common', which occurred in many of the sources, had a double meaning – not just 'usual' but also 'shared' or belonging to the community. This was the sense which emerged from legal discussions. The Roman lawyers Azo (d. 1220) and Accursius (d. 1260), who glossed the famous dictum that 'things are worth as much as they sell for', had both added the significant words *sed communiter*, but commonly.[17] In doing so, they were echoing two other texts of the *Digest* which stated that 'the price of things is not from the affection or utility of single persons, but from their common estimation'.[18] One of Azo's pupils, Laurentius Hispanus, deliberately combined the Roman law texts: 'A thing is worth what it can be sold for, for the price of things is not estimated on the basis of the affection of single individuals, but commonly.'[19] This idea was to be repeated right up to the fifteenth century, when it was taken up by the great preacher Bernardino of Siena.[20] But what did it mean? How were things to be estimated 'commonly'? Almost certainly it meant that the current market price was the result of the workings of the impersonal laws of the market, dominated by the forces of demand and supply, and combined with the objective factors of cost and labour involved in the production and sale of the goods.

DEMAND AND SUPPLY

Support for a 'demand interpretation' can be drawn from Roman law. It also emerges from Aristotle's insistence that demand was the unifying

---

[15] De Roover, 'Just price', p. 422.
[16] Thomas Aquinas, *Summa theologica*, 2a2ae, 77, 3 ad 4, vol. 38, p. 223.
[17] For Azo, Langholm, *Economics*, p. 261; for Accursius, de Roover, *San Bernardino*, p. 20.
[18] *Digest*, 9, 2, 33 and 35, 2, 63.   [19] Quoted by Langholm, *Economics*, p. 261.
[20] Bernardino of Siena, Sermo 33, *Opera omnia*, 4, *Sermones Quadragesimale de Evangelio Aeterno* (Quaracchi, 1956), p. 157, line 36; p. 158, lines 1–2, 8.

factor against which all commodities had to be measured and which came to be expressed in terms of money. As Langholm has shown, Albert the Great extracted, probably by accident, both a 'market' and a 'cost' interpretation from Aristotle's crucial chapter about the farmer and the shoemaker's exchanges. He wrote two commentaries; in the first he used a translation featuring the Latin word *opus*, meaning work, and ironed out the differences in the value of farmers' and shoemakers' products: 'with regard to communal toil and trouble, they are sufficiently measured'. In the second he used a later translation featuring the word *indigentia* – need or demand. It was this which held goods in an exchange together. They ought to be valued 'in relation to use, that is according to their ability in use to supply need, for in that way all are one, and in that way all can be measured by one, which ... is called money'.[21] Albert provided perhaps the first example of the 'cost and demand interpretations rubbing against each other'.[22]

Much the same can be said of his pupil. Aquinas accepted that labour and expenses might be a factor in determining value, although he placed more weight on demand. Using examples from Augustine's *City of God* he cited the scale of natural perfection in which living things were placed above inanimate ones. But men did not always follow this, for they might prefer having bread in the house to having mice; and sometimes a slave girl might be of less value than a pearl.[23] In the human, economic scale, as opposed to God's scale, things were valued according to need and according to money, as Aquinas pointed out, commenting on *Ethics*.[24] On the other hand, he was quite prepared to admit that the price of a thing might increase due to the seller's labour and the risk he encountered.[25]

But this was not the whole picture. What about supply? Aquinas recognized the influence of supply on prices in the moral conundrum about the wheat seller in the famine.[26] The French Spiritual Franciscan Peter Olivi (d. 1298) recognized the impetus of both supply and demand. Combining the two, he explained that the scarcer a thing is, the more we demand it – and the less likely we are to be able to get it and use it. Concentrating on supply, he explained that corn was worth more in times of scarcity than when everyone had plenty. By the same token, earth, air, fire, and water

---

[21] Langholm, *Economics*, p. 187, quoting Albert the Great, *First Commentary on the Ethics*, p. 345; *Second Commentary*, pp. 358–9. See also on these passages, Kaye, *Economy and Nature*, pp. 68–9.
[22] Langholm, *Economics*, p. 190.   [23] Augustine, *City of God*, xi, 16, p. 448.
[24] Thomas Aquinas, Commentary on *Ethics*, 1133a, 31–2: cited in Langholm, *Economics*, p. 230.
[25] Thomas Aquinas, *Summa theologiae*, 2a2ae, 77, 4 ad 2, vol. 38, p. 229.
[26] See p. 136 above.

were cheaper than gold and balsam, because they were abundant, although the four elements were essential for our lives.[27] The theologian Henry of Hesse also appreciated that prices were determined by supply and demand. In terms of supply, wine was going to be more expensive at some times than at others, and more so in areas where grapes did not grow than where they did. In estimating the exchange value of something, what mattered was not the natural value, which would make a mouse worth more than all the gold in the world, but its value in terms of its usefulness. Value had to be decided on the basis of the common need of those who were able to communicate among themselves in a particular region or city.[28]

The scholastics seemed to equate the current market price with the just price, and most allowed that the market price would be determined by the forces of both supply and demand and by labour and cost. Reasoning on the just wage was similar. St Bernardino of Siena, relying on Olivi, declared that the price of goods would be estimated by the community of citizens working together. Similarly, when fixing people's wages their status, office, and dignity would be considered, so that a duke would earn more than a soldier.[29] Antoninus of Florence also opted for 'common estimation'. Wages, like prices, were determined by 'common estimation in the absence of fraud', by which he meant any attempts to interfere with the freedom of the labour market by either employers or employees.[30]

MONOPOLY

The 'natural' price of goods and services could operate only if the free flow of the market was undisturbed. Monopoly disturbed it. In terms of exchange, monopoly meant the creation of artificial scarcities of necessities (as opposed to luxuries) in order to make a cash profit. It violated justice in the form of the just price, because it forced an unjust price on the market and injured the whole of society. Aristotle had vilified it under the heading of 'retail trade', something which violated the mean of justice, because it involved unlimited acquisition: 'There is no limit to the end it seeks; and the end it seeks is wealth of the sort we have mentioned [that is, currency] and the mere acquisition of money.'[31] He made his point with the story of the philosopher Thales of Miletus. Reproached for his poverty, which apparently demonstrated the uselessness of philosophers, he used his knowledge of meteorology to predict a good year for olive

[27] Peter Olivi, *De emptionibus et venditionibus*, ed. Giacomo Todeschini (Rome, 1980), p. 53.
[28] Henry of Hesse, *De contractibus*, pt. 1, ch. 5, p. 187r.
[29] Bernardino, Sermon 35, art. 2, ch. 3, p. 198. Cf. De Roover, *San Bernardino*, pp. 20–4.
[30] Ibid., p. 24.   [31] Aristotle, *Politics*, I, ix, 13, 1257a, p. 26.

growers. He then bought up all the olive presses, and when the seasonal demand became heavy he was able to let them out for whatever price he chose. He thus demonstrated the practical usefulness of philosophy – and made a fortune into the bargain.[32]

Roman law dealt sternly with monopoly. The Emperor Diocletian imposed the death penalty in 301, though his edict was probably repealed soon after.[33] Zeno (474–91) confiscated all the goods of the monopolists and sent them into perpetual exile.[34] Echoing this, Alexander of Hales condemned monopolists as 'abominable', especially those dealing with the necessities of life. Commenting on *Eiciens*, he declared that they should be thrown out of the Church.[35]

In practice, the most common monopolistic offences were the closely related ones of engrossing, forestalling, and regrating. All of these involved interference with the free flow of the market by creating an artificial scarcity, and all of them therefore affected the current market price. In origin the terms were innocuous enough but they gradually became associated with the abuses which their particular branch of commerce occasioned. Engrossing originally meant wholesale dealing (hence the term 'grocer', because he sold in the gross),[36] but it came to mean buying up supplies in advance, often of corn, and withholding them from the market until the price had risen. The illegality of buying up wine and corn in the autumn to induce scarcity and push up prices is specifically condemned by Albert the Great.[37] Condemnation became positive law in England when towns such as London and Bristol legislated that no one should store up grain from one market to another to sell at a higher price. Such offenders risked losing their stock.[38]

Forestallers literally bought up goods (including corn) 'before the stall', that is, on their way to market, and therefore cheaply, to resell them later at a profit. From the mid-thirteenth century, regulations to prevent forestalling were often included in either the statutes of gilds merchant or in the town charters bought from the Crown. The most comprehensive definition (incorporated into a statute of 1307) was that of 1274, drawn up for the use of the King's Marshalsea court clerks. The forestaller was one who

---

[32] Ibid., I, xi, 8, 1259a, p. 31.
[33] Raymond de Roover, 'Monopoly theory prior to Adam Smith: a revision', in Kirschner, ed., *Business, Banking, and Economic Thought*, p. 274.
[34] *Codex*, 4, 59.
[35] Alexander of Hales, *Summa theologica*, 4, bk. 3, pt. 2, tract 2, sect. 2, q. 2, tit. 3, 490, p. 724b. Cf. Langholm, *Economics*, p. 131.
[36] Skeat, notes to William Langland, *Piers Plowman*, B, passus 3, 80, p. 43, n. 82.
[37] Langholm, *Economics*, p. 179.   [38] Lipson, *Economic History*, p. 301.

hurries out before other men...to meet grain, fish, herring or other kinds of goods coming for sale by land or water, thirsting for evil profit...and he contrives to carry off these goods unjustly and to sell much more dearly.

The scale of penalties ranged from fines and confiscation of goods to expulsion from the city.[39] Two examples from Norwich demonstrate the effect of forestalling on prices. In 1374/75 Roger Calf 'bought by forestalment four boats full of oysters at divers times'. The result was that the price for 100 rose by $1\frac{1}{2}$d in one day.[40] There were also complaints about Roger de Bergham who bought 'by forestalment divers kinds of corn, going to meet it in streets and lanes, at gates and bridges... to the great heightening of the market'.[41]

Regraters, or more often regratresses, were originally just retail traders or hucksters. After a catalogue of the frauds committed by Avarice's wife in *Piers Plowman*, Langland says of Rose the regrater that 'She had been a huckster all her life.'[42] Often regraters were in effect bakers' delivery girls. The *White Book of London* demonstrates the origin of the expression 'a baker's dozen', for the regratresses made their profit by reselling single loaves of bread, apparently at the regulation price, previously bought in bulk 'according to the ancient manner', that is, thirteen loaves for the price of twelve from the baker.[43] Ale was often sold by women, and in 1320 regraters – almost certainly regratresses – were forbidden to sell ale on London Bridge.[44]

Regrating, however, could have a more pejorative meaning, and could be equated with monopoly in general. The Scottish-born Oxford philosopher, John Duns Scotus (d. 1308) described those who bought and sold goods merely in order to profit, without adding any service in the form of improvement or transport, as 'regraters'. Such people stood in the way of free exchange and caused prices to rise for buyers and fall for sellers, and so harmed everyone. In his opinion they ought to be banished.[45]

Monopoly applied just as much to wages as prices. There is evidence from the late fourteenth century when labour was especially scarce of people acting as middle men between employer and wage-earner and monopolizing the supply. They were, in effect, setting up employment agencies. In 1381, for example, Henry Maddy of Lincolnshire was described as a

---

[39] R. H. Britnell, '*Forestall*, forestalling and the Statute of Forestallers', *EHR*, 102 (1987), pp. 89–102, at p. 94, and Britnell, *Commercialisation of English Society*, p. 93.
[40] *Leet Jurisdiction in the City of Norwich*, ed. William Hudson, Selden Society, 5 (1892), p. 63.
[41] Ibid., p. 62.
[42] William Langland, *Piers Plowman*, B, passus v, lines 226–7, p. 148.
[43] Riley, *Memorials of London*, p. 232.
[44] Ibid., p. 137.   [45] Langholm, *Economics*, p. 408.

'common forestaller of labourers and servants so that no-one in the neighbourhood is able to hire any servant without his approval and aid', and a painter in the city was described as 'the chief engrosser of craftsmen in the city'.[46] Leaving aside the elastic use of terms like forestaller and engrosser, the implication that the free flow of the market was being disturbed is clear. It is more explicit in the case of a certain Robert Archer who led half a dozen labourers out of his Norfolk village at harvest time in 1378. He was specifically accused of causing a labour shortage and pushing up wages.[47]

Accusations of monopoly and restrictive practices have always stuck firmly to the gilds. Their very nature as societies formed to protect a common interest, either that of the general trade of a town, in the case of the gilds merchant, or that of a particular craft or occupation, in the case of the craft gilds, lent itself to such indictments. The gilds merchant were set up to control the trading interests of a town, and were monopolistic to the extent that either they severely restricted the trading opportunities of non-members, or excluded them altogether. The following example from Southampton is a good illustration:

And no one, except a gildsman, shall buy honey, suet, salt, herring, nor any kind of oil, nor mill-stones, nor fresh leather, nor any kind of fresh skins; nor keep a wine-tavern, nor sell cloth by retail, except on market and fair day.[48]

There is not much sense of the 'free flow' of the market here. If the regulations did not control prices directly, their restrictive character would have done so indirectly. Alan Basset, lord of High Wycombe, destroyed its merchant gild in 1224 specifically because he thought that the town would benefit from freedom of trade for all.[49]

By restricting trade the gilds merchant affected the current market price. The craft gilds, however, affected both the current market price and the current market wage, if only because they covered every aspect of trade and commerce – both those who sold or manufactured goods for a price and those who provided a service for a wage, such as the masons or the carpenters. Membership of each craft gild or mystery was originally limited to those who worked in a particular occupation. The gilds were responsible overall for protecting the livelihood of their members. They controlled

[46] Christopher Dyer with Simon A. C. Penn, 'Wages and earnings in late medieval England: evidence from the enforcement of the labour laws', repr. in Dyer, *Everyday Life in Medieval England* (London and Rio Grande, 1994), p. 178.
[47] Ibid.
[48] Ordinances of Southampton, Charles Gross, *The Gild Merchant*, 2 vols. (Oxford, 1890) 1, p. 47; 2, p. 281, no. 20.
[49] Edward Miller and John Hatcher, *Medieval England: Towns, Commerce and Crafts 1086–1348* (London, 1995), p. 296.

standards of work, working hours and conditions, entry to the craft, the number of apprentices each master might have, wages and, sometimes, prices.

Craft gilds might legitimately fix 'legal' prices; they might also, illegitimately, interfere with the current market price. The effect of restricting entry to a gild and either cornering the market or monopolizing the available work could only be to raise prices. For example, the University of Oxford accused the cordwainers of pushing up the price of shoes by restricting entry to the gild in 1315, in 1321, and yet again in 1465.[50] The most serious violation of the just price was where members of a craft combined to fix a price and deliberately monopolized or upset the current market price. In 1300, for example, the Norwich chandlers had 'fixed' among themselves an extortionate price for a pound of candles, below which they would not sell; they were accordingly fined.[51] A Wyclifite tract cursed all new fraternities, especially merchants, grocers, and victuallers, who 'conspired wickedly together' that none of them 'schal bie over a certeyn pris', knowing full well that what they were buying was worth more.[52] Nor were such practices peculiar to England. In Italy the statutes of many city-states contained clauses forbidding any 'combinations' formed for the purpose of increasing or decreasing prices, and in Florence especially legislation of 1293 and later prohibited all 'conspiracies, monopolies, leagues, or pacts' which aimed to manipulate prices.[53]

The gilds had a specific responsibility to fix wages, which meant that they were not directly concerned with the 'natural' price of labour. Indeed, in fixing wages, they were immobilizing their natural movement. What was likely to affect the laws of supply and demand for labour was the monopoly which the gilds might gain over the work available in a particular area. The lawyers considered that craftsmen should not unite for an unjust purpose – that is, one that was restrictive or monopolistic. The jurist Bartolus, for example, forbade them to make regulations by which 'another is prejudiced, as for instance if they make a law that only certain people and no others can exercise that craft'. He also prohibited them from making agreements that 'a job begun by one man may not be finished by someone else'.[54] Both these actions could have created a scarcity of labour within a particular occupation and allowed the gild masters to fix a high wage.

---

[50] H. E. Salter, *Medieval Oxford*, Oxford Historical Society, 100 (1936), pp. 61–2.
[51] *Leet Jurisdiction in Norwich*, p. 52.
[52] John Wyclif (?), *The Grete Sentence of Curs Expounded*, ed. Thomas Arnold, in *Select English Works of John Wyclif*, 3 (Oxford, 1871), ch. 28, p. 333.
[53] De Roover, 'Just price', pp. 418–38, at p. 433.
[54] Bartolus on *Digest*, 47, 22, 4: quoted by Anthony Black, *Guilds and Civil Society in European Political Thought from the Twelfth Century to the Present* (London, 1984), pp. 17–18.

It might also have had the effect of driving the current market wage for non-members down, because in order to secure any work they would have been tempted to undercut the gild prices.

The fixed or legal price

Bernardino of Siena considered that the just price could be fixed either by the estimation current in the market or by the public authorities for the common good[55] – that is, by the 'natural' or the 'legal' price.[56] Antoninus of Florence advocated price fixing by the State.[57] On the whole the scholastics were more concerned with the natural price than the legal. In the mid- to late fourteenth century Henry of Hesse was one of the first to discuss official price-fixing. He considered it necessary to prevent the rich, the idle, the avaricious, the dishonest, and above all the usurers, from taking advantage of honest workers and the poor.[58] It was only if the authorities failed to fix the price that the parties to the sale contract had to evaluate things.[59] In France the conciliar theorist and Chancellor of the University of Paris, Jean Gerson (d. 1428), who was an admirer of Hesse,[60] recommended that all prices, meaning not just those of essentials, should be fixed by the State. This was because the authorities were in a better position to assess things than the individual.[61]

It seems that the practice of fixing the legal price anticipated the theoretical discussion. Philip the Fair had attempted to fix the price of grain in Paris in 1304.[62] In England prices of essentials were being fixed from the thirteenth century.

As we have seen, price-fixing by king or Parliament was closely linked with weights and measures, especially in legislation like Henry III's Assizes of Bread and Ale (1266).[63] As with weights and measures, there were enormous local variations, and urban or manorial officials gradually came to be responsible for fixing and enforcing prices, although occasionally the government might intervene. For example, in 1301 Edward I fixed the

---

[55] De Roover, 'Just price', p. 423.
[56] Cf. the sixteenth-century Dominican Dominic de Soto, *De justicie et jure*, bk. 6, qu 2, art 5: quoted in Gordon, *Economic Analysis*, p. 237.
[57] Jarrett, *Social Theories*, p. 161.
[58] For discussion see Manuel Rocha, *Travail et salaire à travers la scholastique* (Paris, 1933), pp. 30–5.
[59] Henry of Hesse, *De contractibus*, pt. 1, ch. 12, p. 191r.
[60] Rocha, *Travail et salaire*, p. 23.   [61] Gordon, *Economic Analysis*, p. 230.
[62] Edward Miller, 'The economic policies of governments', in *The Cambridge Economic History of Europe*, 3 (Cambridge, 1963), p. 314.
[63] See chapter 4, pp. 97–8, above.

prices of certain foodstuffs and manufactured goods for the city of York.[64] Edward II's Parliament in the spring of 1315, faced with the emergency of the great famine, determined prices of animals and some foodstuffs.[65] Edward III fixed prices of victuals 'according to the market price' in 1349, at the height of the Black Death epidemic.[66] In 1350 his statute for London laid down detailed price regulations about everything from wine and bran to 'the thousand of tiles' which was to be sold 'at 5s. at the very highest', and the price for making ' a gown garnished with say and with sandel, 18d.'.[67] But in general prices and their enforcement would be left to the civic authorities. Thus, in 1363 civic proclamations were made about the price of victuals in London: 'That the best goose shall be sold for 6d. The best sucking-pig for 8d. The best capon 6d. A hen 4d.'[68] In 1371 best ale was set at 2d a gallon, and in 1418 the price of mussels, oysters, salt, and whiting was fixed.[69] At Coventry in 1498 the mayor listed the price of victuals in a book 'and set it upon the south door of the minster'.[70] For the countryside, the *Manner of holding a manorial court*, written about 1440, ordered

All manner of men what wyll bake brede to sell, loke they sell four loaves for iiiid. and ii loaves for iid. And loke ye kepe the assyse. All manner of brewsters... that they sell a galon of ale of the best for id.ob. and other for id. and other for halfpeny, and kepe the assyse, and that no bruer sell out no burthen tylle the ale founder hath assayed thereof and set a pryce thereupon.[71]

THE FIXED WAGE

The theorists do not seem to have suggested that wages should be fixed by the State, although this happened in England even before the Black Death, when Edward I tried to fix wages for all the construction trades,[72] and many times after it; after the Black Death there is abundant evidence. The wiping out of between a third and a half of the population led to scarcity of labour and a dramatic rise in wages. The chronicler Henry Knighton, for example, observed that by the autumn of 1348 it was not possible to hire a reaper for less than 8d and his food, or a mower for

[64] Britnell, *Commercialisation of England*, p. 93.
[65] Kershaw, 'The great famine', p. 88.
[66] Ordinance of Labourers, ed. Horrox, *The Black Death*, no. 98, p. 289.
[67] Riley, *Memorials of London*, p. 253.   [68] Ibid., p. 312.
[69] Ibid., pp. 348, 666.   [70] Lipson, *Economic History*, p. 300.
[71] Quoted in Jarrett, *Social Theories*, p. 160. A version of this document (omitting the words quoted here) is edited in *EHD*, 4, no. 355, pp. 548–53.
[72] Steven A. Epstein, *Wage Labour and Guilds in Medieval Europe* (Chapel Hill and London, 1991), pp. 112–13.

12d with his food 'for which reason many crops rotted unharvested in the fields'.[73] The customary rate for a reaper, as laid down in 1351 in the Statute of Labourers, was 2d or 3d a day, and that for a mower 5d a day.[74] William Dene, in his Chronicle of the Cathedral Priory of Rochester, recorded that the humble 'turned up their noses at employment and could scarcely be persuaded to serve the eminent unless for triple wages'.[75] The government reacted first by the Ordinance of Labourers of 1349, then by the Statute of 1351. The preamble to the ordinance noted the 'needs of masters and the shortage of employees' and that many people were refusing to work except for excessive wages. Others preferred to 'beg in idleness rather than work for their living'. It tried to peg wages to their pre-Black Death level, to compel the able-bodied, both men and women, to accept work, and to tie labourers to their lords.[76] The statute lamented the lack of observance of the ordinance: the employees having 'no regard to the said ordinance but rather to their own ease and exceptional greed', were demanding double and triple their accustomed wages. It then detailed the exact wages to be paid for each occupation, both rural and urban, and set up special justices of labourers to enforce the statute.[77] The Cambridge Parliament of 1388 reinforced previous legislation in the strongest possible terms and fixed wages for some occupations omitted earlier.[78] In France there was the same conviction that labourers did not, as John II put it in the legislation he issued, want to 'expose their bodies to do any work', and instead spent their time begging, drinking, and whoring.[79] In Aragon the situation was much the same, and Peter IV estimated that the high wages demanded were 'against equality and right reason' – in other words, against the concept of the just wage.[80]

In the aftermath of the plague the supply of labour had diminished, and demand had increased, but employers were not prepared to let wages find their own level in the light of the changed circumstances. Their conception of 'equality and right reason' was to try to ensure that they did not have to pay the 'natural' price for the scarce commodity of labour. Yet however hard they tried, in the final analysis no amount of regulation and legislation was able to withstand the natural laws of the market. The relationship between employer and employee in the town and between

---

[73] The plague according to Henry Knighton, trans. and ed. Horrox, *The Black Death*, no. 19, p. 78.
[74] These were the normal rates as laid down in the Statute of Labourers of 1351, Horrox, *The Black Death*, no. 112, p. 313.
[75] Ibid., no. 19, p. 70.
[76] Ordinance of Labourers, ibid., no. 98, pp. 287–9.
[77] Ibid., no. 112, pp. 312–16.
[78] Additions to the Statute of Labourers, 1388, ibid., no. 117, pp. 323–6.
[79] Epstein, 'The just wage', p. 66.   [80] Ibid.

lord and peasant in the country had changed, and wages did increase enormously.

THE GILDS AND THE JUST WAGE

The gilds had the specific duty of determining wages, and although there was considerable variety among them, their full members were largely master craftsmen. There were, however, three categories of worker associated with them – the master craftsmen, the journeymen, who worked for wages, and the apprentices, who served their masters for a number of years in return for training, board and lodging, and occasionally a small salary.[81] Obviously the fixing of wages applied largely to the journeymen. Whether these were just is open to question. Individual wages seem to have been fixed according to the ability of the journeyman, who would be examined by the gild officials, but there is little sense of the journeyman being in a position to strike a bargain. Most of the evidence comes from London. Ordinances about alien weavers in London, that is, weavers who were not members of the gild, dated 1362, provide one of a number of examples:

if any alien shall come to the said city to work in the said trade, and to make his profit, he shall do nothing in the same before he shall have presented himself to the Masters alien of the said trade, and by the said Masters have been examined if he knows his trade or not; and thereupon, let orders be given by the said Masters what he shall take by the day for his work.[82]

It can hardly be said that such an examination was impartial.

The masters had an overriding interest in enforcing the just or customary wage. One of the results of the post-Black Death labour shortage, however, was to create a community of interest between the civic authorities and the crafts in enforcing government legislation, for it was also the concern of city councils to implement the labour legislation. In London the mayor and aldermen became justices of labourers in 1349. As such, they had to enforce that year's ordinance, and they were given all the necessary punitive powers. In 1350, even before the Statute of Labourers was issued, Edward III had attempted to fix both prices and wages throughout the City of London, and enforcement was to be by 'two to four good men' in each ward.[83]

---

[81] On apprentices' salaries see Epstein, *Wage Labor and Guilds*, p. 110.
[82] *EEH*, section 6, no. 32, p. 195.
[83] Sylvia Thrupp, *The Merchant Class of Medieval London* (Ann Arbor, MI, 1962), p. 74; Riley, *Memorials of London*, pp. 253–8. Cf. p. 144 above.

The relationship between councils and crafts was bonded further by legislation of 1363–4. This envisaged the gilds as controllers of labour and enforcers of statutory policy. It assumed that master craftsmen would govern their workers and keep wages steady. It also imposed the rule of 'one man one craft' by ordering 'that Artificers, Handicraft People, hold them every one to one Mystery, which he will choose... and two of every Craft shall be chosen to survey, that none use other Craft than the same which he hath chosen'.[84] Heather Swanson has convincingly argued that the statute should be seen as part of the labour legislation initiated in 1351. The immediate result was an increase in the number of crafts being founded in the late fourteenth and early fifteenth centuries, as registration of many gild ordinances with civic authorities testifies.[85]

When it came to implementing the 'just' in the sense of 'legal' wage, city and gild officials might cooperate. In London, for example, in 1349 there was trouble over wages amongst the bakers, the cordwainers, and the winedrawers, and several people were imprisoned.[86] There are other, later, instances of cooperation between mayor and aldermen and the craft officials over wage restraint.[87] But from the mid-fourteenth century there are examples throughout Europe of associations being formed by the wage-labourers to 'bargain' with the masters over wages, and of the municipal authorities intervening on the side of the lesser men. This, however, comes under the heading of 'free bargaining'.

Free bargaining

The 'natural' and the 'legal' prices of goods and services were fixed by intangible market forces or by public officials. The two prices could be closely related, because there was nothing to stop the 'natural' price being adopted as the 'legal' price. The 'just' price or wage which emerged from free bargaining, however, was the result of negotiation between two parties, sometimes individuals, and sometimes groups, such as journeymen and masters. In practice, of course, the price arrived at might use the market price, whether legal or natural, as a point of reference.

The private aspect of free bargaining prompted scholastics and lawyers to take different approaches, although both were to reach the conclusion that the concept of justice could not always be a mathematically exact

---

[84] Heather Swanson, *Medieval Artisans: an Urban Class in Late Medieval England* (Oxford, 1989), pp. 112–14.
[85] Ibid., p. 114.
[86] Thrupp, *Merchant Class of Medieval London*, p. 74.   [87] Ibid., pp. 112–13.

one. The scholastics based their ideas on a combination of divine law and Aristotle; the lawyers thought in terms of the law of contract.

The 'natural' and the 'legal' prices had originated at a later stage of civilization than free bargaining, which originally had been an extension of the primitive exchange described by Aristotle. Here it did not matter whether what changed hands was goods for goods or money for goods. As the philosopher observed, 'It makes no difference whether it is five beds that exchange for a house or the money value of five beds.'[88] In this situation there was no differentiation between the 'buyer' and the 'seller', for they were simply parties to the exchange, even if the buyer had paid in money. Such a differentiation might have detracted from strict equality.

Differentiation started with the Roman lawyers. Whereas Aristotle thought in terms of 'exchange', they thought in terms of 'contract'. Both prices and wages came under the main heading of the law of contract – of *emptio-venditio*, buying and selling, in the case of price, and of *locatio-conductio*, placing out and hiring (or more literally taking away)[89] in the case of wages. It was essential for the lawyers that the price of a thing or a service was in money, for if this were not so, the transaction was not sale, but barter, and there could then be no distinction between buyer and seller. This would have made the law of sale unworkable.[90] The distinction made it possible for inequality to creep in between the two. As the jurist Paul declared of both types of contract: 'In buying and selling natural law permits the one party to buy for less and the other to sell for more than the thing is worth: thus each party is allowed to outwit the other. It is the same in letting and hiring [that is, wages].' If the business acumen of the parties was evenly matched, then presumably some sort of rough justice would be achieved, but if not, then one party would be the loser. What Paul was really doing was introducing the idea of free bargaining, and like the later medieval commentators he saw the buyer as disadvantaged.[91]

The notions of inequality and freedom of bargaining led on to the important legal concept of *leasio enormis* (enormous discrepancy). This again was to influence later medieval thinkers. The discrepancy was between the price agreed between the parties and the so-called 'just price', and it allowed the injured party a legal remedy where the contract price had been less than half the true value. In this case the 'just price' could have been either the natural or the legal price. It was assumed that the contract price was a 'mistake' rather than the result of deliberate deceit. The doctrine was originally applied to the conveyance of land, and was introduced to

---

[88] Aristotle, *Ethics*, v, v, p. 121.
[89] Fritz Schulz, *Classical Roman Law* (Oxford, 1951), p. 543.
[90] Nicholas, *Roman Law*, p. 174.   [91] Baldwin, *Just Price*, pp. 21–7.

protect the seller. The buyer who had underpaid could either return the land and have his money back, or keep the land and pay the balance, the discrepancy, to the vendor. But gradually the idea was extended by the medieval Roman lawyers to both buyers and sellers of all types of things. They were legally protected against gross errors of up to 50 per cent.[92]

The lawyers' doctrine of enormous discrepancy was based on human, civil law. When the theologians considered it, they based their conclusions on divine law. This suggested that to accept any price in excess of the just price (by which they meant the current market price) could lead to damnation. Peter the Chanter, for example, cited the case of a grocer who had been excommunicated for selling his wares above the just price. Clearly his 'mistake' was a sin, and he was punished accordingly, rather than being given the benefit of the doubt and allowed to make restitution, as he would have been under Roman law.[93] Thomas of Chobham in his *Summa confessorum* pinpointed the difference between the legal and theological approaches: 'the secular law says that no seller is allowed to receive above half the just price for the goods he sells, but it is a sin if he has received anything above the just price'.[94] Aquinas also highlighted the difference between divine law and human civil law. Roman law allowed a seller to sell for more than the just price, up to half its amount.

Divine law, on the other hand, leaves nothing contrary to virtue unpunished, so that any failure to keep a due balance in contracts of sale is counted to be contrary to divine law. He who profits is, therefore, bound to make restitution to the party who loses out, provided the loss is an important one.[95]

The idea had introduced some doubt about the identity of justice and strict equality. Even Aquinas was here implying that divine law might overlook 'unimportant' losses.

When the theologians discussed free bargaining they synthesized Roman legal ideas with Aristotelian ones. Free bargaining was based on the subjective judgement of individuals, rather than the objective valuation of positive law or the impersonal workings of the market. This subjective element made it difficult to define the just price precisely. As Joel Kaye has demonstrated, it was in this area of market negotiation that the notion of equality gradually changed, starting in the mid-thirteenth century, from the strictly arithmetical one demanded by corrective justice, to one based

---

[92] Ibid. [93] Baldwin, *Peter the Chanter*, 1, p. 268, and 2, n. 61, p. 180.
[94] Thomas of Chobham, *Summa confessorum*, art. 6, d. 4, q. 10a, p. 302. For discussion see Langholm, *Economics*, p. 55; Baldwin, *Just price*, pp. 67–8; *Peter the Chanter*, 1, p. 268, 2, n. 65, p. 189.
[95] Thomas Aquinas, *Summa theologiae*, 2a2ae, 77, 2 ad 1, vol. 38, p. 217.

on geometrical proportion, the commutative justice described by Aristotle in *Ethics* (v, v).[96]

Henry of Ghent (d. 1293) supplied one of the most graphic descriptions of free bargaining in which the notion of equality was still the strict arithmetical one resulting from the application of 'corrective' justice. Both seller and buyer were to be judges of whether they had received too much or too little. They were to move like the arms of the scales until justice was achieved and the tongue of the scales rested in a perpendicular position between arms carrying equal weights.[97]

As Kaye has shown, Godfrey of Fontaines, Henry of Ghent's pupil, adopted the alternative view of equality – that is, the geometrical one based on proportion. He considered that in all contracts of sale a 'convenient estimate' could be made – not according to the inherent value of the thing in question, but according to the sufficient proportions of the use of the thing to the parties.[98] Aquinas, too, admitted that 'we cannot always fix the just price precisely; we sometimes have to make the best estimate we can', and that 'giving or taking a little here or there does not upset the balance of justice'.[99] Henry of Hesse referred directly to Aristotle, *Ethics* (v), and explained that in buying and leasing the just price was not always accepted, but 'something near to the equality of things in proportion to the measure of their market or usual or customary value'. This approximate measure was 'the quantity of human need'.[100] Justice, then, was no more than an approximation. Olivi, too, considered that there had to be latitude in arriving at a just price in free bargaining, and that it should be left to the common consent of buyer and seller. In practice, the common good was best served by accepting most contracts rather than endlessly haggling over minor details.[101]

Two points are axiomatic in free bargaining. The first is that what matters is not so much the objective and mathematically just value of things exchanged, but the more personal value of their usefulness to each party. The second point is that if someone does not feel that he will benefit from a transaction, then he will not bother to exchange. In a bizarre example, Bonaventure likened God to a trader who had given his son in exchange for the redemption of sinful man. This prompted the question of whether God had loved mankind more than Christ, on the basis that

---

[96] Kaye, *Economy and Nature*, esp. ch. 4, pp. 79–115.
[97] Langholm, *Economics*, p. 256.
[98] Godfrey of Fontaines, *Quodlibet*, v, 14, 67: cited in Kaye, *Economy and Nature*, p. 113, and n. 161.
[99] Aquinas, *Summa theologiae*, 2a2ae, 77, 2 ad 1, vol. 38, p. 217.
[100] Henry of Hesse, *De contractibus*, pt. 1, ch. 5, p. 187r.
[101] Langholm, *Economics*, p. 357.

if someone gives one thing for another, he values what he receives more than what he gives: only a fool would exchange a more valuable for a less valuable thing. But God is no fool, so he must have reckoned to gain from the exchange. Of course, Bonaventure demolished this ridiculous idea, but it did make the two crucial points about exchange, that what mattered was subjective value, and that without the hope of gain no one would exchange.[102] Richard of Middleton also focused on the difference between strictly objective value and value to the individual. From this point of view both seller and buyer can benefit.

> The money which the seller has received for a horse sold is of more use to him than the horse would have been, and the horse is more useful to the buyer than the money which he has given for the horse, when the seller needs money more than a horse and the buyer needs a horse more than the money.[103]

Duns Scotus also took up the point that strictly just prices differ from those set by individual need. Establishing justice in exchange calls not only for latitude, but also good will, since the give and take necessary on both sides is the equivalent of making a gift: 'Exchange between men would be difficult if the parties did not intend reciprocally to remit some of that rigorous justice, so that, in so far as they do, a gift may be said to accompany every contract.'[104]

According to Scotus, the justice based on the personal valuation of seller and buyer allowed a seller to indemnify himself against selling at a loss, but it did not allow him to take advantage of a buyer's special need or affection for an object to make an unjust profit.[105] This was Aquinas's rule, which Langholm has aptly called the 'double rule of just pricing'.[106] Aquinas imagined circumstances where the value of a particular thing to the seller was above the normal market price – where he was going to suffer loss by parting with it. In these circumstances he was allowed to charge a price higher than the market, or strictly just, price. But if the buyer valued the thing more highly than the seller, the seller was not allowed to take advantage of this and accept the price the buyer suggested.[107] A loaf of bread was not to be exchanged for a pearl just because it was worth that to a starving man.

In summary, the justice recommended in free bargaining from the time of Aquinas came to be based on proportional rather than arithmetical equality. Strict equality would have removed all incentive for exchanging

---

[102] Ibid., p. 157.
[103] Richard of Middleton, *Super Quatuor Libros Sententiarum*, bk. 3, dist. 33, art. 3 ad 4, p. 390a. See Langholm, *Economics*, p. 333.
[104] Langholm, *Economics*, p. 410.   [105] Ibid.   [106] Ibid., pp. 232–3.
[107] Thomas Aquinas, *Summa theologiae*, 2a2ae, 77, 1, vol. 38, p. 215.

and the result would have been a deadlocked market. It was also recognized that it was not always possible to evaluate individual need in terms of strict justice.

FREE BARGAINING OVER THE JUST WAGE

The concept of 'proportional' equality also entered into free bargaining over the just wage. The theologians were left with an embarrassing legacy in terms of the Parable of the Vineyard, where those who had toiled all day were paid the same as those who were taken on late in the day, some of them having worked for only an hour. When the vineyard owner hired the later workers he promised to pay them 'whatsoever is just' (Matthew 20.4). Not only did this appear to violate 'arithmetical' equality, because the workers were rewarded unequally, but also the justice based on proportion, because those who contributed most were not rewarded according to their effort. Augustine pointed out that the employer had not broken his contract with the original workers because he had paid them what had been agreed. As for the rest, they had been paid by gift rather than under contract, and it was up to the vineyard owner to do what he liked with his own money.[108] As an explanation of the just wage, this was totally unconvincing, but it did sanction free bargaining.

Free bargaining over wages was different from haggling over prices, because of the inequality of employer and employee. Antoninus of Florence, despite opting for the current market wage, discussed free bargaining and aired his concern about inequality. The classical Roman jurists had not bothered much about this. As members of the wealthy, property-owning class, in a system based substantially on slavery, they were content to maintain the *status quo*.[109] Antoninus was not; he recognized that the bargaining power of employer and employee was unequal, because the worker 'is a pauper and has to be satisfied with much less than is needed to support himself and his family'.[110] The Archbishop condemned the payment of less than the 'just' wage, presumably the current market wage, in cases where the worker was not in a position to bargain freely. The worker's need to feed his family was not to be exploited. It was as unjust and sinful to pay less than the just wage in such a situation as it was to pay less than the just price simply because a seller desperately needed the money.[111] Aquinas, too, had pointed out that workers were usually poor people scraping an

---

[108] Augustine, Sermon on the Parable of the Vineyard, *PL*, 38, 530–9: cited in Epstein, 'The just wage', p. 54.
[109] Nicholas, *Roman Law*, p. 184.
[110] De Roover, *San Bernardino*, p. 24.   [111] Ibid., p. 255.

existence.[112] Both thinkers insisted on prompt payment of wages. Antoninus also fulminated against the practice of truck, that is, payment in goods, which was common throughout Europe.[113] Workers needed cash to buy food, so cloth or other goods were useless to them.

SOCIAL STATUS

The economic or social status of a merchant, an employer, or an employee might be a factor in deciding the just price or the just wage. One of Aquinas's justifications of the merchant had been the man 'who uses moderate business profits to provide for his household',[114] implying that he would be maintaining his economic *status quo* rather than improving it. In the following century Henry of Hesse allowed a seller to fix a price for his goods by considering what he needed to maintain his social status and to sustain himself, and by a reasonable estimate of his labour and expenses. If, greedy for money, he charged a higher price, he would commit the sin of avarice.[115] This formed the basis of the extraordinary view challenged by de Roover that the level of the just price depended upon the social status of the merchant.[116]

Status was only a marginal factor in determining the price of goods, but it could be more central in determining the price of labour, especially at the top of the social scale. The medieval Roman lawyers recognized a difference between fees (*salarii*) and wages (*mercedes*).[117] The scholastics followed them. Fees or salaries were earned by professional people, whose skill, knowledge, labour, and experience were all factors in determining their reward. Peter John Olivi argued that something requiring more expert knowledge and skill should be better paid than unskilled labour. The architect would earn more than the stone-cutter. High office was better rewarded because the skill, expertise, and diligence it required was gained 'through lengthy and lasting study, experience, and labour, and at great risk and expense', and also because those fit for it were few and therefore valued more highly.[118] The Franciscan Minister-General Gerald Odonis (d. 1348) agreed that professional people would earn more because they were 'rarer and more necessary in great matters'.[119] The Franciscans were largely concerned with professional status. The Dominican Aquinas was

---

[112] Thomas Aquinas, *Summa theologiae*, 1a2ae, 105, 2 ad 6, vol. 29, p. 287.
[113] De Roover, *San Bernardino*, p. 26; Lipson, *Economic History*, p. 481.
[114] Thomas Aquinas, *Summa theologiae*, 2a2ae, 77, 4, vol. 38, p. 229.
[115] Henry of Hesse, *De contractibus*, pt. 1, ch. 12, p. 191r.
[116] De Roover, 'The just price', pp. 418–20.   [117] Epstein, 'The just wage', p. 59.
[118] Langholm, *Economics*, p. 363.   [119] Ibid., p. 520.

concerned about the status of the client. In discussing the fees of lawyers, physicians, and masters he stipulated:

> The only proviso is that they charge moderate fees having regard to their clients' position, profession and work, and also the customs of the country. It follows that anybody who is dishonest enough to charge excessive fees commits a sin against justice.[120]

The same point about discrimination in fees according to the social standing of the client was made by an Englishman, John of Ardenne, in a medical treatise of about 1376:

> When ... [the surgeon] has made an examination, even though he may think that the patient may be cured, he should warn the patient ... of the perils to come if treatment should be deferred. And if he sees that the patient is eager for the cure, then the surgeon must boldly adjust his fee to the man's status in life. But the surgeon should always beware of asking too little, for this is bad both for the market and the patient.[121]

The medical profession had clearly come a long way since the Roman Empire, when medicine was an occupation of slaves.[122] In this context, Henry of Hesse's idea that a seller's status might dictate a price has been turned upside down, for here it is the client's – the buyer's – social standing and means which matter, not the seller's.

The same idea featured in discussions about teaching. The canonist, and later cardinal, Godfrey of Trani (d. 1245) suggested that scholars should pay their teachers according to their own means and social status.[123] There was no such thing as a just wage for teachers, because knowledge was a gift of God, and could therefore not be sold: 'scientia donum dei est: unde vendi non potest', as Johannes Teutonicus phrased it. On the other hand, teachers needed to eat. The Fourth Lateran Council of 1215 had ordered that every cathedral church should provide a grammar master for the clergy and poor scholars, and every metropolitan a theologian. Teaching was to be free, but the masters were to be provided with benefices to support them. Johannes allowed those who lacked benefices or salaries to ask for fees: indeed, even if they had support, they might still accept

---

[120] Thomas Aquinas, *Summa theologiae*, 2a2ae, 71 ad 4, vol. 38, p. 153.
[121] *EHD*, 4, no. 696, p. 1185. Traditionally medical practitioners were expected to treat the poor either free or at cut price. See Rawcliffe, *Medicine and Society*, p. 143.
[122] Nicholas, *Roman Law*, p. 185.
[123] Gaines Post, Kimon Giocarnis, and Richard Kay, 'The medieval heritage of a humanistic ideal: '*Scientia donum Dei est: unde vendi non potest*', *Traditio*, 11 (1955), pp. 195–234, at p. 207; Gaines Post, 'Masters' salaries and student fees in the medieval universities', *Speculum*, 7 (1932), p. 191, n. 1.

gifts from the rich, though not the poor or the clergy.[124] The obvious solution to the problem was to draw a distinction between knowledge, which was not marketable, and labour, which was. Two thirteenth-century canonists, the Englishman Alanus, and the Italian Arnold of Brescia, arrived at it.[125]

In practice, masters in the late medieval universities did accept fees. At Oxford their payment was compulsory in the fourteenth century.[126] But what about preachers? They, too, were dealing in knowledge, even in sacred knowledge, and should not have been entitled to payment. Arnold of Brescia again divided knowledge from labour, concluding: 'A preacher cannot be said to sell preaching, yet he is allowed to ask for his sustenance.'[127] Pauper as a preaching friar considered that he was 'not bound to travail for nought', emphasizing that 'though he ask for nought, the people is bounden to give him freely'.[128]

COLLECTIVE FREE BARGAINING

The proportion of people in the late medieval English economy who depended for their living either wholly or partly on wages was between a third and a half.[129] The number had increased in the pre-Black Death period in rural areas because of the commutation of labour services for a money rent, which had started in the twelfth century. This meant that manorial lords became dependent upon wage labourers to perform tasks which had previously been done by customary tenants. Sometimes it paid them to be. In the early fourteenth century the abbot of Battle estimated that harrowing work on the manor of Barnhorn would cost him 4d if he hired labour, but 5d if he had to feed his own workers for the necessary two days.[130] In the post-Black death period the proportion of wage-earners increased both in town and country, because when labour was scarce and wages were high and still rising, it paid people to work for

---

[124] Post, '*Scientia donum Dei*', pp. 198–200. For the Fourth Lateran Council, *Decretales*, 5,5,4, col. 770.
[125] Ibid., p. 201.   [126] Post, 'Masters' salaries', p. 198.
[127] Post, '*Scientia donum Dei*', p. 201.
[128] *Dives and Pauper*, pt. 2, Commandment VII, xvii, p. 177, lines 20–6.
[129] R. H. Hilton, 'Some social and economic evidence in late medieval English tax returns', in Hilton, *Class Conflict and the Crisis of Feudalism: Essays in Medieval Social History*, rev. edn (London and New York, 1990), pp. 188–94. Hilton used the problematic evidence of the 1381 poll tax returns for the Gloucestershire Cotswolds region.
[130] Eleanor Searle, *Lordship and Community: Battle Abbey and its Banlieu, 1066–1538* (Toronto, 1974), pp. 176–80. See also John Hatcher, 'English serfdom and villeinage: towards a reassessment', *P & P*, 90 (1981), pp. 10–12; Rigby, *English Society*, p. 75.

the 'current market wage'. It also paid them to work on short-term contracts or take casual work rather than to be tied down to a fixed wage for a long period and risk losing the advantage of any rises in the current wage.[131]

The theorists, basing themselves on Aristotle and Roman law, had assumed that free bargaining over wages took place between two individuals — the employer and the employee. In practice, during the late medieval period there is evidence both of 'collective' free bargaining and even occasionally of current ideas of representation creeping into negotiations. In the towns, wage-earners were an ill-defined group, sometimes shifting between wage-earning and self-employment.[132] A great many people would have been self-employed — among them those who provided a service of some kind, professionals, independent journeymen, day-labourers, and domestic servants.

Collective bargaining over wages emerged in various associations of workers — journeymen gilds, drinking clubs, brotherhoods — often formed under cover of a religious fraternity, or at least closely associated with one.[133] As early as 1303 the journeymen cordwainers of London formed a confederacy, apparently because the masters had lowered their wages. The following year the skinners formed one, and there are many later examples.[134] Sometimes the journeymen would resort to sympathetic strikes. There were accusations against the alien weavers of London in 1362 that if a dispute arose between a master and a workman, the workman would go round and rouse all the others in the trade 'and by covin and conspiracy between them made, they would give orders that no one of them should work or submit to serve until the said master and his workman should have agreed'.[135] The author of the Wyclifite tract had singled out the free masons for the 'great curse'. They conspired together that none of them should take a lower daily wage than they had set, 'though he should by good conscience take much less'. They also 'worked to rule' by refusing to do anything but hew stone, although they knew that by laying a wall a mason 'might profit his master twenty pound by a day's work ... without

---

[131] Nora Kenyon, 'Labour conditions in Essex in the reign of Richard II', reprinted in E. M. Carus-Wilson, ed., *Essays in Economic History*, 2 (London, 1962), pp. 93–5; Dyer and Penn, 'Wages and earnings', pp. 179–89.

[132] Gervase Rosser, 'Crafts, guilds and the negotiation of work in the medieval town', *P & P*, 154 (1997), p. 15.

[133] Rosser, 'Crafts, guilds and work', has drawn attention to these.

[134] Lipson, *Economic History*, p. 403. R. H. Hilton, 'Popular movements in England at the end of the fourteenth century', in Hilton, *Class Conflict*, pp. 79–91, at p. 90.

[135] *EEH*, sect. 6, no. 32, p. 196. Cf. the similar case of the London shearmen in 1350: Riley, *Memorials of London*, p. 247. For discussion of strikes see Lipson, *Economic History*, pp. 406–7.

harm of paining himself'.[136] There is similar evidence of collective action throughout Europe.[137] Occasionally in the commercially advanced Low Countries there is a representative element to negotiations. At Douai, for example, in 1229, after a strike by the tailors, wages were negotiated between representatives of 'all the chief officers of the craft, all the guardians of the goods of the trade, all the merchant clothiers and all the tailors, both masters and journeymen'.[138]

For the countryside the evidence of collective wage bargaining is harder to find, although there is plenty on tenants combining to withstand lordly demands for increased labour services or higher rents.[139] Dyer and Penn, discussing the enforcement of the labour laws of the fourteenth century, have pointed to 'collective links among the rural workforce' and remark significantly: 'There are various hints that the labour market was not a matter of simple negotiations between individual employers and individual workers.'[140]

The collective aspect of free bargaining over the just wage implies that the parties involved were negotiating on terms of near equality. This was not something envisaged by the scholastics, who thought of free bargaining over wages in terms of two individuals. It was an example of economic practice being in advance of theory. Nevertheless, the greater equality of masters and wage-earners achieved through collective bargaining followed the strict principles of the just price of labour.

CONCLUSION

The level of prices and wages could be fixed in different ways. They might be fixed from above by central government or civic authority, from a position of near equality or even from below by free bargaining, or by the self-moving natural laws of the market which, being impersonal, came from neither above nor below. In practice, they might be the result of a combination of these things.

The just wage and the just price were supposed to achieve equality between either seller and buyer or employer and employee. In the area of free bargaining, the most significant theoretical development, based on a combination of Aristotelian and Roman law principles, was the

---

[136] Wyclif (?), *The Grete Sentence of Curs Expounded*, pp. 343–4.
[137] Rosser, 'Crafts, guilds and work', pp. 24–7.   [138] Ibid., p. 25.
[139] R. H. Hilton, 'Conflict and collaboration', in Hilton, *The English Peasantry in the Later Middle Ages* (Oxford, 1975), pp. 62–9; Hilton, 'Peasant movements in England before 1381', in *Class Conflict*, pp. 49–65, esp. pp. 55–60; Christopher Dyer, 'A redistribution of incomes in fifteenth-century England?' *P & P*, 39 (1968), pp. 11–33, at pp. 32–3.
[140] Dyer and Penn, 'Wages and earnings', p. 178.

change in the notion of justice from an exact mathematical balance to something based on geometrical proportion, which allowed considerably more latitude. Ultimately in negotiating prices there could be no such thing as precise equality, because equality would deprive both parties of profit and lead to deadlock. Like Buridan's ass faced with two equal heaps of hay, the result would have been economic inactivity and disaster.

7

THE NATURE OF USURY: THE USURER AS WINNER

INTRODUCTION: DEFINITIONS AND FOUNDATIONS

The just price and usury were once inseparably linked by historians – indeed, for some people the two still constitute the sum total of medieval economic thought. In fact, they are completely different. The just price was accepted by the scholastics as grounded on justice and equality, either arithmetical or proportional, while usury – that is, making a charge for lending money – was grounded on *in*justice and *in*equality.

How was usury defined? Usury was concerned with lending, especially the lending of money, although it could be applied to anything that could be counted, weighed, or measured. The definitions were based ultimately on biblical texts, both Old Testament ones along the lines of 'Take thou no usury...' (Leviticus 25.36), and the New Testament Sermon on the Mount of Luke 6.35, 'Lend, hoping for nothing again.' Two definitions feature in Gratian's *Decretum*, both of them citing patristic texts. They emphasize two different aspects of the question. The first is 'expecting to receive back more than you have given' in a loan, whether of money or anything else,[1] and it underlines the sinful intention of the usurer. It echoed the Luke text, and formed the basis for the all-important idea that the sinful hope was what defined usury. Urban III (1185–87) issued a decretal called *Consuluit*, where he quoted the Luke text, and made the point that usury was a sin of intention.[2] This became the acid test. The

---
[1] Gratian, *Decretum*, C. 14, q. 3, c. 1: col. 735. One of the best discussions of the theory of usury and its sources is G. le Bras, 'La doctrine ecclésiastique de l'usure à l'epoque classique (viie–xve siècle)', *Dictionnaire de théologie catholique*, 15, 2 (1950), cols. 2336–72.
[2] *Decretales*, 5,19,10, col. 814. For discussion see Noonan, *Scholastic Analysis*, p. 18.

author of the *Fasciculus morum*, enshrining a long tradition, proclaimed 'Only the hope or intention creates usury.'[3]

The second of Gratian's definitions was more legalistic: 'Whatsoever exceeds the principal is usury.'[4] This highlighted the familiar idea of balance and equality. It also made the point that although usury applied primarily to money, anything that could be counted, weighed, or measured could be the subject of a loan. The late fourteenth-century English poet John Gower had his own less formal definition: he called usury lending a small pea and receiving back a bean.[5]

Usury was first condemned by the Council of Nicaea of 325, but the ban applied only to clerics.[6] Fourth-century councils at Elvira in Spain, and Carthage in Africa, however, extended the prohibition to the laity. Pope Leo the Great (440–61) in an important letter repeated the ban on clerical usurers, and accused lay practitioners of *turpe lucrum* (shameful gain). Both the Nicaea canon and Pope Leo's letter were included in a collection of canons known as the *Hadriana*, presented by the Pope to the Emperor Charlemagne, who then himself repeatedly legislated against usurers. His capitulary of Nynweger of 806 defined usury officially as 'where more is asked than is given'.[7]

One of the most significant statements about usury was the palea *Eiciens*, the Pseudo-Chrysostom (encountered in chapter 5).[8] Since it touches on most of the basic ideas about usury, it will be used as a framework. What follows is a fairly free translation.

Above all other merchants the most accursed is the usurer, for he sells a thing given by God which was not acquired through being a merchant, and after usury he demands his merchandise back again, taking both his own and that of the other party. A merchant, however, does not demand back something he has sold. Someone might therefore say, 'Isn't someone who lets a field so that he may receive land rent, or a house so that he may receive rent, the same as someone who gives his money out at usury?' Not at all: in the first place, because money should be spent only in buying; secondly, because the man who has a field obtains fruits from it by cultivating it, and a house-owner accepts the use of living in it. Therefore he who lets a field or a house evidently gives up his own use and accepts money

---

[3] *Fasciculus morum*, IV, vii, p. 352 (Latin), line 2.
[4] Gratian, *Decretum*, C. 14, q. 3, c. 3, col. 735. For discussion see T. P. McLaughlin, 'The teaching of the canonists on usury', *Medieval Studies*, 1 (1930), pp. 81–147, at p. 95.
[5] John Gower, *Confessio amantis*, ed. G. C. Macaulay, *The English Works of John Gower*, EETS, 81–2 (1900–1), bk. 5, p. 67, lines 4408–9.
[6] For translated text see Gilchrist, *Church and Economic Activity*, First General Council, Nicaea I, canon 17, p. 155.
[7] Noonan, *Scholastic Analysis*, p. 15; Baldwin, *Just Price*, p. 32.
[8] See ch. 5, pp. 112–13, above.

for it, and in a certain sense it seems as if he exchanges gain for gain, but you get no use from stored money. Thirdly, a field or a house deteriorates in use. Money, however, when it is lent, neither deteriorates nor diminishes.[9]

The most important implications of this condensed passage seem to be these. The usurer is accursed by God, meaning that he is worthy of eternal damnation. He sells something which belongs to God alone, presumably time. He also, by taking both his own money back – his merchandise – and that of the borrower, takes something which belongs to the borrower, which is the equivalent of theft. It is licit to make a profit on something by working on it, as the farmer cultivates his field, but not by doing nothing, which, by implication, is what the usurer does. Then there are the three fundamental points about the nature and use of money which we have already analysed, and which underlie most of the dicussion about usury. Firstly, its proper use is not in loans, but in buying and selling. Secondly, it is a fungible, which is consumed in use, and the use of it cannot therefore be separated from its ownership, as it can in the case of immovable goods like houses and fields. Finally, if it is stored, in this instance in a loan, it will neither increase nor diminish, which is another way of stating that it is sterile: barren money cannot breed.[10]

These three characteristics will underpin our discussion. The starting point is the Church's attitude to usury as mortal sin, followed by a discussion of the sin in question, the lender's theft of money or goods from the borrower. Such a crime automatically required restitution to be made. But usury was also the theft of time, which was owned by God alone for the common benefit of mankind. The question of time leads to discussion of those things which could and could not be changed by time. If time alone could not make barren money fruitful, could it be made to appear so by the application of labour and industry to it? And if this were so, whose labour counted, that of the borrower or the lender?

USURY AS MORTAL SIN

According to *Eiciens* the usurer was 'accursed by God'. The Church regarded usury as a mortal sin – that is, one that deprived the sinner of God's grace and led to eternal damnation if the usurer did not repent and make satisfaction. The Third Lateran Council of 1179 issued an influential, though ambiguous, decree against usury. It denied 'manifest' usurers – a

---

[9] Gratian, *Decretum*, D 87, c. 9 palea, col. 309. For discussion see Noonan, *Scholastic Analysis*, pp. 38–9.
[10] See chapter 3, pp. 74–6, 84–7, above.

term which was to cause some discussion – the communion of the altar, which probably meant that they were to be excommunicated as well as being denied the sacrament of the Eucharist.[11] It also ordered them to make restitution of their ill-gotten gains, and it refused them Christian burial if they died unrepentant.[12]

The French preacher Jacques de Vitry had a suitably dramatic story about a parish priest who refused Christian burial to a local usurer:

But since the dead usurer's friends were very insistent, the priest yielded to their pressure and said, 'Let us put his body on a donkey and see God's will, and what He will do with the body. Wherever the donkey takes it, be it a church, a cemetery or elsewhere, there will I bury it.' The body was placed upon the donkey which, without deviating either to right or left, took it straight out of town to the place where thieves are hanged from the gibbet, and with a hearty buck, the donkey sent the cadaver flying into the dung beneath the gallows. The priest left it there with the thieves.[13]

The point of the story was to underline God's judgement of usurers. The priest's reluctance was also due to the fact that clergy who buried unrepentant usurers in consecrated ground were automatically excommunicated.[14] In such cases the cadavers of usurers had to be exhumed. A council held at Mainz in 1310 even imposed an interdict on any cemetery where a usurer was buried until such time as the body was removed.[15] The preachers positively revelled in this macabre atmosphere. The decomposing bodies of the usurers became host to all manner of diabolical beasts – leeches, spiders, flies, toads, crows, vipers, worms, and so on, and the exhumations were usually enveloped by a nauseating stench.[16] A story from the *Fasciculus morum* is fairly typical. It tells of a usurer who refused to make a will (with the implication that he had not made restitution), but made his wife swear that she would tie 30 marks from his profits to his body, so that wherever he ended up he would be able to make a good bargain. He was duly buried, with the money, but soon afterwards a papal legate arrived and ordered the priest who had buried him to exhume him, throw him on to an open field, and burn him.

---

[11] See McLaughlin, 'Canonists on usury', pt. 2, p. 4 for discussion.
[12] *Decretales*, 5, 19, 3 and 5, 19, 5, col. 812, which reiterate it. Cf. Gilchrist, *Church and Economic Activity*, Lateran III (1179), Canon 25, p. 173.
[13] Jacques Le Goff, *Your Money or Your Life: Economy and Religion in the Middle Ages*, trans. Patricia Ranum (New York, 1988), p. 64.
[14] McLaughlin, 'Canonists on usury', pt. 2, p. 3.   [15] Ibid., p. 9.
[16] Jacques le Goff, 'The usurer and purgatory', in *The Dawn of Modern Banking*, pp. 25–52, esp. pp. 38–43.

Now when the priest and his assistants came to him, they found in the place where the money had been tied ugly toads that gnawed at his miserable decomposing body and countless worms instead of an armband of money. When they saw this, they burned him, and many died of the stench.[17]

The Church viewed usury with the utmost gravity and spared no effort to drive home its sinful nature. Robert of Courçon, Cardinal-Legate for France but a native Englishman, equated usury with the crime of heresy at the Council of Paris in 1213. He encouraged the Parisian faithful to try to convert usurers from their evil ways. If that failed, they were to accuse them publicly and to report the names of all usurers to the ecclesiastical authorities. After three warnings unrepentant usurers were to be excommunicated.[18] This was given universal application at the Council of Vienne of 1311, presided over by Clement V, which declared that anyone who believed or said that usury was not a sin was to be punished as a heretic. The inquisitors were to proceed as they would against anyone accused or suspected of heresy.[19] In late thirteenth-century Pistoia a usurer had already been branded as a heretic with a cross on his chest and thighs.[20]

Heresy, in papal eyes, was a threat to the whole structure of the Christian society. It was not just a question of holding eccentric beliefs, rather it entailed disobedience to the commands issued by the head of that society and was therefore a challenge to the supreme jurisdictional authority of the pope. It was something which could affect the whole corporate unity of the Church, and many medieval writers liken heresy to a foul disease, which if left unchecked will destroy the whole body. A decree of the Council of Lyons in 1274 referred to the 'canker of usury which devours souls and exhausts resources'.[21] Bernardino of Siena was more physical: 'Usury concentrates the money of the community in the hands of a few, just as if all the blood in a man's body ran to his heart and left his other organs depleted.'[22]

Heresy was one crime, but there were others – fornication, murder, and robbery. Antoninus of Florence likened usury to the great harlot of the Apocalypse (17), who 'sitteth upon many waters, with whom the kings of the earth have committed fornication'.[23] Comparisons between murder and usury tended to favour murder. As the Paris master William of Auxerre

[17] *Fasciculus morum*, IV, vii, pp. 353, lines 107–19.
[18] Baldwin, *Peter the Chanter*, I, p. 302.
[19] Gilchrist, *Church and Economic Activity*, Vienne (1311–12), Decree 29, p. 206.
[20] Iris Origo, *The Merchant of Prato* (London, 1960), p. 151.
[21] Gilchrist, *Church and Economic Activity*, Lyons II (1274), Constitution 26, p. 194.
[22] Noonan, *Scholastic Analysis*, p. 74.   [23] Ibid., p. 78.

(1160–1229) allowed, there may be circumstances when murder is morally permissible – in effect, the moral end may justify the immoral means. But not so usury, which is always evil, and is therefore always condemned by the law of morality.[24] And it lasts longer. As Antoninus later observed, crimes like adultery and murder are of limited duration, but 'sleeping or waking [usury] works and never ceases'.[25]

John Bromyard also made the point that the usurer could make a profit even in his sleep. His comparison, however, was the more traditional one with robbery, specified in *Eiciens*:

> The usurer is worse than the robber, because the robber usually steals at night. The usurer, however, robs by day and night, having no regard for time or solemnity, for the profit which accrues to him through a loan never sleeps, but always grows.[26]

Usury was generally regarded as theft. It was an offence against the Seventh Commandment. Under that heading Dives asked whether usury was 'any species of theft' to which Pauper returned the answer that it was indeed 'wol gret thefte'.[27]

The worst theft was from the poor, which would have included most of the usurer's customers. Oppressing them in this way was theft not only because it violated natural justice, but also because the superfluities of the rich belonged by right to the poor. As William of Auxerre realized, usury was 'contrary to that species of justice which obliges us to relieve a neighbour in need'.[28] The emphasis on justice passed into popular penitential literature. The *Fasciculus* author, for example, regarded it as a violation of natural justice: 'A usurer, though he gains worldly riches... is yet in the greatest danger, and this first because he sells to his poor neighbour what he owes him freely by the law of nature, namely help in his need.'[29]

The Aristotelian approach to usury and theft was that the borrower had been parted 'involuntarily' from his goods. In *Ethics*, book 3, Aristotle discussed the philosophical question of the freedom of the will and the extent to which actions are voluntary or involuntary. Some actions he thought were a mean between the two because they 'are mixed, but are more like voluntary actions'.[30] The example he gave was of a captain who jettisoned

---

[24] Langholm, *Economics*, p. 84. [25] Noonan, *Scholastic Analysis*, p. 78.
[26] John Bromyard, *Summa praedicantium*, 2, ch. 12, 'usura', sect. 8, p. 468r.
[27] *Dives and Pauper*, pt. 2, Commandment VII, xxiv, p. 195, lines 1–2. For earlier examples see Noonan, *Scholastic Analysis*, p. 17; Langholm, *Economics*, p. 69. Ambrose's statement to this effect was incorporated into the *Decretum*, C. 14, q. 4, c. 10.
[28] Langholm, *Economics*, p. 77. [29] *Fasciculus morum*, IV, vii, p. 347.
[30] Aristotle, *Ethics*, III, i, p. 49. On coercion in economic relationships see Odd Langholm, *The Legacy of Scholasticism in Economic Thought: Antecedents of Choice and Power* (Cambridge, 1998), esp. pp. 15–29 on the Aristotelian tradition.

his cargo in a storm to save both his ship and its crew. The act was voluntary because he had chosen to do it, but involuntary because he would not normally have considered doing such a thing. It was an action of 'mixed' voluntariness. The scholastics were to take this concept of mixed voluntariness and to apply it to those who paid usury. William of Auxerre explained that there were two kinds of voluntary consent, absolute and conditional. In terms of 'absolute voluntariness' the debtor does not want to have to pay the usurer for the loan. On the other hand, applying conditional consent, he does want to pay because he knows that the usurer will not give him a gratuitous loan. What makes usury theft is that the usurer 'takes alien goods against the owner's will', in this case his 'absolute' will.[31] Many later commentators, Albert the Great, Aquinas, Duns Scotus, and Gerald Odonis among them, echoed this Aristotelian argument. Aquinas provided a fair summary:

he who pays usury suffers injustice not from himself but from the usurer, for granted that the usurer does not apply absolute force he nevertheless applies a certain mixed force on him, in that the necessity of having to accept the loan imposes a serious condition so that he returns more than he is given. And it is similar if one reduced to need were to be sold a certain thing for much more than its worth, for that would be an unjust sale just as a usurious loan is unjust.[32]

The rapacious merchant and the usurer both violated justice by ignoring the balance between the two parties. The difference was that the price agreed by the sale contract was the result of free bargaining, and was assumed to be just. In the case of a loan contract, however, there was little opportunity for bargaining. The borrower had to take it or leave it. An example of this sort of compulsion is provided by the record of a London inquisition of 1453 before the mayor and aldermen at Guildhall. It tells the sad tale of how William Bertram, an attorney of Richard Woodville, Lord Rivers, fell into the clutches of a loan shark. He was forced to agree to borrow £300 from a city salter, Alexander Brook, for six months. He had to pay £59 (a rate of nearly 40 per cent a year) and hand over £700 worth of his master's jewels as security. 'William, in his great necessity and perplexed by great affliction of heart, chose what he thought to be the lesser evil and accepted the conditions imposed.' The story did not end happily. After six months William was unable to repay the loan and Alexander drove an even harder bargain for the next six months. On a loan of £300 Alexander netted a profit of £59 and jewels worth £700, and for the next six months on a loan of £98, a further £50, with jewels worth

---

[31] Langholm., *Economics*, p. 78; Langholm, *Legacy of Scholasticism*, p. 61.
[32] Aquinas, *De malo*, XIII, 4 ad 7, quoted by Langholm, *Economics*, p. 247.

£200, that is, over £1,000 for a total loan of £398 for a year.[33] Avarice in Langland's *Piers Plowman*, when questioned by Repentance on whether he had pity on poor men who were forced to borrow from him, produced his own version of fleecing the poor:

> I have as moche pite of pore men as pedlere hath of cattes,
> That wolde kille hem, yf he cacche hem myght for coueitise
>   of here skynnes.[34]

However unjust, and however much duress was applied by the usurer, a loan was the result of a contract which by definition involved two parties. While the money-lender was evidently committing a mortal sin, the borrower sinned as well, though not mortally, by agreeing to pay usury. The scholastics have no real answer to the problem of how severe the degree of need or duress had to be to exonerate the borrower, bearing in mind, of course, that in extreme necessity all things are common. William of Auxerre thought that necessity justified the payment of usury, but where there was no necessity, it was sinful to pay it. His conclusion was evasive: 'But at which degree of necessity it is sinful and at which degree it is not, that is not determined by theory or usage or knowledge, but by charity.' Albert the Great was even more hesitant. He simply admitted that the problem was too difficult and refused to commit himself.[35]

RESTITUTION

On the understanding that usury was theft, the Third Lateran Council ordered usurers to make restitution of their usurious gains. Once this was done, the balance of justice was seen to be restored. Then, and only then, might they be absolved. The decree had stipulated that 'manifest' usurers had to make restitution. This was enlarged upon by Innocent III when he declared that a repentant usurer would not be 'heard', meaning that he would not be absolved, until he had made restitution.[36] The Second Council of Lyons (1274) toughened the law on restitution by declaring that the wills of usurers who did not make provision for full restitution were invalid.[37] Canon law also decreed that if the usurer himself did not make restitution during his lifetime, then his heirs had to do so.[38] In theory, all usurers were bound to make restitution; in practice, it did not work quite

---

[33] H. E. S. Fisher, and A. R. J. Juřica, eds., *Documents in English Economic History: England from 1000 to 1760* (London, 1977), sect. 6, no. 15, p. 351.
[34] William Langland, *Piers Plowman*, B, passus 5, lines 257–62, p. 150.
[35] Langholm, *Economics*, pp 82. 195; Langholm, *Legacy of Scholasticism*, p. 68.
[36] *Decretales*, 5, 19, 3; 5, 19, 5 (Alexander III); 5, 19, 14 (Innocent III): cols. 812–13; 815.
[37] Gilchrist, *Church and Economic Activity*, Lyons II (1274), const. 27, pp. 195–6.
[38] *Decretales*, 5, 19, 9, cols. 813–14.

like that. The legislation posed awkward questions, such as who qualified as a manifest usurer and who did not, how restitution was to be made in cases where the borrower had died, or vanished over the horizon, or where the distance involved was too great to make restitution practical. It also highlighted the issue of the involvement of both princes and priests in usury.

The manifest usurer could be compelled by the episcopal courts to make restitution, whereas the occult practitioner was merely to be persuaded to do so by his confessor. But who was the manifest usurer? He was the public usurer who openly kept a pawnshop or had been condemned in court or had admitted his usury before witnesses. Sometimes usurers occupied a particular area of a town, as did the prostitutes. The fourteenth-century canonist Henry of Bouhic, echoing earlier opinion, described the manifest usurer as one who was notorious, or had been officially penalized, and who kept a table from which he was prepared to lend money at usury to anyone, just as the harlot in the brothel demonstrated that she was ready for anyone.[39]

The original manifest usurers of Europe were the Jews, who were not subject to the jurisdiction of the Church. They were also not subject to qualms of conscience, for there seemed to be clear sanction for their activities in Deuteronomy 23.19–20, which forbade the Jews to lend at usury to their fellow Jews, but allowed that 'unto a stranger thou mayest lend upon usury'.[40] The 'stranger' in this case was the Gentile.

Usurers, regardless of their faith, were indispensable to secular rulers, which complicated matters of prosecution and subsequent restitution. From the twelfth century onward, monarchs had started to protect them. Peter the Chanter considered that both Jewish and Christian moneylenders were favoured by the French King, who declared all indiscriminately – Jew and Christian alike – as 'his Jews'. This protected them from persecution, for the Church had no jurisdiction over Jewish moneylenders.[41] Innocent III writing to the Bishop of Auxerre in 1207 complained that no one dared to prosecute the numerous usurers in his diocese for 'fear of princes'.[42] Of course, royal protection did not come cheap. In England the king was able to claim the goods of dead usurers, Jew and Christian, layman, and even cleric.[43] Thomas of Chobham expressed his

---

[39] Henry de Bouhic, *Super quinque libris decretalium* (Lyons, 1498), 5. 19. 3, fol. 41r. Peter the Chanter had made the comparison with the prostitute in the twelfth century, Baldwin, *Peter the Chanter*, 1, p. 300.

[40] On the history of this controversial text and the use Christians were able to make of it to justify taking usury from enemies see Benjamin N. Nelson, *The Idea of Usury*, 2nd edn (Chicago, IL, and London, 1969).

[41] Baldwin, *Peter the Chanter*, 1, p. 299.   [42] *Decretales*, 5, 19, 15, col. 815.

[43] Glanvill, *Laws and Customs of England*, 7, 16, p. 89.

astonishment that the Church allowed princes to convert Jewish money with impunity for their own use. Since the Jews had nothing except what they gained from usury, the princes were in effect participating in usury and so were usurers themselves. Thomas assumed that the Church did not punish them because of their power, but pointed out that God would not excuse them.[44] Bishop Robert Grosseteste of Lincoln, writing for the Countess of Leicester, adopted much the same attitude. God had ordered that Jewish captivity should be burdensome. Christian princes were therefore bound to see that Jews did not live in luxury on the profits of usury extorted from Christians. Princes should understand that those who encouraged the practice of Jewish usury would share both the guilt and the punishment of the Jews.[45]

Monarchs developed a conscience only when they had exhausted the financial resources of the Jews, and the Jews had outlived their usefulness, or when they posed a threat to public order. Edward I forbade Jewish usury in 1275, and then expelled the Jews from England in 1290. In France they were banished in 1394, although not for the first time. Their places were taken by merchants of Italy and the Low Countries. When the canonist William Durandus (known as the Speculator) commented on the usury legislation of the Second Council of Lyons (1274) he considered that it was not meant to apply to occult usurers or denizens, but only to manifest foreign usurers, and he cited among others the Italians in England, and other groups in Italy, France, and Provence.[46]

From the twelfth to the first half of the fourteenth century the merchant-usurer, especially the Italian, was persecuted by the Church and held to restitution. Benjamin Nelson has charted his rise to respectability in Italy, showing that by the fifteenth century he was regarded as a merchant prince, an Establishment figure, no longer persecuted. Not surprisingly, the line between restitution and philanthropy became blurred. Initially most restitutions were testamentary, and disguised by a blanket formula which made no reference to usury. By the end of the period, however, acts which might earlier have been considered as restitution were being performed as public acts of charity during the merchant's life. The usurer-pawnbroker's body may have been slung on to unhallowed ground, but the merchant prince often lay in a position of honour in front of the high altar. As Nicholas Bozon, a French friar-preacher, observed: 'The world is now turned upside down; for those who would refuse to give a usurer the kiss of peace

---

[44] Thomas of Chobham, *Summa confessorum*, art 7, dist. 6, q. 11, ch. 4, p. 510.
[45] See J. A. Watt, 'Jewish serfdom', in *The Church and Sovereignty: Essays in Honour of Michael Wilks*, ed. Diana Wood, SCH, subsidia 10 (Oxford, 1991), p. 170, notes 61–2.
[46] Benjamin N. Nelson, 'The usurer and the merchant prince: Italian businessmen and the ecclesiastical law of restitution, 1100–1500', in *The Tasks of Economic History: The Journal of Economic History*, supplement 7 (1947), pp. 104–22, at p. 107.

in church would not now stick at kissing his feet... and these men, whose bodies of old time were buried in the field or the garden are now buried in front of the high altar in church.'[47] A notorious Florentine usurer, Bartolomeo dei Cocci-Compagni, after extensive bequests to the Church, which did not leave enough money to make restitution to the borrowers he had fleeced, was given a state burial in 1389 under the steps to the high altar in Santa Maria Novella.[48] The 'Merchant of Prato', Francesco di Marco Datini, was buried in 1410 in a tomb at the foot of the high altar of Santa Maria Novella in Prato, although some of his dealings had probably been usurious.[49] Enrico Scrovegni of Padua, a usurer and son of a usurer, was buried in a specially commissioned tomb in his own chapel in 1336.[50] The Datinis and Scrovegnis of this world were far above the pawnbrokers and were unlikely to be prosecuted as manifest usurers. They also took care, by various legal devices, as we shall see in chapter 8, that they did not technically commit usury.

Restitution was divided into two types – that of 'certa', where the person wronged, or his heir, was known and available, and that of 'incerta', where the reverse was true. From the twelfth to the early fourteenth centuries there are a good many Italian examples of restitution of 'certa' by international merchant-usurers, but subsequently very few, and most of the restitutions are of 'incerta'.[51] Much of the evidence comes from wills, unsurprisingly in view of the decree of the Second Council of Lyons invalidating the wills of usurers who had not made restitution.[52] Such restitutions are disguised or made to look like philanthropy. For instance, Francesco, the Merchant of Prato, left a dubious legacy of 1,500 florins 'about which my executors are well-informed', which were to be distributed after consultation with doctors of theology and canon lawyers about the good of his soul.[53] Enrico Scrovegni ordered the restitution of ill-gotten gains made by himself and his family, which would have included his notorious usurer father, Reginaldo, whom Dante had consigned to the seventh circle of Hell, the place reserved for such people.[54]

An alternative favoured by leading Italian mercantile families was to try to make restitution of 'incerta' before death, that is, to purchase heaven through patronage of art, architecture, and humane learning, and

---

[47] Nicholas Bozon, *Contés moralisés de Nicole Bozon*, Société des anciens textes françaises (Paris, 1889), p. 35: cited and trans. Coulton, *Medieval Village*, p. 284.
[48] Raymond de Roover, *Money, Banking, and Credit in Mediaeval Bruges: Italian Merchant-Bankers, Lombards, and Money-Changers: a Study in the Origins of Banking* (Cambridge, MA, 1948), n. 13, p. 157.
[49] Origo, *Merchant of Prato*, pp. 338–9.
[50] Giuseppe Basile, *Giotto: the Arena Chapel Frescoes* (London, 1993), p. 9.
[51] Nelson, 'The usurer and the merchant prince', pp. 114–16.
[52] See p. 166, n. 37 above.　　[53] Origo, *Merchant of Prato*, p. 338.
[54] Basile, *Giotto*, p. 19 and n. 14. Cf. Dante, *Inferno*, XVII, lines 64–75.

ostentatious gifts to the Church. In 1300 Enrico Scrovegni bought the site of the Roman ampitheatre at Padua on which to build a palace with a private chapel. It was dedicated partly to the Virgin of Charity, and in 1303–4 Benedict XI granted indulgences to those who visited it. The Scrovegni chapel is famous for the superb cycle of frescos painted by Giotto and his followers, many of which feature the theme of usury. It was founded ostensibly to expiate the sins of Reginaldo, but in reality it was to ensure his own salvation. In the fresco of the Last Judgement, Enrico appears, wearing penitential purple, presenting a model of his chapel to the Virgin, Mary Magdalen, herself a penitent and redeemed sinner, and St John the Evangelist. It is meant to symbolize the restitution of the profits of usury. This tableau appears on the right-hand side of Christ, that is, the side of the saved.[55] Later, the great Cosimo de Medici (1389–1464) consulted Pope Eugenius IV about how to make restitution of his illicitly acquired profits. As a result he endowed the monastery of San Marco in Florence.[56] There no longer seemed to be any doubt on earth about the salvation of the usurer, provided that he was sufficiently prominent. A tiny naked figure clinging to the foot of the Cross and stumbling towards salvation in the Giotto Last Judgement at Padua has been tentatively identified as Reginaldo Scrovegni.[57]

The Church gained greatly from the restitution of 'incerta'. Such prizes were supposed to be given to 'the poor', but this became a cover for any ecclesiastical institution or pious use. According to canon law the bishop fixed the amount of 'incerta' due from usurers in his diocese.[58] This included the Bishop of Rome, and there are several instances in the thirteenth century of popes arranging for their own financiers, the 'merchants of the apostolic camera' to restore 'incerta'. Often licences would be granted by either bishop or pope to ecclesiastical institutions to receive a quota of 'incerta'. Contemporaries complain that this could lead to collusion between a licence-holder and a usurer.[59]

The Church prosecuted 'manifest' usurers and ordered restitution, but in practice a lot of correction was left to the inner forum of individual conscience and to the priest in the secrecy of the confessional. The confessor had to induce the usurer to make restitution before absolution could

---

[55] Basile, *Giotto*, pp. 9–23, esp. pp. 9, 13, 19, n. 14, 285 (for reproduction of Last Judgement); Robert Smith, 'Giotto: artistic realism, political realism', *Journal of Medieval History*, 4 (1978), pp. 267–84, at pp. 272–83.
[56] Nelson, 'The usurer and the merchant prince', p. 119.
[57] Smith, 'Giotto', p. 283.
[58] Second Council of Lyons, 1274: *Sext.*, 5, 5, 2, cols. 1081–2: trans. Gilchrist, *Church and Economic Activity*, pp. 194–5.
[59] Nelson, 'The usurer and the merchant prince', p. 111.

be given. This could lead to duplicity on both sides, for absolution might be given in return for a substantial donation to the confessor's church or monastery. Contemporary literature is full of accusations of false restitution, among them by Peter the Chanter, Robert of Courçon, and Dante.[60] In *Piers Plowman*, when Repentance rebuked Avarice for robbing some merchants in the mistaken conviction that he was making 'restitution', Avarice retorted, 'I thought robbery was restitution.'[61] Later Repentance told him, ' If I were a friar and belonged to an honest house, I should never consent to spend money of yours on vestments or church repairs...if I knew, or had any suspicion, that it came from a man like you.' He refused Avarice absolution until he had made restitution.[62] The implication was that many friars did accept tainted offerings. Richard Fitzralph warned that those who absolved usurers without demanding restitution were themselves implicated in usury.[63] Such examples show how the system of penance and restitution could be abused in favour of the material interests of the Church.

CLERICAL USURY

Clerical involvement might be more direct. The papacy was obliquely involved in lending money at usury to the clergy so that they could pay the money back to it in the form of taxes. This was especially true of the lump sums known as common services, which had to be paid by bishops and abbots at formative moments in their careers. Such lending was done under papal licence and by the pope's bankers. A charge was made for this, which in effect was usury.[64] In England, in 1229, papal tenths (clerical taxes) were being exacted so harshly that the clergy were forced to borrow from the usurers who came over with Stephen, the pope's nuncio, at 'the rate of one noble for the loan of twenty by the month', that is, a yearly rate of 60 per cent. The usurers, known as 'Cahorsins', were Italian bankers. The Bishop of London excommunicated them in 1235, and they were banished in 1240, only to return in 1250 with papal assistance.[65]

---

[60] Ibid., pp. 110–11.
[61] William Langland, *Piers Plowman*, ed. Skeat B, passus v, p. 150, line 238, trans. J. F. Goodridge, *Langland: Piers the Plowman* (Harmondsworth, 1966), p. 68.
[62] Ibid., B, passus v, p. 154, lines 268–77, trans. Goodridge, p. 69.
[63] Wendy Scase, *Piers Plowman and the New Anti-clericalism* (Cambridge, 1989), p. 29.
[64] Lunt, *Papal Revenues in the Middle Ages*, 2, pp. 236–9, nos. 356–63; pp. 257–9, no. 378. On common and petty services and the difficulties in paying them see 1, pp. 461–79, 2, pp. 214–17, 279–80.
[65] Matthew Paris, *Chronica majora*, ed. H. R. Luard, *RS*, 57, 3 (1880), 1229, p. 184; 1235, pp. 328–32; Rogers Ruding, *Annals of the Coinage of Great Britain and its Dependencies*, 3rd edn, 1 (London, 1840), p. 183.

Following the example of their chief bishop, prelates too were involved in the money-lending business. A particularly disgraceful incident occurred in connection with plans for the conquest of Sicily on behalf of the papacy. Henry III of England had been forced into debt to Pope Alexander IV. The Pope tried to persuade the English bishops to lend to the King, so that the King could repay him. The Bishop of Hereford, a Savoyard, 'whose memory exhales a sulphurous odour', as a monastic chronicler judged, invented a scheme to help the Pope. He pretended that he was the official proctor of the English bishops – he had actually tricked two or three of them into consenting to this – and used his position to raise substantial loans with Italian merchants, pledging several of the English monasteries to repay these at interest. The money was sent to the papal camera and the monasteries were left in debt for both the loans, which they had never contracted, far less received, and for interest at a rate of over 20 per cent.[66]

This was an exceptional case. More often English ecclesiastics were simply involved in straight loans. Clerical usury was sufficiently common in twelfth-century England for Richard fitz Nigel in the *Dialogue of the Exchequer* to point out that its practitioners automatically lost all their clerical privileges and were penalized in the same way as laymen.[67] In a usury case which came before the Canterbury consistory court in 1292 a witness called John Bere let slip that the defendant 'took less than the archbishop takes from his debtors'. The Archbishop at the time was the Franciscan, John Pecham, himself hopelessly in debt to the Italians.[68] He had some years earlier, in 1279, castigated the Abbot of Bristol for having taken from a poor man 'more than 100 per cent of usury, which even civil law forbids'.[69] In the late thirteenth century a council held at Exeter had to decree the suspension from both office and benefice of usurious clergy.[70] In the mid-fourteenth century the Archbishop of York, William Melton, made so much profit from money-lending that he was able to build up his private estates, and even to found what was, in effect, a knightly family. His heir, a nephew called William, was knighted soon after inheriting. The records, unsurprisingly, do not reveal whether the Archbishop ever charged usury from the start of a loan, but he frequently charged for loans which were secured by bonds for more than the amount of the principal

---

[66] Lunt, *Papal Revenues in the Middle Ages*, 1, pp. 265–72.
[67] Richard fitz Nigel, *Dialogue of the Exchequer*, EHD, 2, no. 70, p. 550.
[68] Helmholz, 'Usury and church courts', p. 336; on Pecham's indebtedness see Decima Douie, *Archbishop Pecham* (Oxford, 1952), pp. 64–70.
[69] Coulton, *Medieval Village*, p. 286.
[70] D. Wilkins, *Concilia magna Britanniae et Hiberniae*, 4 vols. (London, 1737), 2, p. 146, canon 24.

if that was not repaid on time.[71] Of course, loans were not always made for financial profit. G. L. Harriss has argued convincingly that the enormous loans made to the Lancastrians by Cardinal Beaufort in the fifteenth century were for his own political and dynastic advantage rather than for financial profit.[72] Nor were bishops the only sinners, for the monasteries were equally involved in dubious financial transactions, both borrowing and lending, from the twelfth century onwards. Even a few of the lesser clergy could afford to lend: a Norwich jury recorded in 1290 that 'John the chaplain is an excessive usurer.'[73]

The Church in many cases condoned usury. In England it prosecuted very few cases in the late medieval period – an average of no more than three a year in most diocesan courts.[74] An English confessional manual of the first half of the fourteenth century, the *Memoriale Presbiterorum*, delivered a particularly damning indictment:

Here... usury is exercised by many, both clerics and laymen, every single day, sometimes secretly, sometimes openly... As for the judicial forum, justice is not done against usurers for this reason, that judges of today, in the execution of justice concerning this sin, are lukewarm and remiss and in no way wish to punish it.[75]

In Bruges an even more scandalous situation prevailed. Despite the prohibitions of the Council of Lyons in 1274, which forbade the letting of houses to usurers, and those of Vienne in 1311, which condemned on pain of interdict and excommunication the licensing of public usurers, the chief pawnshops, fourteen in all, were on the property of the provost and canons of the collegiate church of St Donatian. The provost himself granted licences to the usurers. The territory was immune from the jurisdiction of the municipal authorities, and the mainly Flemish and Walloon pawnbrokers were charging higher rates than the Lombards in the rival pawnshop in the municipal area.[76] Both the condoning of usury and their direct involvement in it must have made the role of the clergy as prosecutors and confessors an embarrassing one.

---

[71] L. H. Butler, 'Archbishop Melton, his neighbours, and his kinsmen, 1317–1340', *JEH*, 2 (1951), pp. 54–67.
[72] G. L. Harriss, 'Cardinal Beaufort – patriot or usurer?' *TRHS*, ser. 5, 19 (1969), pp. 129–48. This article is a revision of the view of K. B. McFarlane, 'Loans to the Lancastrian kings: the problem of inducement', reprinted in McFarlane, *England in the Fifteenth Century: Collected Essays* (London, 1981), pp. 57–78.
[73] A. Harding, *The Law Courts of Medieval England* (London, 1973), document 17, p. 159.
[74] R. H. Helmholz, 'Usury and the medieval English church courts', in Helmholz, *Canon Law and the Law of England* (London, 1987), pp. 326–9.
[75] Michael Haren, *Sin and Society in Fourteenth-century England: a Study of the 'Memoriale Presbiterorum'* (Oxford, 2000), p. 164.
[76] De Roover, *Money, Banking and Credit*, pp. 162–3.

TIME, LABOUR, AND INDUSTRY

The amount of restitution owed by a usurer to a borrower or his heirs could be calculated precisely. In the case of theft from God, it could not. *Eiciens* had stated that the usurer 'sells a thing given by God which was not acquired through being a merchant', meaning time. It was a medieval commonplace that time was God's time: it was ecclesiastical time, to be spent in the work God had ordained. Because, like knowledge, it was the free gift of God, it was not to be sold.[77] Time was church time, as Le Goff has shown. In practice it was regulated by liturgical seasons and services, and its passing was sounded by church bells.[78] As ecclesiastical values gave way to secular and mercantile ones in the Renaissance, the mechanical clock started to regulate lives, and man gradually assumed ownership of time. In the early thirteenth century Thomas of Chobham could still declare that 'The usurer does not sell the debtor something which is his own, but time, which belongs to God. It follows that because he sells something belonging to another he ought not to have any profit from it.'[79]

By the late fifteenth century it was different. The Florentine humanist Leon Battista Alberti explained in *The Family* that there are three things given by nature to man. The soul and the body are two of them: the third thing, time, 'is a most precious thing. These hands and eyes of mine do not belong to me as much as that.'[80]

Alberti was perhaps unwittingly resurrecting a Roman law idea that time was owned by the individual. Applying this to usury Peter John Olivi abandoned the idea that time was common, because it was God's time, and suggested that it could be sold if it was owned by the seller. He produced an example of a debtor who decided to repay a loan early in return for a discount. He appeared to be selling the time back to the creditor, so that he ran the risk of being accused of usury, of 'selling time'. But since the time 'belonged' to him, and, on the basis of the Roman law maxim 'Time belonging to the seller can be lawfully sold', there was no question of usury. When the physical possession of something, whether money or anything else, passed from one person to another, time went with it. The time attached to money would be transferred when money was alienated, either by being lent or by being exchanged for something else.[81]

---

[77] Le Goff, *Your Money or Your Life*, ch. 3, pp. 33–45: 'The thief of time'.
[78] Jacques Le Goff, 'Merchant's time and Church's time in the Middle Ages' and 'Labor time in the "crisis" of the fourteenth century', in *Time, Work, and Culture in the Middle Ages*, trans. Arthur Goldhammer (Chicago, IL and London, 1980), pp. 29–42, 43–52.
[79] Chobham, *Summa confessorum*, 7, 6, q.11, p. 504.
[80] Leon Battista Alberti, *The Family*, pp. 27–326, at p. 173.
[81] Langholm, *Economics*, pp. 369–70. See *Digest*, 41, 3, 14 and 19.

Gerald Odonis the future Minister-General of the Franciscan Order seemed to have it both ways. Time for him was both common and individual. Common time could not be sold; individual time could: 'In the first sense time is something common and in no way vendible. In the second sense it is the property of someone, just as a year of a horse lent me is said to be mine.'[82] The main interest of this is that Odonis had drawn the Middle Ages a step closer to the Renaissance concept that time belonged to man.

Eiciens had highlighted some differences between lending money at usury and letting a house or a field and linked these with both time and labour. As the author observed, both a house and a field might deteriorate in use over time, but money, being sterile, did not alter when it was lent. In addition, if someone applied labour to cultivating a field, then fruit could be expected from it, whereas this was not true of fruitless money. The problem faced by late medieval thinkers was how to justify the fact that in practice barren money did appear to increase over time, and to do this without actually destroying either the nature of money as a fungible or the notion of its sterility.

The crucial words here are 'over time', for it was time which naturally caused things either to increase and multiply or to diminish. The time argument was an alternative way of looking at the sterility doctrine.[83] There were some things which were altered by time, and some things which were not. The subject arose in discussion of credit sales. William of Auxerre provided a forceful restatement of traditional time-based arguments against usury, reinforced with metaphysics culled from Augustine, about how all created things, the sun, the earth, the water, for example, 'give of themselves': 'Nothing, however, so *naturally*, gives itself as time; willy-nilly things have time. Because, therefore the usurer sells what necessarily belongs to all creatures generally, he injures all creatures, even the stones...'[84] By placing these words under the heading of credit sales William had spotted that usury in the sense of selling time was as likely to occur in them as it was in a straight loan. Of course, they were not the same thing, but the line between them became blurred. In credit sales merchants almost literally played for time, gambling on the future price of goods. The blurring of the line between credit sales and loans was also due to a famous decretal of Pope Gregory IX, *Naviganti* (1227–34),[85] which although it was about credit sales, could be and was applied by many writers to loans. *Naviganti* allowed a higher price to be charged where payment was deferred over time if there was real doubt about the future

---

[82] Langholm, *Economics*, p. 525.   [83] Ibid., p. 589, for this important observation.
[84] Noonan, *Scholastic Analysis*, pp. 43–4.   [85] *Decretales*, 5, 19, 19, col. 816.

price of the goods – that is, if time had altered their value or quality. The point was enlarged upon by Giles of Lessines (d. post 1303), who, in his *De usuris*, produced the first medieval treatise to be devoted to an economic subject. His contribution was fundamental. He considered that there were certain circumstances in which a seller could ask for a higher price for a credit sale without committing the sin of usury. In the first place, there might be seasonal variations in market prices for crops: for example, corn would be scarcer (and dearer) in the spring than in the autumn. If payment was to be made in the spring, then presumably the spring price could be charged. Secondly, there might be an increase over time in the number, size, or value of natural objects – crops, forests, or animals, which would justify a higher price. Thirdly, Giles lists 'the nature of the thing in relation to local conditions', by which he probably means changes in a local market price due to demand. In all of these three cases, provided that there is no fraud or dishonesty involved, the charging of a higher price for credit is justified because of the increase in the value of the goods over time. But if more is asked simply because seller and buyer agree that payment should be deferred over time, and time has wrought no change in the goods, then the contract is usurious and unjust.[86] Giles specifies that usury can occur even if exactly the same amount is returned, if the value of that amount has meanwhile increased and the lender *intended* to gain from the transaction.[87] The sinful hope of gain was what decided the issue.

English popular writers took up the theme of loans and credit sales. Under the heading of usury, the author of the *Fasciculus morum*, relying on *Naviganti*, discussed cases where it was licit to receive an amount beyond the principal, and specified cases of doubt:

If someone gives you ten measures of grain, wine, or oil, so that at a later time the same amount of grain, wine, or oil may be given back to him, which then is worth more, if he is at the time of handing over in genuine doubt whether their price would go up or down, he must not be called a usurer.[88]

Turning to credit sales, doubt also excuses someone

who sells cloth, grain, wine, or other such goods so that he shall receive more than they are then worth after a certain time, always provided that he does not actually sell them at the time of the contract. But if he sells looking towards a long delay at a much greater price than their value, it is usury.[89]

[86] Langholm, *Economics*, pp. 311–12.   [87] Ibid., pp. 314–15.
[88] *Fasciculus morum*, IV, vii, pp. 351–3, lines 78–83.
[89] Ibid., lines 83–7.

In *Dives and Pauper* the subject is advance payment for goods, something which frequently happened in the English wool trade, although Pauper describes it in terms of a loan:

> If a man or woman lend ten shillings at Easter or in another time to receive as many bushels of wheat in harvest and the wheat be better for that time than is the money, and it be in doubt skilfully [reasonably] whether the wheat shall be more worth or less in time of payment, it is not usury.[90]

As for the *Fasciculus* author, it is the sinful hope that time will make profitable changes which constitutes usury. Pauper warns: 'If a man lend silver, corn, or wine to have again the same quantity in certain time only in hope that the same quantity shall be more worth in time of pay he doth usury.'[91]

LABOUR AND INDUSTRY

Allowing time to take its course and effect its own changes was a lazy way of making a profit. Scholastic thinkers, however, began to realize that it was not actually time that made barren money fertile, but labour and industry, and that whereas time belonged to God, labour belonged to man. In the late medieval period there was growing resentment against people who did not work, whether they were able-bodied beggars, mendicant friars, or companies of freebooting soldiers between military campaigns. In this climate passions were roused against those who made vast profits without lifting a finger – the usurers. The informal definition of usury came to be making a profit without working for it. Thomas of Chobham, writing about 1216, pointed out that the usurer 'wishes to pursue his profit without any labour, even while sleeping, which is contrary to the precept of the Lord, "In labour and the sweat of your face shall you get your bread."'[92] He was much exercised by the comparison of usurers with prostitutes. Why, he questioned, did the Church coerce usurers more severely than prostitutes?[93] One answer was the question of labour. While moralizing that 'No one ought to labour unless they honour God through their labour', he allowed that prostitutes 'hire out their bodies for shameful use, but because they undergo bodily labour, it is lawful for them to keep what they receive for such labour'.[94] It was not just a question of idleness:

---

[90] *Dives and Pauper*, pt. 2, Commandment VII, xxiv, p. 196, lines 32–5. Cf. M. M. Postan, 'Credit in medieval trade', in Postan, *Medieval Trade and Finance* (Cambridge, 1973), pp. 1–27, esp. pp. 5–21.
[91] *Dives and Pauper*, pt. 2, Commandment VII, xxv, p. 200, lines 62–5.
[92] Thomas of Chobham, *Summa confessorum*, q. 11, art. 7, dist. 6, cap. 4, p. 504.
[93] Ibid., q. 6a, art. 7, cap. 2, p. 347.
[94] Ibid., q. 5a, art. 6, dist. 4, pp. 297, 296, respectively.

the usurer took the labour of the borrower, which did not belong to him. This had been hinted at in *Eiciens*, and it was taken up forcefully by Albert the Great. The borrower

> by hard labour has acquired something as profit on which he could live, and this the usurer, suffering no distress, spending no labour, fearing no loss of capital by misfortune, takes away, and through the distress and labour and changing luck of his neighbour collects and acquires riches for himself.[95]

Underlying all these observations was the idea that the true source of economic profit is labour. The most interesting theoretical developments on usury came when this conviction was joined to the concept of the sterility of money. What apparently made hitherto sterile money bear fruit was the application of human labour and industry, but no one was actually allowed to say this, because it would have damaged the doctrine of the sterility of money. It is not always easy to define the term industry as used by the scholastics, but it appears to mean business acumen, sagacity, even perhaps entrepreneurship, as opposed to manual labour.[96]

The terms labour and industry were introduced by William of Auxerre in his *Summa aurea*, when he was examining the duty of the usurer to restore his usurious profits to the borrower. The question which concerned him and others was whether a usurer had to restore profit to the borrower which he had acquired through legitimate business, but based on the illegitimate proceeds of usury – that is, after he had recycled his usurious profit into a respectable venture. William thought that everything should be restored except a 'reasonable amount' for his 'labour and industry'. This was largely because the rest of the profit, after the deduction of the 'reasonable amount', was deadened by its root[97] – in other words, a corrupt root would bring forth only corrupt fruit. The reference is obliquely to Matthew 7.18, 'A good tree cannot bring forth evil fruit, neither can a corrupt tree bring forth good fruit.' By implication, William's biological root metaphor denied that money was sterile, whether it produced good or evil fruit.[98]

By the time of Aquinas both the application of industry to money in economic undertakings and the 'root' argument had become established. Aquinas disagreed with William of Auxerre, however, and upheld the Aristotelian notion that money was sterile. He could not deny that money-lending was profitable, but the profit in any economic enterprise must be due to labour and industry rather than to the money itself, since money

---

[95] Albert the Great, *Super Lucam*, ad 6, 35: quoted by Langholm, *Economics*, p. 197.
[96] For discussion of this see Langholm, *Aristotelian Analysis*, p. 102.
[97] Langholm, *Economics*, p. 87.   [98] Langholm, *Aristotelian Analysis*, pp. 92–3.

could not 'breed'. That meant that it was not necessary to inquire about the 'root' of the profit. 'Root' and 'labour' were unconnected. The question then was who actually owned the labour that generated the profit, for he who applied the labour should enjoy its rewards.

a lender who has extorted such things as money, corn, or wine by way of interest on a loan is bound to restore only what he has actually received from the borrower, since anything that has been made out of such a commodity is the fruit, not of this thing itself, but of human industry.[99]

Richard of Middleton agreed, emphasizing that man owned his labour: 'because man owns his labour and industry, profit which is acquired by *legitimate business from money extorted by usury does not have to be restored*' (my ital.).[100] He also attacked the root metaphor, and in so doing failed to maintain the separation between the sterility doctrine and labour. Money could be made fruitful by the application of care and labour:

Of a sterile thing no one ought to demand a fruit, but money of itself is a sterile thing, for it can bring forth no fruit *except by the labour and solicitude of the user* [my ital.]; therefore you ought not to demand any fruit of your money if you have neither laboured nor been solicitous for that profit.[101]

Richard appeared to have destroyed the sterility doctrine, but whether intentionally or not is an open question.[102]

Duns Scotus, a younger Franciscan contemporary of Richard, agreed that what made money fruitful was not time but labour, in this case the labour of the borrower not the lender:

Money does not from its nature have any fruit, as have other things which may germinate of themselves, but any fruit which does occur is through the labour of another, that is the user [borrower]... therefore he who wishes to get fruit from the money wishes to have the fruit of another's industry.[103]

In tackling the question of recycled usury, Scotus agreed with Richard that legitimate profit did not have to be restored by the usurer to the borrower. After all, it had been acquired by his own industry. Unlike the original profit it could not be restored to the borrower, because the borrower would then be committing usury by receiving the fruit of someone else's industry.

---

[99] Thomas Aquinas, *Summa theologiae*, 2a2ae, 78, 3 ad 3, vol. 38, p. 249.
[100] Richard of Middleton, *Super Quatuor Libros Sententiarum*, 2, bk. 4, dist. xiv, art. 5, q. 6, p. 224b.
[101] Ibid., p. 224a.   [102] Langholm, *Economics*, pp. 338–9.
[103] John Duns Scotus, *Opus Oxoniensis*, bk. IV, dist. xv, q. 24 in *Opera omnia*, 18 (Paris, 1894), p. 293a.

He appreciated the very real danger that this situation would encourage usury.[104] In effect, there was nothing beyond a guilty conscience to prevent the usurer from pocketing a rapid secondary profit before making restitution of the original.

The final twist in the industry argument came from Gerald Odonis commenting on Peter Olivi. Odonis addressed the question of whether the industry of the borrower or the lender should be rewarded. These are the words of the lender: 'I say that I do not sell you your industry but sell you the cessation of my own industry, which to me is harmful and to you profitable. For we cannot both use the same money at the same time.'[105] Odonis seems to be suggesting that money is scarce, and that anyone who lends it is entitled to be compensated for the loss of its use.

CONCLUSION

The palea *Eiciens* had touched on the main aspects of the usury doctrine – usury as a mortal sin, depriving the sinner of salvation, usury as theft, its connection with time, the theft of God's time by the usurer, his attempt to sell it to the borrower, and the fact that time was the factor which made natural things increase or diminish. Money, as a sterile thing, could not be affected by time in this way, but what it could be affected by was the labour and industry of either the lender or the borrower. The borrower's labour was what was at issue more often than that of the lender, and the usurer was condemned for taking the fruits of someone else's labour in demanding more in return than was originally given. Although the focus has been on the malicious actions of the usurer, his sinful intention to profit, and his fate at the final balancing of accounts with God, the impression conveyed is that in this life the usurer gained at the expense of the borrower. It is to the opposite role of the lender as loser, or potential loser, that we now turn.

[104] Ibid., p. 333a. Cf. Langholm, *Economics*, pp. 417–18.
[105] Ibid., pp. 528–9 and *Aristotelian Analysis*, pp. 97–8.

8

THE THEORY OF INTEREST: THE USURER AS LOSER

INTRODUCTION: USURY AND INTEREST

Usury and trewe interest be thinges as contrary as falshed is to trewth. For usury contayneth in it selfe inequalitie and unnaturall dealinge, and trewe interest observeth equitie and naturall dealinge.[1]

This sixteenth-century English quotation sums up the difference between the theories of usury and interest. We have already seen the usurer as winner — the one who gained from a loan at the expense of the borrower. Usurers, however, did not always win. In the mid-thirteenth century Ptolemy of Lucca noted that 'in loans a lender often suffers outrage, because it is in the nature of a borrower for it to be difficult for him to return a loan'.[2] John Bromyard reported complaints by usurers about rich bad debtors who deserved to be charged higher rates of interest because they did not make repayment at the end of a loan. He seemed to think that the false and deceitful debtors were a suitable match for the greedy usurers.[3] Nevertheless, the risk of loss was always staring the usurer in the face.

Our final discussion is about interest, which was supposed to compensate for loss or potential loss. The idea derived from Roman law. In Latin *inter-est* meant something which 'is between'; it meant difference. Payment of *inter-est* was meant to restore the lender's financial position to what it had been before he made the loan, to make up any difference between what was

---

[1] 'Discussion of Usury with proposal to nationalize exchange business' 1570(?), in R. H. Tawney and Eileen Power, eds., *Tudor Economic Documents*, 3 (London, 1924), p. 364.
[2] Quoted in Noonan, *Scholastic Analysis*, p. 129.
[3] John Bromyard, *Summa praedicantium*, pt. 2, ch. 12, 'usura', art. 6, sect. 19, p. 470r.

given and what was returned or was likely to be. As the canonist Raymond of Peñafort explained, 'Interest is not profit, but the avoidance of loss',[4] and Henry of Friemar echoed this when he allowed that interest might be charged to 'avoid a loss, but not to seek a gain'.[5] Payment of *inter-est* was meant to restore the balance of justice: 'Trewe interest observeth equitie and naturall dealinge.' In this sense it could be regarded as a mean.

Although apparently distinct from it, the theory of interest was dangerous to the condemnatory usury doctrine. It was a means of evading it, and of undermining its most fundamental tenets: that a loan should be free, that time, as God's gift, could not be sold, that money was sterile, and that it was a fungible which was totally consumed in use, making its use and ownership inseparable. All of these things were challenged, and the weaknesses in the usury doctrine exposed. What was not challenged, however, was intention – the sinful hope of profit was still what made an action usurious. The criterion which decided whether repayment above the principal was licit or not was always whether it was '*in fraudem usuarum*' – 'with the deceitful intention of usury'. Interest merely restored the balance between the parties.

In an increasingly profit-geared economy there was a need for both credit and ready cash. Bernardino of Siena had a realistic approach to the situation. He observed that 'all usury is profit, but not all profit is usury', and acknowledged both the need for credit and the uncomfortable fact that in an imperfect world no one would lend without the hope of profit.[6] In this climate a number of economic devices grew up, many of them based on Roman law, which appeared to allow payment of an amount above the principal without contravening the usury laws. A fourteenth-century Italian preaching friar was understandably perplexed by their variety:

There are certain cases concerning which even wise and lettered men are in doubt...such as usurious contracts, which are so many...one can hardly understand them. And some men conceal and excuse them under the names of exchange or interest, and others with those of deposit or savings. Some call them purchase and sale, or profits involving hazards or deferred payments, and yet others say they are investments, companies, associations, and other abominable profits.[7]

Against the background of the experiences of people who either demanded or paid interest, these and other so-called 'abominable profits' will be

---

[4] Quoted in Noonan, *Scholastic Analysis*, p. 106. For discussion of the concept of interest see ibid., pp. 105–6.
[5] Quoted in Langholm, *Economics*, p. 527.
[6] Noonan, *Scholastic Analysis*, pp. 32, 73, respectively.
[7] Fra Jacopo Passavanti, *Mirror of True Penitence*, quoted and translated by Origo, *Merchant of Prato*, p. 150.

the specific concern of this chapter. Practical developments led to the evolution of a theory of interest, the avoidance of loss, which ultimately led to a narrowing in scope and a redefinition of what constituted usury. More than anything else, discussion on the Italian *montes*, the civic public debts, led to the establishment of the idea of taking interest from the beginning of a loan, rather than as compensation for default or damage, which logically had to be assessed retrospectively. Discussion on the *montes pietatis*, charitable pawnshops providing loans to the poor, was to lead to a new papal definition of usury which sanctioned labour, expense, and risk as justifications for paying amounts which exceeded the principal.

PRACTICAL ATTITUDES

Usury and interest were in practice the same, because both of them involved repayment above the amount of the principal. Due to the increasing complexity and prevalence of usurious contracts from the second half of the fourteenth century, the canonists started to wonder whether usury cases were still the exclusive preserve of the ecclesiastical courts. Many of them allowed the secular courts to prosecute in cases where it was clear that the contract was usurious, although the establishment of this in doubtful cases was still left to the courts Christian.[8] In practice, by the fifteenth century, in the advanced commercial centres of Italy and the Low Countries, the civic authorities rather than the Church were largely responsible for prosecuting usurers and enforcing canon law, except in the case of the clergy. In Florence, in 1345, when relations with the clergy, and especially the papacy, reached a nadir, the city government decreed that all citizens were immune from the jurisdiction of church courts.[9] The commune itself no longer prosecuted the 'manifest' usurers, the pawnbrokers – only the individual, small-time lenders. This was because pawnbrokers became 'licensed', and often the Establishment merchant-princes, technically usurers themselves, were responsible as city fathers for granting the licences and for prosecuting the unlicensed.[10] In the fourteenth century they would go through the motions of fining public pawnbrokers, but in reality would treat the fines as annual licence fees, in return for which the pawnbrokers were to be 'free and absolved from any further censure, penalty, or exaction', as a text of 1354 stated.[11] In Bruges, where the pawnbrokers renting church property charged more than those in the municipal area, Philip the Bold

---

[8] McLaughlin, 'Canonists on usury', pp. 18–22.
[9] M. B. Becker, 'Three cases concerning the restitution of usury in Florence', *Journal of Economic History*, 17 (1957), pp. 446–7.
[10] Nelson, 'The usurer and the merchant prince', p. 113.
[11] De Roover, *Medici Bank*, pp. 14–15; text at p. 410, n. 32.

imposed heavy fines with the agreement of the Church. As in Florence, these were soon treated as yearly licence fees.[12]

In less-commercialized England prosecution of usurers was undertaken both by church and secular courts, although the royal court did not become involved until the late fifteenth century. In rural areas usury was one of the crimes investigated at a view of frankpledge from as early as the thirteenth century, and there is evidence that some manorial courts prosecuted village usurers.[13] It was even more of a problem in the towns. In London the mayor and aldermen had assumed jurisdiction of usury cases in 1363.[14] In 1376, a parliamentary petition was presented to Edward III, complaining that the 'horrible vice of usury is so spread abroad and used throughout the land that the virtue of charity ... is wellnigh wholly perished'. It requested that, as in London, all urban authorities should be granted jurisdiction over usury cases.[15] In 1487 a statute of Henry VII against usury and unlawful bargains acknowledged the jurisdiction of civic authorities, reserving to the Chancellor authority to examine all 'maner corrupt bargayns, promyses, lones or sales'.[16]

The Church was still responsible overall for prosecuting usurers. Contrary to the strict letter of canon law, people were prosecuted only for charging exorbitant rates for lending, rather than simply for making a charge. The low average of three prosecutions a year in most diocesan courts was perhaps because of the overlapping jurisdiction with the lesser secular courts (as opposed to the royal court). In addition, where prosecutions were brought officially rather than privately the responsibility of presentment fell on the people of a parish, who may have been deterred by neighbourly loyalty. Many cases were settled out of court.[17] The lax attitude of the clergy cannot have helped either.

Popes and prelates would both borrow and lend: lay princes borrowed rather than lent. Compared with merchants, they were a bad risk, for if they died their successors would not necessarily honour their debts, any more than their subjects would while they lived. If secular rulers refused to repay loans there was little that a creditor could do. In the early fourteenth century Philip IV of France decided to cancel all his debts and banish his bankers, which contributed to the ruin of the order of Knights Templar. In mid-century, Edward III was at least partly responsible for the crash

---

[12] De Roover, *Money, Banking, and Credit*, pp. 162–3.
[13] Articles of enquiry by the frankpledge for St Peter's Gloucester, in Titow, *English Rural Society*, p. 190, enquiry to be made 'About Christian usurers'; Helmholz, 'Usury and the medieval English church courts', p. 328. For occurrences in manorial court rolls see Hilton, *English Peasantry*, pp. 46–7, 103–4.
[14] Thrupp, *Merchant Class of Medieval London*, p. 175.
[15] *EEH*, section 6, no. 36, pp. 200–1.
[16] Tawney and Power, eds., *Tudor Economic Documents*, 2, section 3, no. 3, pp. 135–6.
[17] Helmholz, 'Usury and the church courts', pp. 326–9.

of the Florentine firms of the Bardi and Peruzzi when he failed to repay substantial loans contracted in the early stages of the Hundred Years War. Small wonder that rates of usury for lending to princes were set high. Frederick of Austria, for example, had to pay 80 per cent, although Robert of Anjou paid only 30 per cent to his Florentine bankers. Differing reports of Charles VIII of France's loans in 1494 to pay his military expenses for the invasion of Italy record rates of 42 per cent, 56 per cent, and 100 per cent.[18] Yolande of Flanders, Countess of Bar, a member of the ruling house, was always in trouble. In 1364 she had to pledge her exquisite jewelled golden coronet, two tiaras, and twelve silver cups to the Grands Cahorsins of Bruges before they would lend to her, even at usury of 50 per cent.[19] The normal pawnshop rate in fourteenth-century Flanders was $43\frac{1}{3}$ per cent, and the rate for commercial loans was only 10–16 per cent, while in Florence and Pisa it was 7–15 per cent.[20]

ROMAN LAW, INTEREST, AND CONTRACT

Many of the ambiguities in the usury laws discovered by late medieval thinkers originated in Roman civil law. There was some confusion about whether Roman law permitted usury, in the sense of receiving back more than was given. The consensus of the medieval Roman lawyers seemed to be that while technically it did, the permission had no force because it was contrary to divine law and the law of the Church.[21] The theologians, however, considered that Roman law and secular law in general did permit usury, not because usury was just, but because it was for the good of the people. In the fifteenth century Pauper summarized a tradition based on Albert the Great and Aquinas:

By God's law all usury is damned. By emperors' law and by man's law sometimes it is suffered, not for that it is good nor lawful but for to flee the more evil, for oftentime men should perish [perchyn] but they must borrow at usury, for otherwise the covetous rich man will not lend to the needful. And so the law of man rightfully suffereth it for a good end, but the covetous man doth it unrightfully and for a wicked end.[22]

Civil law was clearly more permissive than canon law.

---

[18] Sidney Homer, *A History of Interest Rates* (New Brunswick, NJ, 1963), pp. 100, 106.
[19] De Roover, *Money, Banking, and Credit*, p. 119.
[20] Homer, *Interest Rates*, p. 100.
[21] On this question and the texts of Justinian on which the disagreement was based, see McLaughlin, 'Canonists on usury', pt. 1, pp. 87–92.
[22] *Dives and Pauper*, pt. 2, Commandment VII, xxvi, p. 202, lines 58–65. For the views of William of Auxerre, Albert the Great, Aquinas, and his pupil John of Naples (d. 1336), see Langholm, *Economics*, pp. 85, 196, 238, 477, respectively.

Roman law also provided specific loopholes on which the medieval theory of interest came to be based. The loan contract was that of *mutuum*. Its meaning was clarified by an entirely bogus etymology popularized by Gaius, a second-century lawyer. What was mine passed 'from me' (*meo*), to become 'yours' (*tuum*).[23] Bogus or not, the famous pun made an important point, namely that in a *mutuum* ownership passed: what was mine became yours. With this transfer of ownership went all the associated risks and responsibilities, which meant that they were no longer the burden of the lender. But whatever happened, the *mutuum* had to be repaid.

What about interest? The Romans did charge interest on loans, but they carefully excluded this from the loan contract. It was negotiated by a separate verbal agreement, known as a *stipulatio*. The maximum rate allowed in the Roman Empire was 12 per cent a year. In addition, there were several Roman law contracts, such as partnership (*societas*), deposit (*depositum*), and exchange (*permutatio*), which did not come under the heading of *mutuum*, but which might involve making a profit from money. Medieval thinkers were to take advantage both of the permissive attitude of Roman law to interest and of the various contracts outside the range of the strict loan, the *mutuum*. Legally only a *mutuum* could attract usury: other contracts could not.

The easiest way of side-stepping contractual obligations was to make a gift. A borrower incurred not just a financial debt, but also a moral debt of gratitude to the lender, which might be repaid in this way. To avoid the charge of usury, the gift had to be entirely free. If it were, as Giles of Lessines put it, 'given freely without any idea of compensation, the recipient was guiltless'.[24] The gift relationship could not be contractual. As Duns Scotus recognized, contract deprived an offering of the character of a gift, and so made it illicit.[25] Even if it were not part of a contract, certain conditions had to be fulfilled. The gift (which was not always money) had to be the donor's to give. Scotus explained that the giver had to have both the will and the right to give, that is, the gift must not infringe the rights of a lord or superior. But what really mattered to the scholastics was the criterion of intention. To lend in the main hope of receiving a gift, and thereby a profit, was sinful. A 'secondary' hope, however, was allowed, although it is difficult to see how this could have been distinguished from the primary one. William of Auxerre, Raymond of Peñafort, Hostiensis, and other later thinkers all subscribe to this peculiar idea.[26] In practice, it is hard to conceive of the Italians in England, for example, making enormous loans to the first three Edwards without an eye on revenue from customs and

---

[23] Schulz, *Classical Roman Law*, p. 508.   [24] Langholm, *Economics*, p. 306.
[25] Ibid., p. 408.   [26] Noonan, *Scholastic Analysis*, p. 105.

subsidies, the assignment of direct taxes, licences to export wool without going through the Staple, or the grant of numerous 'free' sacks of wool. The Riccardi of Lucca had total control of the customs for nearly twenty years during the reign of Edward I.[27] Sometimes the giving of 'gifts' came perilously near to an obligation to pay interest. The King would agree to compensate his bankers for their 'damages', but although the compensation was paid ostensibly as a series of 'gifts', he was expected to issue bonds for the amounts, and they were treated as part of the total debt. In just over three years between 1328 and 1331 Edward III ran up a debt of £42,000 with his Florentine bankers, the Bardi, and on this amount he granted £11,000 of 'gifts'. This amounted to an interest rate of 26 per cent.[28]

Gift avoided having to stipulate payment of interest in a contract. Another way of doing it was by a 'fictitious loan', which meant that the amount of the loan stated in the contract was rather more than the actual amount borrowed. As G. L. Harriss has shown, this occurred frequently in the records of the English Exchequer, making it virtually impossible to gauge the rate of interest paid.[29] Yet another trick, popular in merchant loans, was the 'loan by sale', where a loan would be disguised as a sale for the purposes of the records.[30] At the foot of the social ladder it was common for people to work off their debts, and often a substantial amount of interest, by labouring for the creditor without pay. As a fifteenth-century English author puts it: 'If the poor man may not pay thee at his day, thou bindest him by law to work with thee; and for a penny of debt, thou takest two pennyworth of work.'[31] For the rest, it was a case of using contracts other than the *mutuum* to conceal such payments. The reasoning seemed to be that if the contract drawn up was not that of a *mutuum*, ownership and the attendant risk were not necessarily transferred to the borrower. This entitled the lender to claim compensation, or *inter-est*, for damage or loss caused by delay in the repayment of a loan.

The justifications for payment of interest were known as 'extrinsic titles', being dictated by circumstances which were outside the loan. Since a loan was supposed to be free, they could hardly be intrinsic. The three most important 'extrinsic' factors were delay in repayment, loss emerging (*damnum emergens*), and profit withheld (*lucrum cessans*).

---

[27] E. B. Fryde, 'Public credit with special reference to North-western Europe', in *Cambridge Economic History of Europe*, 3, pp. 456–7.
[28] Ibid., p. 456.
[29] G. L. Harriss, 'Fictitious loans', *EconHR*, ser. 2, 8 (1955), pp. 187–99.
[30] Postan, 'Credit in medieval trade', pp. 11–12.
[31] *Jacob's Well*, ed. Arthur Brandeis, EETS, o.s. 115 (Oxford, 1900), p. 124, lines 7–9. Cf. the fourteenth-century *Book of Vices and Virtues*, ed. W. Nelson, EETS, o.s. 217 (London, 1942), p. 32, lines 17–24. For variations of this practice in Europe see Baldwin, *Peter the Chanter*, 1, pp. 278–9.

The 'extrinsic titles' were closely linked, for they were all devices for indemnifying the creditor against the default of the debtor by making up the *inter-est*. This could be done on the basis of a simple penalty for delay, either built into the original loan contract as a specific penalty clause or assessed retrospectively. But how could a payment for delay be assessed – was it to be assessed by the length of time involved, in which case the accusation of selling time might be raised? Or might it be charged as interest to make good any loss or expense the creditor might have sustained as a result of not getting his money back on time? Or should it be assessed on the profits he might have made if he had received his money on the due date and put it to profitable use? All these possibilities were to be aired.

DELAY IN REPAYMENT

It was common practice during the later Middle Ages for penalty clauses to be attached to loan contracts – penalties that became enforceable if the debtor did not honour his repayment obligation. So long as they were not included in the hope that the debtor would default, they were licit. Raymond of Peñafort, summarizing earlier opinions, recognized them, provided they were not a cloak for usury. Suspicion would arise if the creditor were a known usurer or the penalty fixed in proportion to the length of the delay at so much per month or year.[32] For Duns Scotus, in the following century, the condition was that the creditor really preferred to have his money back on time rather than have it later with the penalty attached. To prefer to receive the penalty was both to sell time and the debtor's industry.[33] In practice it was sometimes profitable to receive the penalty, particularly on short-term loans. The public money-lenders of Belgium, for example, collected much of their profit in this way.[34] The influential fourteenth-century notary Roland de Passigiero, founder of a school at Bologna, supplied text-book examples of loan contracts, all of which demanded double the amount of the loan as penalty for delay.[35] In a fourteenth-century English case a village money-lender brought an action against three executors because the deceased had not repaid a debt of 20s. The amount demanded was 100s.[36]

Was it possible to claim interest for delay without damage? Logically it was not, because there was no difference in the situation of the creditor

---

[32] McLaughlin, 'Canonists on usury', p. 141.   [33] Langholm, *Economics*, p. 416.
[34] Noonan, *Scholastic Analysis*, p. 108.   [35] Ibid.
[36] Fisher and Jurica, eds., *Documents in English Economic History*, no. 13, p. 349.

as the result of not having received his money back on time if he had not suffered damage. The title of delay, however, gradually became merged with the penalty for damage, which, because it was fixed in advance, could be claimed if delay occurred, regardless of what the damage was. The mere fact of delay became sufficient title. The thirteenth-century canonist Hostiensis justified it 'because it is sought for the sake of avoiding loss not taking gain'.[37] Many of the scholastics approved.[38]

In practice, the way in which English creditors protected themselves was often by taking a recognizance, a sum of money pledged as security for repayment of a debt on the due date, which would be forfeited if the debtor defaulted. Alternatively a creditor might demand a bond, a sealed letter of obligation, enforceable at law, by which a debtor was bound to pay more than the principal, but which was cancelled if the loan was repaid on time. The most famous bond was that demanded by Shylock of Antonio:

> Go with me to a notary, seal me there
> Your single bond; and, in a merry sport,
> If you repay me not on such a day,
> In such a place, such sum or sums as are
> Express'd in the condition, let the forfeit
> Be nominated for an equal pound
> Of your fair flesh...[39]

Archbishop Melton of York charged a rate of interest secured by bonds of anything from 33.33 to 300 per cent of the debt in the fourteenth century.[40] There were other alternatives, also resorted to by Melton. One of these was to take pledges in valuables, such as silver plate or jewellery, which exceeded the principal in value. Another was to take land as security, in effect a mortgage. The creditor would enjoy the fruits of the land for the duration of the loan, but the amount would not be added to the principal, which meant that the creditor was in effect taking interest. Mortgages had been specifically condemned by Alexander III in 1173 at the Council of Tours.[41] Melton's loan of 1,000 marks to the Earl of Atholl in 1332 brought him the fruits of the manor of Gainsborough for nearly two years.[42] Like modern mortgages, default could lead to forfeiture.

---

[37] Noonan, *Scholastic Analysis*, p. 109.
[38] Langholm, *Economics*, p. 338 (Richard of Middleton); p. 425 (François de Meyronnes); p. 485 (Durand of Saint-Pourçain); p. 416 (Duns Scotus).
[39] Shakespeare, *The Merchant of Venice*, I, 3, lines 145–51.
[40] Butler, 'Archbishop Melton', pp. 58–9.
[41] McLaughlin, 'Canonists on usury', p. 114.   [42] Butler, 'Archbishop Melton', p. 61.

DAMAGE, LOSS, AND PROFIT WITHHELD

Usually, and logically, the justification for charging interest for delay was linked to the damage or expense incurred by the lender. Aquinas certainly approved of interest in such cases. 'Somebody who makes a loan is within his rights to settle terms of compensation for the loss of any advantage which he is entitled to enjoy, for this does not amount to selling the use of money, but is a question of avoiding loss.'[43] The most distressing loss, tackled by several thinkers, was where the creditor himself was forced by his own lack of money to borrow at usury.[44] The position is set out in the *Fasciculus morum*:

> If you have to repay me one hundred shillings by a certain day and cannot do it, so that I have to recoup it at usury in order to carry on my business, you must pay that usury, if I have paid it. And if I have not paid it, you have to free me from that obligation.[45]

Thomas of Chobham in the previous century had painted a heart-rending picture of a creditor being thrown out of his home for not having paid the rent, being too poor to buy essentials, and being unable to pay for his daughter's wedding, all through the default of someone else.[46]

It was obvious that hunger, homelessness, and embarrassment were damaging. What was less easy to assess was 'profit withheld', that is, a situation where the lender might have made a profit with the money he had lent if it had been returned on time. Aquinas firmly rejected profit withheld:

> One is, however, not entitled to make a contract to secure compensation for the loss that consists in not being able to use the money lent in order to make a profit, because one should not sell something which one has not yet got and which one may be prevented... from getting.[47]

Others disagreed. As a German Aristotelian commentator, probably Henry of Friemar, pointed out, 'to miss an expected gain is also a kind of loss' and he allowed compensation for this loss.[48] Duns Scotus justified it on the basis that 'anyone may lawfully keep himself indemnified'.[49]

So far we have looked at cases involving delay. There has been no suggestion that interest, in the modern sense, might be charged from the beginning of a loan. This was far more contentious.

---

[43] Thomas Aquinas, *Summa theologiae*, 2a2ae, 78, 2 ad 1, vol. 38, p. 243.
[44] For example, Raymond of Peñafort and Alexander of Hales; see Noonan, *Scholastic Analysis*, p. 109.
[45] *Fasciculus morum*, IV, vii, p. 350 (Latin), lines 74–8.
[46] Thomas of Chobham, *Summa confessorum*, art. 7, d. 6, q. 11, ch. 7, p. 513.
[47] Thomas Aquinas, *Summa theologiae*, 2a2ae, 78, 2 ad 1, vol. 38, p. 243.
[48] Langholm, *Economics*, p. 548.   [49] Ibid., p. 416.

INTEREST FROM THE START OF A LOAN

The crack in the usury theory occurred in connection with indemnity, because if someone was entitled to protect himself from damage or loss of potential profits when he made a loan, it would have to be assessed at the outset and a premium added. This might be seen as *inter-est*, in the sense of compensation, if the loss or damage occurred. But suppose no loss occurred? In this case it would be more like the modern concept of interest, meaning profit rather than compensation, and this was where the danger lay. It could be regarded as a charge for the 'use' of money, which hitherto had been inseparable from its substance; it could be a charge for the time involved in the loan, although time was supposed to be non-vendible. Above all, it could be seen as a denial of the precept that loans should be free. If they were not free, if they might be profitable, then the implication was that money itself could make a profit. Understandably both scholastics and canonists were cautious about allowing interest from the beginning of a loan. When they did so, it was usually in connection with profits withheld rather than loss or damage sustained. After all, as Aquinas had observed, if a lender expected to lose, he should not have lent in the first place.[50] It was also strictly limited to the 'charitable' rather than the commercial sphere. A merchant who lent to a needy neighbour might indemnify himself, provided he made the loan with a charitable intent and not for deliberate gain.

The first to admit interest from the beginning of a loan on the basis of profit withheld was probably Hostiensis:

> I think... that if some merchant, who is accustomed to pursue trade and the commerce of the fairs and there profit much has, *out of charity to me*, who needs it badly, lent money with which he would have done business, I remain obliged from this to his *interesse*, provided that nothing is done in fraud of usury... and provided that the said merchant will not have been accustomed to give his money in such a way to usury.[51]

Turning to the mendicants, Odd Langholm has suggested that both Peter Olivi and Gerald Odonis allowed interest from the beginning of a charitable loan.[52] Bernardino of Siena in the fifteenth century repeats the example of the merchant making a pious loan, and declares that he may demand compensation for profits he might have made, because he 'gives not money in its simple character, but he also gives his capital' — an important word.[53] His words might indicate that money, or capital, is of itself

---

[50] Aquinas, *Commentary on Sentences*, 4: quoted by Langholm, *Economics*, p. 246.
[51] Noonan, *Scholastic Analysis*, p. 118.   [52] Langholm, *Economics*, pp. 370–1, 526.
[53] Noonan, *Scholastic Analysis*, p. 126.

fruitful, thus undermining the sterility doctrine. This was not so. Neither he nor his mendicant predecessors, such as Aquinas, regarded money *of itself* as fruitful. The only way in which it could be made to appear so was if the merchant applied his labour or industry to it.[54] Bernardino's explanation represents the opinion of all three:

> that money was truly worth more to its owner than itself because of the industry with which he would have used it... and therefore the receiver of the money not only deprives the owner of his money, but also *of all the use and fruit of exercising his industry in it and through it*.[55]

The friars had with difficulty maintained the idea of the sterility of money. They had also preserved the concept of justice as fairness and equilibrium, because what was charged was interest in the sense of compensation – the balancing of resources – for actual or anticipated loss or damage. But it had stretched the doctrine of charity to its limits. This had ordered giving, not loans, far less loans on which a profit might be made. Nor did it expect works of charity to be performed without any cost to the giver. This was taking Aquinas's idea that someone should not be charitable to the extent that he endangered his own 'status' to unreasonable lengths.

RISK

Lending was a risky business, but was it permissible to charge interest for the risk of losing the principal? On the whole, lawyers and scholastics thought not. There were two problems in trying to reach a consistent theory of what later came to be called risk of the principal – *periculum sortis*. One of these was a matter of logic. In a loan, as distinct from a sale, ownership passed to the borrower, and risk was an inherent part of ownership. Since the risk no longer belonged to the creditor, he could not reasonably ask for payment for it during the period of the loan. Whatever happened to the principal in the hands of the debtor, whether it increased, decreased, or simply vanished, and whatever the purpose of the loan, whether consumption or investment, it concerned the debtor alone. But, come what may, the principal had to be returned to the lender at the end of the loan period. The 'risk' suffered by the lender was that of default, but that was already covered by other penalties. Bernardino made just this point. Since the debtor always has to indemnify the lender against default, the peril of the lender is imaginary. In any case, the risk involved

---

[54] See chapter 7, pp. 178–9, above.   [55] Noonan, *Scholastic Analysis*, p. 127.

in lending is inherent, and to profit from it is to profit from the very act of lending.[56]

The other problem was that there was no real precedent on which to draw. True, there was the relatively permissive second part of Gregory IX's decretal *Naviganti*. This appeared to indemnify the seller against the risk that the price would have risen by the time payment was actually made, and that he would therefore lose the difference between the original price and the later price. A few thinkers, Alexander of Hales and Duns Scotus among them, accepted risk as a title to interest, and cited this section of *Naviganti*.[57] But generally thinkers rejected risk as a title to interest. For one thing, it was not always easy to distinguish risk of losing the capital from simple delay. For another, security was usually taken for a loan, as we saw in the case of William Bertram, who pledged £700 worth of jewels for a £300 loan.[58] Even if a pawn was difficult to shift in the market, it still represented some value and deadened the effect of the risk.[59] Added to this there was the first part of *Naviganti*, on sea loans and partnerships, which condemned risk as a title to profit.

PARTNERSHIP

Once the theorists stepped outside the bounds of the loan contract, most of the foundations of the usury doctrine were ignored, contradicted, or just cast aside. This was especially true in the case of the partnership or *societas*.[60] Roman law had provided for two types of business association. One was where two or more people joined forces, the one putting up the money, the other the labour. Both shared the ownership of any merchandise and both shared in the risk of loss and the gain through profit on the venture. Here ownership and risk stayed together. The other was the sea loan where a 'loan' was made to a shipowner on the understanding that the lender would bear all the risk for the duration of the voyage, for which he was entitled to charge double the normal rate of interest. Once the shipowner, the 'debtor', had docked safely, he assumed all the risk, and if he traded unsuccessfully, he still had to repay the full amount. At this point the arrangement seemed to be a straight loan, because ownership and risk had passed to the debtor, but during the voyage a kind of partnership had existed, although the risk was not assumed by both parties.[61] Sea loans were popular in Mediterranean ports as a primitive form of maritime

[56] Ibid., p. 131.   [57] Langholm, *Economics*, pp. 140, 416.
[58] See chapter 7, pp. 165–6, above.   [59] Noonan, *Scholastic Analysis*, p. 129.
[60] On the workings of partnership in practice see Postan, 'Credit in medieval trade', pp. 16–21.
[61] Noonan, *Scholastic Analysis*, pp. 134–5.

insurance from the twelfth century until the mid-thirteenth, despite their very high cost. Charges of between 40 and 50 per cent of the loan were common.[62]

The popularity of sea loans waned abruptly when Gregory IX condemned them, along with partnerships, in *Naviganti*.[63] In practice, the partnership seems to have been part of the fabric of commercial society and to have caused little comment. Indeed, given the doubts about authenticity and authorship of *Naviganti*, which may have been written by Raymond of Peñafort,[64] it is possible that the Pope never intended to damn partnerships. Earlier, Johannes Teutonicus in the *Glossa ordinaria* to the *Decretum* had accepted them. If someone invests money with a businessman, so forming a partnership in which risk is shared, then the contract is legal, he declared.[65] Robert of Courçon and Thomas of Chobham had also approved, because the investor, the passive partner, still owned part of the money and assumed part of the risk, ownership and risk being inseparable. It followed that part of the profit should also be his. But if ownership was transferred to the merchant, as in a straight loan, and the investing partner expected his principal back and a half share of the profits, then this was clearly usury.[66]

These commentators were writing before *Naviganti*; Aquinas was not, though he chose to ignore it. Referring back to the *Glossa ordinaria*, he pronounced partnership licit:

Somebody who commits his money to a merchant or a craftsman in a sort of partnership does not hand over the ownership, and so it is still at his risk that the merchant trades or the craftsman works. The lender is, therefore, entitled to ask for a part of the profit of the undertaking in so far as it is his own.[67]

This raises several issues. Coming from one who had argued strongly elsewhere that the ownership and use of money could not be separated, due to its nature as a fungible,[68] it is remarkable, for the investor still 'owned' the money while the merchant 'used' it. There was another problem: if the merchant traded or the craftsman worked, then the profit should

---

[62] Raymond de Roover, 'The organization of trade', in *The Cambridge Economic History of Europe*, 3 (Cambridge, 1965), pp. 53–5.
[63] *Decretales*, 5, 19, 19, col. 816.
[64] As compiler of the *Decretals*, Raymond may have been either the recipient of *Naviganti*, as 'Brother R', or the author, with Gregory as the signatory. The authenticity of the wording is also questionable, given the contrast in attitude between the two parts: G. C. Coulton, 'An episode in canon law', *History*, 6 (1921), pp. 67–76.
[65] Noonan, *Scholastic Analysis*, p. 135.   [66] Langholm, *Economic Analysis*, pp. 51, 56.
[67] Thomas Aquinas, *Summa theologiae*, 2a2ae, 78, 2, ad 5, vol. 38, p. 245. For discussion see Noonan, *Scholastic Analysis*, pp. 143–5.
[68] See chapter 3, p. 75, above.

legitimately have been theirs alone, otherwise the investor was profiting either from the labour of others or from sterile money. Again Aquinas had himself argued this.[69] Finally, there was the question of risk. *Naviganti* had seemed to separate ownership from risk, for the investor had relinquished ownership of the money by lending it, but retained the risk.[70] Yet to Aquinas risk seemed to be an essential part of ownership.

Naviganti was not ignored by Giles of Lessines, although he thought along similar lines to Aquinas. He rejected the risk run by the passive partner as a title to profit. Yet if he retained ownership *and* risk (contrary to *Naviganti*) he was allowed to profit. This situation was like a master who sent his servant out to do business for him.[71] Despite its dangers, the theologians on the whole accepted the partnership contract. The acceptance of risk was a mark of ownership, and since ownership remained with the investor, the contract was licit.

The canonists discussed, and censored, the riskless partnership, where the investor could recoup his capital even if disaster struck. There were two reasons for condemning it. One was the Roman law maxim that a partnership had a 'right of brotherhood in it'.[72] The other was the canonists' doctrine, as stated by Johannes Teutonicus in the Gloss, that only if the risk was shared by both partners was the partnership contract licit.[73] The *Fasciculus morum* accordingly listed partnership 'when someone gives his commodity to some merchant on the condition that he shares his gains but not his losses' as a type of cloaked usury.[74] St Antoninus in the following century repeated the canonists' condemnation, adding that whenever an investing partner's capital is safe the partnership is usurious.[75]

Was there any exception to this? Innocent III had written a letter to the Archbishop of Genoa, *Per vestras*, which seemed to allow a husband to invest his wife's dowry with a merchant, and without risk to the capital.[76] The canonist Johannes Andreae later defended this on the basis that the end justified the means. The good of marriage justified the riskless investment.[77] The other hint at acceptance came from the canonist Hostiensis in discussing partnerships. He accepted arrangements where the investing partner was liable only for major catastrophes, and suggested that if all was lost, the investor was merely *advised*, rather than ordered,

---

[69] Cf. Noonan, *Scholastic Analysis*, p. 145. Cf. chapter 7, pp. 178–9, above.
[70] Noonan, *Scholastic Analysis*, pp. 137–8 for discussion of *Naviganti*.
[71] Langholm, *Economics*, p. 318.
[72] *Digest*, 22, 2: 3 and 6; *Codex*, 4, 33; 1: Noonan, *Scholastic Analysis*, pp. 134, 141–2.
[73] McLaughlin, 'Teaching of the canonists', p. 104, n. 193.
[74] *Fasciculus morum*, IV, vii, p. 349.   [75] Noonan, *Scholastic Analysis*, p. 151.
[76] *Decretales*, 4, 20, 7, cols. 729–30.   [77] Noonan, *Scholastic Analysis*, p. 149.

not to press for repayment of his share.[78] If he chose to ignore that advice, he would press for full repayment, which would mean that he had not borne any of the risk. However well intentioned, or perhaps totally un-intentioned, this was a dangerous argument, because riskless profit undermined all the basic usury condemnations – an effortless profit would be made over time, and money would appear to have increased itself.

LIFE RENT OR CENSUS

There could be an element of riskless profit in a census or life rent. It was something like an annuity. A capital sum would be paid over by the 'buyer', in return for a fixed income either for so many years, for the rest of his life, or even in perpetuity to be inherited by his descendants. This income would be paid by the 'seller'. Originally the returns were paid in kind, which presented no problem, because the transaction was clearly a sale. As the economy became more monetary, however, it was fixed in cash, and was paid as a life rent.[79] But did this make it a loan? On the basis of sinful intention, Henry of Ghent thought it did.[80] The buyer hoped to live long enough to get back more than he had paid; the seller hoped to have to pay out less than he had received. This sort of reasoning was applied by religious and monastic houses, who sold annuities in kind, known as corrodies – food, clothing, and sometimes board and lodging – in return for a cash payment. Usually this was a measure of financial desperation, and the house gambled on the hope that the corrodian would not live long enough to be a drain on resources.[81]

A corrody was clearly a sale. Giles of Lessines thought that the life rent was a sale, provided that the risk was shared and the price was just. The problem was to prove that the total of future rent payments to a long-lived buyer, which might exceed the amount of the principal, was not actually worth more. Giles, as Langholm has argued, used an original argument, that of time preference. Things paid over in future are not as valuable or useful as things paid over now, and should therefore be given a lower value.[82] The other original contribution came from Richard of Middleton. He, too, saw the rent contract as one of sale, but he suggested that what was sold was not money itself but a *right to receive* a particular sum of money over an agreed time span, or even for ever. He was probably the first to apply this legalistic idea to money. Earlier scholastic arguments about it had relied on its physical properties as coinage. Difficulties arose, as for Giles of Lessines, in fixing a just price for a perpetual rent. Richard

[78] Ibid., pp. 140–2. [79] For discussion see ibid., pp. 154–64.
[80] Langholm, *Economics*, p. 273.
[81] R. N. Swanson, *Church and Society in Late Medieval England* (Oxford, 1993), pp. 236–7.
[82] Langholm, *Economics*, pp. 316–19.

expressed the time preference argument in natural law terms: it is naturally more desirable to have something for oneself than for one's heirs.[83] The reasons were probably the difficulties involved in collecting future payments, especially from heirs, and the likely effects of inflation, which would erode the value of the fixed payments.

On balance, the census or life-rent did appear to flout the usury prohibitions. The longevity of a buyer meant that he would receive sums above the principal. Once he had received back the amount of the principal, then he was clearly making a riskless profit. On the part of the seller, the sinful hope was there that the buyer would die.

BANKING AND DEPOSIT

The usury prohibitions, including *Naviganti*, contributed directly to the development of banking. This was because the legislation did not condemn money-changing, one of the functions of merchant-bankers, and it was possible to use this heading for a number of transactions which actually concealed loans. The other point was that money-changing of one currency for another always involved an element of risk, due to fluctuating exchange rates, so there was no question of a changer making a riskless profit.

The development of banking is a complex and by no means uniform story. Local and international banking both originated with merchants. At the local level some merchants undertook money-changing as a corollary of their normal business activities. Originally it had been undertaken by goldsmiths and moneyers. As the reputations of the money-changing merchants grew, this aspect of their work became increasingly important. They became merchant money-changers. They gradually started to attract deposits of money for safe-keeping, and this enabled them to settle amounts outstanding, both among their own customers, and between their own customers and those of other local banks, by transferring money from one deposit account to another. They had, in effect, become merchant-bankers.[84] The other group consisted of wealthy international Italian merchants whose fortunes were founded on staple commodities such as wool

---

[83] Ibid., pp. 339–40.
[84] The literature on the development of banking is considerable, but see especially Edwin S. Hunt and James M. Murray, *A History of Business in Medieval Europe, 1200–1550* (Cambridge, 1999), pp. 64–5; de Roover, *Money, Banking, and Credit*, pp. 247–83; de Roover, 'Organization of trade', pp. 66–70; de Roover, 'New interpretations of the history of banking', repr. in Kirshner, ed., *Business, Banking, and Economic Thought*, pp. 200–38; Robert S. Lopez, 'The Dawn of Medieval Banking', in *The Dawn of Modern Banking*, pp. 1–23; Abbott Payson Usher, *The Early History of Deposit Banking in Mediterranean Europe* (Cambridge, MA, 1943), pp. 2–233.

and grain, and who used to full advantage the opportunities of the economic expansion of the thirteenth and early fourteenth centuries. The outstanding examples, dubbed the 'super-companies', were the Bardi, the Peruzzi, and the Acciaiuoli of Florence, although other towns of north-central Italy also produced them. The companies combined the roles of general and commodity traders, manufacturers, and bankers, and specialized in the wool, cloth, and grain trades. Their widespread presence, tight organization, and enormous resources meant that they were ideally suited to act as bankers, exchangers, and collectors, and to advance money to the pope, the Roman curia, and to European princes, especially the kings of England. The companies used the funds deposited with them to finance their various ventures and to advance money to their 'customers'.[85]

Deposit was originally a Roman contract, and it meant the handing over of a movable good for safekeeping. It involved no transfer of ownership or even of use, and the transaction was free. Eventually the exact thing deposited had to be returned to the depositor. This worked perfectly well in the case of non-fungibles. It presented problems, however, in the case of fungibles. Of course, they could be shut up in a box and ultimately returned untouched to the depositor. In the post-classical (Byzantine) era a new contract, the 'irregular deposit', came into existence in connection with fungibles, especially money, where the equivalent amount of the deposit was to be returned. Here ownership passed, as in a loan, to the depositee, who was allowed the 'use' of the money, for which interest was paid. Sometimes the original agreement actually provided for the depositee to change the money into a *mutuum* and use it,[86] which underlined the difficulty of distinguishing between them.

In late medieval practice there were two types of deposit, the unconditional deposit, which did not bear interest, and was made to enable funds to be transferred on the customer's behalf. The other, the controversial one, was the 'time deposit', made for a certain period, and returning not interest, but *discrezione* – discretionary gifts from banker to client.[87]

Deposits attracted little attention until the fifteenth century, partly because there were no papal decretals to occasion comment. The papacy was too close to its bankers, both as depositor and borrower, to condemn banking practices. In the thirteenth century the English chronicler Matthew Paris criticized English magnates who deposited money

---

[85] Hunt and Murray, *History of Business*, pp. 99–122; Edwin S. Hunt, *The Medieval Super-companies: a Study of the Peruzzi Company of Florence* (Cambridge, 1994); de Roover, *Medici Bank*; de Roover, 'Organization of trade', pp. 70–89.
[86] W. W. Buckland, *A Textbook of Roman Law from Augustus to Justinian*, 3rd edn, rev. Peter Stein (Cambridge, 1968), pp. 469–70.
[87] De Roover, *Medici Bank*, pp. 100–7; Hunt and Murray, *History of Business*, pp. 209–12.

with Italian bankers 'after the manner of the Roman curia'.[88] In the fourteenth century the Avignon popes often borrowed from the super-companies, which meant that they were using money from deposited reserves. Clement VI, for example, bought the city of Avignon from Joanna of Naples in 1348 for 80,000 florins, having borrowed from Italian bankers.[89] In 1427 Martin V had a personal deposit of nearly 1,200 florins with the Medici bank in Rome, while the papal treasury had one of about 24,500.[90] The popes were hardly in a position to condemn deposits.

Bernardino and Antoninus had no such reservations, and both declared deposits usurious. Bernardino was clear that to deposit with a merchant or banker for a fixed rate of interest was usury.[91] Yet he allowed that if the same deposit were left with an exchange-dealer, provided that it was not done with an eye to profit, the depositor might accept a gift from the dealer', and this was not usury. Antoninus, however, did not exonerate the exchange-dealers, and considered deposits the deceit of the idle rich:

> The nobles, who do not wish to work, in case they lack money as they gradually consume, give it to a merchant or a money-changer, principally intending to receive something annually at their [the depositee's] discretion, the capital, however, being kept safe. And although they call this a deposit, yet it is clearly usury.[92]

In other words, it was a riskless investment.

EXCHANGE-DEALING

Exchange was a complicated subject, if only because there were several types. Of these the most important were petty exchange, the bill of exchange, and dry exchange. What made any sort of exchange-dealing suspect was that interest was invariably concealed within it.

Petty exchange was the straight exchange of one currency for another in one place. William of Moerbeke's mistranslation of the word for 'trade' in Aristotle's *Politics* as *campsoria* led the scholastics initially to condemn money-changing on the basis that it was an unnatural use of money. Exchanging money for money meant that it was both the medium term in the exchange and also the end term. John of Paris summarized this attitude. Referring to the three unnatural uses of money as detailed by

---

[88] Matthew Paris, *Chronica majora*, 5, p. 245. On the papacy and its bankers in general see Y. Renouard, *Les Relations des papes d'Avignon et des compagnies commerciales et bancaires de 1326 à 1378* (Paris, 1941); W. E. Lunt, *Papal Revenues in the Middle Ages*, 2 vols. (New York, 1934).
[89] Renouard, *Les Relations*, p. 60. [90] De Roover, 'Organization of trade', p. 85.
[91] Noonan, *Scholastic Analysis*, p. 174. [92] Ibid., p. 174 (my translation).

Aristotle, of which *campsoria* – money-changing – was one, he declared that all three were evil and perverse. Those who practised them mistook a means for an end. They sought the limitless accumulation of money by exchanging it for itself.[93] Writing nearly a century later Nicholas Oresme branded all exchange, that is, the trade of money for money, as unnatural. Exchange was an occupation which defiled the soul, as certain vulgar occupations, like cleaning the sewers, defiled the body.[94]

Alternatively, Giles of Lessines and Alexander Lombard (d. 1314) approved of petty exchange. Rejecting the idea that money was both the medium and the end in an exchange they argued that petty exchange was neither a sale nor a loan, but a form of barter.[95] Alexander was convinced that changing one kind of money for another was no more than an exchange of commodities, and therefore not usury. Indeed, without money-changing, money could not serve its true purpose. Merchants brought back money with them from abroad rather than goods to trade with, and when those from many different areas came together they carried many different currencies. They would be lost without the changers.[96] Many of the scholastics even allowed the changer to charge interest for his labour and expenses. Giles of Lessines went further and allowed the changer to make a profit justified by risk.[97] These arguments were similar to those of the merchant-bankers themselves. To them, an exchange transaction was not a loan (*cambium non est mutuum*), but either an exchange (*permutatio*), in the sense that barter was an exchange, or a buying and selling of foreign currency (*emptio-venditio*).[98]

The idea of an exchange as buying and selling led to complications, if only because money was supposed to be non-vendible. Henry of Ghent found a way round this which involved using the two different valuations of money – its official, or ghost, value as a measure of exchange, and its intrinsic value, based on its metal content. That way, money was both a commodity and a means of exchange, which meant that it could be both the medium and the end in an exchange. If money was worth more in weight that its official value, that is, if the official value was not a just one, then the surplus could be sold as a commodity. 'Up to the just price exchange ought to be free', declared Henry, 'and surplus weight... [the changer] may sell in the form of weight not money and thus receive more in so far as it is owing him for the weight...'[99]

---

[93] Langholm, *Economics*, pp. 395–6. For Albert the Great and Aquinas see pp. 178, 237, respectively.
[94] Nicholas Oresme, *De moneta*, ch. 17, p. 27.
[95] Langholm, *Economics*, pp. 314, 437.   [96] Ibid., p. 437.
[97] Ibid., p. 314.   [98] De Roover, *Medici Bank*, p. 11.
[99] Langholm, *Economics*, pp. 209–10.

On the whole these arguments triumphed, and petty exchange became widely accepted. Even the censorious Antoninus allowed it on the basis that it was neither sale nor loan,[100] but not so the bill of exchange. This was the device by which the merchant-bankers made their loans, by concealing them in the bill. At its simplest a bill of exchange was an agreement to discharge a debt somewhere abroad, at a future date, and in a foreign currency. Since it involved both a time span and foreign currency, the bill of exchange was a combination of a credit and an exchange transaction. It probably originated in twelfth-century Genoa, and its development was advanced by the Champagne fairs. The decline of the fairs in the late thirteenth century by no means spelt the decline of the bill of exchange.[101] It was far too useful, since it avoided the necessity of transporting specie over long distances. By the late fourteenth and fifteenth centuries it provided a welcome alternative to the often illegal export of bullion.[102] This did not stop Antoninus condemning it on grounds of sinful intention, along with all forms of credit in exchange dealings. An especially pernicious form was dry exchange, a fictitious exchange by which money was advanced under the pretence of an exchange contract that made it repayable abroad and in another currency. In fact, it was usually repaid in the same place and in the same currency.[103]

By the fifteenth century Laurentius Ridolfis observed that if bills of exchange were illegal, many would be damned.[104] Bills were an essential tool in the business of the Italian merchant-bankers. They were also popular with the English, especially with wool-dealers and merchants.[105] Yet for over a century, starting in 1387, English laws known as employment laws attempted to ban their use. They prevented the import of bullion, and interfered with the royal prerogative of fixing exchange rates, both of which had a critical effect on supplies to the Mint. If the rate were more favourable abroad merchants would find a way of exporting their specie or bullion, regardless of the legal prohibitions. Finally, the hated Italians often exported their takings by bills of exchange, which did nothing to increase the popularity of paper transactions.[106]

---

[100] Noonan, *Scholastic Analysis*, pp. 188–90.
[101] De Roover, 'Organization of trade', p. 95; *Money, Banking, and Credit*, pp. 53–9; Hunt and Murray, *History of Business*, pp. 65–6.
[102] Munro, 'Bullionism and the bill of exchange', pp. 173–4.
[103] Raymond de Roover, 'Cambium ad Venetias: Contribution to the History of Foreign Exchange', in Kirschner, ed., *Business, Banking and Economic Thought*, pp. 239–59; 'What is dry exchange? A contribution to the study of English mercantilism', in ibid., pp. 183–99. See also de Roover, *Medici Bank*, p. 443, n. 53; *San Bernardino*, pp. 33–8.
[104] Noonan, *Scholastic Analysis*, p. 185.
[105] Postan 'Credit in medieval trade', pp. 11–13.
[106] Munro, 'Bullionism and the bill of exchange', pp. 198–205.

THE MONTES

The merchant-bankers were large public lenders. In the early fourteenth century the French Dominican Durand of Saint-Pourçain (d. 1334) hit on the revolutionary idea that the State should enter the money-lending business. He recognized the need for credit and suggested that there should be a state money-lender, who would lend freely to all (thus evading the charge of usury), and who would be paid an annual salary by the government. There would be nothing unjust about this, because it would simply be a wage for performing a public service. But Durandus had to admit that he had never heard of such a thing in practice.[107] The suggestion was not entirely far-fetched. In northern Italy, in the early fourteenth century, communes such as Genoa, Venice, and Florence set up not a public money-*lender*, as suggested by Durandus, but a public money-*borrower*, in the form of a state fund, known as a *mons*. The citizens were compelled to 'lend' or rather to buy shares in this, and were paid a paltry rate of interest – 5 per cent in late fourteenth-century Florence. Did this constitute usury? Could interest from the beginning of a loan be justified? The Franciscans thought it could; the Augustinians disagreed. The Augustinian case was quite simple: interest could be justified only if a debtor defaulted, and never from the beginning of a loan. By operating the *montes* the communes were encouraging usury, and the citizen-creditors who received the interest were committing it.[108]

Paving the way for the Franciscan case was Peter Olivi in the thirteenth century, even before the *montes*. He defended the payment of interest in the case of forced government loans in cases where the creditor was a merchant who had been forced to sacrifice money intended for business, and so had been deprived of profit on it.[109] This was the extrinsic title of 'profit withheld'. The Franciscan Astesanus in his *Summa* for confessors in 1317 argued that the commonplace 'no one would lend in the expectation of loss' could not apply to compulsory loans. He considered that the interest was compensation for damages suffered by the merchants, but that it was permissible only if the creditor would rather have had his money than the interest.[110]

Summarizing Franciscan views, Laurentius Ridolfis defended the charge that interest from the beginning of a loan constituted usury. The commune, he pointed out, was like a debtor in perpetual delay, because no date was ever set for redemption. If interest was allowed in delay, it could hardly be otherwise in a case of perpetual delay. In reply to the more general

[107] Langholm, *Economics*, pp. 485–6.　[108] Noonan, *Scholastic Analysis*, p. 122.
[109] Langholm, *Economics*, pp. 370–1.　[110] Noonan, *Scholastic Analysis*, p. 120.

accusation that the State promoted usury, he concentrated on the factor of intention. Usury involved the intention to make a profit from a loan, but in this case it could not apply, because the loans were compulsory. In any case, with interest of 5 per cent there was precious little profit to be had. On the contrary, the citizens suffered great hardship, and they should be compensated accordingly. This compensation should be both for damage sustained and for the deprivation of expected profits.[111] Laurentius was recommending payment of both damage arising and profit withheld *from the beginning of a loan*, and this was a crucial point. So strongly did he feel about it that he predicted dire ruin if interest were not paid: the creditors would 'be driven to desperation and would plot against the republic to the serious loss of body and soul and danger to the republic'.[112] Such impassioned pleading deserved to succeed. Payment of interest from the outset on state loans became widely accepted. In the fifteenth century both Bernardino and Antoninus were to endorse it.[113]

The most controversial public money-lenders were the *montes pietatis*, in effect public pawnshops for the poor. The storm they raised was to lead the papacy to a new definition of usury. The first was founded in Perugia in 1462 as a result of Franciscan pressure. It was to serve as the model for many others, and a century later some 214 of them had sprung up throughout Italy, many of them as a result of Franciscan initiative. They aimed to provide small loans to the poor on the security of pawns and on payment of a small charge, usually amounting to about 5 per cent. An equally if not more important aim was to oust the Jews from the money-lending business by providing the same service as they did to the community, but at a fraction of the cost. Although expelled from England and France, the Jews had played an increasingly prominent role in the economic life of the Italian city-states from the thirteenth century. Their legal monopoly of the pawnbroking business in Florence from 1437 sealed their unpopularity, which, as in other cities, acted as a catalyst for the founding of the *mons*. The Franciscans, especially Bernardino of Siena, attacked the evils of Jewish usury and urged cities to set up *montes* to help the poor.[114] In Florence this theme, hitherto opposed by the Dominicans, was taken up by the Dominican preacher Savonarola in the 1490s.[115] The statutes of the Florentine *mons*, established in 1496, emphasized its

---

[111] Ibid., p. 122. [112] Ibid., pp. 122–4. [113] Ibid., pp. 124, 126, 128.
[114] See Anscar Parsons, 'Bernardine of Feltre and the *montes pietatis*', *Franciscan Studies*, 1, no. 1 (1941), pp. 11–32; Parsons, 'Economic significance of the *montes pietatis*', ibid., no. 3, pp. 3–28.
[115] F. R. Salter, 'The Jews in fifteenth-century Florence and Savonarola's establishment of a *mons pietatis*', *Cambridge Historical Journal*, 5 (1935–7), pp. 193–211.

charitable purpose: 'to be able to lend to poor persons against pawns with as low an interest rate as possible'.[116] What constituted 'poor persons' was not specified, but Richard Trexler has suggested strongly that what was envisaged at a time of economic and military crisis was not the totally indigent, as suggested by Franciscan historians, but the 'shame-faced poor', the downwardly mobile.[117]

CONCLUSION: THE FINAL SOLUTION?

The papacy was drawn into the debate over the questionable morality of the *montes pietatis*. The fact that the poor were compelled to pay interest to cover running expenses led the Dominicans to rekindle the debate about taking interest from the beginning of a loan, to say nothing of the immorality of exploiting the poor.[118] They lost their case. At the Fifth Lateran Council in 1515 Leo X gave the *montes pietatis* his blessing, in the bull *Inter multiplices*. Although previous popes had approved individual *montes*, starting with Pius II for Orvieto in 1464, this was the first time that the practice of taking interest from the beginning of a loan had been given universal sanction. The basis for this was both to cover expenses and to indemnify against loss. Leo also arrived at a redefinition of usury which begged a good many questions. Far from the original definition – demanding back more than was originally lent, or making a repayment beyond the principal, Leo stated: 'Usury means nothing else than gain or profit drawn from the use of a thing that is by its nature sterile, *a profit that is acquired without labour, cost, or risk*.'[119] He had undermined most of the foundations of the usury doctrine. By accepting the charging of interest by the *montes* from the beginning of a loan he had denied that loans were free, and also, by implication, suggested that time could be sold. By suggesting that a profit *could* be made, provided that it involved labour, cost, or risk, he was sanctioning the main extrinsic titles to interest, and so hinting that barren money could be made fruitful by the application of any of these three. By isolating 'use' he implied that ownership did not pass to the borrower, and so separated ownership and use, and demolished the character of money as a fungible consumed by that use. All that appeared

---

[116] Carol Bresnahan Menning, *Charity and State in Late Renaissance Italy: the Monte di Pietà of Florence* (Ithaca, NY and London, 1993), pp. 11–35; quotation at p. 87.
[117] Richard C. Trexler, 'Charity and the defence of urban elites in the Italian communes', in Frederick Cople Jaher, ed., *The Rich, the Wellborn, and the Powerful: Elites and Upper Classes in History* (Urbana, IL, 1973), pp. 64–109, esp. 82–5.
[118] Gilchrist, *Church and Economic Activity*, p. 115. See also de Roover, *Money, Banking, and Credit*, p. 145.
[119] Leo X, Lateran V (1515): Gilchrist, *Church and Economic Activity*, pp. 115, 224.

to be left intact was the condemnation of the totally idle lender making an effortless profit, and the acid test of intention, whether a loan had been made 'in fraudem usurarum'. Leo's definition had narrowed the scope of usury and had sanctioned the payment of interest, condemning the one and approving the other.

Leo X canonized the attitude that 'Usury and trewe interest be thinges as contrary as falshed is to trewth', in effect, admitting that the Church had come to terms with economic practice. If his definition had been issued a century earlier, it might have settled the usury issue for all Christians. But by the sixteenth century the papacy was a shadow of its former self, robbed of its authority by the Protestant reformations in Europe. In 1551 Edward VI forbade the taking of interest because 'Usury is by the word of God utterly prohibited, as a vice most odious and detestable', and threatened the 'divers greedy, uncharitable and covetous persons' of England with God's wrath and vengeance if they practised it.[120] Paradoxically it was the Protestants, with their biblically based faith, who kept the usury debate alive by returning to the traditional scholastic attitudes.

[120] *EHD*, 5, no. 150, p. 1011.

CONCLUSION

This book has tried to survey some of the fundamental issues in economic thought as they evolved in the pre-Reformation period and to relate them to economic practice. In a work of synthesis there is no claim to reach original or definitive conclusions, but simply to bring together a few observations.

The period from the twelfth to the fifteenth century was marked by dramatic developments in economic thought and practice within the framework of a changing society. Although still a Christian society in the sense that its members were baptized into the Church, ecclesiastical domination, especially that of pope and priests, was weakening. The laity was assuming a more influential role, and as a result secular concerns and values, both economic and cultural, were becoming as important as sacred ones. In political terms, Europe was fragmenting into a number of independent national states, each fiercely defending its sovereignty. A combination of demographic and monetary factors had led to an acceleration in the economy, demonstrated by an expansion of trade, commerce, and industry, the growth or foundation of towns and markets, and more intensive cultivation of the countryside. The emergence of a new merchant class was a direct result of all this. The famines and epidemics of the fourteenth century, which reversed the population trend and checked economic growth, did not halt commercial progress.

The most important development was that of an increasingly monetized economy, which heralded a transition to secular values. Everything came to have its price. This meant not just land and property, but also commodities, which were valued according to a monetary price, and the labour of individuals, which commanded a price for labour, a wage. Even money itself might be treated as a commodity with a price that could rise and fall like any other. At a time of social mobility money came to be able to buy status, as the sumptuary legislation which graded people according to income showed. On the international stage possession of wealth in terms of coinage or bullion was becoming associated with a nation's political power.

As money came to be seen as the life-blood of the State, especially in early Renaissance Italy, so the theoretical position of wealth and poverty was gradually reversed: wealth was exalted and poverty decried. The statement of a fifteenth-century Italian merchant-prince that a copious body of misers is the essential foundation of the State is a far cry from the total poverty espoused by St Francis and his followers in the early thirteenth century. The belittling of poverty was accompanied by blame, especially of the able-bodied and undeserving poor, and a harder and more discriminatory attitude to relieving them developed. Yet the decline in spontaneous giving was balanced by a growth in post-mortem charity.

The glorification of riches was preceded by the justification of hitherto sinful trade and the status of the merchant. The merchant's role was pivotal in both the internal economy and in international trading relations. As essential tools of his trade a number of commercial practices involving credit developed, such as bills of exchange, deposit and exchange banking, sea loans, and partnerships. In the eyes of the Church these all involved an element of usury, that is, making a charge for lending money, and were damnable. Damnable or not, the merchant expected Christian burial – in some cases in majestic state before the high altar.

One of the most significant aspects of medieval economic thought was the emergence of the concept of interest on loans and its divorce from usurious, and therefore sinful, profit. Ultimately this meant that money came to be regarded not just as a convenient medium of exchange, but as capital. And capital, given the right treatment, could and did grow. The possibility arose of being able to make a riskless, and almost effortless, profit. This more than anything heralded the transition from an economy which was based on natural resources to one which was based on money, and sanctioned many of the monetary considerations that underlie modern economies. It is nicely ironic that it was the Pope himself who finally 'justified' the taking of interest, in the sense of compensation, and separated it from its sinful cousin usury.

The connection between economic and political ideas was close, in the sense that wealth and power were often linked. Possession of property, for example, gave a title to dominion or lordship. The economic attributes of medieval sovereignty were especially important – things such as the control of weights and measures and coinage – and the way in which these were exercised was an indication of the constitutional structure of a country. A sovereign who considered himself absolute needed to maintain his authority over them. Nicholas Oresme significantly associated medieval 'democracy' with popular ownership of the coinage.

An important difference between economic and political ideas is that political ideas often anticipate practice, whereas economic ideas do the reverse. Until the Reformation the Church still dominated the expression of economic ideas, and it was ecclesiastics, often friars, who were faced with the problem not just of Christianizing Aristotle, but of justifying economic practice retrospectively. Private property rights, wealth, trade, mercantile status, the different roles of money, and above all the theory of interest all fall under the heading of retrospective justification.

This is not to say that all economic thought was backward-looking. Perhaps the most forward-looking idea was that of a public money-lender. There are also anticipations of the thought of John Locke and the notion of labour as a title to property by John of Paris and Sir John Fortescue. What is remarkable is the existence by the fifteenth century of economic practices usually associated with a later age. There is a sense of collective wage-bargaining, of capital formation and investment, and even, with the establishment of the *montes*, of share dealing. In England especially there is also in both theory and practice the set of ideas characterizing the mercantile system, such as protectionism, the encouragement of exports, especially of finished goods like cloth, the control of the trade routes, and the anticipation of Gresham's Law in bullionist policies. The wealth of a country in terms of coinage and bullion, as well as an excess of exports over imports, was an essential part of its national sovereign status: economic and political nationalism were inseparable. Such notions, where they were expressed, however, were expressed by laymen rather than ecclesiastics.

Despite its practical emphasis, medieval economic thought was not without ideals. Since most of it was expressed by ecclesiastics as an aspect of theology, it is not surprising that it had a strong ethical content. Even when economics became a discrete discipline, no longer controlled by the Church, it still raised moral and ethical issues. In England the nineteenth-century debates on issues such as the Poor Laws, the abolition of slavery, or the Corn Laws are instances of this, and legislation about usury was still being issued in the eighteenth century.[1] Among our present concerns are the balancing of wealth between developed and underdeveloped countries, and applying moderation to our exploitation of natural resources.

The ethical ideal of medieval economic thought was the imposition of a mean in the sense of the balance of justice, or righteousness. It featured

[1] *Statutes of the Realm*, 9 (1882), 13 Ann. (1715), c. 15.

in every aspect of the medieval economy – the balance between private and communal rights to property, the redistribution of resources between rich and poor, the use of money as an impartial mean against which all things could be measured, dealings between buyer and seller, producer and consumer, employer and employee, and borrower and lender. It was not possible, however, to reach an exact balance. As Aquinas appreciated 'We sometimes have to make the best estimate we can, with the result that giving or taking a little here or there does not upset the balance of justice.'[2] The mean, in the sense of the balance of justice, was based not on precision but on more flexible reason and common sense. It was a question of virtue rather than econometrics:

> The mean of virtue does not depend on the quantity of external goods employed, but on the rule of reason... This rule in fact measures not only the quantity of the thing used, but also the condition of the person, and his intention, the fitness of place and time, and such things that are required in acts of virtue.[3]

Leaving virtue aside, what prevailed in the monetized market-place, as Joel Kaye has demonstrated, was geometrical, proportional equality rather than strict arithmetical equivalence. In purely practical terms economic exchange between individuals or nations could never be based on strict equality. Faced with such exactitude, Buridan's ass was literally spoilt for choice. If the inequality that creates the incentive to exchange had been removed from the medieval economy, then it too would have suffered a demise.

---

[2] Thomas Aquinas, *Summa theologiae*, 2a2ae, 77, 2, vol. 38, p. 217.
[3] Thomas Aquinas, *Summa contra gentiles*, vol. 3, 2, ch. 134, pp. 143–4.

APPENDIX

NOTES ON THE MAIN WRITERS AND ANONYMOUS WORKS MENTIONED IN THE TEXT

Albert the Great, St (*c.* 1200–80), Bishop of Ratisbon, was a distinguished Dominican Master of Theology, who taught at both Paris and Cologne, and counted Thomas Aquinas among his pupils. He had a brilliant and versatile mind and was a prolific writer. He is known as the *Doctor universalis*. With Aquinas and William of Moerbeke he was one of the three Dominicans commissioned by the papacy to examine the works of Aristotle and to assimilate their principles into Christian thought. As a result his great *Summa theologiae* applied Aristotelian methods and principles to theology. His contributions to economic thought occur in the *Summa* and in his commentaries on Aristotle's works, especially the *Ethics* and the *Politics*.

Alexander of Hales (*c.* 1186–1245) was born at Halesowen (West Midlands). He studied and taught theology at Paris, returning briefly to England in 1231–2, when he was Archdeacon of Coventry, but soon returned to Paris, where in 1236 he became a Franciscan. He continued to hold his chair of theology, which became a Franciscan one. Bonaventure was his pupil. The *Summa theologica* which bears his name is important because it was one of the first works to be based on a knowledge of all Aristotle's philosophical works, but it is not known how much was written by him and how much by his followers.

Ambrose, St (*c.* 339–97) was Bishop of Milan and, like Augustine, one of the Four Doctors of the Church. After a career in law and administration he became Governor of Aemilia-Liguria and was based at Milan. In 374, after the death of the bishop, Ambrose was chosen by the people to succeed him, although he was not even baptized. As bishop he was a celebrated preacher, an upholder of orthodoxy, especially against the Arians, and asserted his authority over successive Western Roman emperors and over Theodosius the Great. His most important works are the *De sacramentis* and the *De officiis ministrorum*, written to guide the clergy. He also left sermons, letters, and hymns.

Antoninus, St (1389–1459), Archbishop of Florence, joined the Dominican Order at the age of fifteen, becoming attached to the party of the Strict Observants. He rose to be Superior of the Reformed Tuscan and Neapolitan Congregations, prior of Fiesole (1425) and of San Marco in Florence (1439). He was the friend of Eugenius IV and attended the Council of Florence (1439). As bishop he was an exemplary pastor, who was especially concerned for the poor, and a renowned preacher. His economic ideas are valuable as coming from one who had first-hand knowledge of the Florentine woollen industry. His main works are the lengthy *Summa theologica moralis* and a chronicle of universal history.

Augustine, St, Bishop of Hippo (354–430) is one of the most influential theologians in history and is honoured as one of the Four Doctors of the Church. He was born at Thagaste (North Africa) to a Christian mother, St Monica, and a pagan father. He studied at Carthage, and then taught there before moving to Rome, and on to Milan, where he held a chair of rhetoric. While in Africa he joined the sect of the Manichees, but in Milan he was influenced both by the preaching of Ambrose and by reading the works of the Christian Neoplatonists. In July 386 a dramatic experience in a Milan garden led him to abandon his career, thoughts of marriage, and the Manichaeans. He was baptized by Ambrose in 387. Back at Thagaste he and some friends lived an ascetic community life. He was ordained in 391, somewhat against his will, and was consecrated bishop in 395. He was involved in controversy with the Donatists, the Pelagians, and the Manichaeans. He wrote numerous theological works, including tractates on St John's Gospel, commentaries on the Psalms, and composed a Rule for monks and nuns. His most famous works are the autobiographical *Confessions* and the *City of God*, written as a defence of the Christian faith against pagan accusations that the sack of Rome by the Goths in 410 was due to the abandonment of the old gods.

Bartolus of Sassoferrato (1313/14–57) was a famous Roman jurist. At the age of fourteen he was sent to Perugia, where he studied law under Cinus de Pistoia, and then studied briefly at Bologna. He became a doctor of law at nineteen. He was made professor of law at Pisa, and a magistrate, in 1339, before moving back to Perugia to teach for the rest of his life. He was the teacher of the celebrated canonist Baldus de Ubaldis (d. 1400).

He was a prolific writer, commenting on the *Digest* and the *Codex*. He also wrote tracts on city government (*De regimine civitatum*) and on tyranny (*Tractatus de tyrannia*).

Bernardino of Siena, St (1380–1444), was a great Franciscan reforming preacher. He was born at Massa Marittima, where his father was governor, and joined the Franciscans when he was twenty-two, and from 1417 was reputed to be the greatest preacher of his age. For the last six years of his life he was Vicar General of the Friars of the Strict Observance in Italy, and their popularity in fifteenth-century Italy is largely due to him. His surviving works are mainly sermons. Once thought to be an original economic thinker, he is now seen as deriving his ideas from earlier Franciscans.

Bonaventure, St (*c.* 1217–74) (Giovanni di Fidanza) was an influential Franciscan theologian who rose to be Minister General of the Franciscan Order in 1257, and Cardinal Bishop of Albano in 1273. He studied theology at Paris under Alexander of Hales, himself becoming a doctor of theology and teaching until 1257. He seems to have been a master of compromise, and he steered the Order through a time of division and turmoil, codifying its customs in the Statute of Narbonne (1260), and writing the official Life of St Francis, accepted as such by the Order. His commentary on the *Sentences* of Peter Lombard is his major surviving work.

Christine de Pisan (1365–1430) was remarkable as Europe's first known professional woman writer. She was born in Venice, where her father, Thomas de Pizzano (a town near Bologna) was a counsellor to the government of Venice. After her father became physician and astrologer to Charles V of France she moved there, in 1369, and married a nobleman from Picardy, Etienne de Castel, ten years later. A decade on saw her left as a penurious widow with three children to support, which she did through her writing. She entered a convent in 1418. Her works are numerous and varied, ranging from poetry to tracts on political thought.

Coluccio Salutati (1331–1406) was Chancellor of Florence, 1375–1406, after holding office at Lucca. Renowned as a great letter-writer and Latinist, he was a friend of Petrarch. Apart from his letters he wrote several humanistic treatises and in 1400 a work of political thought, *De tyranno* (On tyranny) in which, contrary to the enthusiasm for Florentine liberty which emerges from his letters, he supported monarchy.

Dives and Pauper is an anonymous prose dialogue, written almost certainly by a Franciscan, between a preaching friar, Pauper, who assumes the role of teacher, and a rich layman, Dives. Its main subject is the Ten

Commandments, but it is prefaced by a dialogue on Holy Poverty. It was written in Middle English between 1405 and 1410. The author displays considerable knowledge of theology and canon law, but the work also contains a great deal of political and social comment. He has been identified as the author of the sermons in MS Longleat 4.

Durandus of Saint-Pourçain (d. 1332) was a French Dominican theologian and nominalist philosopher at Paris. He held the bishoprics of Limoux (1317), Le Puy-en-Velay (1318), and Meaux (1326). His contribution to economic thought (as opposed to political, for which he is better known) occurs in his Commentary on the *Sentences* and a Paris *quodlibet* in which he discussed usury.

Fasciculus morum – an early fourteenth-century preachers' handbook in the form of a treatise on the Seven Deadly Sins and their opposite virtues. It was written in Latin, almost certainly by a Franciscan. It is extant in twenty-eight manuscripts, which demonstrates its popularity. It has many *exempla* on economic and social topics such as usury.

Gerald Odonis (c. 1290–1348) was master of theology, probably at Paris. In 1329 he was 'elected' Minister-General of the Franciscans in succession to the deposed Michael of Cesena, due to the influence of his friend Pope John XXII. He defended John during the controversy over the Beatific Vision and was a member of the commission which condemned Durandus of Saint-Pourçain's views on it. He was created patriarch of Alexandria by Clement VI and ultimately Bishop of Catania, where he became a victim of the Black Death. He wrote commentaries on the *Sentences* and on Aristotle's *Ethics*, and his main contribution to economic thought is in connection with the payment of interest.

Giles of Lessines (1230/40–c. 1304) was a Dominican theologian, philosopher, and natural scientist from Lessines (Hainaut, Belgium). Probably a pupil of Albert the Great at Cologne, and also of Aquinas at Paris, he did not himself become a master in theology. His treatise *De usuris*, written between 1278 and 1284, is the first known medieval treatise on an economic subject and made a fundamental contribution to scholastic discussions on usury, especially on the time factor it involved.

Giles of Rome (Aegidius Romanus) (c. 1243/7–1316) was probably descended from the Colonna family. He was born in Rome, but while still young entered the Order of Augustinian Hermits at Paris, and subsequently became a pupil of Thomas Aquinas. He became Prior General of the Order in 1292, and Archbishop of Bourges in 1295. He became attached to the papal court of Boniface VIII, and the Pope's famous bull *Unam sanctam* may well have been based on Giles's *De ecclesiastica potestate*, completed in 1302. Giles was a prolific writer on theological and philosophical subjects and a commentator, commenting on some of Aristotle's works, on the *Sentences* of Peter Lombard, and on parts of the Bible. His best-known work, the *De regimine principum*, was written for his pupil, the future Philip IV the Fair of France (*c.* 1285), before he entered the service of the Pope. Giles returned to Philip's service after the death of Boniface VIII, and helped in his persecution of the Templars.

Gratian (fl. *c.* 1140), known as the 'father of the science of canon law', was famed for his *Decretum*, which collected, synthesized, and commented on earlier collections. It appeared *c.* 1140. He was possibly a monk of the Camaldulensian monastery at Bologna. Apart from this nothing is known of his life.

Guido Terreni (d. 1342) was a native of Perpignan, a master of theology at Paris, and a member of the Carmelite Order, who rose to be Prior General in 1318. He became Bishop of Majorca in 1321 and of Elne in 1332. He was heavily involved in the apostolic poverty controversies in the early 1320s, on which he wrote *De perfectione vitae*, dedicated to John XXII. He was also a commentator on canon law, on the Bible, on Aristotle's *Politics*, and on the *Ethics,* from which most of his economic thought comes.

Henry of Bracton (d. 1268) was a royal justice in the time of Henry III of England. The treatise *On the Laws and Customs of England*, a survey of the English common law, was formerly attributed to him because some versions bear his name. It now seems likely that it was written in the 1220s and 1230s and that Bracton was one of the later editors. It survives in over fifty manuscripts and was popular in the fourteenth and fifteenth centuries, but had no successors.

Henry of Friemar (*c.* 1245–1346) was a German theologian from Friemar, near Gotha, who studied at Bologna. He became German provincial of the Order of Augustinian Hermits and moved to Paris, where from 1305 he held the Augustinian chair of theology. He returned to Germany about ten years later, and held several high offices in the Order. He eventually settled at Erfurt, where he died. He left many devotional works and sermons, but also a commentary on Aristotle's *Ethics* (unpublished), a *Tractatus de vitiis* (Concerning the vices), and a *Tractatus de decem praeceptis* (On the Ten Commandments). His main contributions to economic thought were about money, price, and value.

Henry of Ghent (1217–93) was a theologian and philosopher, who studied first at the cathedral school of Tournai, then arts and theology at Paris, becoming a master of theology in 1275, and soon establishing a reputation as a great teacher. He became a canon of Tournai in 1267, archdeacon of Bruges in 1276, and of Tournai in 1278, but continued to teach at Paris. He was part of the commission which examined the works of the 'Averroist' philosophers in Paris which formed the basis for the condemnation of 1277. He also opposed the privileges of the mendicant orders. His main works include an unfinished *Summa theologica*, composed of ordinary questions arising during his teaching work, several *quodlibets*, and questions on the *Physics* and the *Metaphysics* of Aristotle.

Henry of Hesse (?1340–97), also known as Henry of Langenstein, was a pupil of John Buridan at Paris and a follower of William of Ockham. Originally an astronomer, he transferred to the theology faculty in about 1375, and became a master in theology and Vice-Chancellor of the University. The conciliarist Jean Gerson was his pupil. Later he helped to set up the new university of Vienna, where he became a professor. Henry is known mainly for his work in support of the conciliarists during the Great Schism (1378–1417). His main contribution to social and economic thought is on the theory of the just price, and occurs in two chapters of his tract *De contractibus et origine censuum*.

Hostiensis (Henricus de Segusio) (c. 1190–1271) was a celebrated canonist, who featured in Dante's *Divine Comedy* (*Paradise*, 12, 82–97). A native of Susa, in the diocese at Turin, he studied law at Bologna and then moved to Paris where he taught canon law. He spent some time in England as part of the household of Eleanor of Provence, wife of Henry III. He became Bishop of Sisteron (on the river Durance) in 1244, archbishop of Embrun in 1250, and Cardinal-Bishop of Ostia (hence his name) in 1261. His best-known work is the *Summa*, later known as *Summa aurea*, although it was his later Commentary on the *Decretals* which justified payment of interest from the beginning of a charitable loan on the basis of the potential profit lost by the lender.

Huguccio (d. 1210) was born at Pisa, studied and lectured on canon law at Bologna, and was the teacher of Pope Innocent III. In 1190 he became Bishop of Ferrara, where he often acted as papal judge-delegate. His great work, the *Summa super corpore Decretorum*, written at the request of his students, and completed *c.* 1190, has won universal acclaim, but is still unpublished.

Jean de Meun(g) (d. c. 1305) was born at Meung sur Loire. He studied arts at Paris. He continued the prose romance, *Romance of the Rose*, started by Guillaume de Lorris, which was one of the most popular literary works of the medieval period. He also translated into French Boethius,

Consolation of Philosophy and the Life and Letters of Heloise and Abelard. There is much social comment in the *Romance of the Rose*, especially on the able-bodied but idle poor.

Johannes Andreae (c. 1270–1348), a famous canonist, was the illegitimate son of a concubine called Novella. He studied theology and civil and canon law at Bologna, and later held prestigious teaching appointments both at Padua and Bologna, where he finally settled in 1320. He was sent on several diplomatic missions on behalf of the Bolognese civil authorities. He was apparently only the second married layman to become a professor of canon law, and Christine de Pisan records that he allowed his daughter Novella to lecture for him when he was ill. His most important works are the *Glossa ordinaria* on the *Sext.* and the *Clementines*, a commentary on the *Decretales* called *Novella super Decretalibus*, and the *Novella* on the *Sext.* His name is associated wrongly with a theory on the inherent value of fungibles. When he died of the plague in 1348 he was a wealthy man.

Johannes Teutonicus (c. 1170–1245) was a native of Saxony, but studied and taught at Bologna. He returned to Germany in 1218 as Provost of Halberstadt. He was a canonist, whose *Glossa ordinaria* on the *Decretum* was very influential and covered many economic and social topics. He also collected the later decrees of Innocent III, glossed the decrees of the Fourth Lateran Council, and made his own collection of decretals, the *Compilatio quarta*.

John of Ayton (*c.* 1307–*c.* 1349) was an English canonist, the product of study at Oxford and Cambridge, where he later taught, before becoming a canon of Lincoln cathedral. He held various minor benefices, and was in the service of the Archbishop of York and the Bishop of Durham, Richard de Bury. His most famous works are his Gloss on the Constitutions of the papal legates Otto and Ottobuono, and a pastoral work on the Seven Deadly Sins, the *Septuplum*. The gloss was very popular.

John Bromyard (d. *c.* 1352) was a Dominican from Hereford Convent, who possibly studied at Oxford. His main works are the *Opus trivium*, which was a handbook for preachers derived from divine, canon, and civil law, and arranged alphabetically, and its much larger revised version, the *Summa praedicantium*, also arranged alphabetically, and probably completed in 1348–9. The *Summa* was very popular and is full of social comment. Bromyard is not to be confused with another of the same name, also a Dominican from the Hereford convent, who lived about fifty years later.

John Buridan (*c.* 1292–1358) was a Franciscan philosopher, theologian, and mathematician. He studied and taught at Paris, where he was rector of the University in 1328 and also 1340. He taught Nicholas Oresme. His main works are commentaries on the *Politics* and the *Ethics* of Aristotle. No reference to the story of the ass has ever been found in his work.

John Chrysostom, St (347–407), Archbishop of Constantinople, was trained in law and rhetoric at Antioch and became a monk of an austere mountain community until ordained deacon and then priest (386). He quickly became famous as a preacher and scriptural commentator. He was consecrated Archbishop in 398 at the wish of the Emperor Arcadius. He soon proved to be too rigorous a moral reformer: charges were trumped up against him, and he was deposed and exiled, though subsequently recalled and then exiled again. His main surviving works are his biblical commentaries and his treatise on the priesthood.

John Duns Scotus (*c.* 1265–1308) was a Franciscan philosopher and theologian, who was born probably near Duns (Berwickshire). He was ordained priest in Northampton in 1291. He studied at Oxford 1288–1301 and lectured there on the *Sentences*, 1298–9, and possibly also at Cambridge. He became regent master at Paris in 1305 and transferred to the Franciscan house at Cologne in 1307, where he lectured as professor of theology. His main work is his commentary on the *Sentences*, but he also commented on works of Aristotle and Porphyry.

John Fortescue, Sir (*c.* 1394–*c.* 1476) was a celebrated lawyer and Chief Justice of the King's Bench in the time of Henry VI of England. He wrote in defence of the Lancastrians. His most famous works are *De laudibus legum Angliae (In Praise of England's Laws)* and *The Governance of England: Otherwise Called the Difference between an Absolute and a Limited Monarchy*. He is associated with the idea of the English 'political and royal lordship', that is, the balanced constitution of King and Parliament, which emphasized the idea of parliamentary consent to issues such as taxation.

John of Paris (*c.* 1240–1306) was a French Dominican writer on a wide range of subjects, natural philosophy, theology, metaphysics, and politics, who was an outstanding teacher at the University of Paris. He was a disciple of Aquinas, although he was an opponent of papal supremacy. In the dispute between Philip IV and Boniface VIII he sided with the King, as was demonstrated in his *De potestate regia et papali* (On royal and papal power), written in 1302. He supported calls for the accusation of the Pope before a general council. He himself died under a cloud, having been censured by an episcopal court under Giles of Rome, and forbidden to teach. Death intervened before his appeal could be heard by Clement V. His ideas on labour as a title to private property anticipate those of the seventeenth-century thinker John Locke.

John of Salisbury (*c.* 1120–80) took his name from his birthplace. He was one of the leading scholars of the twelfth-century renaissance, a humanist, a classicist, a theologian, and a political thinker, who studied at Paris under Peter Abelard. He was secretary to Archbishop Theobald of Canterbury, in which capacity he often visited the Roman curia. He was both servant and friend to Theobald's successor, Thomas Becket, and was present at his murder. He became Bishop of Chartres in 1176. His most celebrated writing is the *Policraticus*, in which he described the kingdom as a body, in which the ruler and different groups of people and their functions corresponded to different parts of the body.

John Wyclif (*c.* 1328–84) was a controversial English theologian, philosopher, and political thinker, whose ideas became the basis for the heresy known as Lollardy. Most of his life was spent in Oxford, at Balliol, where he was master, then at Queen's, and finally at Canterbury Hall, where he was warden. He became a doctor of divinity in 1372 and played a leading part in the faculty of theology. In 1374 he was sent to Bruges on a mission to negotiate about papal dues and taxes. The same year he became rector of Lutterworth (Leicestershire). He entered the service of John of Gaunt, who brought him to London, where he preached several anti-clerical sermons. When tried for heresy he was protected by Gaunt or members of the royal family, until 1379, when he was condemned at Oxford for his views on the Eucharist. In 1381 he retired to Lutterworth. He was finally condemned posthumously by the Council of Constance in 1415. Of his numerous and lengthy works the best known are *On Divine and Civil Dominion*, *On the Truth of Holy Scripture*, *Concerning the Church*, *On the Office of King* (written for Richard II), *Concerning the Power of the Pope* (for Urban VI), and *Concerning the Eucharist*. The idea most often associated with him is that of dominion and grace, by which anyone not in a state of grace (something known only to God) was denied the right to govern or to own property.

Laurentius Ridolfis (fl. 1400s) was a Florentine layman and, surprisingly, a teacher of canon law. He was sometimes used as an ambassador by the Florentine Republic. His main economic work, written in 1403, is the *Tractatus de usuris* (Concerning Usury), in which he discussed interest and exchange-dealing.

Leon Battista Alberti (1402–72) was a true Renaissance man who shone in a number of different fields. He was a humanist scholar, a mathematician, a natural scientist, author, artist, and architect. He was educated at Genoa, Padua, and Bologna, in classics, mathematics, and canon law respectively. He became a papal secretary, and in this capacity travelled widely, spending much time in Florence. His most important works were *Della pittura* (1436), which greatly influenced painting, the *Della famiglia*, written in the 1430s, a discussion between members of his own family about domestic life, and the *De re aedificatoria* (completed 1452, published 1485), a practical and important treatise on architecture.

The Libelle of Englyshe Polycye is an anonymous English mercantilist tract, written between 1436 and 1438. It is fiercely nationalistic and recommends a protectionist policy and control of the sea routes.

Matteo Palmieri (1406–75) was a Florentine humanist, the son of a prosperous Florentine mercantile family. He held several governmental appointments. His most important work is the treatise *Della vita civile* (1431–8).

Nicholas Oresme (*c.* 1320–82) Due to his association with both the Court of Charles V of France and the University of Paris he held a succession of high offices, eventually becoming Bishop of Lisieux in 1377. He was a mathematician and a natural philosopher, and was the pupil of John Buridan. He wrote an important set of *quaestiones* on Aristotle's works on natural philosophy in order to attack contemporary astrologers. Towards the end of his life he translated Aristotelian works into French, and commented on them, for Charles V. These included the *Politics* and the *Ethics*. His famous work *De moneta* (On the Coinage) was written for Charles V and made important contributions to ideas on manipulation of the currency.

Peter John Olivi (d. 1298) was a Spiritual Franciscan and theologian who was heavily involved in the controversy over the absolute poverty of Christ. He taught at Paris, Montpellier, Florence, and Narbonne. He was condemned for heresy in 1282, and although his orthodoxy was vindicated later, he was condemned posthumously by the Council of Vienne (1311) and by John XXII. His works, of which most are unpublished, include a postill on the Apocalypse, *quaestiones* on the *Sentences*, *quodlibets*, and biblical commentaries. His main contributions to economic thought were on usury and interest. He is now acknowledged as one of the main sources for the economic ideas of St Bernardino.

Peter the Chanter (*c.* 1150–97) was a theologian and a celebrated teacher of theology at Paris, who gathered a distinguished circle of followers, including Robert of Courçon and Thomas of Chobham. In 1171 he was a canon of Notre Dame and a teacher of theology, and from 1184 was cantor there. His election to the bishopric of Tournai was condemned as irregular, but he eventually became dean of the cathedral chapter of Rheims. His works are wide ranging, and include extensive biblical commentaries. The best known, and for a long time his only published work, is the *Verbum abbreviatum*.

Poggio Bracciolini (1380–1459) was a Florentine humanist and one of the outstanding figures of the early Renaissance. He was a great Latinist with a passion for collecting classical Latin manuscripts. His appointment as a secretary at the papal curia was interrupted briefly by a period of exile in England, but resumed during 1423–52. He ended his life as Chancellor of Florence. He wrote many Latin dialogues, some of them obscene. The *De avaritia*, in which he lauded avarice as the basis for the smooth running of the city-state, was written in 1428.

Ptolemy (Bartholomew) of Lucca (d. *c.* 1328) was a Dominican, Prior of Lucca, then of Santa Maria Novella at Florence. He spent much time at the papal court at Avignon, finally becoming bishop of Torcello in 1318. He is mainly known for his completion of his teacher, Aquinas's, work *De regimine principum*, which he finished about 1300.

Raymond of Peñafort (c. 1180–1275) studied and taught rhetoric and logic at Barcelona before moving on to Bologna to study, and then to teach, canon law. On his return to Barcelona in the 1220s he became a canon and provost of the cathedral chapter, but resigned when he entered the Dominican Order. In 1230 he was summoned to Rome by Pope Gregory IX, who created him papal chaplain and penitentiary, and commissioned him to make an official collection of the decretals which had appeared since Gratian's *Decretum*, promulgated as the *Decretales* of Gregory IX, or the *Liber Extra*, in 1232. In order to complete the collection, Raymond may have written some of the decretals himself, such as *Consuluit*. He may also have been responsible for *Naviganti*. Soon after returning to Catalonia he was elected Master-General of the Dominican order, in which role he revised the Order's constitutions. Apart from the *Decretales*, he is celebrated for glosses on the *Decretum*, the writing of a *Summa* on canon law, and a *Summa de penitentia*. He commissioned Thomas Aquinas to write the *Summa contra gentiles* to help in his work of converting Jews and Muslims.

Reginald Pecock (*c.* 1393–1461) was a Welshman, educated at Oxford, and then, in 1431, appointed master of Whittington College, London. He became bishop of St Asaph in 1444 and Chichester in 1450. He was a strong Lancastrian supporter, and his unpopularity with the Yorkists led to accusations of heresy and his deposition from the see of Chichester in 1457. He died as a prisoner in Thorney Abbey. He wrote mainly to refute the doctrines of the Lollards, among them those on the poverty of the clergy. The most famous is the *Repressor of Over Much Blaming of the Clergy*.

Richard Fitzralph (*c.* 1295–1360) was celebrated as a scholar, preacher, and controversialist. He held a number of high offices, Chancellor of Oxford University (1332), Chancellor of Lincoln Cathedral (1334), Canon of Lichfield (1335), Dean of Lichfield (1337) and finally Archbishop of Armagh (1347). He spent much time at the papal court at Avignon in connection with controversies being discussed there. On his third and final visit (1357 until his death) he was involved in the controversy between the secular clergy and the mendicant orders on the subject of apostolic poverty, which he opposed. In this connection he wrote his best-known work, the *De pauperie Salvatoris* (On the Poverty of the Saviour), which influenced Wyclif's ideas on dominion and grace.

Richard of Middleton (Mediavilla, *c.* **1249–1302),** was probably English (from Middleton Stoney, Oxon. or Middleton Cheyney, Northants) but may have been French. He was a Franciscan philosopher and theologian, with an interest both in economics and science. In 1283 he was appointed to a commission to examine the works of Peter John Olivi, and from 1284 (the year he obtained his mastership in theology) to 1287 he was regent master in theology at the Franciscan studium in Paris. His main works are his Commentary on the *Sentences*, several questions and *quodlibets*, and some academic sermons. His most important contributions to economic thought concern usury and interest.

Robert of Courçon (*c.* 1160–1219) was an Englishman from either Devonshire or Derbyshire, who may have studied at Oxford before going to Paris, where he became a student of Peter the Chanter and a friend of the future Innocent III. After obtaining his mastership he taught at Paris. He was a canon of Noyon and then of Paris, before being created cardinal-priest by Innocent III. He was frequently used as a papal legate and was employed as legate to France in 1213 to preach the Crusade. As legate he held numerous local councils, where he promulgated often unpopular reforms. His most memorable was that of Paris in 1213 to reform abuses, especially that of usury. In 1215 he issued new statutes for the university which proscribed the study of Aristotle's *Metaphysics* and other works and strictly controlled teaching of what was known of the *Ethics*. He returned to Rome to take part in the Fourth Lateran Council, and was sent by Honorius III, Innocent's successor, on the Fourth Crusade. He died in Damietta. His main work is his *Summa* (probably incomplete), written *c.* 1208, which examines penance and usury, a subject which he felt strongly about and took practical measures to repress.

Rufinus (d. 1192) was a celebrated canonist who studied and taught at Bologna, where he was also a canon of the cathedral. He later became bishop of Assisi and then, *c.* 1180, Archbishop of Sorrento. He is renowned for his *Summa* on the *Decretum* (*c.* 1159).

Thomas Aquinas, St (*c.* 1225–74), known as the Angelic Doctor, is the most celebrated theologian of the late medieval period. He is famed especially for his synthesis of Aristotelian principles with those of the Church. Originally a student at Naples, where he joined the Dominican Order in 1244, the rest of his life was divided between Paris and Cologne, where he both studied, under Albert the Great, and taught, and Italy, where he spend time at the papal court. His most famous work is the great *Summa theologiae*, the first part of which was written in Italy 1259–68, the second in Paris from 1268. He also commented on Aristotle's *Politics* and *Ethics* (1269–72), wrote part of a political tract, the *De regimine principum* (completed by Ptolemy of Lucca), and the *Summa contra gentiles* (1259–64). He died on the way to the Council of Lyons, and was canonized by John XXII for his views on property. He is traditionally taken to be the main writer on economic thought of the period, although it now appears that many of his ideas were not original.

Thomas Brinton (*c.* 1330–89) was a Benedictine monk of Norwich Cathedral Priory who studied law probably at Cambridge and certainly at Oxford, where he obtained a doctorate in canon law in 1364. By then he had already been appointed a papal penitentiary. During the next few years he spent much time at Avignon and built up a reputation as a preacher. He probably went to Rome with Urban V when the papacy briefly returned there. He was appointed Bishop of Rochester in 1373. As such he was heavily involved in politics. He was an envoy to the French at Calais in 1380, a member of the commission which tried the rebels in 1381, and in 1382 both attended the Black Friars Council which tried Wyclif and was appointed to a commission to inquire into the state of the realm. His outspoken sermons dealt with many of the social issues of the day, and demonstrated his opposition to Wyclif.

Thomas of Chobham (1158/68–*c.* 1235) was an Englishman, probably from Chobham in Surrey, who became sub-dean of Salisbury. It is likely that he was a pupil of Peter the Chanter in Paris, where he may also have taught. His main work, the *Summa confessorum*, is a handbook of penance, which appeared in about 1216, just after the Fourth Lateran Council had made annual confession compulsory. It was very influential, especially in England, where it was an important source for *Dives and Pauper*.

William Langland (*c.* 1332–*c.* 1400) was born in Shropshire, and educated at Malvern Priory. In later life he lived in London and was married, although he was also in minor orders. He is famous as the author of the long alliterative poem, *The Vision of William concerning Piers the Plowman*, which exists in three versions, of unequal length – the A text, written about 1362, the B Text, started in 1377, and the C Text, written in the 1390s. It is full of social comment and is especially critical of the clergy and religious and the able-bodied poor. Langland may also have written *Richard the Redeless*, a poem of advice to Richard II, in 1399.

William of Auxerre (c. 1150–1231) was a master in theology at Paris, possibly a former pupil of Richard of St Victor. He became archdeacon of Beauvais. In 1230 he was sent as an envoy to Gregory IX to try to reach a settlement in a dispute between the university and citizens of Paris. Gregory was sufficiently impressed by him to retain him as his own adviser, and in 1231 he was appointed to head a commission of three to 'correct' the prohibited works of Aristotle. He died in Rome. His main work is the *Summa aurea* (Golden Summa), written between 1215 and 1220, which was very popular. It is really a commentary on the *Sentences*, and it contained a treatise on usury. In terms of economic thought it was important as a precursor of Aquinas's *Summa theologiae*. It made use of the limited number of Aristotelian works available at the time and emphasized the importance of natural law as a basis for economic affairs.

Wynnere and Wastoure is an unrhymed alliterative poem in Middle English, dated between 1352 and *c.* 1370. It is in the form of a debate between the characters of the title and is largely about national economic matters. It may have influenced William Langland in his writing of *Piers Plowman*.

GLOSSARY OF TERMS

Appropriation – transfer of parish church and its endowments to a monastery, cathedral, college or other corporate institution, so that the institution became the 'rector'.

Assart – piece of forest or waste land reclaimed or cleared for productive use.

Assay – trial of metal or ore for quality.

Assize – (1) enactment of legislative assembly; (2) regulation of bread or ale according to the price of grain; (3) statute regulating weights and measures of articles for sale in the market-place; (4) a judicial inquest.

Benefice – ecclesiastical office held in return for duties, to which an income was attached.

Bullion – unminted gold or silver.

Chantry – endowment, either in perpetuity or for a term of years, of a priest to celebrate Mass for the soul of the founder and, often, his/her family. Sometimes the endowment would be a piece of real property which would produce an income. The founding of a chantry by a wealthy person might involve the building of a chapel or an altar in a cathedral or church.

Copyhold tenure – method of landholding developed in the fifteenth century by which a peasant would possess a copy of the entry on the manorial court roll recording his admission to the tenement. Abolished in 1922.

Corrody – pension in form of lodging at a religious house, or allowance of food and clothing, given to lay person, often in return for lump sum payment.

Court leet – court through which a magnate exercised jurisdiction within his estates, which usually included the view of frankpledge (see below). Held twice a year, but became obsolete in seventeenth century.

Court baron – manorial court held by lord, or, more usually, his steward, for recording of transfer of customary holdings, the enforcement of the customs of the manor, disputes between tenants, debts, and trespass. Usually held every three to four weeks.

Debasement – term loosely applied to manipulation of the coinage. Strictly speaking it meant adulteration of the precious metal content of a bi-metallic coin by changing its ratio in relation to base metal, the other component, rather than merely altering the weight of the coin.

Demesne land – land retained by the lord and cultivated by him (with peasant labour) or leased out, as opposed to tenant (or villein) land held by hereditary peasant tenants.

Enclosure – the enclosing of land formerly held in strips in open or common fields by erecting fences or hedges. It might be done by the lord, often for pasture, or by a tenant who had consolidated his strips and wanted exclusive rights over the enclosed land.

Engrossing – advance buying of supplies, usually of corn, and withholding them from the market until the price had risen. The term originally meant wholesale dealing (hence the term 'grocer' because he sold in the 'gross').

Fief – land held from a lord by a tenant in return for an oath of loyalty and performance of personal service.

Forestalling – buying of goods on their way to market, literally 'before the stall', cheaply, and reselling them at a profit.

Frankpledge – the obligation of unfree men over twelve years of age to be sworn into *tithings*, that is, groups of ten, for the purpose of keeping the peace. Members were responsible for the good conduct of the group and had to report any crimes which came to their knowledge. A view of frankpledge, a periodic court, would be held at intervals for production of members of the tithing and for the reporting of crimes (see court leet above).

Friar – one who renounced all property, both individual and corporate, and was supposed to live by alms. The four main orders of mendicant friars were the Franciscans, the Dominicans, the Carmelites, and the Austin Friars.

Fungible – an object that is consumed in use, with the result that its use cannot be separated from its ownership.

Journeyman – a craftsman who had finished his apprenticeship and worked for wages, but was not yet a master craftsman and a member of a gild of masters.

Manor – the smallest unit of estate administration and a unit of lordship to which a court was attached.

Monopoly – exclusive control of either goods or labour in a particular trade or industry which interfered with the free flow of the market.

Rector – incumbent of parish who received the full revenues (tithes, offerings, etc.). If a parish was 'appropriated' to an institution, that institution would become the rector.

Regrating – the buying up of goods in order to re-sell at a profit, without adding to or improving them. Although originally it meant retail trading, it came to be associated with monopoly.

Scholastics – academic philosophers and/or theologians of the twelfth to fifteenth centuries, associated especially with the universities of Paris and Oxford, who based their teaching on the Bible, the Fathers of the Church, and on Aristotle, and whose method was to teach by lecture and reasoned argument.

Specie – coinage.

Tenant-in-chief – tenant holding land directly from the Crown.

Tithe – the tenth part of the produce of everything subject to natural increase in a parish, which was allowed to the rector for his maintenance. In the towns it was a personal tax on income.

Truck – payment of workers in kind rather than in money and associated especially with the cloth-making industry.

Usury – making a charge for a loan, usually of money.

Vassal – someone, usually a tenant, under the protection of a lord, to whom homage and fealty is sworn.

Villein – unfree tenant tied to a manorial lord and to a holding of land, who held strips of land in the open or common fields and who owed servile dues to his lord.

SELECT BIBLIOGRAPHY

PRIMARY SOURCES

Ælfric of Eynsham, *Colloquy*, ed. Michael Swanton, *Anglo-Saxon Prose* (London, 1975), pp. 107–15
Albert the Great, *Ethicorum* (Second commentary), *Opera omnia*, 7 (Paris, 1891)
Alexander of Hales, *Summa theologica*, 4 vols. (Quaracchi, 1924–48)
Aristotle, *On Rhetoric: A Theory of Civic Discourse*, trans. George A. Kennedy (New York and Oxford, 1991)
 The Nicomachean Ethics, ed. and trans. David Ross, rev. J. L. Ackrill and J. O. Urmson (Oxford, 1980)
 The Politics, ed. and trans. Ernest Barker (Oxford, 1946)
Aspin, Isabel S. T., ed., *Anglo-Norman Political Songs*, Anglo-Norman Texts, 11 (Oxford, 1953)
Augustine, *City of God*, ed. David Knowles, trans. Henry Betteson (Harmondsworth, 1972)
Benedict, *The Rule of St Benedict*, ed. and trans. Justin McCann (London, 1976)
Bernard Mandeville, *The Fable of the Bees*, ed. F. B. Kaye, 2 vols. (Oxford and Cambridge, 1924)
Bernardino of Siena, *Opera omnia*, 9 vols., ed. College of St Bonaventure (Quaracchi, 1950–65)
Bland, A. E., Brown, P. A., and Tawney, R. H., eds, *English Economic History: Select Documents* (London, 1914)
The Book of Vices and Virtues, ed. W. Nelson Francis, EETS, o.s. 217 (1942)
Christine de Pisan, *The Book of the Body Politic*, pt. 3, trans. Kate Langdon Forhan, in Cary J. Nederman and Kate Langdon Forhan, ed. and trans., *Medieval Political Theory – a Reader: The Quest for the Body Politic, 1100–1400* (London and New York, 1993), pp. 230–47
 The Treasure of the City of Ladies or The Book of the Three Virtues, ed. and trans. Sarah Lawson (Harmondsworth, 1985)

Cicero, *De Officiis*, ed. and trans. Walter Miller, LCL, 21 (London and Cambridge, MA, 1913)
Conrad of Megenberg, *Yconomica*, ed. Sabine Kruger, *MGH Staatsschriften des späteren Mittelalters*, 3, pt. 5, vol. 1 (1973)
Decretales Gregorii IX, ed. Ae. Friedberg, *Corpus iuris canonici*, 2 (Leipzig, 1879)
Decretum Gratiani, ed. Ae. Friedberg, *Corpus iuris canonici*, 1 (Leipzig, 1879)
Didache or The Teaching of the Twelve Apostles, ed. and trans. James A. Kleist, Ancient Christian Writers, 6 (Westminster, MD, 1948)
Dives and Pauper, ed Priscilla Heath Barnum, *EETS*, 275 (Oxford, 1976); 280 (1980)
Dobson, R. B., ed., *The Peasants' Revolt of 1381* (London, 1970)
English Historical Documents, 1, ed. Dorothy Whitelock (London, 1955)
English Historical Documents, 2, ed. David Douglas (London, 1953)
English Historical Documents, 3, ed. Harry Rothwell (London, 1975)
English Historical Documents, 4, ed. A. R. Myers (London, 1969)
English Historical Documents, 5, ed. C. H. Williams (London, 1967)
Fasciculus morum: a Fourteenth-century Preachers' Handbook, ed. and trans. Siegfried Wenzel (Pennsylvania, PA, 1989)
Fisher, H. E. S. and Juřica, A. R. J., eds., *Documents in English Economic History: England from 1000 to 1760* (London, 1977)
Friedberg, Ae., ed., *Corpus iuris canonici*, 2 vols. (Leipzig, 1879)
Geoffrey Chaucer, *The Canterbury Tales*, ed. Larry D. Benson, *The Riverside Chaucer*, 3rd edn (Oxford, 1988)
Gilchrist, John, ed. and trans., 'Selected Canons and Constitutions of the General Councils', in *The Church and Economic Activity in the Middle Ages* (London, 1969), Appendix 1, pp. 141–225
Giles of Rome, *De ecclesiastica potestate* (On Ecclesiastical Power), trans. R. W. Dyson (Woodbridge and Dover, NH, 1986)
De regimine principum (Rome, 1556)
Given-Wilson, Chris, ed., *Chronicles of the Revolution, 1397–1400: The Reign of Richard II* (Manchester, 1993)
Glanvill, *The Treatise on the Laws and Customs of the Realm of England commonly called Glanvill*, ed. and trans. G. D. G. Hall, Oxford Medieval Texts (Oxford, 1993)
Guillaume de Lorris and Jean de Meun, *The Romance of the Rose*, trans. Frances Horgan (Oxford, 1994)
Habig, Marion A., ed., *St Francis of Assisi: Writings and Early Biographies: English Omnibus of the Sources for the Life of St Francis*, 3rd edn rev. (London, 1979)
Henry de Bouhic, *Super quinque libris Decretalium* (Lyons, 1498)
Henry of Bracton, *De legibus et consuetudinibus Angliae*, 4 vols, ed. G. E. Woodbine and trans. Samuel E. Thorne (Cambridge, MA, 1968)
Henry of Hesse (Langenstein), *De contractibus*, in John Gerson, *Opera omnia*, 4 (Cologne, 1484), pp. 185–224
Henry Knighton, *Knighton's Chronicle 1337–1396*, ed. and trans. G. T. Martin, Oxford Medieval Texts (Oxford, 1995)
Horrox, Rosemary, ed. and trans., *The Black Death* (Manchester, 1987)

Jacob's Well: An English Treatise on the Cleansing of Man's Conscience, ed. Arthur Brandeis, EETS, o.s. 115 (1900)

Jeremy Bentham, *Defence of Usury*, ed. W. Stark, *Jeremy Bentham's Economic Writings*, 1 (London, 1952), pp. 121–207

Johannes Andreae, *Commentaria ad Decretales* (Venice, 1581)
  Glossa ordinaria ad Sext., in *Corpus iuris canonici*, 3 (Lyons, 1624)

John of Ayton, *Commentaria ad Constitutiones Othonis et Othoboni*, in Lyndwood, *Provinciale* (Oxford, 1679)

John Bromyard, *Summa praedicantium*, 2 vols. (Venice, 1586)

John Duns Scotus, *Opus Oxoniensis*, bk. IV, dist. xv, q. 2: *Opera omnia*, 18 (Paris, 1894), pp. 256–341

John Fortescue, *The Governance of England*, in Shelley Lockwood, ed., *Sir John Fortescue, On the Laws and Governance of England* (Cambridge, 1997), pp. 83–123
  In Praise of the Laws of England, in Lockwood, ed., *Laws and Governance of England*, pp. 3–80

John Gower, *Confessio amantis*, ed. G. C. Macaulay, *The English Works of John Gower*, EETS, 81–2 (1900–1)

John Locke, *The Second Treatise of Government*, ed. Peter Laslett, *Locke: Two Treatises of Government* (Cambridge, 1988), pp. 265–428

John of Paris, *On Royal and Papal Power*, ed. and trans. J. A. Watt, Pontifical Institute of Medieval Studies (Toronto, 1971)

John of Salisbury, *Policraticus*, ed. and trans. Cary J. Nederman (Cambridge, 1990)

John Wyclif (?), *The Grete Sentence of Curs Expounded*, ed. Thomas Arnold, *Select English Works of John Wyclif*, 3 (Oxford, 1871), pp. 267–337

Leet Jurisdiction in the City of Norwich, ed. William Hudson, Selden Society, 5 (1892)

Leon Battista Alberti, *The Family*, ed. and trans. Guido A. Guarino, *The Albertis of Florence: Leon Battista Alberti's 'Della Famiglia'* (Lewisburg, 1971)

Lewis, Ewart, ed. and trans., *Medieval Political Ideas*, 2 vols (New York, 1974)

The Libelle of Englyshe Polycye, ed. George Warner (Oxford, 1926)

Lopez, Robert S., and Raymond, Irving W., eds, *Medieval Trade in the Mediterranean World: Illustrative Documents* (New York and London, 1955)

Margery Kempe, *The Book of Margery Kempe*, trans. B. A. Windeatt (Harmondsworth, 1985)

Matteo Villani, *Cronaca*, ed. F. Gherardi Dragomanni, *Chroniche Storiche*, 5 (Florence, 1846)

Matthew Paris, *Chronica majora*, ed. H. R. Luard, RS, 57, 3 (1880)

Mommsen, T., Krueger, P., Schoell, R., and Kross, W., eds, *Corpus iuris civilis*, 3 vols. (Frankfurt, 1968–70)

Monroe, Arthur Eli, ed., *Early Economic Thought: Selections from Economic Literature prior to Adam Smith* (Cambridge, MA, 1924)

Nicholas Oresme, *The 'De moneta' of Nicholas Oresme and English Mint Documents*, ed. and trans. C. Johnson (London and Edinburgh, 1956)

Pecham, John, *Registrum epistolarum Fratris Johannis Pecham*, ed., C. T. Martin, RS, 77, 2 vols. (1884)

Peter Lombard, *Sententiae in IV libros distinctae*, 4 vols. (Rome, 1981)
Peter Olivi, *De emptionibus et venditionibus*, ed. Giacomo Todeschini (Rome, 1980)
Plato, *The Laws*, trans. A. E. Taylor, Everyman's Library, 275 (London, 1960)
Poggio Bracciolini, *Dialogus contra avaritiam (de avaritia)*, ed. G. Germano and A. Nardi (Livorno, 1994)
Ptolemy of Lucca, *De regimine principum*, trans. James M. Blythe, *On the Government of Rulers: De regimine principum. Ptolemy of Lucca, with Portions attributed to Thomas Aquinas* (Philadelphia, 1997)
Reginald Pecock, *The Repressor of Over Much Blaming of the Clergy*, ed. Churchill Babbington, *RS* (1860)
Richard of Middleton, *Super quatuor libros Sententiae* (Brescia, 1591)
Riley, H. T., ed. and trans. *Memorials of London and London Life in the Thirteenth, Fourteenth, and Fifteenth Centuries* (London, 1868)
Rymer, T. *Foedera*, 3 (London, 1740; repr. Farnborough, 1967)
Statutes of the Realm, 1–9 (London, 1810–28)
Tawney, R. H. and Power, Eileen, eds., *Tudor Economic Documents*, 3 (London, 1924)
Thomas Aquinas, *Summa contra gentiles*, trans. The English Dominican Fathers, 4 vols. in 5 (London, 1924–9)
  Summa theologiae: Latin Text and English translation, 61 vols., ed. T. Gilby *et al.* (London, 1964–80)
Thomas Brinton, *The Sermons of Thomas Brinton, Bishop of Rochester (1375–1389)*, 2 vols., ed. M. A. Devlin, Camden series 3, 85, 86 (London, 1954)
Thomas of Chobham, *Summa confessorum*, ed. F. Broomfield (Louvain and Paris, 1968), *Analecta mediaevalia Namurcensia*, 25
Thomas Mun, *England's Treasure by Forraign Trade or The Ballance of our Forraign Trade is the Rule of our Treasure* (London, 1664), in J. R. M. McCulloch, ed., *Early English Tracts on Commerce* (Cambridge, 1970), pp. 115–209
Walter of Henley, *Husbandry*, ed. Dorothea Oschinsky, *Walter of Henley and Other Treatises on Estate Management and Accounting* (Oxford, 1971)
Wieruszowski, Helene, ed., *The Medieval University* (Princeton, NJ, 1966)
Wilkins, D., *Concilia magna Britanniae et Hiberniae*, 4 vols. (London, 1737)
William Langland, *The Vision of William Concerning Piers the Plowman*, ed. W. Skeat, 2 vols. (Oxford, 1924, repr. 1969)
William of Sarzano, *Tractatus de summi pontificis*, ed. R. del Ponte, *Studi medievali*, ser. 3, 12 (1971), pp. 1020–94
Wright, T., ed., *Political Poems and Songs*, *RS* 14 (1859)
Wynnere and Wastoure, ed. Stephanie Trigg, *EETS* 297 (Oxford, 1990)

SECONDARY WORKS

Aston, M. E., '"Caim's Castles": poverty, politics and disendowment', in Aston, *Faith and Fire: Popular and Unpopular Religion, 1350–1600* (London and Rio Grande, 1993), pp. 95–131

Aston, T. and Philpin, C. H. E., eds., *The Brenner Debate: Agrarian Class Structure and Economic Developments in Pre-industrial Europe* (Cambridge, 1985)

Ault, Warren O., *Open-Field Farming in Medieval England* (London, 1972)

Baeck, Louis, *The Mediterranean Tradition in Economic Thought* (London, 1994)

Bainbridge, Virginia, 'The medieval way of death', in Michael Wilks, ed., *Prophecy and Eschatology*, SCH, subsidia 10 (1994), pp. 183–204

Baker, J. H., *An Introduction to English Legal History*, 3rd edn (London, 1990)

Baldwin, Francis Elizabeth, *Sumptuary Legislation and Personal Regulation in England* (Baltimore, MD, 1926)

Baldwin, J. W., *Masters, Princes, and Merchants: the Social Views of Peter the Chanter and his Circle*, 2 vols. (Princeton, NJ, 1970)

  'The medieval merchant before the bar of canon law', in *Papers of the Michigan Academy of Sciences, Arts, and Letters*, 44 (1959), pp. 287–99

  The Medieval Theories of the Just Price: Romanists, Canonists and Theologians in the Twelfth and Thirteenth Centuries, Transactions of the American Philosophical Society, n.s. 49, pt. 4 (Philadelphia, PA, 1959)

Barker, Ernest, *The Political Thought of Plato and Aristotle* (repr. New York, 1959)

Baron, Hans, 'Franciscan poverty and civic wealth as factors in the rise of humanistic thought', *Speculum*, 13 (1938), pp. 1–37

Basile, Giuseppe, *Giotto: the Arena Chapel Frescoes* (London, 1993)

Bec, Christian, *Les Marchands écrivains à Florence 1375–1434* (Paris, 1967)

Becker, Marvin B., 'Three cases concerning the restitution of usury in Florence', *Journal of Economic History*, 114 (1956), pp. 445–50

Beckwith, Sarah, 'A very material mysticism', in David Aers, ed., *Medieval Literature* (Brighton, 1986), pp. 34–57

Beer, Max, *Early British Economics from the Thirteenth to the Middle of the Eighteenth Century* (London, 1938)

Benson, Robert Louis, and Constable, Giles, with Lanham, Carol D., *Renaissance and Renewal in the Twelfth Century* (Toronto and London, 1991)

Beveridge, William, *Prices and Wages in England from the Twelfth to the Nineteenth Century*, 1 (London, 1939)

Black, Anthony, *Guilds and Civil Society in European Political Thought from the Twelfth Century to the Present* (London, 1984)

Bloomfield, Morton, W., *The Seven Deadly Sins: an Introduction to the History of a Religious Concept, with Special Reference to Medieval English Literature* (East Lansing, MI, 1952)

Bolgar, R. R., *The Classical Heritage and its Beneficiaries* (Cambridge, 1954)

Bolton, Brenda, *The Medieval Reformation* (London, 1983)

  'The poverty of the Humiliati', in Flood, ed., *Poverty in the Middle Ages*, pp. 52–9

Bolton, J. L., *The Medieval English Economy, 1150–1500* (London, 1980)

Brand, Paul, *The Making of the Common Law* (London, 1992)

Bredero, A. H., 'Le moyen-âge et le purgatoire', *Revue d'histoire ecclésiastique*, 78 (1983), pp. 429–54

Brenner, R., 'Agrarian class structure and economic development in pre-industrial Europe', *P & P*, 70 (1976), pp. 30–75

Bridbury, A. R., *Medieval English Clothmaking: an Economic Survey* (London, 1982)

Britnell, Richard H., *The Commercialisation of English Society, 1000–1500*, 2nd edn (Manchester, 1996)

'*Forestall*, forestalling and the Statute of Forestallers', *EHR*, 102 (1987), pp. 89–102

Britnell, Richard H. and Campbell, Bruce M. S., eds., *A Commercialising Economy: England 1086 to c. 1300* (Manchester, 1995)

Brown, E. A. R., '*Cessante causa* and the taxes of the last Capetians. The political applications of a philosophical maxim', in Joseph R. Strayer and Donald E. Queller, eds., *Post Scripta, Essays on Medieval Law and the Emergence of the European State in Honor of Gaines Post, Studia Gratiana*, 15 (1972), pp. 565–87

'The tyranny of a construct: feudalism and historians of medieval Europe', *American Historical Review*, 79 (1974), pp. 1063–88

Brundage, James A., *Medieval Canon Law* (London and New York, 1995)

Buckland, W. W., *A Textbook of Roman Law from Augustus to Justinian*, 3rd edn, rev. Peter Stein (Cambridge, 1968)

Burgess, Clive, '"A fond thing vainly imagined": an essay on Purgatory and pious motive in late medieval England', in S. J. Wright, ed., *Church and People: Local Studies in Lay Religion, 1350–1750* (London, 1988), pp. 56–84

Burns, J. H., ed., *The Cambridge History of Medieval Political Thought* (Cambridge, 1988)

Butler, L. H., 'Archbishop Melton, his neighbours, and his kinsmen, 1317–1340', *JEH*, 2 (1951), pp. 54–67

Carlyle, A. J. and Carlyle, R. W., *A History of Medieval Political Theory in the West*, 6 vols. (Edinburgh and London, 1930–6)

Cazelles, R., 'Quelques reflections à propos des mutations de la monnaie royale française, 1295–1360', *Le Moyen âge*, 72 (1966), pp. 83–105

Challis, C. E., ed., *A New History of the Royal Mint* (Cambridge, 1992)

Chiffoleau, J., *La Comptabilité de l'au-delà. Les hommes, la mort et la religion dans la région d'Avignon à la fin du moyen-âge. Collection de l'Ecole française de Rome*, 47 (Rome, 1980)

Chown, John F., *A History of Money from AD 800* (London, 1994)

Cipolla, Carlo M., 'Currency depreciation in medieval Europe', *EconHR*, ser. 2, 15 (1963), pp. 413–21

Money, Prices and Civilization in the Mediterranean World, Fifth to Seventeenth Century (Princeton, NJ, 1956)

Clapp, B. W., Fisher, H. E. S., and Juřica, A. R. J., eds., *Documents in English Economic History* (London, 1976)

Clarke, M. V., *Medieval Representation and Consent* (London, 1936)

Coleman, Janet, 'Medieval discussions of property: *ratio* and *dominium* according to John of Paris and Marsilius of Padua', *History of Political Thought*, 4 (1983), pp. 209–98

'Property and poverty' in Burns, ed., *Cambridge History of Medieval Political Thought*, pp. 607–48

Coulton, G. C. 'An episode in canon law', *History*, 6 (1921), pp. 67–76
   The Medieval Village (Cambridge, 1925, repr. New York, 1989)
Cunningham, William, *Growth of English Industry, Early and Middle Ages* (London, 1922)
d'Alverny, M. T., 'Translations and Translators', in Benson and Constable, eds., *Renaissance and Renewal*, pp. 421–62
Dawson, James Donne, 'Richard Fitzralph and the fourteenth-century poverty controversies', *JEH*, 34 (1983), pp. 315–44
Day, John, *The Medieval Market Economy* (Oxford, 1987)
Demant, V. A., ed., *The Just Price* (London, 1930)
de Roover, Raymond, *Business, Banking and Economic Thought in Late Medieval and Early Modern Europe: Selected Studies of Raymond de Roover*, ed. Julius Kirschner (Chicago, IL, 1974)
   'The concept of the just price; theory and economic policy', *Journal of Economic History*, 18 (1958), pp. 418–38
   Money, Banking and Credit in Mediaeval Bruges: Italian Merchant-bankers and Moneychangers. A Study in the Origins of Banking (Cambridge, MA, 1948)
   'Monopoly Theory prior to Adam Smith: a revision', in Kirschner, ed., *Business, Banking, and Economic Thought*, pp. 273–305
   'The organization of trade', in Postan, Rich, and Miller, eds., *Cambridge Economic History of Europe*, 3, pp. 42–118
   The Rise and Decline of the Medici Bank (Cambridge, MA, 1963)
   San Bernardino of Siena and Sant' Antonio of Florence. The Two Great Economic Thinkers of the Middle Ages (Boston, MA, 1967)
   'The Scholastic attitude toward trade and entrepreneurship' in Kirschner, ed., *Business, Banking and Economic Thought*, pp. 336–45
   'Scholastic economics. Survival and lasting influence from the sixteenth century to Adam Smith', in Kirschner, ed., *Business, Banking and Economic Thought*, pp. 306–35
   'What is dry exchange? A contribution to the history of English mercantilism', in Kirschner, ed., *Business, Banking and Economic Thought*, pp. 183–99
Dod, B. G., 'Aristoteles latinus', in Kretsmann, Kenny, and Pinbourg, eds., *The Cambridge History of Later Medieval Philosophy*, pp. 45–79
Dolley, R. H. M. and Metcalf, D. M., 'The reform of the coinage under Eadgar, a turning point in the monetary policy of the English state', in R. H. M. Dolley, ed., *Anglo-Saxon Coins* (London, 1961), pp. 136–68
Douie, Decima, *Archbishop Pecham* (Oxford, 1952)
Duffy, Eamon, *The Stripping of the Altars: Traditional Religion in England, 1400–1580* (New Haven, CT, and London, 1993)
Dyer, Christopher, 'The consumer and the market in the later middle ages', *EconHR.*, ser. 2, 42 (1989), pp. 305–27
   'A redistribution of incomes in fifteenth-century England?' *P & P*, 39 (1968), pp. 11–33
   Standards of Living in the Later Middle Ages. Social change in England, c. 1200–1520 (Cambridge, 1989)

Warwickshire Farming, c. 1349–1530. Preparations for Agricultural Revolution, Dugdale Society Occasional Papers, 27 (Oxford, 1981)

Dyer, Christopher, with Penn, Simon A. C., 'Wages and earnings in late medieval England: evidence from the enforcement of the labour laws', repr. in Dyer, *Everyday Life in Medieval England* (London and Rio Grande, 1994), pp. 167–89

Edwards, J. G., 'The *plena potestas* of English Parliamentary representatives', in E. B. Fryde and Edward Miller, eds., *Historical Studies of the English Parliament* (Cambridge, 1970), pp. 136–49

Epstein, Steven A., 'The theory and practice of the just wage', *Journal of Medieval History*, 17 (1991), pp. 53–69

Wage Labour and Guilds in Medieval Europe (Chapel Hill, NC, and London, 1991)

Faith, Rosamond, *The English Peasantry and the Growth of Lordship* (Leicester, 1997)

Fanfani, A., *Catholicism, Protestantism, and Capitalism* (London, 1935)

Fasolt, Constantin, *Council and Hierarchy: the Political Thought of William Durant the Younger* (Cambridge, 1991)

Feavearyear, A. E., *The Pound Sterling: a History of English Money*, 2nd edn rev. E. Victor Morgan (Oxford, 1963)

Ferguson, A. B., *The Articulate Citizen and the Renaissance* (Durham, NC, 1965)

Fleming, Robin, *Kings and Lords in Conquest England* (Cambridge, 1991)

Flood, David, 'Franciscan Poverty: a Brief Survey', Introduction to Gedeon Gál and David Flood, eds., *Nicolaus Minorita: Chronica. Documentation on Pope John XXII, Michael of Cesena and the Poverty of Christ* (St Bonaventura, New York, 1996), pp. 31–53

Flood, David, ed., *Poverty in the Middle Ages*, Franziskanische Forschungen, 27 (Werl, Westfalia, 1975)

Fryde, E. B., 'Edward III's wool monopoly of 1337', in Fryde, *Studies in Medieval Trade and Finance* (London, 1983), pp. 133–49

'Public Credit with special reference to North-western Europe', in Postan, Rich, and Miller, eds, *The Cambridge Economic History of Europe*, 3, pp. 430–553

Gordon, Barry, *Economic Analysis before Adam Smith: Hesiod to Lessius* (London, 1975)

Gross, Charles, *The Gild Merchant*, 2 vols. (Oxford, 1890)

Gurevich, Aron I., *Medieval Popular Culture: Problems of Belief and Perception*, trans. János M. Bak and Paul A. Hollingsworth (Cambridge, 1988)

Harding, Alan, *England in the Thirteenth Century* (Cambridge, 1993)

The Law Courts of Medieval England (London, 1973)

Haren, Michael, *Sin and Society in Fourteenth-century England: a Study of the 'Memoriale Presbiterorum'* (Oxford, 2000)

Harriss, G. L., 'Cardinal Beaufort – patriot or usurer?' *TRHS*, ser. 5, 19 (1969), pp. 129–48

'Fictitious loans', *EconHR*, ser. 2, 8 (1955), pp. 187–99

King, Parliament, and Public Finance in Medieval England to 1369 (Oxford, 1975)

Harvey, Barbara, *Living and Dying in England, 1100–1541: the Monastic Experience* (Oxford, 1995)

Westminster Abbey and its Estates in the Middle Ages (Oxford, 1977)

Harvey, P. D. A., ed., *The Peasant Land Market in Medieval England* (Oxford, 1984)

Haskins, Charles Homer, *The Renaissance of the Twelfth Century* (Cleveland and New York, 1970)

Hatcher, John, 'English serfdom and villeinage: towards a reassessment', *P & P*, 90 (1981), pp. 3–39

Hatcher, John, and Bailey, Mark, *Modelling the Middle Ages: the History and Theory of England's Economic Development* (Oxford, 2001)

Helmholz, R. H., 'Usury and the medieval English church courts', in Helmholz, *Canon Law and the Law of England* (London, 1987)

Hilton, R. H., *Class Conflict and the Crisis of Feudalism: Essays in Medieval Social History*, rev. edn (London and New York, 1990)
  'Conflict and collaboration', in Hilton, *English Peasantry*, pp. 62–9
  The English Peasantry in the Later Middle Ages (Oxford, 1975)
  A Medieval Society: the West Midlands at the End of the Thirteenth Century (London, 1966)
  'Peasant movements in England before 1381', in Hilton, *Class Conflict*, pp. 49–65
  'Some social and economic evidence in late medieval English tax returns', in Hilton, *Class Conflict*, pp. 188–94

Hilton, R. H., ed., *Peasants, Knights, and Heretics. Studies in Medieval English Social History* (Cambridge, 1976)

Holmes, G. A., 'The Libel of English Policy', *EHR*, 76 (1961), pp. 193–216

Homer, Sidney, *A History of Interest Rates* (New Brunswick, NJ, 1963)

Horne, Thomas A., 'Mercantilism', in *The Blackwell Encyclopaedia of Political Thought* (Oxford, 1991), pp. 335–6

Horrox, Rosemary, *The Black Death* (Manchester, 1994)

Hoven, Birgit van den, *Work in Ancient and Medieval Thought* (Amsterdam, 1996)

Hudson, Anne, *Lollards and Their Books* (London and Roncaverte, 1985)
  The Premature Reformation (Oxford, 1988)

Hudson, Anne, ed., *Wyclif: Political Ideas and Practice. Papers by Michael Wilks* (Oxford, 2000)

Huizinga, Johan, *The Waning of the Middle Ages* (1924, repr. Harmondsworth, 1965)

Hunt, Edwin S., *The Medieval Super-companies: a Study of the Peruzzi Company of Florence* (Cambridge, 1994)

Hunt, Edwin S., and Murray, James M., *A History of Business in Medieval Europe, 1200–1550* (Cambridge, 1999)

Hyams, Paul R., 'The end of feudalism?', *Journal of Interdisciplinary History*, 27 (1996–7), pp. 655–62
  King, Lords, and Peasants in Medieval England: the Common Law of Villeinage in the Twelfth and Thirteenth Centuries (Oxford, 1980)

Jarrett, Bede, *Social Theories of the Middle Ages* (London, 1926)

Jones, Norman L., *God and the Money Lenders: Usury and the Law in Early Modern England* (Oxford, 1989)

Kantorowicz, E. H., *The King's Two Bodies* (Princeton, NJ, 1957)

Kaye, Joel, *Economy and Nature in the Fourteenth Century: Money, Market Exchange, and the Emergence of Scientific Thought* (Cambridge, 1998)

Kenyon, Nora, 'Labour conditions in Essex in the reign of Richard II', repr. in E. M. Carus-Wilson, ed., *Essays in Economic History*, 2 (London, 1962), pp. 91–111

Kershaw, Ian, 'The great famine and agrarian crisis in England, 1315–1322', in Hilton, ed., *Peasants, Knights, and Heretics*, pp. 85–132

Kirschner, Julius, ed., *Business, Banking, and Economic Thought in Late Medieval and Early Modern Europe: Selected Studies of Raymond de Roover* (Chicago, IL, and London, 1974)

Knowles, David, *The Evolution of Medieval Thought*, 2nd edn, ed. D. E. Luscombe and C. N. L. Brooke (London and New York, 1988)

Kretsmann, N., Kenny, A., and Pinbourg, J., eds., *The Cambridge History of Later Medieval Philosophy* (Cambridge, 1982)

Kula, Witold, *Measures and Men*, trans. R. Szreter (Princeton, NJ, 1986)

Lambert, M. D., *Franciscan Poverty: the Doctrine of the Absolute Poverty of Christ and the Apostles in the Franciscan Order, 1210–1323* (London, 1961)

Landreth, Harry and Colander, David C., *History of Economic Thought*, 3rd edn (Boston, MD, and Toronto, 1994)

Langholm, Odd, *The Aristotelian Analysis of Usury* (Oslo, 1984)
  Economics in the Medieval Schools: Wealth, Exchange, Value, Money and Usury according to the Paris Theological Tradition, 1200–1350 (Leiden, 1992)
  The Legacy of Scholasticism in Economic Thought: Antecedents of Choice and Power (Cambridge, 1998)
  Wealth and Money in the Aristotelian Tradition (Oslo, 1983)

Lawrence, C. H., *The Friars: the Impact of the Early Mendicant Movement on Western Society* (London, 1994)

Le Bras, G., 'Conceptions of Economy and Society', in *Cambridge Economic History of Europe*, 3, pp. 554–75
  'Le doctrine ecclésiastique de l'usure à l' époque classique (viie–xve siècle), *Dictionnaire de théologie catholique*, 15, 2 (1950), cols. 2336–72

Le Goff, Jacques, *The Birth of Purgatory*, trans. Arthur Goldhammer (London, 1984)
  'Labor time in the "crisis" of the fourteenth century', in *Time, Work, and Culture*, pp. 43–52
  Medieval Civilization, trans. Julia Barrow (Oxford, 1988)
  'Merchant's time and Church's time in the Middle Ages' in Le Goff, *Time, Work, and Culture*, pp. 29–42
  Time, Work and Culture in the Middle Ages, trans. A. Goldhammer (Chicago, IL, and London, 1980)
  'The usurer and purgatory', in *The Dawn of Modern Banking*, pp. 25–52
  Your Money or Your Life: Economy and Religion in the Middle Ages, trans. Patricia Ranum (New York, 1988)

Lesnick, Daniel R., *Preaching in Medieval Florence: the Social World of Franciscan and Dominican Spirituality* (Athens, OH, and London, 1989)

Lipson, E., *The Economic History of England, 1. The Middle Ages* (London, 1947)

Little, Lester K., 'Evangelical poverty, the new money and violence', in Flood, ed., *Poverty in the Middle Ages*, pp. 11–26
  'Pride goes before avarice: social change and the vices in Latin Christendom', *American Historical Review*, 76 (1971), pp. 16–59
  Religious Poverty and the Profit Economy in Medieval Europe (London, 1978)
Little, Lester K. and Rosenwein, Barbara H., 'Social meaning in the monastic and mendicant spiritualities', *P & P*, 63 (1974), pp. 4–32
Livingstone, E. A., ed., *The Oxford Dictionary of the Christian Church*, 3rd edn (Oxford, 1997)
Lloyd, T. H., *The English Wool Trade in the Middle Ages* (Cambridge, 1977)
  'Overseas trade and the English money supply in the fourteenth century', in Mayhew, ed., *Edwardian Monetary Affairs*, pp. 96–124
Lopez, Robert S., *The Commercial Revolution of the Middle Ages, 950–1350* (Cambridge, 1976)
  'The Dawn of Medieval Banking', in *The Dawn of Modern Banking*, pp. 1–23
Lunt, W. E., *Papal Revenues in the Middle Ages*, 2 vols. (New York, 1934)
Maček, Josef, *The Hussite Movement in Bohemia* (London and Prague, 1965)
McFarlane, K. B., 'Loans to the Lancastrian kings: the problem of inducement', repr. in McFarlane, *England in the Fifteenth Century: Collected Essays* (London, 1981), pp. 57–78
McGovern, John F., 'The rise of new economic attitudes – economic humanism, economic nationalism – during the later middle ages and the Renaissance, A.D. 1200–1500', *Traditio*, 26 (1970), pp. 217–53
McGuckin, J. A., 'The vine and the elm tree: the patristic interpretation of Jesus' teachings on wealth', in Sheils and Wood, eds., *The Church and Wealth*, pp. 1–14
McIllwain, C. H., *The Growth of Political Thought* (New York, 1931)
McIntosh, Marjorie Keniston, *Autonomy and Community: The Royal Manor of Havering, 1200–1500* (Cambridge, 1986)
McLaughlin, T. P., 'The teaching of the canonists on usury', *Medieval Studies*, 1 (1930), pp. 81–147; 2 (1940), pp. 1–22
Maddicott, J. R., 'Trade and industry and the wealth of King Alfred', *P & P*, 123 (1989), pp. 3–51
Mate, Mavis, 'Coping with inflation: a fourteenth-century example', *Journal of Medieval History*, 4 (1978), pp. 95–106
  'High prices in fourteenth-century England', *EconHR*, ser. 2, 28 (1975), pp. 1–16
  'Monetary policies in England, 1272–1307', *British Numismatic Journal*, 41 (1972), pp. 34–79
  'The role of gold coinage in the English economy, 1338–1400', *British Numismatic Chronicle*, ser. 7 (1978), pp. 126–41
Mayhew, N. J., 'From regional to central minting, 1158–1464', in Challis, ed., *Royal Mint*, pp. 83–178
  'Money and prices in England from Henry II to Edward III', *Agricultural History Review*, 35 (1987), pp. 121–32

'Numismatic evidence and falling prices in the fourteenth century', *EconHR*, ser. 2, 27 (1974), pp. 1–15

Mayhew, N. J., ed., *Edwardian Monetary Affairs*, British Archaeological Report, 36 (Oxford, 1977)

Mayhew, N. J., and Walker, D. R., 'Crockards and pollards: imitation and the problem of fineness in a silver coinage', in Mayhew, ed., *Edwardian Monetary Affairs*, pp. 125–46

Menning, Carol Bresnahan, *Charity and State in Late Renaissance Italy. The Monte di Pietà of Florence* (Ithaca, NY, and London, 1993)

Meynial, Edouard, 'Roman Law' in C. G. Crump and E. F. Jacob, eds., *The Legacy of the Middle Ages* (Oxford, 1948), pp. 363–99

Miller, Edward, and Hatcher, John, *Medieval England: Towns, Commerce and Crafts 1086–1348* (London, 1995)

Milsom, S. F. C., *The Legal Framework of English Feudalism* (Cambridge, 1976)

Miskimin, Harry A., *Cash, Credit, and Crisis in Europe, 1300–1600* (London, 1989)

'Monetary movements and market structure – forces for contraction in fourteenth- and fifteenth-century England', in *Cash, Credit, and Crisis*, no. 7, pp. 470–90

Money, Prices, and Foreign Exchange in Fourteenth-century France (New Haven, CT, 1963)

Mitchell, Sydney Knox, *Taxation in Medieval England* (New Haven, CT, 1951)

Moisa, Maria A., 'Fourteenth-century preachers' views of the poor: class or status group?', in R. Samuel and G. Stedman Jones, eds., *Culture, Ideology and Politics: Essays for Eric Hobsbawm* (London, 1982), pp. 160–75

Mollat, M., *The Poor in the Middle Ages: An Essay in Social History*, trans. Arthur Goldhammer (New Haven, CT, and London, 1986)

Monroe, Arthur Eli, *Monetary Theory Before Adam Smith* (Cambridge, MA, 1923)

Moorman, R. H., *Church Life in England in the Thirteenth Century* (Cambridge, 1945)

A History of the Franciscan Order from its Origins to the Year 1517 (Oxford, 1968)

Morris, Colin, *The Discovery of the Individual, 1050–1200* (London, 1972)

Munro, John H., 'Bullionism and the bill of exchange in England, 1272–1663: a study in monetary management and popular prejudice', in *The Dawn of Modern Banking*, pp. 169–220

Wool, Cloth, and Gold: The Struggle for Bullion in Anglo-Burgundian Trade (Toronto, Ont., 1972)

Murray, Alexander, *Reason and Society in the Middle Ages* (Oxford, 1978)

Nederman, Cary J., 'Aristotle as authority: alternative Aristotelian sources of late medieval political theory', in Nederman, *Medieval Aristotelianism*, no. 15, pp. 31–44

Medieval Aristotelianism and its Limits (Aldershot, 1997)

Nef, J. U., 'Mining and metallurgy in medieval civilisation', in *The Cambridge Economic History of Europe*, 2 (Cambridge, 1952)

Nelson, B. N., *The Idea of Usury: from Tribal Brotherhood to Universal Otherhood*, 2nd edn (Chicago, IL, and London, 1969)

'The usurer and the merchant prince: Italian businessmen and the ecclesiastical law of restitution, 1100–1500', in *The Tasks of Economic History. The Journal of Economic History*, supplement 7 (1947), pp. 104–22

Nelson, Janet L., 'Wealth and wisdom: the politics of Alfred the Great', *Kings and Kingship, Acta*, 11 (1984), pp. 39–43

Nicholas, Barry, *An Introduction to Roman Law* (Oxford, 1962)

Noonan, J. T., *The Scholastic Analysis of Usury* (Cambridge, MA, 1957)

O'Brien, George, *An Essay on Medieval Economic Teaching* (London, 1920)

Origo, Iris, *The Merchant of Prato* (London, 1960)

The World of San Bernardino (New York, 1962)

Owst, G. R., *Literature and Pulpit in Medieval England*, 2nd edn (Oxford, 1961)

Parel, Anthony and Flanagan, Thomas, eds., *Theories of Property: Aristotle to the Present* (Waterloo, Ont, 1979)

Parsons, Anscar, 'Bernardine of Feltre and the *montes pietatis*', *Franciscan Studies*, 1, no. 1 (1941), pp. 11–32

'Economic significance of the *montes pietatis*', *Franciscan Studies* 1, no. 3 (1941), pp. 3–28

Paton, Bernadette, *Preaching Friars and the Civic Ethos: Siena, 1380–1480* (London, 1992)

Post, Gaines, 'Masters' salaries and student fees in the medieval universities', *Speculum*, 7 (1932), pp. 181–98

Studies in Medieval Legal Thought (Princeton, NJ, 1964)

Postan, M. M., 'Credit in medieval trade', in *Medieval Trade and Finance*, pp. 1–27

Essays in Medieval Agriculture and General Problems of the Medieval Economy (Cambridge, 1973)

The Medieval Economy and Society: an Economic History of Britain, 1100–1500 (London, 1972)

Medieval Trade and Finance (Cambridge, 1973)

Postan, M. M. and Hatcher, J., 'Population and class relations in feudal society', *P & P*, 78 (1978), pp. 24–37

Postan, M. M., Rich, E. E., and Miller, E., eds., *The Cambridge Economic History of Europe*, 3, *Economic Organization and Policies in the Middle Ages* (Cambridge, 1965)

Prestwich, Michael, 'Currency and the economy of early fourteenth-century England' in Mayhew, ed., *Edwardian Monetary Affairs*, pp. 45–58

Pullan, Brian, *Rich and Poor in Renaissance Venice: the Social Institutions of a Catholic State to 1620* (Oxford, 1971)

Putnam, Bertha, *The Enforcement of the Statute of Labourers, 1349–1359* (New York, 1908)

Rawcliffe, Carole, *Medicine and Society in Later Medieval England* (Stroud, 1995)

Reddaway, T. F., *The Early History of the Goldsmiths' Company, 1327–1509* (London, 1975)

Renouard, Yves, *Les Relations des papes d'Avignon et des compagnies commerciales et bancaires de 1326 à 1378* (Paris, 1941)

Les Hommes d'affaires italiens au moyen-âge (Paris, 1949)

Reynolds, Susan, *Fiefs and Vassals: the Medieval Evidence Reinterpreted* (Oxford, 1994)

Rigby, S. H., *English Society in the Later Middle Ages: Class, Status and Gender* (London, 1995)

Robinson, W. C., 'Money, population and economic change in late medieval Europe', *EconHR*, ser. 2, 12 (1959), pp. 63–76

Rocha, Manuel, *Travail et salaire à travers la scholastique* (Paris, 1933)

Roll, Eric, *A History of Economic Thought*, 3rd edn (London, 1954)

Roney, Lois, 'Winner and Waster's "Wyse Wordes": Teaching economics and nationalism in fourteenth-century England', *Speculum*, 69 (1994), pp. 1070–100

Rosser, Gervase, 'Communities of parish and gild in the late Middle Ages', in S. J. Wright, ed., *Parish Church and People: Local Studies in Lay Religion* (London, 1988), pp. 29–55

  'Crafts, guilds and the negotiation of work in the medieval town', *P & P*, 154 (1997), pp. 3–31

Rubin, Miri, *Charity and Community in Medieval Cambridge* (Cambridge, 1987)

  'Development and change in English hospitals, 1100–1500', in L. Granshaw and R. Porter, eds., *The Hospital in History* (London, 1990), pp. 51–4

Ruding, Rogers, *Annals of the Coinage of Great Britain and its Dependencies*, 3rd edn, I (London, 1840)

Salter, F. R., 'The Jews in fifteenth-century Florence and Savonarola's establishment of a *mons pietatis*', *Cambridge Historical Journal*, 5 (1935–7), pp. 193–211

Salter, H. E., *Medieval Oxford*, Oxford Historical Society, 100 (1936)

Scase, Wendy, *Piers Plowman and the New Anti-clericalism* (Cambridge, 1989)

Schlatter, Richard, *Private Property: the History of an Idea* (London, 1951)

Schulz, Fritz, *Classical Roman Law* (Oxford, 1951)

Schumpeter, Joseph, *A History of Economic Analysis* (London, 1954)

Searle, Eleanor, *Lordship and Community: Battle Abbey and its Banlieu 1066–1538* (Toronto, Ont., 1974)

Sheils, W. J., and Wood, Diana, eds., *The Church and Wealth*, SCH, 24 (Oxford, 1987)

Slack, Paul, *The English Poor Law, 1581–1782* (Basingstoke and London, 1990)

Smith, Robert, 'Giotto: artistic realism, political realism', *Journal of Medieval History*, 4 (1978), pp. 267–84

Southern, R. W., *Scholastic Humanism and the Unification of Europe*, I (Oxford, 1997)

Spufford, Peter, *Handbook of Medieval Exchange* (London, 1986)

  Money and its Use in Medieval Europe (Cambridge, 1988)

Stark, W., *The Contained Economy: an Interpretation of Medieval Economic Thought*, Aquinas Papers, 26 (London, 1956)

Steenberghen, Frederick van, *The Philosophical Movement of the Thirteenth Century* (Edinburgh and London, 1955)

Swanson, Heather, *Medieval Artisans: an Urban Class in Late Medieval England* (Oxford, 1989)

Swanson, R. N., *Church and Society in Late Medieval England* (Oxford, 1993)
  The Twelfth-century Renaissance (Manchester, 1999)
Tanner, Norman, *The Church in Late Medieval Norwich, 1370–1532* (Toronto, Ont., 1984)
Tate, W. E., *The Parish Chest*, 3rd edn (Cambridge, 1969)
Thrupp, S., *The Merchant Class of Medieval London*, repr. (Ann Arbor, MI, 1962)
Tierney, Brian, 'The decretists and the "deserving poor"', *Comparative Studies in Society and History*, 1 (1958–9), pp. 360–73
  Medieval Poor Law (Berkeley and Los Angeles, CA, 1959)
Titow, J. Z., *English Rural Society 1200–1350* (London, 1969)
Trexler, Richard C, 'Charity and the defence of urban elites in the Italian communes', in Frederick Cople Jaher, ed., *The Rich, the Wellborn, and the Powerful: Elites and Upper Classes in History* (Urbana, IL, 1973), pp. 64–109
Ullmann, Walter, *The Individual and Society in the Middle Ages* (London, 1967)
University of California, Centre for Medieval and Renaissance Studies, ed., *The Dawn of Modern Banking* (New Haven, CT and London, 1979)
Usher, Abbott Payson, *The Early History of Deposit Banking in Mediterranean Europe* (Cambridge, MA, 1943)
Vauchez, André, *Sainthood in the Later Middle Ages*, trans. Jean Birrell (Cambridge, 1988)
Viner, Jacob, *Essays on the Intellectual History of Economics*, ed. Douglas A. Irwin (Princeton, NJ, 1991)
  'Mercantilist Thought', in Irwin, ed., *Essays on the Intellectual History of Economics*, pp. 262–77
  Religious Thought and Economic Society: Four Chapters of an Unfinished Work by Jacob Viner, ed. Jacques Melitz and Donald Winch (Durham, NC, 1978)
Vinogradoff, Paul, *Roman Law in Medieval Europe* (Oxford, 1929)
Walker Bynum, Caroline, 'Did the twelfth century discover the individual?', in Walker Bynum, *Jesus as Mother: Studies in the Spirituality of the High Middle Ages* (Berkeley, Los Angeles, CA, and London, 1982), pp. 82–109
Watson, Andrew, 'Back to gold – and silver', *EconHR*, ser. 2, 20 (1967), pp. 1–34
Watt, J. A., 'Jewish serfdom' in Diana Wood, ed., *The Church and Sovereignty: Essays in Honour of Michael Wilks*, SCH, subsidia 10 (Oxford, 1991), pp. 153–72
Webb, Diana M., 'A saint and his money: perceptions of urban wealth in the lives of Italian saints', in Sheils and Wood, eds., *Church and Wealth*, pp. 61–73
Weber, Max, *The Protestant Ethic and the Spirit of Capitalism* (London, 1930, repr. 1992)
Wilks, Michael, 'Predestination, property, and power: Wyclif's theory of dominion and grace', in Hudson, ed., *Wyclif. Political Ideas*, pp. 16–32
  The Problem of Sovereignty in the Later Middle Ages (Cambridge, 1963)
  '*Thesaurus ecclesiae*', in Hudson, ed., *Wyclif. Political Ideas*, pp. 147–77
  Wyclif. Political Ideas and Practice. Papers by Michael Wilks, ed. Anne Hudson (Oxford, 2000)
Williams, Ann, *The English and the Norman Conquest* (Woodbridge, 1995)
Winroth, Anders, *The Making of Gratian's 'Decretum'* (Cambridge, 2000)

Wolff, Ph. *The Awakening of Europe* (Harmondsworth, 1968)
Wood, Diana, 'John of Ayton's "Grumbling Gloss": a northern churchman's view of society' in Wood, ed., *Life and Thought in the Northern Church, c.1100–c. 1700: Essays in Honour of Claire Cross* (Woodbridge, 1999), pp. 37–55
' "Lesyng of Tyme": Perceptions of idleness and usury in late Medieval England', *SCH* 37 (2002), pp. 107–16
Woodcock, Brian L., *Medieval Ecclesiastical Courts in the Diocese of Canterbury* (Oxford, 1951)
Yunck, John A., *The Lineage of Lady Meed. The Development of Mediaeval Venality Satire* (Notre Dame, 1963)
Zupko, Ronald Edward, *British Weights and Measures. A History from Antiquity to the Seventeenth Century* (Madison, WI, 1977)

INDEX

Note: Page references in **bold** type indicate entries in Notes on the Main Writers, and those in *italics* indicate Glossary entries.

Acciaiuoli merchant-bankers 198
accumulation 82–4, 200
Accursius 8, 136
action, voluntary/involuntary 164–5
Adelard of Bath 12
Aegidius Romanus *see* Giles of Rome
Aethelberht of Kent 77, 79
agriculture, intensification 5, 206
aids 38, 39
Alan de Lyndeseye 115
Alan of Lille 44
Alanus (canonist) 155
Albert the Great, St **210**
   and Aristotle 11, 210
   Ethicorum 74
   and just price 135–6, 137, 139
   and mercy 56
   and money 74, 137
   pupils 137, 210, 213, 222
   Summa theologiae 210
   Super IV Sententiarum 56
   and usury 165, 166, 178, 185
   and wealth 51
Alexander III, Pope 56–7, 189
Alexander IV, Pope 172
Alexander of Hales **210**
   and interest 190, 193
   and just price 135

   and merchants 117
   and monopolists 139
   and natural law 22
   pupils 210, 212
   Summa theologica 22, 135, 139, 210
Alexander Lombard, and exchange 189
Alfred the Great of Wessex 92
almsgiving 42, 44
   and beggary 47
   and discrimination 42, 43, 58–9, 60–3, 207
   and gold coinage 129
   and heavenly credit 63–7, 68
   and justice 55–6
   method of giving 66
   post-mortem 43, 59, 65, 207
   and Seven Corporal Acts of Mercy 55
   and usury 65–6
Ambrose, St **210–11**
   and almsgiving 61, 62
   De officiis ministrorum 211
   De sacramentis 211
   De Tobia admonitio 84
   Expositio Evangelii secundum Lucam 50
   and usury 84, 164
   and wealth 50, 55, 56

Antoninus of Florence, St **211**
  and interest 203
  and just wage 138, 152–3
  and merchants 114
  and petty exchange 201
  and prices 143
  and usury 163–4, 195, 199
Antoninus, St, *Summa theologica moralis* 114, 211
apprentices 142, 146
appropriation 58, *224*
Aquinas, St Thomas *see* Thomas Aquinas, St
aristocracy
  and expenditure 122
  and landownership 33
  and poor relief 59
Aristotle
  and almsgiving 62
  commentaries on 6, 7, 10, 73, 210
  Ethics 11, 62, 221
    commentaries on 104, 210, 213, 214, 216, 219, 222
    and justice 13, 133–4, 150
    and money 71–2, 76, 82, 104, 105, 138, 148
    and prices and wages 132–4, 150
    and usury 164–5
    and virtue 13, 51, 133
  and exchange 148
  and Franciscans 210
  influence on economic thought 10–12
  and just price 133, 134, 136–7
  and justice 13–14, 55, 133–4
  and the mean 13, 62, 133–4, 164–5
  Metaphysics 215, 221
  and money 70, 71–2, 73, 76, 87, 121, 134, 199–200
  Physics 215
  Politics 11
    commentaries on 210, 214, 216, 219, 222
    and merchants 111
    and money 71–2, 73, 82, 87, 104, 105
    and property 23
    and usury 84–5
  and property 23, 40, 55
  and trade 72, 82, 111, 138–9
  and wealth 51, 62, 73, 82–3, 138
Arnold of Brescia 155

artisans, and improved social status 43, 46–7
assart *224*
assay 94, 97, *224*
assize 35, 97–8, *224*
Assize of Bread and Ale (1266) 97–8, 143
Assize of Measures (1197) 93, 96
Astesanus, *Summa* 202
Athelstan of England 92–3, 114
Augustine of Hippo, St **211**
  and almsgiving 60, 61, 62, 63–4, 66
  City of God 20, 21, 137, 211
  Confessions 211
  Enarratio in Psalmos 55, 60, 66, 88, 116, 211
  and God as author of human law 19–21
  In Ioannis Evangelium Tractatus 20
  and just wage 152
  and justice and almsgiving 55
  and money 88
  and property as result of Fall 32
  Sermones 20, 152
  and trade 113, 115–16
  and wealth 50, 55
Augustinians 85–6, 202
  see also Gerardo of Siena; Giles of Rome; Henry of Friemar
avarice
  attitudes to 53–4
  and civic humanism 52, 53, 118
  and manipulation of weights and measures 99
  of merchants 113–14, 153
  and money 82–3
'Averroists' 215
Azo (Roman lawyer) 136

Baldus de Ubaldis 8, 211
  and civic humanism 49
  and trade 118
banking 5, 103, 171, 187, 197–9, 200, 207
Bardi Company 120, 130, 185, 187, 198
bargaining
  collective 155–7, 208
  and just price 148–52, 157–8, 165
  and just wage 19, 152–3, 157–8
Baron, Hans 49
barter 72, 78–80, 87, 111
  and petty exchange 200
Bartholomew of Lucca *see* Ptolemy of Lucca

Index

Bartolus of Sassoferrato 8, **211–12**
  and civic humanism 49
  De regimine civitatum 212
  and gilds 142
  Tractatus de tyrannia 212
  and trade 118
Basil of Caesarea 56, 64, 65, 84
Bede, the Venerable 64
Beer, Max 126
beggary 145
  attitudes to 44, 47–8, 58, 59, 67
  and mendicants 48–9, 50
  and wealth 42–3
Benedetto Cotrugli, *On Commerce and the Perfect Merchant* 119
Benedict XI, Pope 170
Benedictines 26, 58
  see also Thomas Brinton
benefice *224*
Bentham, Jeremy 85
Bernard of Clairvaux, St, *De consideratione* 50
Bernardino of Siena, St 6, **212**, 219
  and interest 191–2, 203
  and just price 136, 138, 143
  and merchants 114
  and *montes* 203
  and usury 163, 182, 199, 203
betterment, economic 3–4
Bible
  and accumulation 83
  and almsgiving 60
  and coinage 92
  and God as standard 91
  and merchants 112
  and need 60
  and scholasticism 7
  and usury 159
  and wealth 50, 54
  and weights and measures 98
bill of exchange 5, 81, 201, 207
Black Death (1348) 46, 144, 146, 213
Bonaventure, St **212**
  and Alexander of Hales 210, 212
  Apologia pauperum 29
  and avarice 53
  and exchange 150–1
  and mercy and justice 55
bonds 189

Boniface VIII, Pope 24, 217
  and *Liber Sextus* 9
  Unam sanctam 213
Boniface IX, Pope, and Lollards 33
boundaries, measurement 95
Brinton, Bishop of Rochester *see* Thomas Brinton
bullion 78, 79, *224*
  export of 125–6, 128–31, 201
  and mercantile system 111, 125–31
  shortage 80, 81, 100, 108–9, 122, 125, 128–9
bullionism 111, 125–31, 208
'Buridan's Ass' 1, 10, 14, 134, 158, 209

Cahorsins 171, 185
Cambridge Parliament (1388) 145
canon law 2, 8, 21, 214
  and almsgiving 61, 65
  and coinage 104
  and interest 183, 184, 189, 195–6
  and money 74, 86–7
  and necessity 38
  and poverty 46, 48, 50, 57–8
  and prices 135
  and trade 113, 115
  and usury 65, 160, 166–70
  and wages 154–5
canonists *see* Guido Terreni; Henry of Bouhic; Hostiensis; Huguccio; Johannes Andreae; Johannes Teutonicus; John of Ayton; Laurentius Ridolfis; Peter de la Palu; Raymond of Peñafort; Rufinus; William Durandus
Carmelites *see* Guido Terreni
Carta Mercatoria (1303) 93, 96
Cassiodorus, and merchants 112
Cathars 27
census (life rent) 196–7
certa/incerta 169–70
'chain of being' 4
chantry *224*
charity
  and attitudes to poverty 44
  and discrimination 42, 43, 58–9, 60–3, 207
  institutional 58–9, 120
  as investment 66–7, 68
  and loans 191–2
  monastic 3, 58–9

charity (*cont.*)
  post-mortem 43, 59, 65, 207
  and reciprocity 42–3
  and self-control 54
  and Seven Corporal Acts of Mercy 55
  and usury 168, 169
  see also almsgiving
Charlemagne, Emperor 77, 92, 129, 160
Charles V of France 48, 105, 108, 212, 219
Charles VIII of France 185
Chiffoleau, J. 67
chresmatic, trade as 72, 82
Christine de Pisan **212**, 216
  The Book of the Body Politic 70, 120
  and merchants 120
Church
  disendowment 30, 32–3
  and economics 2–5, 208
  as landowner 3
  and responsibility for the poor 56–7
  and society 2–3
  stewardship of property 31, 55
Cicero, Marcus Tullius 10, 37, 136
Cinus de Pistoia 211
Ciompi, revolt 43
Cistercians, and poor relief 58
Clement I, Pope 26
Clement V, Pope 163, 217
  Clementines 9, 216
Clement VI, Pope 199, 213
Clement of Alexandria 45
clergy
  and poverty 30, 32, 220
  and usury 162, 171–3
  and wealth 32, 83
cloth industry 80, 99, 123–4
Codex 8
coinage 70, 73–4, 77, 78–81, 84
  clipping 87, 100, 127–8, 131
  control of 92–3, 100–7, 207–8
  counterfeiting 100, 127, 128, 131
  debasement 81, 102–5, 107–9, 122, 127–8, 131, *225*
  feudal 108
  minting 100–1
  recoinage 128
  standardization 92, 94–5, 128
  and trade 90
  see also currency; gold; money; silver

Coleman, Janet 24
Coluccio Salutati 118, **212**
commerce
  and 'commercial revolution' 50, 79, 110, 130
  and development of towns 5
common services 171
community of the realm 37, 39, 105–7
Confirmation of the Charters (1297) 40
Conrad of Megenberg, *Yconomica* 85
consent
  and currency 105, 106, 107, 109
  and taxation 38–40, 41, 106, 217
contract
  law of 148, 150, 186
  loan contracts 165–6, 186–8
  sale contract 165
copyhold tenure *224*
corporation, Church as 30–1
Corpus iuris canonici 9
Corpus iuris civile 7, 8
corrody 196, *225*
Cosimo de Medici 170
courts
  court baron *225*
  court leet *225*
  ecclesiastical 2, 167, 183–4
  seigneurial 34, 36, 184
craftsmen
  and improved social status 43, 46–7
  master craftsmen 146–7
  and trade 112, 113
  see also gilds
credit
  through almsgiving 63–7
  through patronage 169–70
  via the State 202–3
credit sales 81, 175–6
crusades, and dissemination of Aristotelian ideas 10–11
Cunningham, William 126
cupidity *see* avarice
currency, bi-metallic 129
  see also coinage

Dyer, Christopher 36
Dyer, Christopher and Penn, Simon A. C. 157

Ælfric of Eynsham 64, 116

famines 46, 59, 144, 206
Fasciculus morum **213**
   and almsgiving 64, 66, 67
   and avarice 54
   and partnership 195
   and usury 65–6, 160, 162–3, 164, 176–7, 190
fees and salaries 153–5
fief 34, *225*
Florence
   cloth industry 80, 211
   and mercantilism 6
   and monopolies 142
   and *montes* 203–4
   and usury 183, 185, 187
Florence, Council (1439) 211
forestalling 139–40, 141, *225*
Fortescue, Sir John *see* John Fortescue, Sir
France
   and coinage 102, 104–5, 107–8
   and Jews 168, 203
   and mercantile system 120
   and sovereignty 107
   and taxation 39–40
   and vagrancy 48, 145
Francis of Assisi, St 27–9, 207
Franciscans
   and discrimination in almsgiving 61
   and interest 202
   and *montes pietatis* 203–4
   and papacy as steward of property 29, 30–1
   and poverty 27–9, 75
   and social status 153
   Strict Observants 212
   see also Alexander of Hales; Bernardino of Siena; Bonaventure, St; Gerald Odonis; John Buridan; John Duns Scotus; Peter John Olivi; Richard of Middleton
François de Meyronnes 189
frankpledge 184, *225*
fraternities 64–5, 142
   and collective bargaining 156
fraud, by merchants 114
Frederick of Austria 185
friars *225–6*
   and begging 48–9, 50
   and usury 171
   see also mendicant orders

funerals, and doles 65
fungible 198, 216, *226*
   money as 75–6, 86, 161, 175, 182, 194, 204

Gaius (lawyer) 8, 186
Geoffrey Chaucer, *Canterbury Tales* 123–4
Gerald of Abbeville, and control of coinage 100
Gerald Odonis **213**
   and interest 191
   and usury 165, 175, 180
   and wages 153
Gerardo of Siena, and usury 85–7
gift exchange 42, 186–7
gilds 64–5
   and collective bargaining 156
   craft gilds 141–2
   gilds merchant 139, 141
   and monopoly 141–2
   and wages 142–3, 146–52
Giles of Lessines **213**
   De usuris 176, 186, 213
   and exchange 200
   and ownership and risk 195, 196
Giles of Rome (Aegidius Romanus) **213–14**, 217
   and Church property 31, 33
   De ecclesiastica potestate 31, 92, 213–14
   De regimine principum 83, 118, 213
   and monasticism 25
   and papacy as sovereign 91–2
   and trade 117–18
   and wealth 83
Giordano of Pisa
   and poverty 43
   and wealth 45, 51
Girolamo Savonarola 203
Glanvill, *Treatise on the Laws and Customs of the Realm of England* 95, 167, 214
God, as standard 91
Godfrey of Fontaines, and just price 150
Godfrey of Trani, and wages and fees 154
gold, as currency 81, 128–31
Good Parliament (1376) 47–8
Gordon, Barry 30, 73
Gratian **214**
   and communal life 25–6
   Decretum 8, 9, 18, 56, 112, 159, 214
   and discrimination in almsgiving 60–1

Gratian (*cont.*)
   and trade 112–13
   and usury 159–61
'Great Bullion Famine' 80, 125
Gregory I the Great, Pope, *Regula pastoralis*
   55–6
Gregory IX, Pope 223
   and apostolic poverty 29
   Decretales 9, 220
   Naviganti 175–6, 193, 194–5, 197, 220
   Parens scientiarum 11
   see also Ugolino
Gresham, Thomas 127
Gresham's law 127–8, 131, 208
Guido Terreni **214**
   and accumulation 83
   De perfectione vitae 214
   and money 80, 104
   and need as measure of value 74

Hadriana 160
hall-marking of silver 93–4
Harriss, G. L. 39, 173, 187
Harvey, Barbara 26, 58–9
Henricus de Segusio *see* Hostiensis
Henry II of England
   and common law 35, 36
   and poor relief 59
Henry III of England
   and coinage 100
   and common law 35
   and papacy 172
   and prices 143
   and taxation 39
   and weights and measures 97
Henry IV of England, and coinage 109
Henry V, Emperor, and poor relief 59
Henry VII of England, and usury 184
Henry of Bouhic, and usury 167
Henry of Bracton **214**
   On the Laws and Customs of England 95, 214
Henry of Friemar **214**
   and interest 182, 190
   and merchants 114
   and money 74, 81, 87–8
   Tractatus de vitiis 214

Henry of Ghent **214–15**
   and accumulation 83
   and census 196
   and exchange-dealing 200
   Summa theologica 215
   and wages 150
Henry of Hesse **215**
   and avarice 83, 153
   De contractibus et origine censuum 3, 138, 143, 150, 153, 215
   and price 143, 150, 153, 154
   and supply and demand 138
Henry Knighton
   Chronicle 47, 144–5
   and social distinction 47
   and wages 144–5
Henry of Langenstein *see* Henry of Hesse
heresy, and usury 163
hoarding, and national economy 122–3, 129, 130
Homobonus of Cremona 116
Honorius III, Pope 221
Hostiensis (Henricus de Segusio) **215**
   Commentary on the *Decretals* 9, 215
   and gift 186
   and interest 189, 191
   and partnership 195–6
   Summa aurea 215
Huguccio **215**
   Summa super corpore Decretorum 9, 215
   and trade 113
humanism, civic
   and poverty 49
   and wealth 52, 84
humanism, economic 117, 118
Humiliati 27, 44

idleness 47–50, 52–3, 61, 67, 145
individualism, development 18–19
industry, as title to profit 177–80, 192
Ine of Wessex, laws 78
inequality, and reciprocity 42–3
inflation
   and coinage 101, 103, 128
   and poor relief 58–9
   and rent 197
Innocent III, Pope 116, 166, 167, 195, 215, 221
Innocent IV, Pope 29, 215
Institutes 8, 18

intention 209
  and almsgiving 66
  and interest 196, 201
  and trade 113, 117
  and usury 159–60, 176, 182, 186, 188, 191, 203, 205
interest
  attitudes to 183–5
  and deposits 5, 186, 198, 207
  and exchange-dealing 199–201
  and extrinsic titles 187–90, 204
  and fictitious loans 187
  and gifts 186–7
  and justice 182
  and loan contract 186–8, 193
  and loans by sale 187
  and partnerships 193–6
  as profit withheld 190, 191, 202–3, 204, 207
  and risk 181–3, 187, 192–3, 196, 200
  in Roman law 185–8
  from start of a loan 172, 183, 191–2, 202–3, 204, 215
  and usury 4, 75, 181–4, 185–6, 191, 194, 202–3, 204–5, 207
Irnerius 7–8
Italy
  and civic humanism 49, 84
  and mercantile system 6, 118–20, 207
  and merchant-bankers 197–9, 201
  and monopolies 142
  and *montes* 202
  and *montes pietatis* 203
  and usurers 168–9

Jacob's Well 187
Jacopo Passavanti, Fra 182
Jacquerie 43
Jacques de Vitry
  Historia occidentalis 44, 115
  and usury 162
Jean Gerson 143, 215
Jean de Meun(g) **215–16**
  and almsgiving 62–3
  and avarice 54
  and beggary 48
  and poverty 45–6
  and sufficiency 42, 62
  and wealth 51
  see also The Romance of the Rose

Jews
  and control of coinage 100, 128
  as manifest usurers 167–8
  and money-lending 203
Johannes Andreae **216**
  Glossa ordinaria 46, 216
  Novella super Decretalibus 9, 216
  and partnership 195
  and poverty 46
  and stewardship 31
  and usury 86
Johannes Teutonicus **216**
  and beggary 48
  Compilatio quarta 216
  and discrimination in almsgiving 62
  Glossa ordinaria 9, 194, 195, 216
  and need 60
  and partnerships 194, 195
  and rights of the poor 59–60
  and teachers 154–5
  and tithe 57
John II the Good of France 102, 105
John XXII, Pope 31, 213, 214, 219, 222
  Cum inter nonnullos 29
  Extravagantes 9
John, king of England
  and poor relief 59
  and taxation 39
John of Ardenne, and social status 154
John of Ayton **216**
  Commentaria ad Constitutiones Othonis et Othoboni 217
  and charity 54
  and money 46, 65
John Bromyard **216**
  Opus trivium 216
  Summa praedicantium 115, 216
  and merchants 114–15
  and money 69–70
  and poor relief 57
  and poverty 45
  and usury 164, 181
  and weights and measures 98, 99
John Buridan **216**
  and 'Buridan's Ass' 1, 10, 14
  and money 81
  pupils 10, 104, 215, 219
John Chrysostom, St **216–17**
  and almsgiving 60

John Duns Scotus **217**
    and interest 186, 188, 189, 190, 193
    and just price 151
    and money 179–80
    and regraters 140
    and usury 165
John the Fearless of Burgundy 108
John Fortescue, Sir **217**
    De laudibus legum Angliae 38, 40, 217
    and *dominium regale et politicum* 38
    and economic nationalism 118
    and mercantile system 120, 124
    and natural law 22–3, 25
    On the Laws and Governance of England 38, 118, 124, 217
    and property 24–5, 41, 208
    and taxation 40
John Gerson 143, 215
John Gower, *Confessio amantis* 160
John Hus 27
John of Naples 185
John of Paris **217**
    and money-changing 199–200
    On Royal and Papal Power 24, 31, 217
    and pope as steward 31
    and property 24, 25, 41, 208
John Pecham
    and debt 172
    and poor relief 57
John of Salisbury **218**
    and community of the realm 37, 38
    and money 70, 105
    Policraticus 37, 70, 105, 218
John Wyclif **218**, 222
    and community of property 27
    Concerning the Church 218
    Concerning the Eucharist 218
    Concerning the Power of the Pope 218
    and dominion and grace 29–30, 218, 221
    The Grete Sentence of Curs Expounded 157
    and just price 142
    and king as steward 32–3
    On Divine and Civil Dominion 218
    On the Office of King 218
    On the Truth of Holy Scripture 218
    and poverty 29–30, 49
journeyman 146, 147, 156, *226*
jurisdiction, casual 38

justice
    and almsgiving 55–6
    corrective and distributive 13–14, 126, 133–4, 149–52, 158
    and interest 182
    and the mean 13–14, 71, 90, 133–4, 192, 208–9
    and mercy 56
    and monarchy 35, 107
    and prices 132–3, 135–6, 138, 143, 157–8, 159
    and reciprocity 13
    and trade 113, 165
    and usury 164–5, 166
    and wages 132–3, 146–52, 154, 157–8
justices of labourers 145, 146
Justinian
    Codex 8, 212
    and control of weights and measures 91
    Corpus iuris civilis 7, 8, 48
    Digest 8, 84, 135, 136, 195, 212
    Institutes 8, 18
    Novella 8
    and usury 185

Kaye, Joel 134–5, 149–50, 209

labour
    legislation 46, 47, 145, 146–7, 157
    natural price 142, 152
    and ownership of money 106
    and prices 134, 137, 138, 206
    services 33, 34, 36, 78, 79, 80, 155, 157
    shortages 19, 43, 46, 47, 140–1, 142, 144–5, 146, 155–6
    as title to profit 116, 117, 161, 177–80, 192, 204
    as title to property 24–5, 41, 82, 208, 217
    and usury 175, 177–80
    and work ethic 52–3, 67
    see also wages
'ladder of perfection' 61, 137
laity
    and accumulation 83
    and charitable institutions 59, 64
    and poor relief 57, 67
    role 206, 208
land
    enclosure 36, 96, *225*
    measurement 95

sales 148–9
  as security for loan 189
  shortage 19
landownership
  and the Church 3
  private 18, 19, 33–6
  and tenancy 19, 34
  see also property
Langholm, Odd ix, 6, 68, 85–6, 104, 107, 117, 134, 137, 151, 176, 191, 196
Lateran Council, Third (1179) 56–7, 161–2, 166
Lateran Council, Fourth (1215) 154, 216, 221, 222
Lateran Council, Fifth (1515) 204
Laurentius Hispanus 136
Laurentius Ridolfis **218**
  and bills of exchange 201
  Tractatus de usuris 218
  and usury and interest 202–3
law
  and the Church 2–3
  common 19, 35–6
  and dialecticians 8–9
  divine *see* natural law
  God as author 19–21
  human 17, 18, 19–21
  international 21
  and necessity 38, 60, 106–7
  and property 17–18, 19, 41
  sumptuary 46–7, 122, 207
  systematization 7–8
  see also canon law; natural law
Le Goff, J. 114
Le Songe du Vergier 48
leasio enormis (enormous discrepancy) 148–9
Leo I the Great, Pope 112, 160
Leo X, Pope, *Inter multiplices* 204–5
Leon Battista Alberti **218–19**
  Della famiglia 53, 174, 219
  De re aedificatoria 219
  Della pittura 219
Leonardo Bruni, and wealth 52
The Libelle of Englyshe Polycye 10, 120, 122, 123–4, 126–7, **219**
liberality 62, 118
life rent (census) 196–7
literacy, growth 5–6
loans
  and banking 197–9
  and census 196–7
  compulsory 202–3
  and damage 183, 189, 190, 203
  and delay in repayment 188–9
  fictitious 187
  and interest from start 172, 183, 191–2, 202–3, 204, 215
  loan contract 186–8, 193
  and recognizances 189
  by sale 187
  sea loan 193–4, 207
  see also interest; risk
Locke, John 25, 40, 41, 82, 208, 217
logic
  and mathematics 12
  and theology 11–12
Lollardy 218, 220
  and 'Twelve Conclusions' 32–3
lordship
  and jurisdiction 107
  and property 18, 207
  serial 33
  and tenure 19, 34–6
  and weights and measures 96–7
Louis VII of France
  and coinage 108
  and poor relief 59
Louis IX of France, and poor relief 59
luxury trade 122
Lyons, Second Council (1274) 64, 163, 166, 168–9, 173, 222

Magna Carta (1215)
  and protection of property 37–8
  and standardization of weights and measures 93
Mainz, Council (1310) 162
Manner of holding a manorial court 144
manor 34, *226*
Margery Kempe 67
Martin V, Pope 199
mathematics, and the mean 12–14
Matteo Palmieri **219**
  Della vita civile 49, 219
  and poverty 49
  and wealth 52
Matteo Villani, *Cronaca* 47
Matthew Paris, *Chronica majora* 171, 198–9
Mayhew, N. J. 79, 101

mean, the
    and almsgiving 62, 68
    and interest 182
    and justice 13–14, 71, 90, 133–4, 192, 208–9
    and mathematics 12–14
    and money 12–13, 74
    and poverty 29
    and reciprocity 13, 42–3
    and standard 90
    and sufficiency 42, 51, 62, 68
    and virtue 133
    and wealth 53–4
measure *see* standard
medicine, and medical fees 154
Memoriale Presbiterorum 173
mendicant orders
    and Aristotle 7
    and begging 48–9, 50, 53
    and economic thought 1
    and poverty 27–30, 44–5
    and towns 5–6
    and usury and interest 171, 191–2
    and wealth 50–1
    see also Dominicans; Franciscans
mercantile system 110–31, 208
    and balance of trade 123–5, 126–7, 130, 131
    and bullionism 111, 125–31, 208
    and 'circular flow of wealth' 121–3
    and civic humanism 49
    see also merchants; trade
merchants
    and avarice 113–14
    and banking 5, 103, 197–8, 200–1, 202, 207
    changing attitudes to 115–17, 153, 207
    and the Church 4, 206
    and common good 117
    condemnation of 111–15
    and development of towns 5–6, 19, 26
    exaltation 117–20
    and 'false shewing' 114
    and mendicant orders 27
    and usury 168–71, 183
    and wealth 50, 53
mercy
    and justice 56
    Seven Corporal Acts of Mercy 55
mints 100–1, 102, 131

Miskimin, Harry A. 122
mobility
    geographic 19, 46
    social 3, 19, 36, 43, 46–7, 83, 207
moderation *see* mean, the
monarchy
    and control of coinage 88, 89–90, 91–3, 100–7, 108–9
    and control of weights and measures 89–90, 93–6, 100
    and divine law 20
    as embodiment of the realm 37, 38, 39, 105–7
    and poor relief 59
    and revenues 36–8
    and stewardship 32–3, 41
    and usury 167–8, 184–5
monasticism
    and communal life 25–7
    and poor relief 58
    and rejection of materialism 26–7
    and usury 173
money 69–88
    and avarice 82
    as capital 81–4, 207–8
    as commodity (metallist theory) 70–1, 73–6, 81, 87, 88, 200, 206–7
    and economic exchange 19, 69, 71–2, 74–5, 86, 87–8, 134, 207
    export of 125–6, 128–31
    Franciscan attitude to 27–8
    as fungible 75–6, 86, 161, 175, 182, 194, 204
    'ghost' (money of account) 70, 76–8, 86–7, 200
    and mathematics 12
    as a mean 12–13, 74
    as measure of value (sign theory) 70, 71–2, 73–4, 76–8, 86, 87, 102, 134
    nature and use of 72–6
    and need 74, 81, 134
    ownership and use 105–6, 108, 161, 182, 191, 194, 198, 204
    properties 87–8
    real 70, 76, 78–81, 86–7, 129
    and social status 46–7, 69, 207
    as sterile 84–7, 161, 175, 177, 178–9, 180, 182, 191–2, 195, 204
    as store of value 70, 81–4, 87–8
    and taxation 79

value of 76, 79–81, 86–7, 200
and wealth 41, 73, 111
see also banking; coinage; exchange-dealing; usury
money-changing 85, 103, 197, 199–201
monopoly *226*
and gilds 141–2
and prices and wages 133, 138–44
in trade 111, 123, 124
montes 183, 202–4, 208
montes pietatis 183, 203
morality, and economics 1–2, 7, 208–9
mort d'ancestor 35
mortgages 189
Mun, Thomas 110, 125, 126–7
Munro, John H. 109, 122–3
Murray, Alexander 12
music, and the mean 13
mutuum 186, 187, 198

nationalism, economic 70, 117–19, 121–5, 131, 207–8
natural law 223
and census 197
changing 21–3, 41
and coinage 103
and common good 22, 23–4, 41
and human law 17, 18, 19–33
and private property 17, 18–20, 21–3, 25, 37, 41, 55
and usury 185
and wages and prices 132, 148–9
necessity
and law 38, 60, 106–7
and taxation 38, 39
and usury 166
Nederman, Cary J. 10
need
and almsgiving 56–7
and discrimination in giving 58–9, 60–3, 207
and law 59–60
as measure of value 74, 81, 134, 137–8, 150–1
Nelson, Benjamin N. 168
Neoplatonism, Christian 211
Nicaea, Council (325) 160
Nicholas III, Pope, *Exiit qui seminat* 29
Nicholas Bozon 45, 168–9

Nicholas of Lyre 7
Nicholas Oresme 216, **219**
and coinage 102, 103, 104–6, 108, 127, 208
De moneta 10, 81, 82, 102, 103, 104, 127, 219
and exchange 200
and mendicants 49
and money 81–2, 106–7
Norman Conquest
and appropriation 58
and landownership 33–4
and weights and measures 93
novel disseisin 35
Novella 8

Offa of Mercia 92
On England's Commercial Policy 127
On the Laws and Customs of England 95, 167, 214
Ordinance of Labourers (1349) 46, 47, 144, 145
Ordinances (1311) 108
ownership
and feudal tenure 34–5
and risk 193, 194–5
transfer 186
and use 28–9, 35–6, 41, 75–6, 161, 182, 191, 198, 204
Oxford University 10, 142, 155, 218

Pandects 8
papacy
and banking 171, 198–9
and Franciscans 28–9
and interest 207
and *montes pietatis* 204
and poor relief 59
and pope as steward 30–1, 33, 41
revenues 125, 129
as sovereign 91
and usury 170, 171–2, 184, 203, 204–5
Paris, Council (1213) 163
Paris University 1, 11, 219, 223, 226
parish, and poor relief 3, 57–8, 59
Parliament
and Church 32
and coinage 101, 108–9, 131
and control of standards 90, 95

Parliament (*cont.*)
  and prices 143–4
  and taxation 38, 40
  and vagrancy 47–8
  and wages 145
partnership (*societas*) 5, 186, 193–6, 207
pastoralia, as source 9
Paul (Roman jurist) 8, 73, 82, 148
pawnbrokers 167–8, 169, 173, 183, 203
  see also montes pietatis
peasants
  and economy 78
  and improved social status 43, 46–7
  and land ownership 34–6
Peasants' Revolt (1381) 43
Peregrine of Oppeln 44–5
periculum sortis 192
Peruzzi Company 130, 185, 198
Peter IV of Aragon 145
Peter Abelard 12, 218
Peter of Blois, and poverty 44
Peter the Chanter **219–20**, 221, 222
  and coinage 103
  and just price 149
  and usury 167, 171
  Verbum abbreviatum 220
Peter John Olivi 6, **219**, 221
  De emptionibus et venditionibus 138
  and interest 191, 202
  and just price 150
  and supply and demand 137
  and usury 174, 180
  and wages 153
Peter Lombard, *Sentences* 7–8, 55, 212, 213, 217, 219
Peter de la Palu 104
Peter of Poitiers, and poverty 44
Philip IV the Fair of France 24, 102, 104, 143, 184, 213, 217
Philip VI Valois of France 102, 107, 130
Philip Augustus of France, and poor relief 59
Philip the Bold of Burgundy 108, 183–4
Philip the Good of Burgundy 124
pignotte 59
Pius II, Pope 204
Placuit 135

Plato
  Laws 90–1, 112
  and merchants 111–12
  Republic 23
pledges in kind 189
Poggio Bracciolini **220**
  and avarice 52, 53
  De avaritia 49, 52, 53, 70, 118, 220
  and mendicants 49
  and money 70
  and work 53
Poitiers, Battle (1356) 105
Poor Men of Lyons 27, 44
poor relief 57–9
'poor tables' 57
population
  fall in 19, 43, 144, 206
  increase in 5, 19, 57–8
poverty
  apostolic 26, 27–30, 44–5, 207, 214, 219, 221
  attitudes to 43–50, 67, 207
  and beggary 47–8
  and civic humanism 49, 50
  of the clergy 30, 32, 220
  deserved and undeserved 50, 60–2, 207
  and mendicant orders 27–30
  and rights of the poor 3, 56–60
  and sin 46
  and usury 164
  and wealth 42–3
prayer, for the dead 65, 66–7, 68
preachers, payment 155
prices 90
  and demand and supply 136–8, 142
  and free bargaining 148–52, 165
  and gilds 141–2
  just 74, 132–3, 135–6, 138, 142, 143, 148–51, 157, 200
  and labour 134, 137, 138, 206
  market/natural 133, 135–6, 138–9, 141–2, 144, 145, 147–9, 151, 157
  monopoly 138–44
  negotiated 133
  official/legal 133, 143–4, 147–8, 157
  and usury 159
  see also inflation
profit
  and interest 181–3, 190, 191–2, 194–5, 203, 204, 207, 215

labour as title to 116, 117, 161, 177–80, 192, 204
  and need 151, 158
  and regraters 140
  and risk 116, 117, 182, 193, 195–6, 197, 200, 204
  and seignorage 102, 107
  withheld 190, 191, 202–3
property 17–41, 207
  common 25–7
  and common good 23–4
  definitions 17–19
  ecclesiastical 30–1
  and equality 14, 20
  labour as title to 24–5, 41, 82, 208, 217
  and mendicant orders 27–30
  and monastic ideal 25–7
  as natural 24–5
  ownership and use 28–9, 41
  and stewardship 30–1, 32–3, 55
  and taxation 36–40, 41
proportion, *see also* equality, proportional
Protagoras 90
protectionism 10, 111, 123–5, 208, 219
Pseudo-Chrysostom *see Eiciens*
Ptolemy of Lucca **220**, 222
  De regimine principum 89, 118, 220
  and economic nationalism 118
  and usury 181
  and weights, measures and coinage 89, 102
Purgatory 5, 64, 67
Pythagoras and harmony and proportion 13
Pythagoreans, and the mean 13

quodlibets 8, 213, 215, 219, 221

Ralph of Acton, and reciprocity 42–3
Ranulf de Glanvill 35
Raymond of Peñafort 9, **220**
  and interest 182, 186, 188, 190 n.44
  and *Naviganti* 194, 220
reciprocity
  and the mean 13, 42–3
  and prayer 67
recognizances 189
rector *226*

Reginald Pecock **220**
  Repressor of Over Much Blaming of the Clergy 51, 52, 220
  and wealth 51–2
regrating 139, 140, *226*
Remigio de' Girolami, and merchants 120
rent
  in kind 33, 79, 80, 97
  life rent (census) 196–7
  in money 33, 79, 155, 157
representation 105–6, 109
Richard I of England, and weights and measures 93, 96, 114
Richard II of England 33, 38
Richard Aylesbury 125–6
Richard Caistor 57–8
Richard fitz Nigel, *Dialogue of the Exchequer* 117, 172
Richard Fitzralph **221**
  De pauperie Salvatoris 29, 221
  and poverty 29, 49
  and usury 171
  and work 53
Richard Leicester 103, 125, 126
Richard of Middleton (Mediavilla) 189, **221**
  and census 196–7
  and free bargaining 151
  and money 179
  Super Quatuor Libros Sententiarum 151, 179
  and usury 85
Richard of St Victor 223
riches *see* wealth
rights, natural
  of the poor 56–60
  and private property 23–4
risk
  and interest 181–3, 187, 192–3, 196
  and ownership 193, 194–5
  of the principle 192
  and profit 116, 117, 193, 195–6, 197, 200, 204
Robert of Anjou 185
Robert of Courçon 219, **221**
  and almsgiving 62, 63
  and partnership 194
  Summa 221
  and usury 163, 171
Robert Grosseteste 11, 68, 74

Roland de Passigiero 188
Roman law
  and consent 39
  and corporations 30–1
  and *dominium* 36
  and equality 8–9, 149
  and interest 181–2, 185–6
  and money 73, 75, 82, 84, 92
  and necessity 38, 60
  and partnership 193, 195
  and prices and wages 133, 135, 136, 139, 148–9, 152, 153, 156
  and property 18
  and time 174
  and vagrancy 48
  see also Justinian
Romance of the Rose 44, 45–6, 48, 54, 215–16
  and almsgiving 62–3
  and sufficiency 42, 51, 62
Roney, Lois 121
Rubin, Miri 64
Rufinus **221–2**
  and natural law 21–2
  Summa Decretorum 21, 222
  and trade 113
Rule of St Benedict 26
Rule of St Francis (1223) 27

salaries and fees 153–5
Salomon de Ripple 99–100
salvation
  and almsgiving 42, 44, 64
  and fraternities 65
  for merchants 115, 116, 120
  and Purgatory 64, 67
  and usurers 169–70, 180
  and wealth 43, 50–2, 53, 59
savings *see* accumulation
Savonarola 203
scholastics **226**
  and civic humanism 49
  and coinage 101–2
  and economic thought 1–2, 4, 6–7
  and interest 186, 189, 190, 194–5, 196–7, 200
  and law 8, 21
  and logic and dialectics 11–12
  and mercantile system 110, 111, 115
  and 'mixed' voluntariness 164–5

  and money 69–70, 73, 76, 80–4, 85, 196
  and money-changing 199–200
  and trade 85, 115
  and usury 165–6, 177–80, 186, 189
  and wages and prices 132–3, 135–8, 143, 147–57, 159
  and wealth 53–4
scutage 38
sea, control of 10, 111, 123–4, 219
sea loan 193–4, 207
Second Rule of St Francis 28–9
seignorage 102, 107
self-control, and charity 54
self-employment 156
Seneca, Lucius Annaeus, *De clementia* 43–4
Sentences 7, 8
  commentaries on 8, 212, 213, 217, 221, 223
  and justice and almsgiving 55
  quaestiones on 219
services
  common 171
  labour 33, 34, 36, 78, 79, 80, 155
  military 33, 34, 38
Seven Corporal Acts of Mercy 55
Shakespeare, William, *The Merchant of Venice* 189
silver
  and hall-marking 93–4
  and monetary economy 79, 80
  shortage 125, 128–31
sin
  and almsgiving 64
  and poverty 46, 61–2
  and private property 17, 20, 25, 26, 32
  and trade 112, 116, 149
  and usury 4, 159, 161–6, 180
Smith, Adam, *The Wealth of Nations* 110, 111
society
  as body 70
  and 'chain of being' 4
  and change 4–5
  and law 18
'Song against the King's Taxes' 131
sovereignty
  and coinage 88, 89–90, 91–3, 100–7, 108–9, 207–8
  in France 107–8
  national 4, 36, 110, 123–5, 206, 208

of papacy 91–2
and weights and measures 93–6, 100, 207–8
Spain
  and dissemination of Aristotelian ideas 11
  and wages 145
specie *226*
spending, and national economy 122
standards
  control of 89–90, 91, 100, 109
  God as 91
  origins 90–3
  policing 96–8
  varying 93–6, 128
State
  and fixing of prices 143
  and fixing of wages 144–7
  as money-lender 202–3, 208
  see also sovereignty, national
status, social
  and almsgiving 43, 62, 63
  and money 46–7, 69, 207
  and price 153
  and wages 133, 138, 153–5
Statute of Labourers (1351) 46, 145, 146
Statute of Purveyors (1352) 108–9
Statute of Stepney (1299) 128
Statute of Treasons (1352) 100
Statute of Westminster I (1275) 100
stewardship 55
  of king 32–3, 41
  of pope 30–1, 33, 41
stipulatio 186
Strict Observants
  Dominican 211
  Franciscan 212
strikes 156–7
sufficiency, and the mean 42, 51, 62, 68
supply
  and price 137–8, 142
  and wages 145
Swanson, Heather 147

Taborites 27
taxation
  and consent 38–40, 41, 106, 217
  in money 79
  papal 171
  of property 36–40, 41
  and seignorage 102

teachers, and fees 154–5
tenants
  free 34–6
  servile 34
  tenants-in-chief 34, 38, *226*
tenure 19
  copyhold 36, *224*
  feudal 34–6
  freehold 36
Thales of Miletus 138–9
theft
  usury as 164–5, 174, 180
  withholding of alms as 55–6
Theodosius the Great 211
theology
  and economics 1, 208
  and logic 11–12
Thomas Aquinas, St 6, **222**
  and accumulation 83
  and Albert the Great 210, 222
  and almsgiving 56, 61, 62–3
  and Aristotle 11, 23, 222
  and avarice 53–4
  and casual jurisdiction 38
  Commentary on Sentences 74, 191
  De regimine Judaeorum 37 n.77
  De regimine principum 220, 222
  and interest 190, 191
  and just price 132, 136, 137, 149–51
  and just wage 132, 152–4
  and the mean 51, 209
  and merchants 117, 153
  and money 73, 74–5, 76, 137, 178–9, 192, 194–5
  and natural law 22, 24, 37, 55
  and need 60, 74, 151
  and poverty 29, 45–6, 55
  and private property 23–4
  pupils 213, 217, 220
  and social status 153–4
  and society 4
  Summa contra gentiles 4, 46, 51, 209, 220, 222
  Summa theologiae 8, 22, 23–4, 54, 55, 56, 60, 61, 63, 73, 75, 83, 117, 132, 136, 137, 149, 150, 151, 153, 154, 179, 190, 194, 209, 222, 223
  and taxation 37, 38
  and usury 75, 165, 178–9, 185
  and wealth 51, 53–4, 55, 73

Thomas Brinton **222**
  and almsgiving 66
  and merchants 113–14, 120
Thomas of Chobham 219, **222**
  and partnership 194
  Summa confessorum 222
    and interest 190
    and just price 149
    and merchants 116–17
    and usury 167–8, 174, 177
Tierney, Brian 60–1
time
  and profit 117, 161, 204
  and usury 161, 174–7, 180, 182, 188, 191
tithe 3, *226*
  and poor relief 57, 58
tithings 225
Tours, Council (1173) 189
towns
  and increasing wealth 50–1
  rise of 5, 26, 206
Tractatus de decem praeceptis 214
trade
  balance 111, 122, 123–5, 126–7, 130, 131
  and bullionism 111, 125–31, 208
  changing attitudes to 115–17, 206, 207
  as chresmatic 72, 82
  and the Church 4
  and coinage 101
  condemnation of 111–15
  control of 92
  exaltation 117–20
  international 5, 78
  luxury 122
  and money 72, 79, 90
  and protectionism 10, 111, 123–5, 208, 219
  restriction 141–2
  retail 84–5, 111, 132–8
  see also wool trade
truck system 153, *226*
'Twelve Conclusions' 32–3

Ugolino of Segni
  and Franciscans 28–9
  see also Gregory IX, Pope
Urban III, Pope, *Consuluit* 159
Urban V, Pope 222
urbanization, increase in 5, 26

use
  and free bargaining 150
  and ownership 28–9, 35–6, 41, 75–6, 161, 182, 191, 198, 204
usury 75–6, 159–80, *226*
  and almsgiving 65–6
  clerical 171–3
  definitions 75, 159–61, 204–5
  and deposits 186, 199
  and interest 4, 75, 181–4, 185–6, 191, 194, 202–3, 204–5, 207
  and just price 159
  and labour and industry 175, 177–80
  and manifest usurers 161–2, 166–70, 183
  and money as sterile 84–7, 161, 175, 177, 178–9, 180, 182, 191–2, 195, 204
  and *montes* 202
  prosecution of 170, 173, 183–4
  and restitution 166–71, 174, 179–80
  as sin 4, 159, 161–6, 180
  as theft 164–5, 174, 180
  and time 161, 174–7, 180, 182, 188, 191, 204
  see also banking; loan

vagrancy 47–8, 145
vassal, vassalage 34, 59, *226*
Vienne, Council (1311) 163, 173, 219
villein 18, 34, 36, 46, *226*
virtue, as a mean 133, 209
voluntariness, 'mixed' 164–5

wages
  fixed 144–6, 157
  and free bargaining 19, 147–52, 154–7, 208
  and gilds 142, 146–52
  just 132–3, 138, 145, 146–52, 154, 157
  and labour 46, 132, 206
  market wage 141–3, 152, 156, 157
  money 80
  and monopoly 140–1
  restraint 111
  rise in 144–6, 155–6
  and salaries 153–5
Waldensians 27
Walter of Henley, *Husbandry* 83–4, 99
wealth
  and accumulation 82–3
  and almsgiving 55–6, 62

attitudes to 50–3, 67, 84, 207
  'circular flow' 121–3
  and civic humanism 49, 50
  clerical 32
  and justice 55
  monastic 26
  and money 41, 73, 111
  and poverty 42–3, 54–5
  and work 52–3
Weber, Max 52
weights and measures
  control of 89–90, 100, 207
  offences against 98–100, 114
  origins 90–3, 109
  policing of standards 96–8
  standardization 92
  varying standards 93–6, 143
wergeld payments 77
White Book of London 140
William of Auxerre **223**
  and gift 186
  Summa aurea 178, 223
  and usury 163–4, 165–6, 175, 178, 185
William Dene, Chronicle 145
William Durandus (the Speculator), and usury 168
William Durant the Younger
  and beggary 48–9
  and coinage 102–3

William Langland **222–3**
  Piers Plowman 128, 223
    and avarice 54, 99
    and regraters 140
    and usury 166, 171
  Richard the Redeless 223
William of Malmesbury 26
William Melton 172–3, 189
William of Moerbeke 11, 85, 199, 210
William of Ockham, influence 215
William of Sarzano, *Tractatus de Summi Pontificis* 31
wills, of usurers 162, 166, 169
wool staple 101, 123, 124, 187
wool trade 208
  and bills of exchange 201
  and bullion 128, 130
  and deceit 114
  and international politics 123, 124, 131
  and usury 177, 187
work
  dignity of 24, 43, 52–3, 67
  and poverty 47–9
  and wealth 52–3
Wyclif, John *see* John Wyclif
Wynnere and Wastoure 121–3, **223**

Yolande of Flanders 185

Zeno, Emperor 139

Cambridge Medieval Textbooks

Already published

Germany in the High Middle Ages *c.* 1050–1200
HORST FUHRMANN

The Hundred Years War
England and France at War *c.* 1300–*c.* 1450
CHRISTOPHER ALLMAND

Standards of Living in the Later Middle Ages:
Social Change in England, *c.* 1200–1520
CHRISTOPHER DYER

Magic in the Middle Ages
RICHARD KIECKHEFER

The Papacy 1073–1198: Continuity and Innovation
I. S. ROBINSON

Medieval Wales
DAVID WALKER

England in the Reign of Edward III
SCOTT L. WAUGH

The Norman Kingdom of Sicily
DONALD MATTHEW

Political Thought in Europe 1250–1450
ANTONY BLACK

The Church in Western Europe from the Tenth
to the Early Twelfth Century
GERD TELLENBACH
Translated by Timothy Reuter

The Medieval Spains
BERNARD F. REILLY

England in the Thirteenth Century
ALAN HARDING

Monastic and Religious Orders in Britain 1000–1300
JANET BURTON

Religion and Devotion in Europe *c.* 1215–*c.* 1515
R. N. SWANSON

Medieval Russia, 980–1584
JANET MARTIN

The Wars of the Roses: Politics and the Constitution in England,
c. 1437–*c.* 1509
CHRISTINE CARPENTER

The Waldensian Dissent: Persecution and Survival, *c.* 1170–*c.* 1570
GABRIEL AUDISIO
Translated by Claire Davison

The Crusades, *c.* 1071–*c.* 1291
JEAN RICHARD
Translated by Jean Birrell

Medieval Scotland
A. D. M. BARRELL

Roger II of Sicily: A Ruler between East and West
HUBERT HOUBEN
Translated by Graham A. Loud and Diane Milburn

The Carolingian Economy
ADRIAAN VERHULST

Medieval Economic Thought
DIANA WOOD

Women in Early Medieval Europe, 400–1100
LISA M. BITEL

Other titles are in preparation